CIVIL PROCEDURE

EIGHTH EDITION

STEVEN L. EMANUEL

Founder and Editor-in-Chief, the *CrunchTime*® series, *Emanuel Law Outlines*® and *Emanuel Bar Review*

Harvard Law School, J.D. 1976

Member (Ret.) NY, CT, MD and VA bars

The Emanuel *CrunchTime*® Series

ASPEN PUBLISHING

To contact Customer Service, e-mail customer.service@aspenpublishing.com,
call 1-800-950-5259, or mail correspondence to:

Aspen Publishing
Attn: Order Department
1 Wall Street
Burlington, MA 01803

1 2 3 4 5 6 7 8 9 0

ISBN 979-8-8941-0975-6

ABOUT ASPEN PUBLISHING

Aspen Publishing is a leading provider of legal education content and digital learning solutions in the United States and globally. Our innovative products and platforms—designed based on best practices in learning science—engage students and enhance outcomes. From textbooks and audiobooks authored by renowned experts to digital platforms and products like LEAF, Connected eBooks, Connected Quizzing, PracticePerfect, and JD-Next, we empower the next generation of legal professionals with innovative, trusted, and accessible resources.

The Aspen Casebook Series, affectionately known as the "red and black" casebooks among law faculty and students, includes hundreds of highly regarded textbooks across more than 80 disciplines. These range from foundational courses like Torts and Contracts to emerging electives such as Sustainability and the Law of Policing. Our study aids, including the popular *Examples & Explanations* series, help law students master complex topics with clarity and confidence.

Aspen's expertise extends to undergraduate education with our Paralegal, Criminal Justice, and Business Law series, offering the same hallmark quality to a broader audience. JD-Next, our groundbreaking online law school prep course and admissions test, provides a realistic preview of law school, equips students with essential skills for academic success, and evaluates their readiness for legal studies.

Aspen Publishing Is Proud to Be a UWorld Company

Since 2003, UWorld has been a global leader in developing high-quality learning tools for students preparing for high-stakes exams. With a commitment to excellence, UWorld has helped millions of students in undergraduate, graduate, and professional programs in fields such as medicine, nursing, finance, and law achieve their academic and career goals.

Founded by Chandra S. Pemmasani, M.D., during his medical residency, UWorld began focusing on medical education and has since expanded into various academic fields, including law. In 2020, UWorld launched its Legal vertical, starting with its comprehensive Multistate Bar Exam (MBE®) Question Bank, followed by the acquisition of Themis Bar Review, which integrated resources to provide a complete bar exam preparation experience. In 2024, UWorld expanded its offerings by acquiring Aspen Publishing, enhancing its suite of legal education products.

Today, UWorld offers an unparalleled range of study materials that blend active learning methods with expert content, ensuring students and educators can access the most effective resources. From bar preparation to law school success, UWorld is committed to supporting the next generation of legal professionals. Learn more at uworld.com.

About the Author

As a student at Harvard Law School in the 1970s, **Steve Emanuel** wrote concise outlines for his courses and sold them in the law school dining hall to his fellow students. His outlines were such an immediate hit that soon after graduation, Steve quit the practice of law and started his own company to publish the *Emanuel Law Outlines®* series and other study-aid series he helped write.

For more than 40 years, Steve's full-time job has been to update the *Emanuel Law Outlines®* — and other study aids he's written or published, like the *Law in a Flash* series — to reflect changes in the law, in casebooks, and on topics tested in bar exams. Over 2 million copies of study aids written by Steve have been sold. Steve is a retired member of the New York, Connecticut, Maryland, and Virginia bars, and has passed the California bar exam.

TABLE OF CONTENTS

Preface

Thank you for buying this book.

The *CrunchTime* series is intended for people who want Emanuel quality, but don't have the time or money to buy and use the full-length *Emanuel Law Outline* on a subject. We've designed the Series to be used in the last few weeks (or even less) before your final exams.

This book includes the following features, some of which have been extracted from the corresponding *Emanuel Law Outline* on *Civil Procedure*:

- ***Flow Charts*** — We've reduced most principles of *Civil Procedure* to a series of 13 Flow Charts and Tables, ***almost none of which are published in the full-length Emanuel or elsewhere.*** We think these will be especially useful on open-book exams. For a list of the Flow Charts and Tables, see p. 2.
- ***Capsule Summary*** — This is a 123-page summary of the subject. We've carefully crafted it to cover the things you're most likely to be asked on an exam. The Capsule Summary starts on p. 33.
- ***Exam Tips*** — We've compiled these by reviewing dozens of actual essay questions asked in past law-school and bar exams, and extracting the issues and "tricks" that surface most often on exams. Although there are also Exam Tips in the full-length *Emanuel*, ***the ones here are considerably more extensive***. The Exam Tips start on p. 161.
- ***Short-Answer*** questions — These questions are generally in a Yes/No format, with a "mini-essay" explaining each one. The questions start on p. 205.
- ***Multiple-Choice*** questions — These are in a Multistate-Bar-Exam style. They were created specially for this CrunchTime and have never been published elsewhere. They start on p. 261.
- ***Essay*** questions — These questions are actual ones from past Harvard Law School exams, together with our extensive model answers. They start on p. 293.

Good luck in your Civil Procedure course. If you'd like any Aspen publication, you can find it at your bookstore or at **www.AspenPublishing.com**.

If you'd like to contact me, you can email me at **semanuel@westnet.com**.

Steve Emanuel
Larchmont NY
February 2026

FLOW CHARTS & TABLES

TABLE OF CONTENTS
to
FLOW CHARTS & TABLES

Flow Charts

Tables

Note: The cross-references in the Flow Charts' footnotes (e.g., "See IV(D)(1), *infra*" or "See p. 105, *supra*") are to the full-length *Emanuel Law Outline* on Civil Procedure.

Figure 2-1

Personal Jurisdiction over a Defendant Corporation

Use this chart to figure out whether the Forum State ("FS") may constitutionally exercise personal jurisdiction over a defendant corporation ("D"). Other abbreviations used: P = the plaintiff (who may be either a human or a business entity); the "court" = a state court located in the FS (unless identified as a federal court, in which case the court means a district court that sits in the FS.) [1]

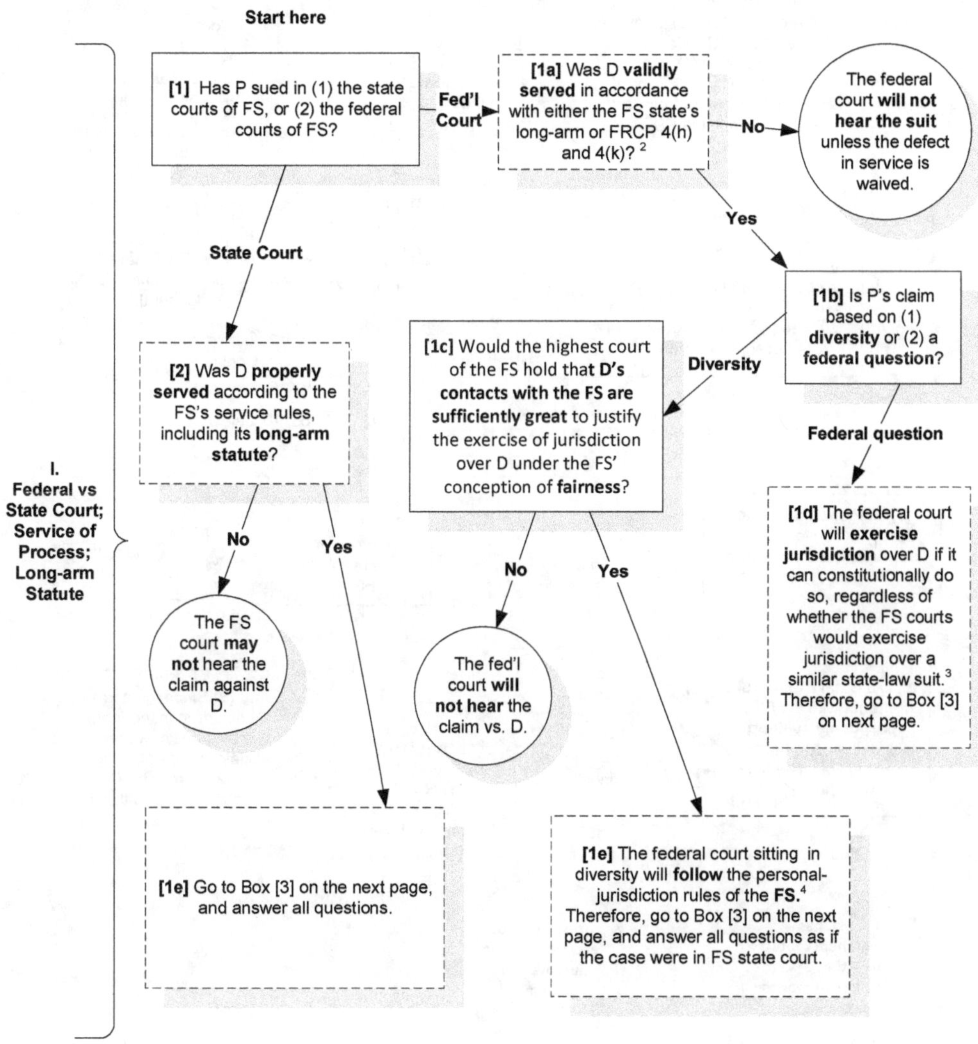

See footnotes starting at "Notes" (after p. 6 of chart)

Figure 2-1
Personal Jurisdiction over a Defendant Corporation (p. 2)

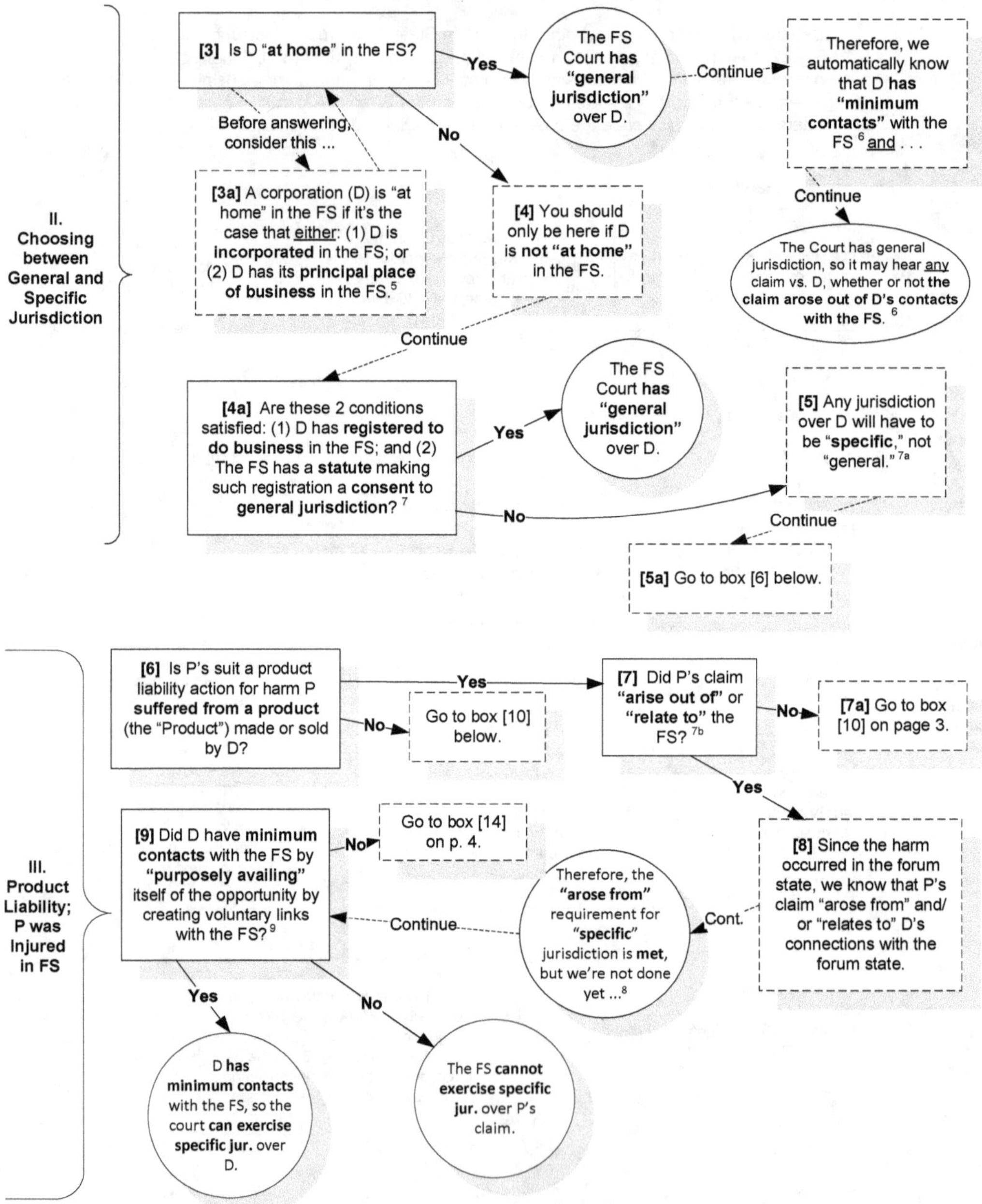

See footnotes after 6th page of chart

Figure 2-1
Personal Jurisdiction over a Defendant Corporation (p. 3)

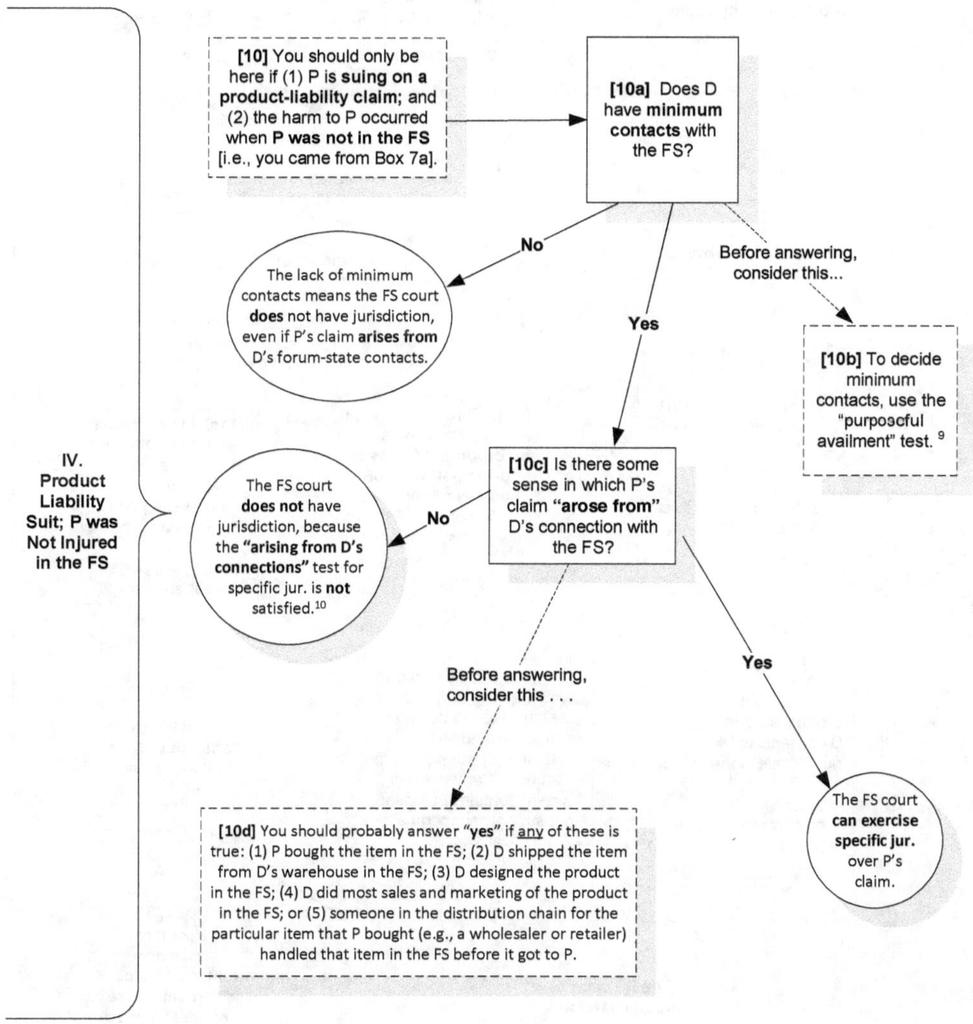

See footnotes after 6th page of chart

Figure 2-1
Personal Jurisdiction over a Defendant Corporation (p. 4)

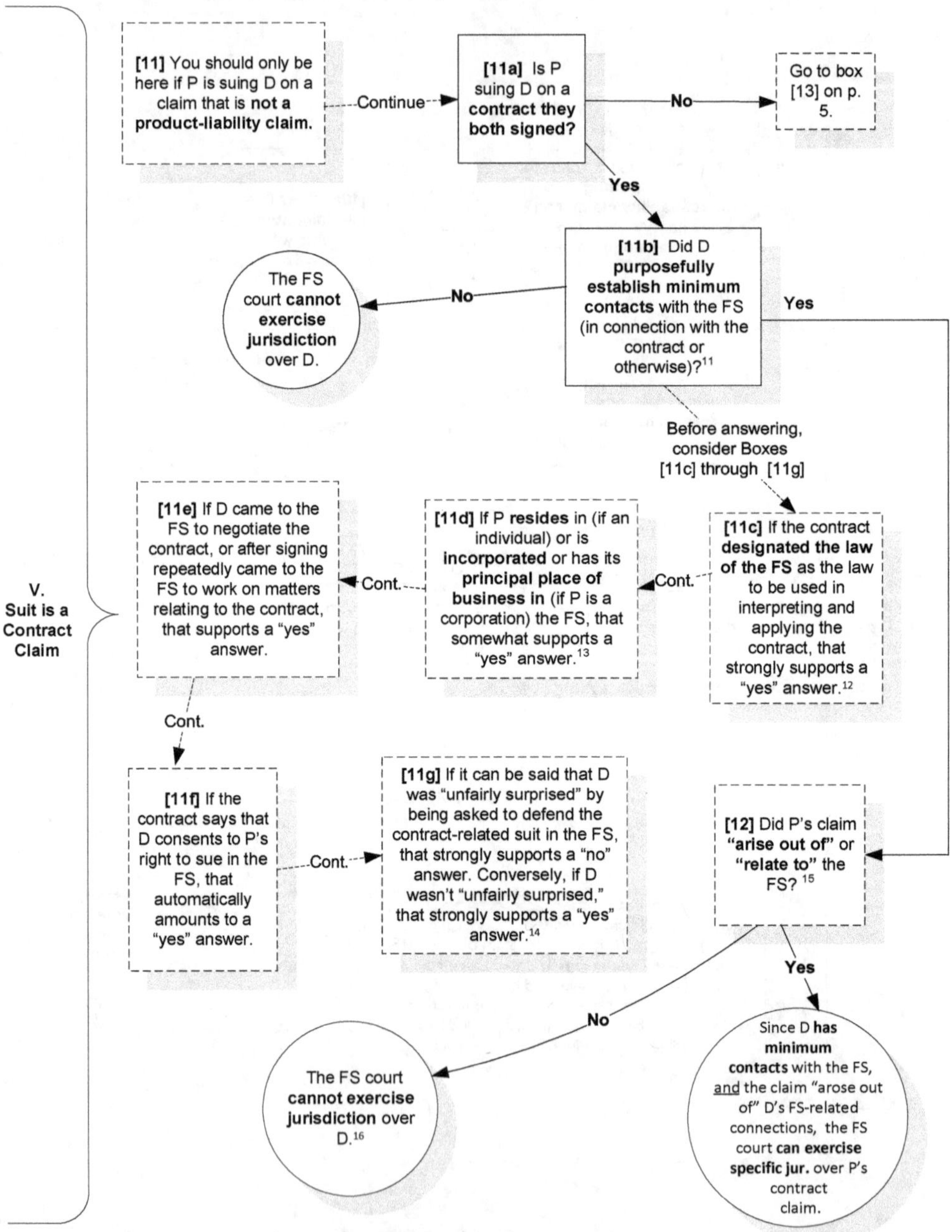

See footnotes after 6th page of chart

Figure 2-1

Personal Jurisdiction over a Defendant Corporation

(p. 5)

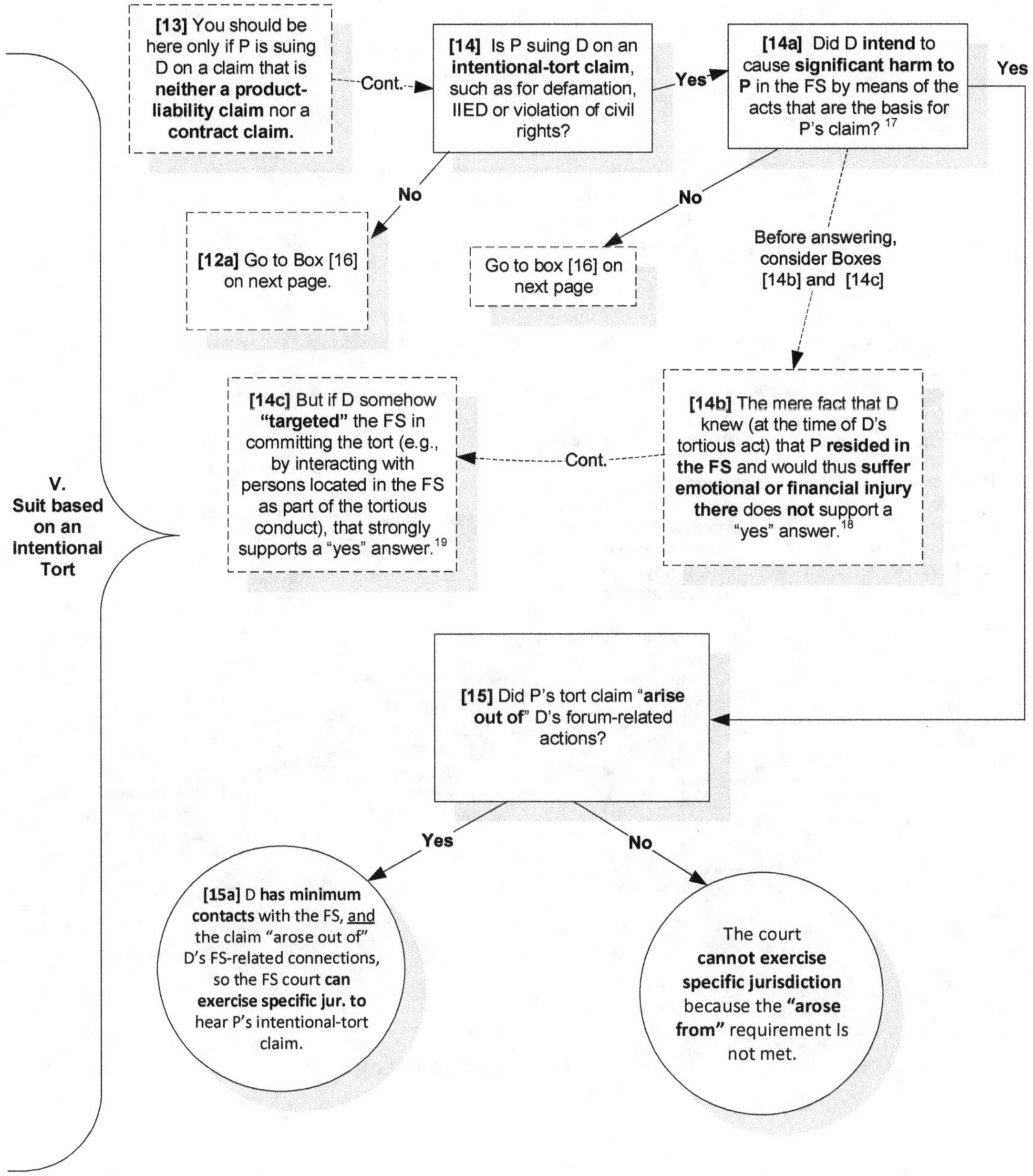

Figure 2-1
Personal Jurisdiction over a Defendant Corporation
(p. 6)

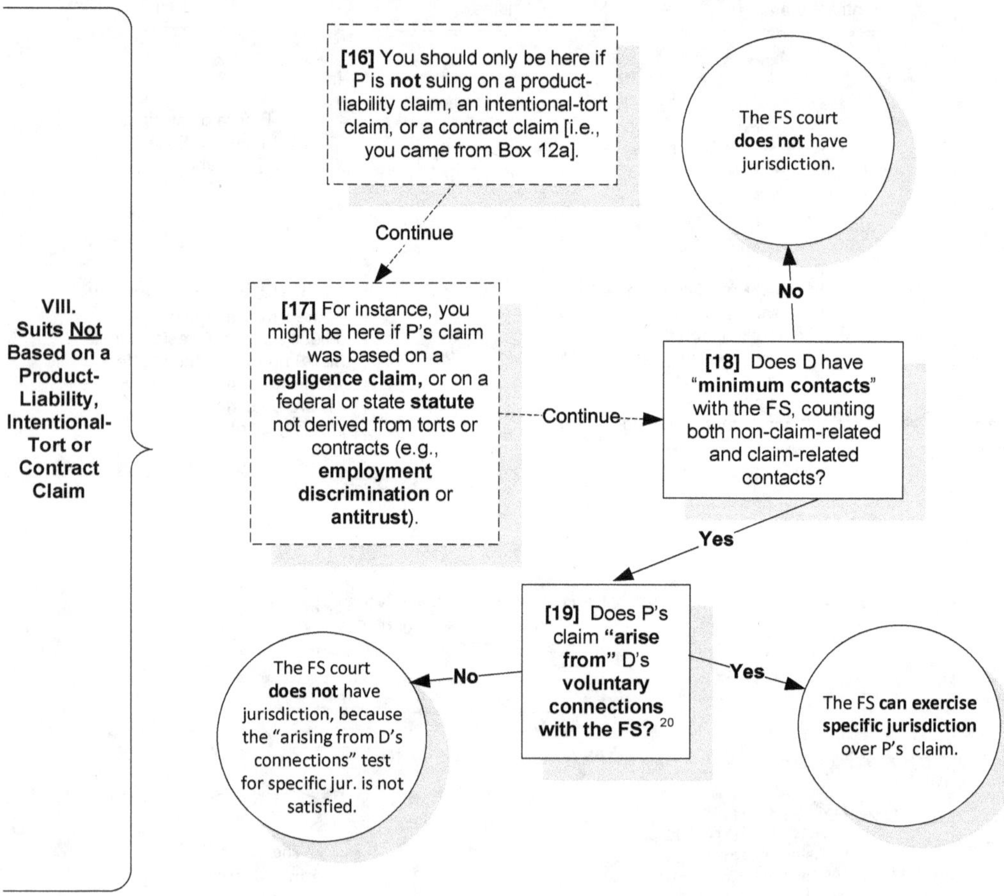

See footnotes on next page

Notes to **Figure 2-1** (Personal Jurisdiction over a Defendant Corporation)

1. References of the form "Ch.xx" are to places in this volume, i.e., *Emanuel Law Outline of Civil Procedure*, 26th Edition ((c) 2018). Thus a reference to "Ch. 2(III)(A)(2)(b)" would mean Chap. 2 of this volume, roman-numeral III, Paragraph (A)(2)(b). References of the form "Box [nn]" are to the boxes in this Flowchart.

2. As to service on a corporation generally, see Ch.2(VI)(C)(2). Rules 4(h)(1)(A) and 4(e)(1), taken together, say that service on a corporation in a federal action may be made by any method that would be valid for a state-court action against that same corporation.

3. See Ch.2(VI)(D)(1), including the Example under (VI)(D)(1)(a).

4. That is, in diversity cases, the federal courts exercise only the jurisdiction that is allowed by the law of the state in which they sit, even if that state law does not go to the limits of what the state could do commensurate with due process. See Ch.2(VI)(D)(2) and the Example under it.

5. See *Goodyear Dunlop v. Brown*, establishing that general jurisdiction against a corporate defendant D exists only where D is "at home" in the forum state. D is "at home" if D is either incorporated in the forum state or has its principal place of business there,

6. When a defendant corporation, D, is either incorporated in the forum state or has its principal place of business there, D is automatically be deemed to have "minimum contacts" with the forum state. Consequently, once D is established to be "at home" in the forum state, we know that it would not violate D's 14th Amendment due process rights for D to be required to defend *any* claim brought against it in the state's courts, whether the claim arose from D's forum-focused activities ("specific" jurisdiction) or not ("general" jurisdiction).

7. Example: Pennsylvania passes a statute saying that (1) no company can do in-state business without registering; and (2) such registration constitutes consent to be sued in-state on any claim (i.e., general jurisdiction). *Held*, this scheme is constitutional. *See Mallory v. Norfolk Southern Ry.*

7a. See *Goodyear Dunlop v. Brown*, establishing that general jurisdiction against a corporate defendant D exists only where D is "at home" in the forum state. Therefore, as soon as we know that D is not "at home" in the FS (Box 4 tells us this), we know that the state cannot exercise general jurisdiction over D. (For the one exception, see Box 4a and note [8].) Consequently, any jurisdiction by the forum state over D would have to be specific rather than general (i.e., would have to cover only claims arising out of D's connections with the forum state).

7b For "arise out of or relate to" status, all that's required is that there be an "affiliation between the forum and the underlying controversy," usually an "activity or occurrence" in the FS. And this activity/occurrence need not be an act committed by the defendant. (So the fact that P was injured in the FS suffices for "arise out of or "relates to" the FS.) Plus, there's no "causal" requirement -- the activity/occurrence need not have resulted from D's voluntary connections with the FS.

Example: Assume that D (Ford Motor Co.), a nationwide business, has minimum contacts with the FS. P, who purchased a Ford outside the FS and is not domiciled in the FS, has an accident in the Ford while in the FS, and sues D for product liability. The fact that the accident took place in the FS is enough to meet the requirement that the claim must "arise out of or relate to" the FS. And the fact that D's in-state minimum contacts (e.g., maintaining in-state dealers) were not the "but-for cause" of the accident is irrelevant. *Ford Motor Co. v. Montana.*

8. The reason "we're not done yet" – even though we know that P's claim meets the "arose out of forum-state connections" requirement for specific jurisdiction – is that there are *two* quite independent requirements for specific jurisdiction: (1) the "arose out of" requirement; and (2) the minimum-contacts requirement. And by this point in the analysis, we still haven't addressed requirement (2) (something that will happen in Box [9]).

9. Minimum contacts exist only if D has "purposely availed" itself of the privilege of doing business in the forum state. Or, to frame the same standard another way, D must have "targeted" the FS by establishing voluntary links between D and the FS, rather than merely "predicting that its goods will reach the forum State."

Some things that would probably constitute "purposeful availment" (or "targeting"):

[1] D marketed its goods nationally, including

Footnotes continue on next page

Notes (p. 2) to **Figure 2-1** (Personal Jurisdiction over a Defendant Corporation)

occasional sales would occur in the FS;

[1] D sold and repaired its goods in-state via one or more authorized dealers. (See *Ford Motor v. Montana*, the Example in this note.)

[2] D had a significant number of employees located in the FS, even if not doing work that related to P's claim;

[3] D qualified to do business in the FS (typically done by filing with the Sec'y of State).

[4] D had some significant contractual relationship with in-FS persons (e.g., suppliers to D).

Example (based on [1] above): D, a carmaker, has local dealers in each state (including the FS), sells its cars nationally through the dealer network, and requires each dealer to repair cars for local customers. D also conducts nationwide sales and marketing that reaches every state. These practices satisfy the "purposely avail" or "targeted the forum" standard; therefore, you know that D has minimum contacts with the forum state. (Plus, the fact that P was injured in the FS satifies the "arose out of" requirement). Cf. *Ford Motor Co. v. Montana* (similar facts).

10. If the claim did not "arise out of" (or "relate to") the FS, the court does not have specific jurisdiction no matter how great D's minimum contacts with the forum state. For more about the "arose out of" requirement, see note 8.

11. See note 9 for what's required to conclude that D purposefully established minimum contacts with the FS.

12. See *Burger King v. Rudzewicz*: The fact that franchise agreement between P (the franchisee) and D (the franchisor) designated Florida law as controlling strongly indicated that P had "purposely availed himself of the benefits and protections" of Florida law; held (based on this among other factors), P had minimum contacts with Florida, so he could be sued there. See Ch.2(IV)(I)(1)(b)(i).

13. See *Burger King v. Rudzewicz* (summarized in prior note): The fact that the suit involves a contract, one party to which is headquartered in the forum state and is supervising the contract from there, points to the conclusion that the other (out-of-state) party has minimum contacts with the forum state. See Ch.2(IV)(I)(2)(a).

14. Again, see *Burger King v. Rudzewicz*: Where D (the franchisee) signed a franchise agreement with Florida-based P (the franchisor), and D knew he was entering a "substantial and continuing relationship with [P's] Miami headquarters," D had fair notice that he might be sued in Florida, and was therefore not unfairly surprised when such a relationship occurred. Consequently, D had minimum contacts with Florida, and could be sued there without violation of his due process rights.

15. Before you answer "yes," know that the conclusion that the claim "arose out of" D's forum-state related connections assumes that P is meaningfully affiliated with the forum state. This assumption will be correct in the usual situation in which P, who resides in or has significant operations in the forum state, sues D, an out-of-stater, on the contract. Thus in *Burger King v. Rudzewicz* (notes 12-14 above), where P (the Florida-based franchisor) brought suit in Florida against D (the Michigan-based franchisee) for breach of the franchise agreement, the court assumed without discussion that the suit "arose out of" Florida-related activities, leaving only the separate issue of whether D had minimum contacts with Florida (which, the court found, D had). But in the unusual scenario in which P sues D on a contract and neither P nor D has significant operations in or connections with the forum state, then it may not be reasonable to say that the requirement that the claim "arise out of" forum-state-related activities is automatically satisfied.

16 Remember from earlier in this chart (e.g., Box [7] and note 7b) that for specific jurisdiction the claim must "arise out of" or "relate to" activities in the FS. That's true even if D unquestionably has mimimum contacts with the FS (but in a way that has nothing to do with P's claim).

17. Example: D stands in State *A* near the border with State *B*, and throws a rock at P, who is standing in State *B*; the rock hits P. D has intended to cause significant effects in State *B*, even though D's act was committed in (or at least "from") State *A*. Therefore, you would answer "yes" to the question in Box [14a]. That answer would then lead you to conclude that (1) D has minimum contacts with State *B*; (2) a suit for battery by P in State *B* court "arose out of" D's voluntary State-*B*-related connections; and (3) State *B* can therefore exercise personal jurisdiction (of the "specific" variety) over P's claim. See Ch.2(III)(E)(1), Example.

18. Example: D, while at her house in Texas, steals a car from the driveway next door. At the time of the theft, D knows that the car belongs to P, and that P is a resident of New Mexico who is visiting his brother in Texas.

Notes (p. 3) to **Figure 2-1** (Personal Jurisdiction over a Defendant Corporation)

D also knows that P plans to drive the car back to New Mexico and use it there. P sues D for conversion in New Mexico state court. D has no connections with New Mexico other than as stated above.

On these facts, you would answer "no" to Box [14a] – the mere fact that D knew that P would suffer emotional or financial harm in New Mexico from D's act in Texas will not be enough to justify the conclusion that D intended to cause significant effects in New Mexico. Therefore, the New Mexico court will not have personal jurisdiction over P's conversion suit.

19. Example: P, a resident of New York, is seeking the nomination of her party for president of the U.S. D, a corporation that offers campaign-related services, is incorporated in Russia, and has its headquarters there. D is hired by X, a candidate opposing P, to help X win the upcoming Iowa primary. Computer hackers employed by D, and based in Russia, hack into a computer server owned by P and located in New York; these hackers then steal from P's server the confidential personal information – including social media profiles – of thousands of Iowa voters thought to be leaning in favor of P. D then infiltrates false information into these Iowa voters' social media feeds, intending to persuade the voters to back X rather than P. P loses the Iowa primary to X in a close race. P sues D in the Iowa state courts, alleging that D's conduct constituted conversion of P's property. D asserts that the Iowa court lacks personal jurisdiction over it.

On these facts, you should answer "yes" to the question in Box [14c]. D's extreme focus on inducing Iowa voters to change their vote should be deemed to be activity that "targeted" Iowa, i.e., that was intended to cause significant effects in that state.

20. Example: D Corp. is a large Internet software company incorporated in Delaware and with its principal place of business in Washington state. P, an individual, resides in Minnesota. While P is interviewing at D's Washington headquarters for a job as a programmer, she slips on an icy sidewalk outside of the headquarters building. The sidewalk and the building are owned and maintained by D. P returns to Minnesota, and sues D for negligence in Minnesota state court. D receives tens of millions of dollars of annual revenue from business customers located in Minnesota, and maintains an office in the state with 300 employees, who perform various sales and programming functions.

On these facts, you would answer "no" to the question in Box [19]: P's claim for negligence does not "arise out of" any voluntary connection that D has with Minnesota. Therefore, even though D has more than enough voluntary connections with Minnesota to constitute "minimum contacts" with that state, the Minnesota courts cannot exercise specific jurisdiction over P's claim.

Figure 2-2: **Federal Jurisdiction — First Analysis**

Is there **subject-matter jurisdiction** (either diversity or federal question)? [1]

Is there **personal jurisdiction** over **each** D (either *in personam* or *quasi in rem*)? [2]

Was each D **served** adequately? [3]

Does the district where the case is pending satisfy the **venue** requirement? [4]

Did D receive **notice** and an **opportunity** to be **heard**?

The answer to all questions must be "yes" for the action to proceed.

For more detail, see Fig. 2-3, next page

Footnotes:

1. See Fig. 3-1 (p. 105) for a detailed analysis of diversity. Where multiple claims, plaintiffs or defendants are involved, be sure to consider the possibility that **supplemental jurisdiction** may eliminate the need for some claims or parties to satisfy the diversity, amount in controversy or venue requirements.
2. Most importantly, D must have **minimum contacts** with the state where the fed. ct. sits. See Fig. 2-1 (p. 38) for details on analyzing *in personam* jurisdiction.
3. Normally, if D is out-of-state he must be someone who could be reached by the **long-arm** of the **state** where the federal court sits. Rule 4(k)(1)(A).
4. Normally, the district must be where all Ds reside, or where a substantial part of the events at issue occurred. See 28 U.S.C. §1391(a) and (b).

Figure 2-3: **Federal Jurisdiction — Detailed Analysis**[1]

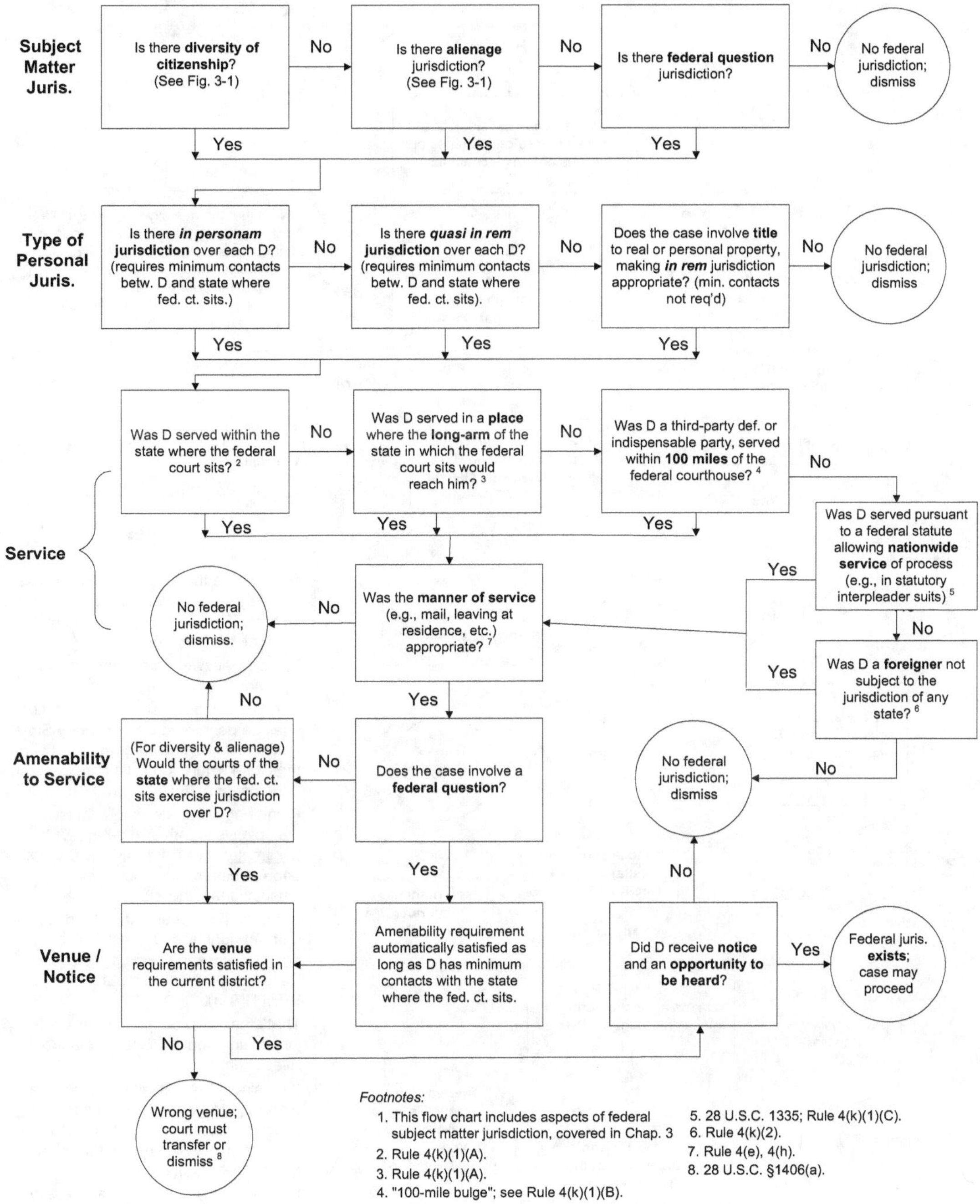

Footnotes:

1. This flow chart includes aspects of federal subject matter jurisdiction, covered in Chap. 3
2. Rule 4(k)(1)(A).
3. Rule 4(k)(1)(A).
4. "100-mile bulge"; see Rule 4(k)(1)(B).
5. 28 U.S.C. 1335; Rule 4(k)(1)(C).
6. Rule 4(k)(2).
7. Rule 4(e), 4(h).
8. 28 U.S.C. §1406(a).

Figure 3-1: **Analysis of Diversity**

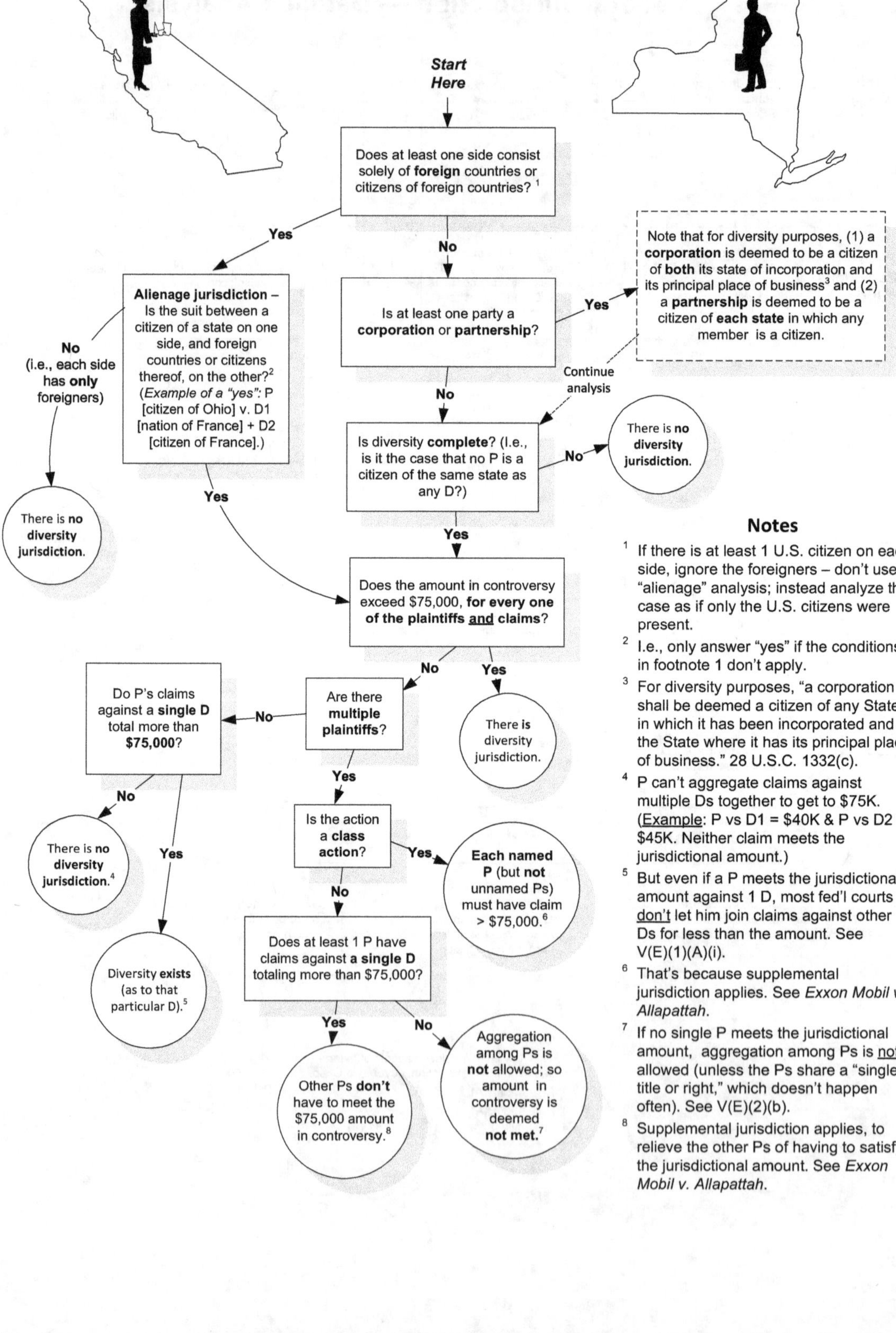

Notes

1 If there is at least 1 U.S. citizen on each side, ignore the foreigners – don't use "alienage" analysis; instead analyze the case as if only the U.S. citizens were present.

2 I.e., only answer "yes" if the conditions in footnote 1 don't apply.

3 For diversity purposes, "a corporation shall be deemed a citizen of any State in which it has been incorporated and of the State where it has its principal place of business." 28 U.S.C. 1332(c).

4 P can't aggregate claims against multiple Ds together to get to $75K. (Example: P vs D1 = $40K & P vs D2 = $45K. Neither claim meets the jurisdictional amount.)

5 But even if a P meets the jurisdictional amount against 1 D, most fed'l courts don't let him join claims against other Ds for less than the amount. See V(E)(1)(A)(i).

6 That's because supplemental jurisdiction applies. See *Exxon Mobil v. Allapattah*.

7 If no single P meets the jurisdictional amount, aggregation among Ps is not allowed (unless the Ps share a "single title or right," which doesn't happen often). See V(E)(2)(b).

8 Supplemental jurisdiction applies, to relieve the other Ps of having to satisfy the jurisdictional amount. See *Exxon Mobil v. Allapattah*.

Figure 3-2: **Supplemental Jurisdiction**

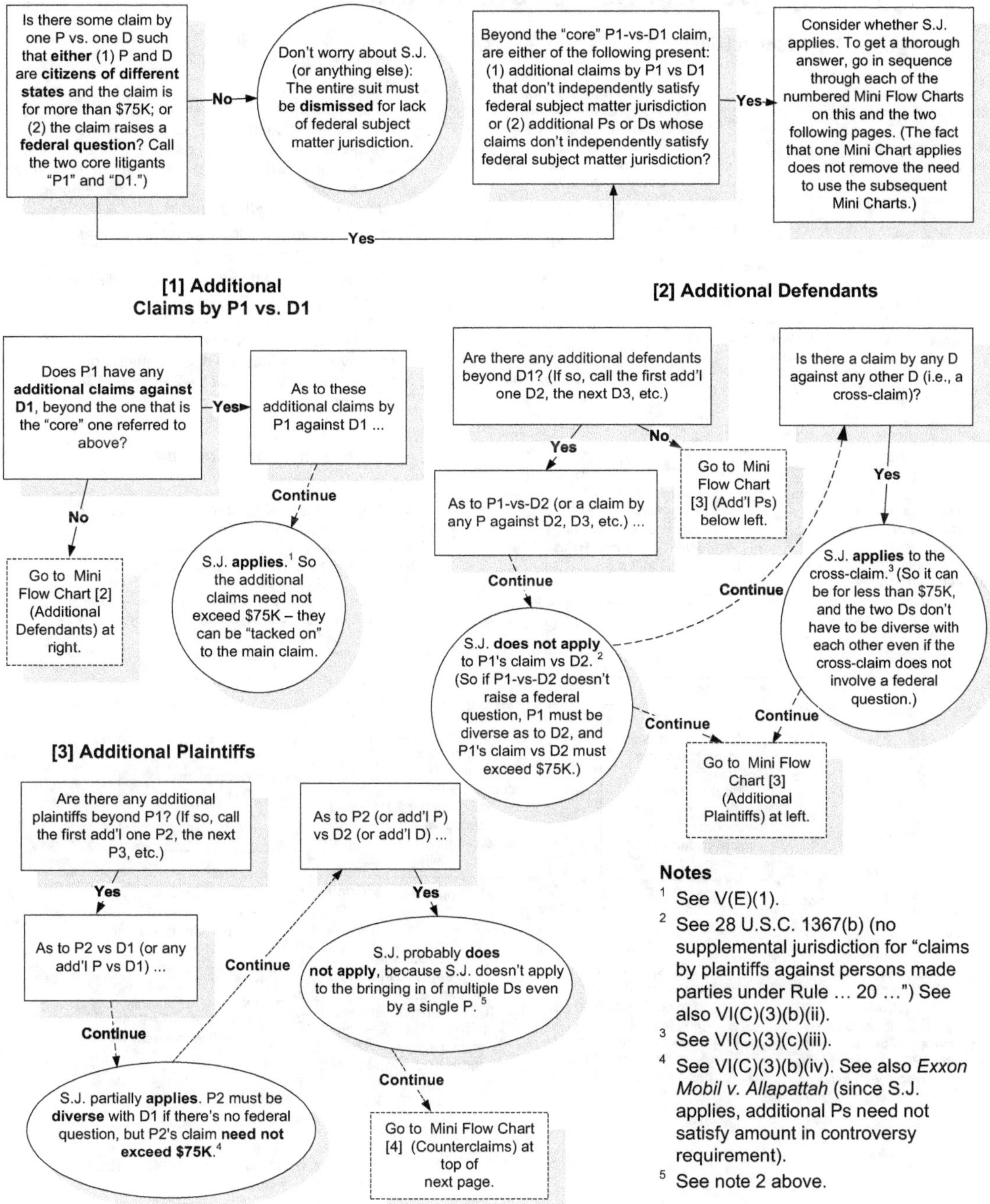

Notes

[1] See V(E)(1).

[2] See 28 U.S.C. 1367(b) (no supplemental jurisdiction for "claims by plaintiffs against persons made parties under Rule … 20 …") See also VI(C)(3)(b)(ii).

[3] See VI(C)(3)(c)(iii).

[4] See VI(C)(3)(b)(iv). See also *Exxon Mobil v. Allapattah* (since S.J. applies, additional Ps need not satisfy amount in controversy requirement).

[5] See note 2 above.

Continued on next page

Figure 3-2

Supplemental Jurisdiction (p. 2)

[4] Counterclaims

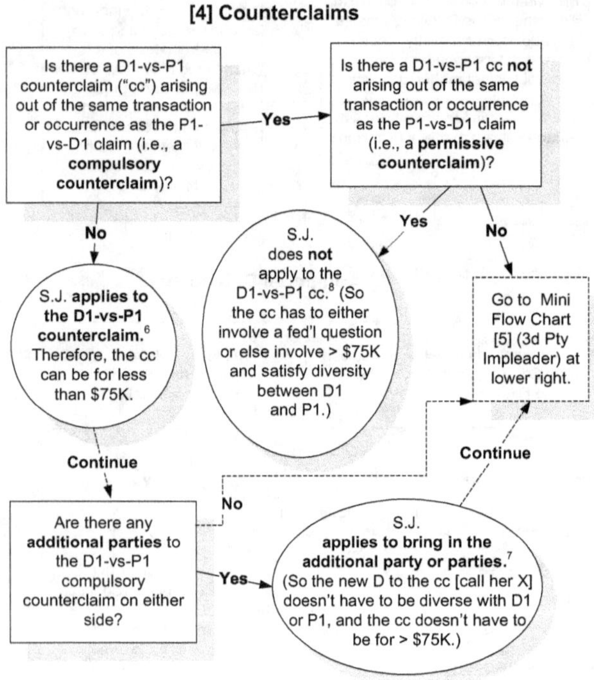

Notes

[6] See VI(C)(3)(c)(i).

[7] See VI(C)(3)(c)(ii).

[8] This is true because (by hypothesis) the counterclaim doesn't arise out of the "same transaction or occurrence" as the P1-vs-D1 claim, so it's almost certainly not part of the "same case or controversy" as the P1-vs-D1 claim, as required for supplemental jurisdiction by 28 U.S.C. 1367(a).

[9] See VI(C)(3)(c)(iv), and Example 3 following it.

[10] See VI(C)(3)(c)(iv).

[11] Because (by hypothesis) the TPD-vs-TPP claim doesn't arise out of the "same transaction or occurrence" as the TPP-vs-TPD claim, it almost certainly doesn't arise out of the "same case or controversy" as that claim, as required for supplemental jurisdiction by 28 U.S.C. 1367(a).

[12] See VI(C)(3)(b)(i).

[5] Third-Party Impleader

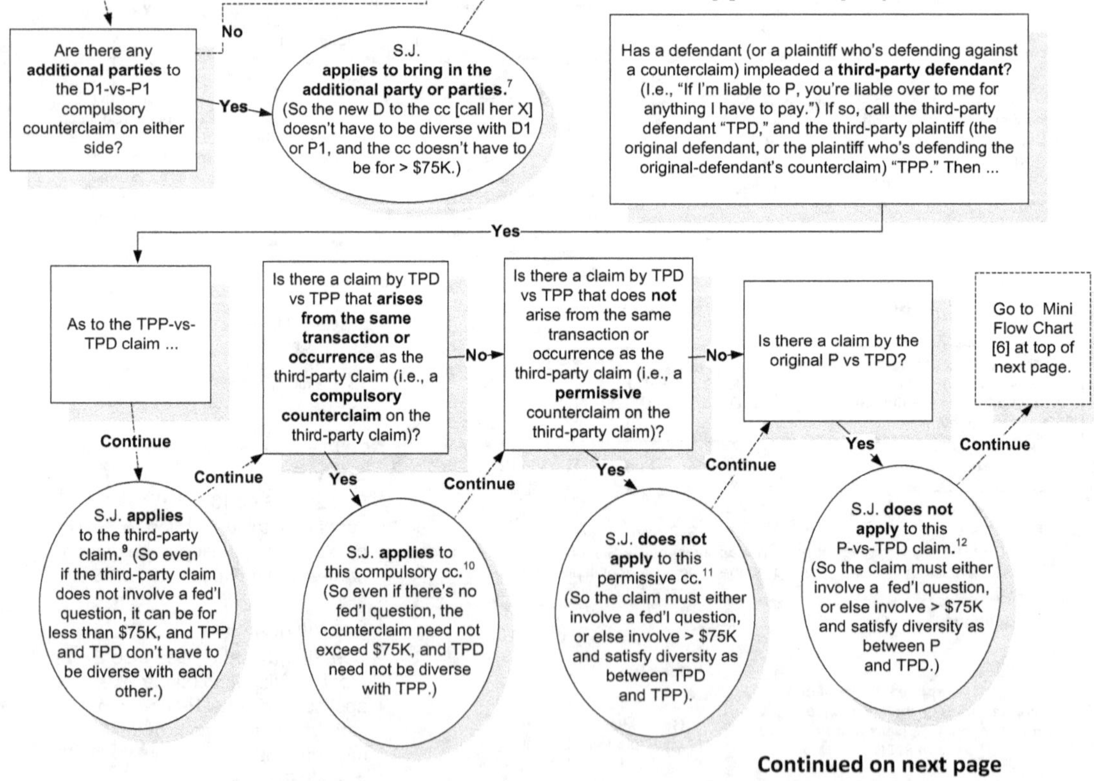

Continued on next page

Figure 3-2

Supplemental Jurisdiction (p. 3)

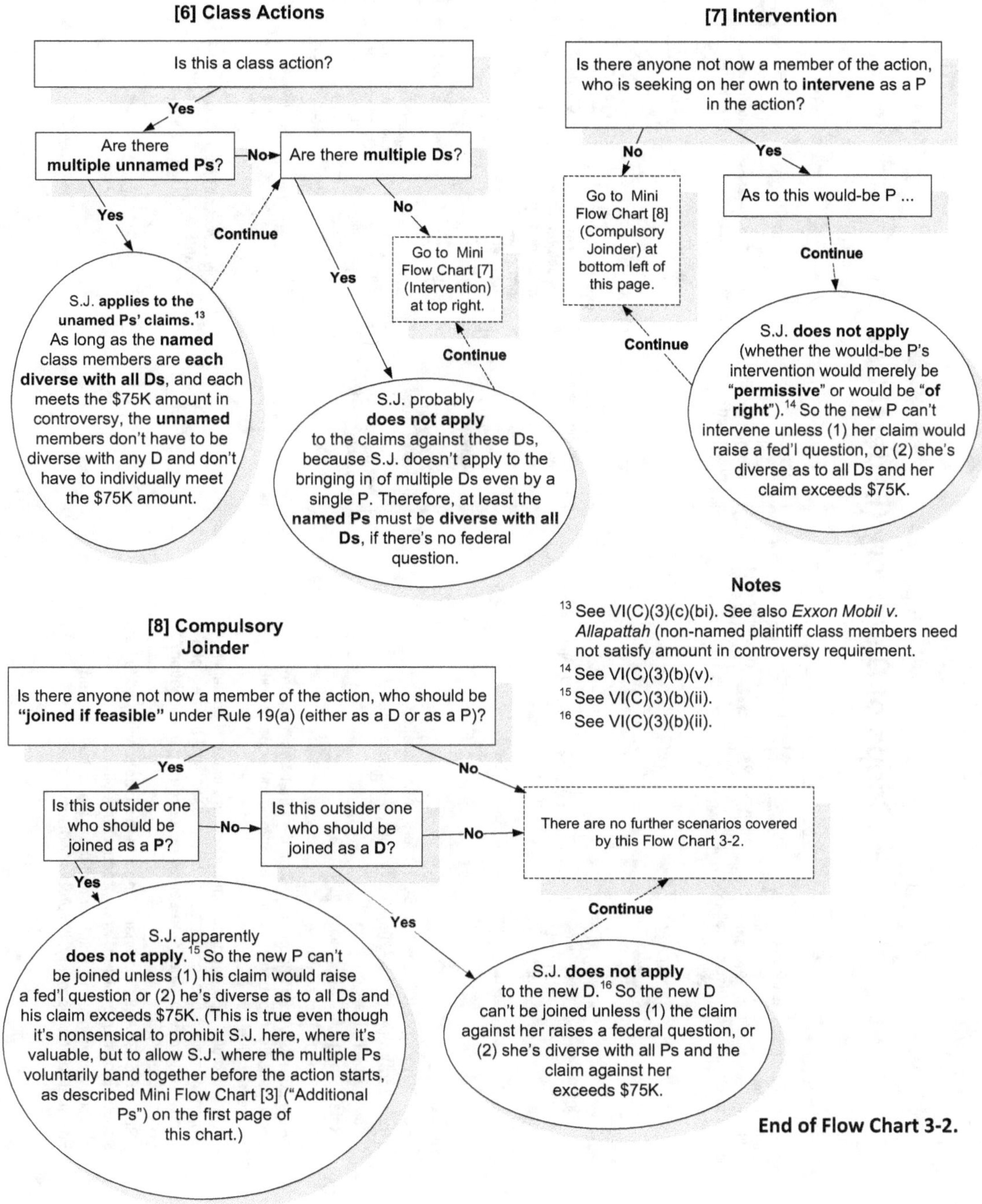

Notes

[13] See VI(C)(3)(c)(bi). See also *Exxon Mobil v. Allapattah* (non-named plaintiff class members need not satisfy amount in controversy requirement.

[14] See VI(C)(3)(b)(v).

[15] See VI(C)(3)(b)(ii).

[16] See VI(C)(3)(b)(ii).

End of Flow Chart 3-2.

Figure 5-1

Scope of Discovery (Federal Courts)

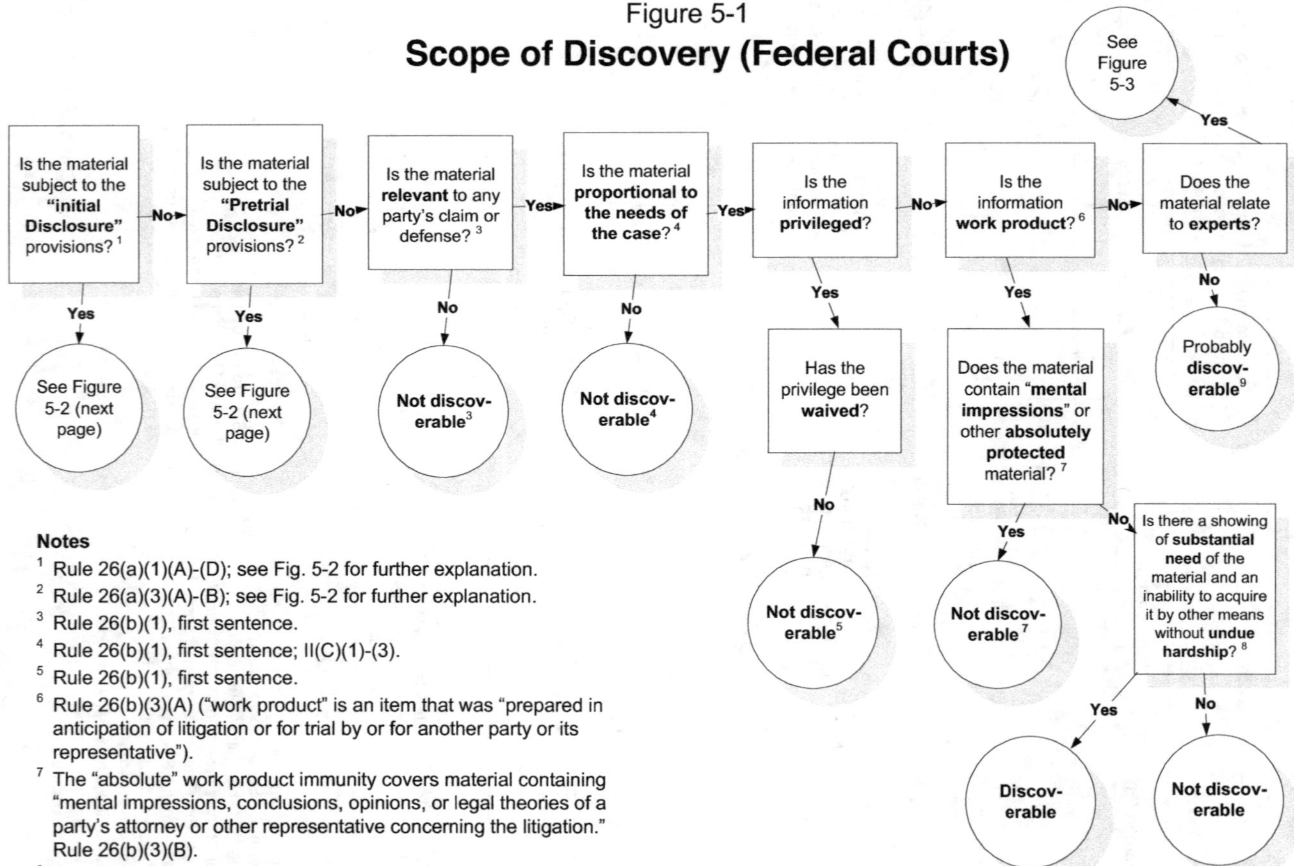

Notes

1. Rule 26(a)(1)(A)-(D); see Fig. 5-2 for further explanation.
2. Rule 26(a)(3)(A)-(B); see Fig. 5-2 for further explanation.
3. Rule 26(b)(1), first sentence.
4. Rule 26(b)(1), first sentence; II(C)(1)-(3).
5. Rule 26(b)(1), first sentence.
6. Rule 26(b)(3)(A) ("work product" is an item that was "prepared in anticipation of litigation or for trial by or for another party or its representative").
7. The "absolute" work product immunity covers material containing "mental impressions, conclusions, opinions, or legal theories of a party's attorney or other representative concerning the litigation." Rule 26(b)(3)(B).
8. Rule 26(b)(3)(A)(ii); material falling into this category is said to be covered by the "qualified" work product immunity.
9. If you've gotten to this point without the material having been disqualified for discovery, it's probably discoverable.

Figure 5-2
Discovery: Automatic Disclosure

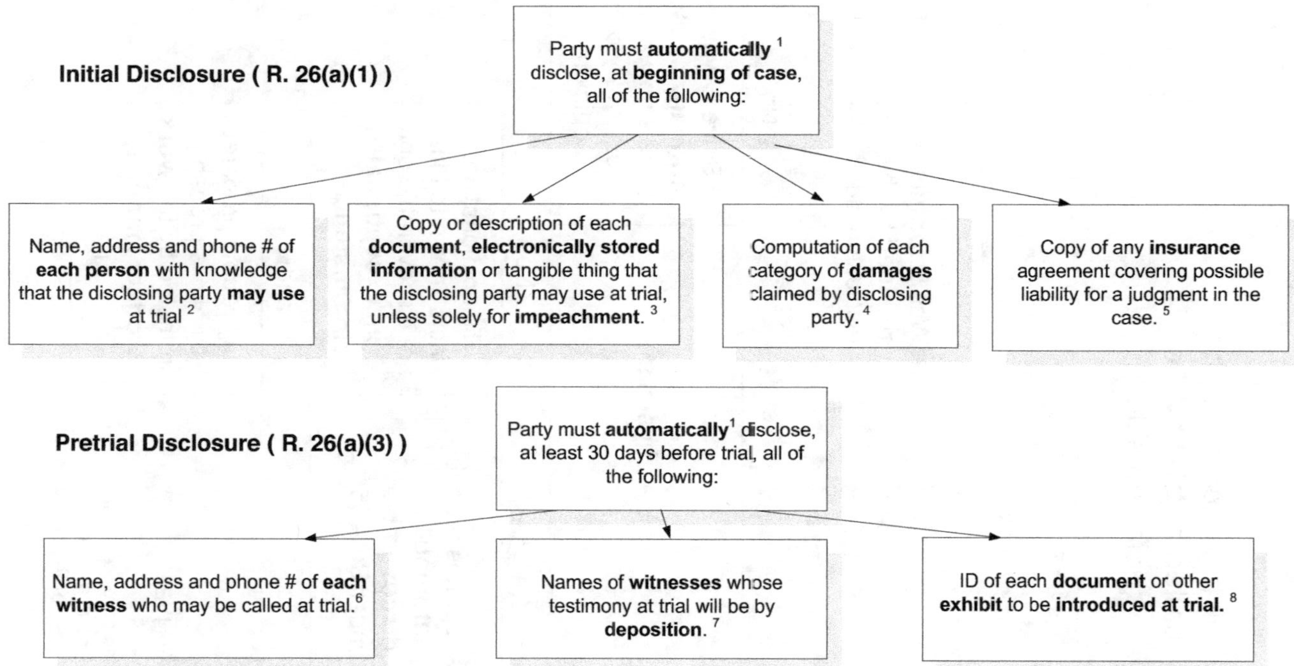

1 "Automatically" means "Without awaiting a discovery request"; see Rule 26(a)(1).

2 Rule 26(a)(1)(A)(i) (requires listing of "each individual likely to have discoverable information – along with the subjects of that information – that the disclosing party may use to support its claims or defenses, unless the use would be solely for impeachment").

3 Rule 26(a)(1)(A)(ii) .

4 Rule 26(a)(1)(A)(iii) (also requires furnishing of "documents or other evidentiary material ... on which such computation is based[.]")

5 Rule 26(a)(1)(A)(iv).

6 Rule 26(a)(3)(A) (also requires disclosing party to distinguish between witnesses she "expects" to present and those whom she "may call if the need arises.").

7 Rule 26(a)(3)(A)(ii) (also requires a transcript of the testimony to be presented, if the deposition was taken by non-stenographic means, such as by videotape).

8 Rule 26(a)(3)(A)(iii) (requires an "identification" of each exhibit; also requires party to distinguish between items which he "expects" to offer and those he "may offer if the need arises.").

Figure 5-3

Discovery Concerning Experts

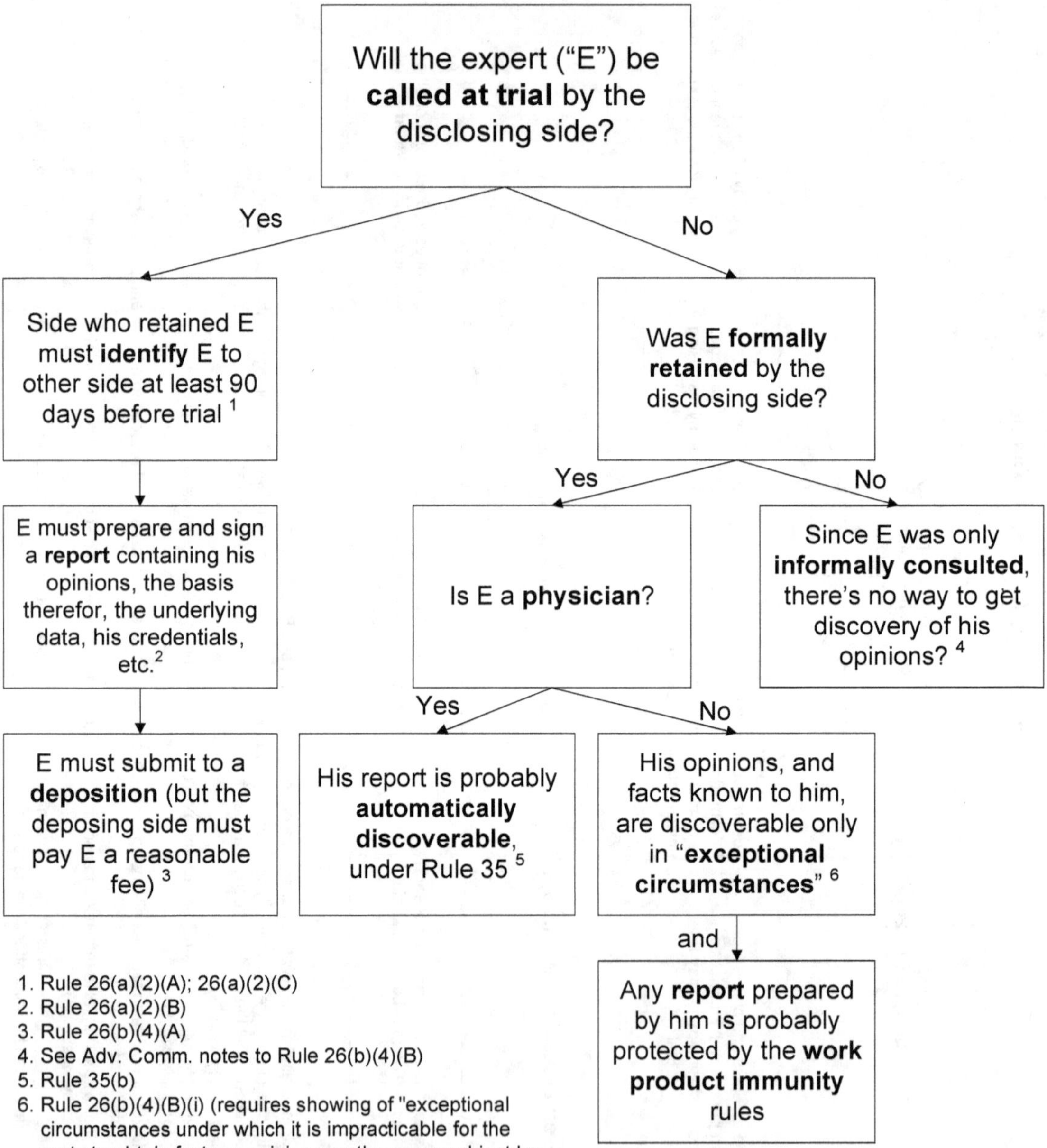

1. Rule 26(a)(2)(A); 26(a)(2)(C)
2. Rule 26(a)(2)(B)
3. Rule 26(b)(4)(A)
4. See Adv. Comm. notes to Rule 26(b)(4)(B)
5. Rule 35(b)
6. Rule 26(b)(4)(B)(i) (requires showing of "exceptional circumstances under which it is impracticable for the party to obtain facts or opinions on the same subject by other means.")

Figure 6-1

Analyzing *Erie* Problems

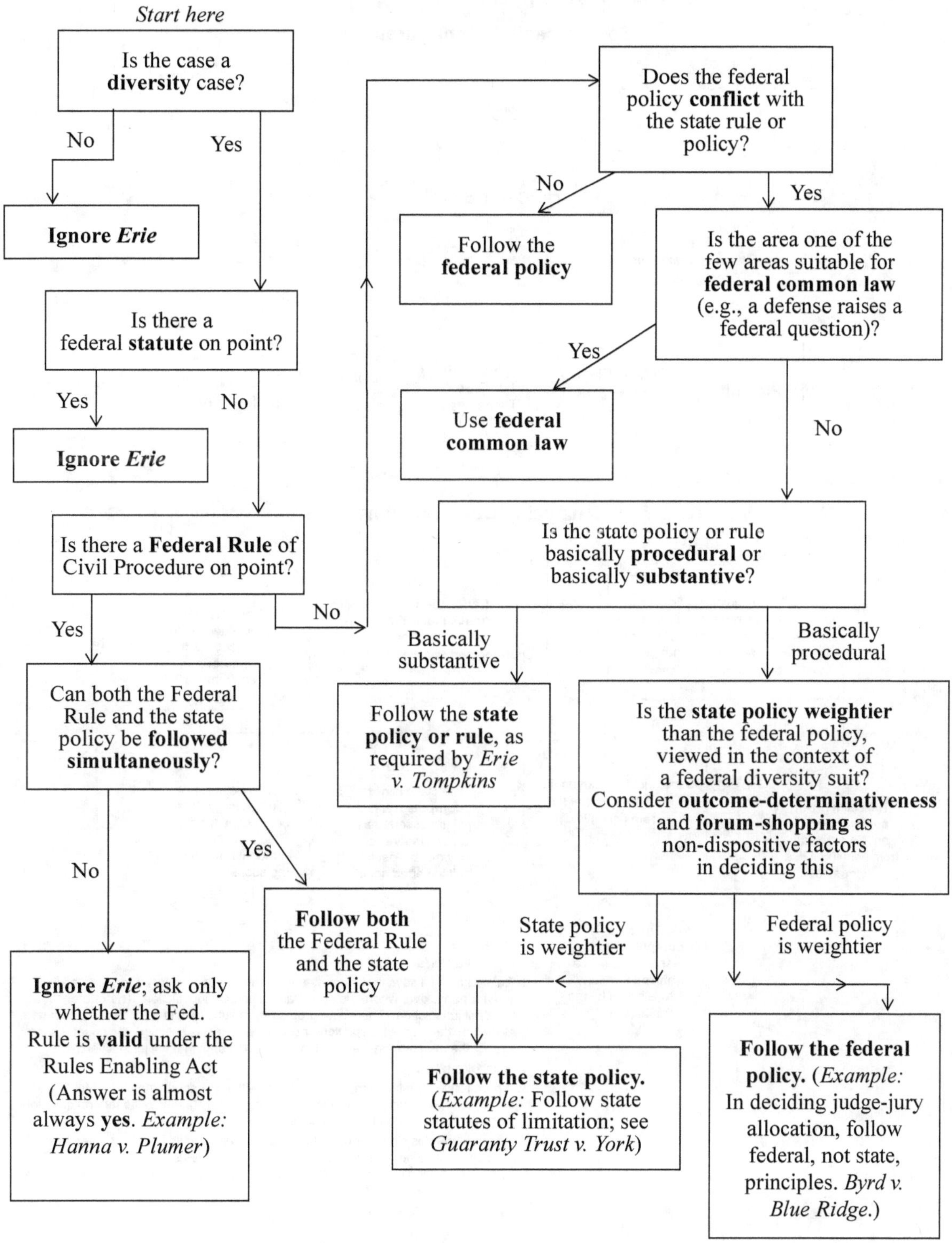

Figure 8-1: Counterclaims

Some Possible Configurations

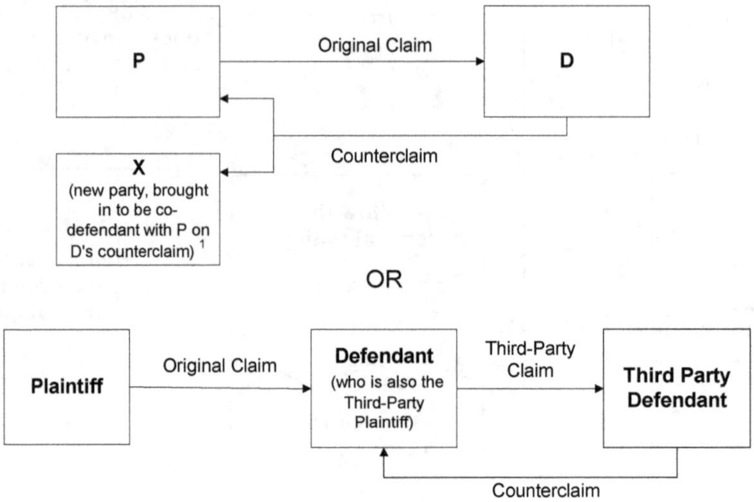

Analyzing Counterclaims

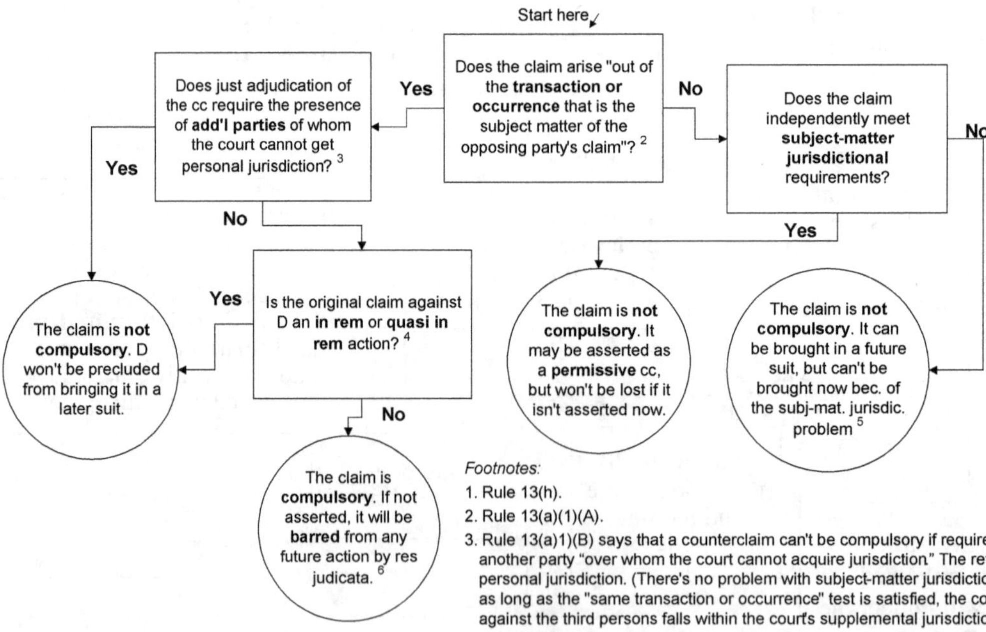

Footnotes:

1. Rule 13(h).
2. Rule 13(a)(1)(A).
3. Rule 13(a)1)(B) says that a counterclaim can't be compulsory if requires adding another party "over whom the court cannot acquire jurisdiction." The reference is to personal jurisdiction. (There's no problem with subject-matter jurisdiction, because as long as the "same transaction or occurrence" test is satisfied, the counterclaim against the third persons falls within the court's supplemental jurisdiction.)
4. Rule 13(a)(2)(B).
5. A permissive counterclaim is probably not within the court's supplemental jurisdiction, and must therefore independently satisfy (if there's no federal question present) diversity and amount in controversy.
6. Observe that this circle represents the only situation in which the counterclaim is compulsory. In other words, the claim must satisfy 3 tests to be compulsory: (1) "same transaction or occurrence"; (2) no unreachable additional parties necessary, and (3) no *in rem* or *quasi in rem*.

Table 8-1
Analyzing Joinder of Parties

Type of Party Jnd.	Permissive v. Compulsory	Requirements as to Claims	Requirements as to Jurisdiction
Plaintiffs	**Permissive** (Rule 20)	(1) Each P must have at least one claim arising out of a ***common "transaction, occurrence*** or series of transactions or occurrences" [R. 20(a)(1)(A)]; and (2) There must be at least one ***question of law or fact common*** to all Ps that will arise in the action. [R. 20(a)(1)(B)]	***Supplemental jurisdiction applies*** as to ***amount in controversy,*** but ***not*** as to the requirement of ***complete diversity***. Therefore, if no federal question is present all Ps must be ***diverse*** with D, but only one P has to have a claim > \$75K (and others with claims < \$75K can use supplemental jurisdiction to join). See *Exxon Mobil v. Allapattah.*
Plaintiffs	**Compulsory** (Rule 19)	[Cannot exist under Rule 20. Very occasionally, "involuntary plaintiff" can be joined under Rule 19(a).]	***Supplemental jurisdiction*** probably does ***not*** apply, so usual diversity and amount in controversy rules would apply.
Defendants	**Permissive** (Rule 20)	(1) All Ds must be faced with at least one claim arising out of a ***common "transaction, occurrence*** or series of transactions or occurrences" [R. 20(a)(2)(A)]; and (2) There must be at least one question of law or fact common to all Ds that will arise. [R. 20(a)(2)(B).]	**Subject matter jur.:** ***Supplemental jurisdiction*** does ***not*** apply, so if no fed. question is present, P must be diverse with all Ds, and the amt. in contr. must be satisfied as to each D. (This prob. means that P must have claim greater than \$75K against <u>each</u> D.) See IV(C)(2), *supra.* **Personal jur.:** Each D must be personally served, have ***min. contacts*** with the state where the fed. ct. sits, and be reachable by the long-arm of the state where the federal court sits. Also, ***venue*** requirements must be satisfied. See IV(C)(1), *supra.*
Defendants	**Compulsory / Necessary, but not Indispensable** (Rule 19(a)) [D must be joined if service can be validly made on him, and if his presence wouldn't destroy diversity. Otherwise, action proceeds without D.]	Same requirements as for "Permissive," *plus* a D must be joined (if possible) if either: (1) in D's absence ***complete relief*** can't be accorded among those already parties [R. 19(a)(1)(A)]; or (2) a judgment in D's absence will either (a) as a practical matter ***impair*** D's interest or (b) leave an existing party subject to substantial risk of "double, multiple, or otherwise ***inconsistent obligations***." [R. 19(a)(1)(B)]	**Subject matter jur.:** Same as for Ds/ Permissive. So ***supplemental jurisdiction*** does ***not*** apply. Thus if no federal question is present, P must be ***diverse*** with all Ds, and ***amount in controversy*** must be satisfied as to ***each*** D. (Probably P must have claim greater than \$75K against <u>each</u> D.) See IV(D)(3), *supra.* **Personal jur.:** Same as for "Permissive." So each D must be personally served, have ***minimum contacts***, etc. Also, venue reqs. must be satisfied.

Continued on Next Page

Table 8-1
(Continued from Previous Page)

Type of Party Jnd.	Permissive v. Compulsory	Requirements as to Claims	Requirements as to Jurisdiction
Defendants	**Compulsory / Indispensable** (Rule 19(b)) [D must be joined if possible. If D can't be joined bec. of jurisdictional problems, whole action must be **dismissed.**]	Same reqs. as "Compulsory / Necessary," *plus* D is "indispensable," judged by looking at prejudice to D or to those already parties, possibility of framing remedy to avoid this prejudice, adequacy of remedy that can be given in D's absence, and whether P will have adequate remedy if action is dismissed.	Same as for "Compulsory / Necessary." Only difference is the ***consequence*** of problems of jurisdiction: If D is "indispensable," action must be dismissed (whereas if D is merely "necessary," action can go on w/o D if D's joinder is not possible.)
Defendants + Plaintiffs	[Combine the analysis: first analyze the "multiple plaintiffs," then analyze the "multiple defendants."]		

Table 8-2

CLASS ACTIONS

Type of Class Action	Requirements	Examples	Notice	Opt-Out Options	Effect on Future Actions by Same P
23(b)(1)	Individual actions by or against the class would create: (a) ***inconsistent decisions*** forcing an opponent of the class to observe incompatible standards; *or* (b) ***impairment of the interests*** of members of the class who are not actually a party to the individual actions	(1) A number of ***taxpayers*** wish to have a municipal bond issue declared invalid, and others wish to have the terms of the issue changed. If taxpayers bring individual suits, the municipality may be forced to observe incompatible standards concerning the bonds. See R. 23(b)(1), Clause A. (2) Members of an ***association*** wish to prevent a financial reorganization of the association. If one member sues individually and loses, the reorg. will proceed. The reorg.'s effect will thus spread to members who wished to prevent it. See R. 23(b)(1), Clause B. (3) ***Mass-tort*** cases: If individual suits are brought, plaintiffs with early suits may bankrupt the defendant, leaving nothing for the latter plaintiffs. Examples: airline crashes; asbestos cases; IUD and breast-implant suits.	Court "may" (but is not required to) direct ***"appropriate notice"*** to the class. FRCP 23(c)(2)(A). This will not necessarily be individual (e.g., mail) notice — it may instead be mass notice such as by newspaper or Website publication.	Class members may ***not*** opt out. (However, if an absent member lacked minimum contacts with the state where the federal court sits, the absentee might be able to claim that binding her violated her due process rights.)	Since no one may opt out, ***all*** class members are ***bound*** by the disposition. See Rule 23(c)(3).

Continued on next page

Table 8-2

CLASS ACTIONS (cont.)

Type of Class Action	Requirements	Examples	Notice	Opt-Out Options	Effect on Future Actions by Same P
23(b)(2)	The party opposing the class has acted or refused to act on grounds generally applicable to the class.	***Civil rights*** cases, where discrimination against the whole class is alleged, and an injunction prohibiting further discrimination is sought.	Same as for (b)(1) actions.	Same as for (b)(1) actions.	Same as for (b)(1) actions.
23(b)(3)	The court makes two findings: (1) ***Common questions*** of law or fact ***predominate*** over any questions affecting only individual members. (2) The class action is ***superior*** to other available methods for fair and efficient adjudication of the controversy.	This is the most common type of class action. (1) Often used in ***securities fraud*** cases (it's impractical for most investors who've been harmed to sue individually, bec. the amount lost is too small to justify the cost of a suit). (2) ***Antitrust*** cases (consumers who've been injured by anti-competitive conduct, such as price-fixing). (3) Occasionally, ***mass-tort*** cases (but (b)(1) is more common in the tort context, especially where there's a danger the defendant will be bankrupted by individual suits).	"***Best notice practicable*** under the circumstances" must be given to all class members. Rule 23(c)(2)((B). This means ***individual*** notice (e.g., by mail) to all class member whose names can be obtained with reasonable certainty. *Id.* The named plaintiffs must front the cost. If they can't or won't, class action must be dismissed. *Eisen.*	Class members have the ***right to opt out***. Rule 23(c)(2).	The judgment will affect each class member (whether favorable to the member or not), ***unless the member opted out.***

Table 8-3

Comparison: Statutory and Rule Interpleader

	Statutory	Rule 22
When there is no federal question, what kind of diversity must exist?	Some pair of claimants must be diverse with each other.	The stakeholder must not have the same citizenship as any claimant.
Where may service of process be made?	Anywhere in the U.S.	Ordinary rules for federal civil suits must be followed.
How much money must be in controversy?	More than $500	More than $75,000 (unless a federal question is present).
Must the stakeholder deposit the amount in dispute in court?	Yes	No
May the stakeholder claim that he is not liable to any of the claimants?	Yes	Yes

CAPSULE SUMMARY

SUMMARY OF CONTENTS OF CAPSULE SUMMARY

CAPSULE SUMMARY

CHAPTER 1

INTRODUCTION

I. CIVIL PROCEDURE GENERALLY

A. **A road map:** Here is a ***"road map"*** for analyzing a Civil Procedure problem:

1. **Personal jurisdiction:** First, make sure that the court has ***"personal jurisdiction"*** or ***"jurisdiction over the parties."*** You must check to make sure that: (1) D had ***minimum contacts*** with the forum state (whether the court is a state or federal court); and (2) D received such ***notice and opportunity to be heard*** as to satisfy the constitutional requirement of due process.

2. **Venue:** Then, check whether ***venue*** was correct. In federal court suits, the venue requirement describes what judicial ***district*** the case may be heard in. Essentially, the case must be heard either: (1) in any district where the ***defendant resides*** (with special rules for multi-defendant cases; or (2) in any district in which a ***substantial part of the events*** giving rise to the claim occurred. See 28 U.S.C. §1391.

3. **Subject-matter jurisdiction:** If the case is a federal case, you must then ask whether the court has ***subject-matter*** jurisdiction. Essentially, this means that one of the following two things must be true:

   a. **Diversity:** Either the case is between ***citizens of different states*** (with "complete diversity" required, so that no plaintiff is a citizen of the same state as any defendant) and at least $75,000 is at stake; or

   b. **Federal question:** The case raises a ***"federal question."*** Essentially, this means that plaintiff's right to recover stems from the U.S. Constitution, a federal treaty, or an act of Congress. (There is no minimum amount required to be at stake in federal question cases.)

4. **Pleading:** Next, you must examine whether the ***pleadings*** are proper.

5. **Discovery:** Next, you may have a complex of issues relating to pre-trial ***discovery***.

6. **Ascertaining applicable law:** Now, figure out ***what jurisdiction's law*** should be used in the case. The most important problem of this type is: In a diversity case, may the federal court apply its own concepts of "federal common law", or must the court apply the law of the state where the federal court sits? If the state has a ***substantive law*** (whether a statute or a judge-made principle) that is on point, ***the federal court sitting in diversity must apply that law***. This is the "rule" of ***Erie v. Tompkins***. (*Example:* In a diversity case concerning negligence, the federal court must normally apply the negligence law of the state where the court sits.)

7. **Trial procedure:** Next, you may face a series of issues relating to ***trial procedure.***

8. **Multi-party and multi-claim litigation:** If there is more than one claim in the case, or more than the basic two parties (a single plaintiff and a single defendant), you will face a whole host of issues related to the ***multi-party*** or ***multi-claim*** nature of the litigation. You must be prepared to deal with the various methods of bringing multiple parties and multiple claims into a case. In federal courts:

   a. **Counterclaim:** D may make a claim against P, by use of the ***counterclaim.*** See FRCP 13. Check whether the counterclaim is ***"permissive"*** or ***"compulsory."*** (Also, remember that third parties, who are neither the original plaintiff nor the original defendant, may make a counterclaim.)

   b. **Joinder of claims:** Once a party has made a claim against some other party, she may then make ***any other claim*** she wishes against that party. This is ***"joinder of claims."*** See Rule 18(a).

   c. **Joinder of parties:** Multiple parties may ***join*** their actions together. Check to see whether either "***permissive*** joinder" or "***compulsory*** joinder" is applicable. Also, remember that each of these two types of joinder can apply to ***either multiple plaintiffs*** or ***multiple defendants***. See FRCP 19 and 20.

   d. **Class actions:** Check whether a ***class action*** is available as a device to handle the claims of many similarly-situated plaintiffs, or claims against many similarly-situated defendants. See FRCP 23. Look for the possibility of a class action wherever there are 25 or more similarly-situated plaintiffs or similarly-situated defendants.

   e. **Intervention:** A person who is not initially part of a lawsuit may be able to enter the suit on his own initiative, under the doctrine of ***intervention***. See FRCP 24. Check whether the intervention is "of right" or "permissive."

   f. **Interpleader:** Where a party owes something to two or more other persons, but isn't sure which, that party may want to use the device of ***interpleader*** to prevent being made to pay the same claim twice. After checking whether interpleader might be desirable, decide whether the stakeholder should use "***statutory*** interpleader" or "Rule interpleader." See 28 U.S.C. §1335 (statutory interpleader) and FRCP 22 (Rule interpleader).

   g. **Third-party practice (impleader):** Anytime D has a potential claim against some ***third person*** who is not already in the lawsuit, by which that third person will be liable to D for some or all of P's recovery against D, D should be able to ***"implead"*** the third person. (*Example:* Employee, while working for Employer, hits Victim with a company car. Victim sues Employer in diversity, under the doctrine of *respondeat superior*. Under traditional concepts of indemnity, Employer will be able to recover from Employee for any amount that Employer is forced to pay Victim. Therefore, Employer should "implead" Employee as a "third party defendant" to the Victim-Employer action.) See FRCP 14(a). Once a third-party defendant is brought into the case, consider what other claims might now be available (e.g., a counterclaim by the third-party defendant against the third-party plaintiff, a cross-claim against some other third-party defendant, a counterclaim against the original plaintiff, etc.).

h. Cross-claims: Check to see whether any party has made, or should make, a claim against a ***co-party***. This is a ***cross-claim***. See FRCP 13(g).

i. Jurisdiction: For any of these multi-party or multi-claim devices, check to see whether the requirements of ***personal jurisdiction*** and ***subject-matter jurisdiction*** have been satisfied. To do this, you will need to know whether the doctrine of ***"supplemental"*** jurisdiction applies to the particular device in question. If it does not, the new claim, or the new party, will typically have to ***independently*** meet the requirements of federal subject-matter jurisdiction. (*Example:* P, from Massachusetts, sues D, from Connecticut, in diversity. X, from Massachusetts, wants to intervene in the case on the side of D. Because supplemental jurisdiction does not apply to intervention, X must independently satisfy the requirement of diversity, which he cannot do because he is a citizen of the same state as P. Therefore, X cannot intervene.)

9. Former adjudication: Lastly, check whether the results in some ***prior litigation*** are ***binding*** in the current suit. Distinguish between situations in which the ***judgment*** in the prior suit is binding on an entire cause of action in the present suit (under the doctrines of ***merger*** and ***bar***), and the situation where a ***finding of fact*** is binding on the current suit, even though the judgment itself is not binding (the ***"collateral estoppel"*** situation).

a. Non-mutual collateral estoppel: Where a ***"stranger"*** to the first action (one not a party to that first action) now seeks to take advantage of a finding of fact in that first suit, consider whether this ***"non-mutual"*** collateral estoppel should be allowed.

b. Full Faith and Credit: Lastly, if the two suits have taken place in ***different jurisdictions***, consider to what extent the principles of ***Full Faith and Credit*** limit the second court's freedom to ignore what happened in the first suit.

CHAPTER 2

JURISDICTION OVER THE PARTIES

I. GENERAL PRINCIPLES

A. Two kinds of jurisdiction: Before a court can decide a case, it must have jurisdiction over the ***parties*** as well as over the ***subject matter***.

1. Subject-matter jurisdiction: ***Subject-matter*** jurisdiction refers to the court's power to decide the ***kind*** of case before it. (*Examples of subject-matter jurisdiction issues:* (1) Does the federal court for the District of New Jersey have the power to decide cases in which the two parties are citizens of different states? (2) Does the Binghamton Municipal Court have the power to decide cases involving more than $1,000?)

2. **Jurisdiction over the parties:** Jurisdiction over the ***parties*** refers to whether the court has jurisdiction to decide a case ***between the particular parties***, or ***concerning the property***, before it. (*Examples of issues concerning jurisdiction over the parties:* (1) Does Court X have jurisdiction over D, who is a citizen of State X, but who is temporarily out of the state? (2) Does Court Y have jurisdiction over property in State Y where the action is one by P to register title to the land in his name?)

B. **Jurisdiction over the parties:** There are two distinct requirements which must be met before a court has jurisdiction over the ***parties***:

1. **Substantive due process:** The court must have ***power*** to act, either upon given property, or on a given person so as to subject her to personal liability. The Constitution's Fourteenth Amendment Due Process Clause imposes this requirement of power to act, as a matter of ***"substantive due process."***

2. **Procedural due process:** Also, the court must have given the defendant ***adequate notice*** of the action against him, and an ***opportunity to be heard.*** These, taken together, are requirements of ***procedural due process***, also imposed by the Fourteenth Amendment's Due Process Clause.

C. **Three kinds of jurisdiction over the parties:** There are ***three different kinds*** of jurisdiction which a court may exercise over the parties — one of these three ***must be present*** for the case to go forward.

1. **In personam:** ***In personam*** jurisdiction, or jurisdiction over the defendant's "person," gives the court power to issue a judgment against her ***personally***. Thus ***all*** of the person's ***assets*** may be seized to satisfy the judgment, and the judgment can be sued upon in other states as well.

2. **In rem:** ***In rem*** jurisdiction, or jurisdiction over a ***thing***, gives the court power to adjudicate a claim made about a ***piece of property*** or about a ***status***. (*Examples:* An action to quiet title to real estate, or an action to pronounce a marriage dissolved.)

3. **Quasi in rem jurisdiction:** In ***quasi in rem*** jurisdiction, the action is begun by seizing property owned by (***attachment***), or a debt owed to (***garnishment***) the defendant, within the forum state. The thing seized is a pretext for the court to decide the case without having jurisdiction over the defendant's person. Any judgment affects only the property seized, and the judgment cannot be sued upon in any other court.

4. **"Minimum contacts" requirement:** If jurisdiction in the case is ***in personam*** or ***quasi in rem***, the court may not exercise that jurisdiction unless D has ***"minimum contacts"*** with the state in which the court sits.

   a. **"Purposefully directed" towards the forum state:** The requirement of minimum contacts usually means that D has to have taken ***actions*** that were ***purposefully directed*** towards the forum state.

Examples of the required action: (1) D sold goods in the state, or (2) D is a corporation that has incorporated in the state, (3) D has visited the state, and been served with process while there, or (4) D has bought property in the state, etc.

b. **Consequence of lack of contacts:** Without such minimum contacts between D and the forum state, exercise of jurisdiction would violate D's 14th Amendment federal constitutional right to due process. For more about due process, see Par. (D), "Due process," below.

D. **Due process:** The exercise of jurisdiction by a state court must satisfy the defendant's rights under the ***due process*** clause of the ***14th Amendment.*** Thus if D is entirely lacking in ***connections with the forum state***, it will violate D's 14th Amendment due process rights for a court of the forum state to exercise *in personam* jurisdiction over D. Nearly all of the Supreme Court cases about jurisdiction in Civil Procedure courses concern this due process requirement.

1. **"Specific" versus "general" jurisdiction:** The Supreme Court's cases on the due process aspects of *in personam* jurisdiction make an important distinction between two categories of personal jurisdiction: (1) ***"specific"*** jurisdiction; and (2) ***"general"*** jurisdiction.

a. **"Specific" jurisdiction:** ***"Specific"*** jurisdiction refers to a court's exercise of personal jurisdiction to hear a claim ***related to, and arising out of,*** the defendant's voluntary ***contacts with the forum state.***

i. **Lesser contacts required:** In general, a ***smaller degree*** of contact between the defendant and the forum state is required for a state court to exercise specific jurisdiction over the defendant than for it to exercise general jurisdiction. But the defendant will still be required to have some voluntary contacts (also referred to as ***"minimum contacts"***) with the forum state.

Example: D, an individual, contracts to sell a laptop computer to P, also an individual. D lives in Texas and P resides in Arkansas. D assembles the laptop in Texas and personally delivers it to P's Arkansas home address, where D installs it. D has no business connections with Arkansas other than this one sale and delivery to P. Ten months later, the laptop's batteries malfunction, the laptop catches on fire, and P is burned. P sues D in Arkansas state court for his injuries.

If the Arkansas state court hears the case and decides whether D should be personally liable for damages, the type of personal jurisdiction that the court will be exercising is ***"specific*** jurisdiction" — that is, the suit relates to and arises out of D's contacts with the forum state, Arkansas (since the suit relates to a computer as to which D voluntarily traveled to Arkansas to make delivery and installation).

Because the suit is based on specific jurisdiction, all that's required is that D have "minimum contacts" with Arkansas. And here, even the relatively small degree of voluntary connection between D and Arkansas amounts to "minimum contacts," thereby preventing the Arkansas court's hearing of the case from being a violation of D's 14th Amendment due process rights.

b. "General" jurisdiction: By contrast, ***"general"*** jurisdiction refers to a situation in which the state court is exercising *in personam* jurisdiction to hear a claim that ***does not arise out of or relate to the defendant's contacts with the forum state.***

i. Extensive contacts required: The U.S. Supreme Court requires, as a matter of fairness to the defendant, ***much more extensive contacts*** between the defendant and the forum state when the state court is exercising general jurisdiction (as opposed to specific jurisdiction) over that defendant.

In fact, where the defendant is an ***individual***, in most cases a state court may as a constitutional due process matter exercise general jurisdiction over that defendant ***only*** if the defendant is ***domiciled in***, or else ***personally served with process in***, that state.

Example: Same basic fact pattern as in the above example. Now, however, some time after D has delivered the computer to P in Arkansas, P drives through Texas on a vacation, and happens to stop off to see D at D's house there. Towards the end of the visit, when P is standing in D's driveway, D accidentally runs him over. P brings a negligence suit against D in Arkansas for P's injuries from the Texas accident.

This suit, unlike the one in the prior Example, will have to be based on ***"general"*** (not specific) jurisdiction, since P's claim has nothing to do with any voluntary contact between D and Arkansas (the forum state). Since the case has to be based on general jurisdiction over D or not brought at all, D's federal constitutional due process rights probably mean that the Arkansas court will not have personal jurisdiction over D to hear the case, unless either (1) D changes his domicile to Arkansas prior to suit; or (2) D is served by P at a moment when D happens to be temporarily in Arkansas.

c. "Specific" form more common: The substantial majority of state-court litigations that you will encounter in your Civil Procedure course — including most of the Supreme Court opinions you'll read — involve specific rather than general jurisdiction.

E. Long-arm statutes: Even where the requirements of due process (minimum contacts between D and the forum state, etc.) are satisfied, the defendant may not be served ***outside*** of the forum state unless the forum state has enacted a ***statute*** authorizing out-of-state service under certain circumstances. Such statutes allowing the courts of a state to obtain jurisdiction over persons ***not physically present*** within the state at the time of the service are called "***long-arm*** statutes."

1. Links to forum state: Long-arm statutes allow jurisdiction on the basis of specified ***links between the defendant and the forum state***, such as domicile there, ownership of property in the state, commission of a tortious act inside the state, etc.

2. **Substitute service:** Long-arms typically provide for "substitute" means of ***service***, since in-state personal service is not possible. (*Example:* A long-arm statute might allow the plaintiff to cause the defendant to be served out of state by registered mail.)

F. **Flow Chart:** For an overview of how to analyze state-court jurisdiction problems, see the Flow Chart printed as Figure 2-1.

II. JURISDICTION OVER INDIVIDUALS

A. **Different categories:** In most states, there are a number of different criteria which will enable the court to take personal jurisdiction over an individual. Some of the most common (each of which will be considered in detail below) are:

1. ***Presence*** within the forum state;
2. ***Domicile*** or ***residence*** within the forum state;
3. ***Consent*** to be sued within the forum state;
4. ***Driving a car*** within the forum state;
5. Committing a ***tortious act*** within the state (or, perhaps, committing an out-of-state act with in-state tortious consequences);
6. Ownership of ***property*** in the forum state;
7. Conducting ***business*** in the forum state;
8. Being ***married in***, or living while married in, the forum state.

Note: Regardless of the criteria used by the state and its long-arm for establishing personal jurisdiction over the individual, due process requires that the individual have ***minimum contacts*** with the forum state before personal jurisdiction may be exercised over her. The meaning of "minimum contacts" is discussed further below in the treatment of jurisdiction over corporations.

B. **Presence:** Jurisdiction may be exercised over an individual by virtue of his ***presence within the forum state*** at the time he is served with process. That is, even if the individual is an out-of-state resident who comes into the forum state only briefly, personal jurisdiction over him may be gotten as long as ***service was made*** on him while he was in the forum state.

Example: D and his wife, P, separate while residing in New Jersey. P moves to California with their children. D visits California on business, and stops briefly to visit the children. While D is visiting, P serves him with process in a California suit for divorce. D never visits the state again.

Held, California can constitutionally assert personal jurisdiction over D based on his presence in the state at the time of service, even though that presence was brief, and even though D had virtually no other contacts with the state. [*Burnham v. Superior Court*]

C. **Domicile:** Jurisdiction may be exercised over a person who is ***domiciled*** within the forum state, even if service takes place outside of the forum state.

1. **Meaning of "domicile":** A person is considered to be domiciled in the place where he has his ***current dwelling place***, if he also has the ***intention to remain*** in that place for an ***indefinite period.***

D. **Residence:** Some states allow jurisdiction to be exercised on the basis of D's ***residence in the forum state***, even though he is absent from the state. A person may have several residences simultaneously. (The Supreme Court has not yet passed on the due process validity of jurisdiction based solely on residence, so this remains presumptively a valid method of gaining jurisdiction.)

E. **Consent:** Jurisdiction over a party can be exercised by virtue of her ***consent***, even if she has no contacts whatsoever with the forum state.

> **Example:** P, who does not reside in Ohio or have any other contacts with Ohio, brings suit against D in Ohio. By filing the suit in Ohio, P will be deemed to have consented to Ohio's jurisdiction. D may then counterclaim against P. Even if P dismisses his own suit, his consent to the action will be binding, and the Ohio courts will have personal jurisdiction over him on the counterclaim.

F. **Non-resident motorist:** Most states have statutes allowing the courts to exercise jurisdiction over ***non-resident motorists*** who have been involved in ***accidents in the state***.

> **Example:** P is a resident of the forum state. D, not a resident of the forum state, is driving his car in the forum state, and has a collision with P's car. Even if D has no other contacts with the state, a non-resident motorist statute will probably be in force in the state, and will probably give the forum state's courts jurisdiction over a tort suit by P against D.

1. **Service on state official:** Most of the non-resident motorist statutes provide for in-state service of process on a ***designated state official*** (e.g., the Director of Motor Vehicles) and for ***registered mail service*** on the out-of-state defendant himself.

2. **Specific jurisdiction only:** Non-resident motorist statutes, when they exist, confer only ***specific jurisdiction.*** That is, they confer jurisdiction only for a suit involving the in-state auto accident.

G. **In-state tortiousness:** Many states have statutes allowing their courts jurisdiction over persons committing ***tortious acts within the state***.

> **Example:** D, an out-of-stater, gets into a fight with P at a bar in P's home state. P wants to bring a civil battery claim against D in the state. If, as is likely, the state has a long-arm provision governing tortious acts within the state, P will be able to get personal jurisdiction over D in the battery action.

1. **Out-of-state acts with in-state consequences:** Some "in-state tortious acts" long-arm clauses have been interpreted to include acts done ***outside the state*** which produce ***tortious consequences within the state***. In a ***products liability*** situation, a vendor who sells products that he knows will be used in the state may constitutionally be required to defend in the state, if the product causes injury in the state. [*Gray v. American Radiator Corp.*]

H. **Owners of in-state property:** Many states exercise jurisdiction over ***owners of in-state property*** in causes of action arising from that property.

I. **Conducting business:** States often exercise jurisdiction over non-residents who conduct ***businesses*** within the state. Since states may regulate an individual's business conduct in the state, they may constitutionally exercise jurisdiction relating to that doing of business.

   1. **Limited to specific jurisdiction:** Again, however, the statement that this type of unincorporated-business long-arm is constitutional assumes that the jurisdiction being exercised under the long-arm is ***specific***, rather than general, jurisdiction. In other words, probably the statute can constitutionally apply only to a suit ***arising out of the non-resident unincorporated business' in-state business activities***.

J. **Limits of due process as to lawsuits against individuals:** The Supreme Court has never squarely articulated a test for determining whether a state's exercise of personal jurisdiction over an out-of-state *individual* violates that person's right to ***constitutional due process.***

   1. **Rules for cases involving corporations:** But cases involving *corporate* defendants imply that a defendant who is an individual ***cannot constitutionally be subjected to a state's jurisdiction unless either:***

      [1] **General jurisdiction based on domicile:** The defendant is ***domiciled in*** (or, perhaps, has a residence in) the forum state. And in that case, it's probably constitutional for even *general* jurisdiction to be exercised over her — i.e., even jurisdiction for a suit having nothing to do with the defendant's in-forum-state activities.

   or ...

      [2] **Specific jurisdiction based on minimum contacts:** The suit relates to and arises out of the defendant's ***voluntary ties to the forum state*** (e.g., conduct that the defendant voluntarily took in the forum state, such as driving a car in the forum state). That is, the situation is one in which the defendant can be said to have ***"minimum contacts"*** with the forum state. And in this minimum-contacts situation, probably *only specific* jurisdiction — jurisdiction for a claim arising out of the voluntary in-state activities — would satisfy D's right to due process.

III. "MINIMUM CONTACTS" GENERALLY; INTRODUCTION TO "SPECIFIC" JURISDICTION, INCLUDING SPECIFIC JURISDICTION OVER OUT-OF-STATE CORPORATIONS

A. **General principles covered in this section:** In this Section III, we're going to concentrate on the requirements that must be met before a forum state may exercise jurisdiction over an ***"out-of-state" corporate defendant.***

   1. **Federal due process issue:** Our focus will be on one central constitutional issue: when does a forum state's exercise of personal jurisdiction over an out-

of-state corporation ***violate the corporation's constitutional due process rights***?

a. **"Minimum contacts":** The out-of-state corporate defendant's right to due process means, essentially, that the defendant must have ***"minimum contacts"*** with the forum state.

2. **Specific versus general jurisdiction:** When a court purports to exercise personal jurisdiction over an "out of state" corporation, the court is necessarily exercising ***"specific jurisdiction"*** — not "general jurisdiction" — over that type of corporation.

   a. **Conclusion as to foreign corporation:** Therefore, if you see that a corporate defendant D is ***not headquartered in or incorporated in the forum state*** (i.e., D is a "foreign corporation"), you automatically know that any personal jurisdiction exercised by the forum state ***must be of the "specific" variety*** — so if the suit doesn't arise out of (or relate to) D's forum-state connections, you can immediately be *certain* that there is *no* type of personal jurisdiction (i.e., neither general nor specific) that the courts of the forum state can exercise over D.

   b. **Conclusion as to domestic corporation:** Conversely, as soon as you determine that corporate defendant D ***is*** a ***"domestic" corporation*** — i.e., one headquartered in the forum state, or with its principal place of business in the forum state, or both — then you know that the forum state ***can exercise general jurisdiction over D.*** And once you know that this corporation is subject to the general jurisdiction of the forum state, you know that ***all due process limits*** on the state's power to exercise personal jurisdiction over the corporation ***essentially disappear.***

3. **Minimum contacts always required in specific-jurisdiction cases:** If the suit arises out of D's forum-state connections, specific jurisdiction can exist even if D's forum-state connections that are *not* related to the suit are very sparse. But this statement is true *only* if the defendant's ***total connections*** with the forum state, taken together, ***constitute "minimum contacts"*** with the forum state. In other words, ***even in specific-jurisdiction cases, the court still has to ensure that D has minimum contacts with the forum state.***

   a. **"Arising out of" or "relating to" the forum state:** There is a ***second important requirement*** before an out-of-state defendant will be subject to specific jurisdiction in the forum state: the plaintiff's claim "must ***arise out of or relate to"*** the forum state.

   Example: P buys a car manufactured by D. The sale takes place in P's home state of Rhode Island, and the car was made in Michigan. P is injured in Rhode Island when the car crashes due to a defective steering wheel. Because the statute of limitations on a Rhode Island claim has already run, P sues in Maine state court, where the action is timely. D targets Maine (and every other state) with marketing efforts, and maintains a network of local dealership network there, thus giving D minimum contacts with Maine. But the accident has nothing to do with Maine.

P's claim cannot be said to have "arisen out of" or been "related to" Maine. Therefore, the Maine court can't exercise specific jurisdiction over D, and the suit can't go forward.

i. **Tort cases:** Many cases involve a tort suit (e.g., a product liability suit) brought in the federal or state court in the ***state where the plaintiff's injury occurred.*** The fact that the injury occurred in the forum state is enough to meet the requirement that the claim "arise out of or relate" to the forum state. (So in the above example, if the crash had occurred in the forum state, Maine, the suit would be able to go forward.)

B. Foreign corporations generally: A state is much more limited in its ability to exercise jurisdiction over a ***foreign*** corporation (i.e., a corporation not incorporated in the forum state and not headquartered there) than over a domestic corporation.

1. **Minimum contacts:** The forum state may exercise personal jurisdiction over the corporation only if the corporation has ***"minimum contacts"*** with the forum state "such that the maintenance of the suit does not offend 'traditional notions of fair play and substantial justice.' " [*International Shoe Co. v. Washington*]

2. **Dealings with residents of forum state:** Usually, a corporation will be found to have the requisite "minimum contacts" with the forum state only if the corporation has somehow ***voluntarily sought*** to ***do business*** in, or with the residents of, the forum state.

Example 1 (minimum contacts found): D has no activities in Washington except for the activities of its salesmen, who live in the state and work from their homes. All orders are sent by the salesmen to the home office, and approved at the home office. The salesmen earn a total of $31,000 per year in commissions.

Held, the company has minimum contacts with Washington. [*International Shoe Co.*]

Example 2 (minimum contacts found): D is a Texas insurance company. It does not solicit business in California. However, it takes over, from a previous insurance company, a policy written on the life of X, a California resident. D sends X a new policy; X sends premiums from his California home to D's out-of-state office. X dies; P (the beneficiary under the policy) is a California resident. P sues D in California for payment under the policy.

Held, D has minimum contacts with California, and can thus be sued *in personam* there in a suit by P for payment on the policy. [*McGee v. International Life Insur. Co.*]

Example 3 (minimum contacts not found): D is a Delaware bank, which acts as trustee of a certain trust. S, the settlor of the trust, is a Pennsylvania resident at the time she sets up the trust. Years later, she moves to Florida. Later, her two children, also Florida residents, want to sue D in Florida for a judgment that they are entitled to the remaining trust assets. D has no other contacts with Florida.

Held, D does not have minimum contacts with Florida, and therefore, cannot be sued *in personam* there. [*Hanson v. Denckla*]

Note: The key idea is that D will be found to have minimum contacts with the state only if D has ***purposely availed*** itself of the chance to do business in the forum state. Thus in *McGee* (Example 2 above), the insurance company offered a policy to someone who it knew was a resident of the forum state. In *Hanson* (Example 3 above), by contrast, the trustee never voluntarily initiated business transactions with a resident of the forum state or otherwise voluntarily did business in the state — it was only S's unilateral decision to move to the forum state that established any kind of connection with that state, so minimum contacts did not exist.

IV. SPECIFIC JURISDICTION AND MINIMUM CONTACTS — THE MODERN CASES

A. The modern cases, generally: We're now going to look in detail at the Court's modern-era cases on two issues about when a court can exercise specific jurisdiction over a claim: (1) whether D does or doesn't have "minimum contacts" with the forum state; and (2) whether P's claim "arises out of" some contact with the forum state, so as to trigger specific jurisdiction.

B. The modern cases, generally: We're now going to look in detail at the Court's modern-era cases on two issues about when a court can exercise specific jurisdiction over a claim: (1) whether D does or doesn't have ***"minimum contacts"*** with the forum state; and (2) whether P's claim "arises out of" the forum state.

C. Two requirements: There are ***two requirements*** that have to be met in order for the forum state to exercise specific jurisdiction over a suit:

[1] D must have ***"minimum contacts"*** with the forum state. Generally, this means that D must have ***"purposefully availed"*** itself of the ***opportunity to do business in the state***;

and

[2] P's claim must ***"arise out of, or relate to,"*** the forum state. But this requirement can be met even if D has ***not*** performed any activities in the forum state. So, for instance, the requirement is met if the event on which the claim is based occurred solely through the in-state activities of P.

Example of [2]: D, a car maker, makes a car in Ohio and sells the car in Ohio to P. Because of a defect in the car, P is injured in an accident that occurs in Indiana. P wants to sue D in a product liability action brought in Indiana. Assuming that D has minimum contacts with Indiana (requirement [1] above), the fact that the accident occurred in Indiana is *enough* to meet requirement [2], that the claim ***"arose out of or related to"*** something that happened in Indiana. In other words, the fact that D did nothing in Indiana that contributed to the accident does not prevent the "arise out of" requirement from being met, since P was injured there.

1. **Product liability suits:** Most of the modern cases about specific jurisdiction have arisen in the context of ***product liability suits.***

D. Suit based on products that cause injury in the forum state: A lot of issues of personal jurisdiction have arisen in ***products liability*** suits in which the plaintiff claims that the out-of-state defendant corporation made or sold — from a location ***outside the plaintiff's home state*** — a product that later found its way ***into the plaintiff's home state***, causing personal injury to the plaintiff there. The plaintiff then sues in her home-state courts, where the defendant has few or no contacts apart from the fact that the plaintiff's injury occurred there.

1. **Suit asserts "specific jurisdiction":** Throughout the discussion of product-liability cases in this Par. (B), we'll be assuming that the suit by the injured plaintiff asserts ***"specific jurisdiction"*** over the manufacturer. Remember, "specific" jurisdiction means jurisdiction in a case in which the claim ***"arises out of*** or ***relates to"*** something that happened in the forum state.

2. **Summary on out-of-state vendors:** Here (in Pars. 3 and 4) is an attempt to summarize some of the relevant principles about when an out-of-state or foreign product seller should be required to defend a product liability suit brought in the state where the injury occurred.

3. **"Purposeful availment" required for minimum contacts:** The mere fact that a product ***finds its way*** into the forum state and ***causes injury there*** is ***not enough*** to subject the out-of-state manufacturer or vendor to personal jurisdiction there. Instead, the defendant must be shown to have had ***minimum contacts*** with the forum state. Generally, this requires that D made some conscious ***effort to market in the forum state*** (a/k/a a ***"purposeful availment"*** of the privilege of doing business in the forum state). Or as it's often put, D must have had enough conduct relating to the forum said that D should ***"reasonably anticipate being haled into court there."***

   Example: The Ps purchase a car in New York. Some time later, the Ps are driving the car through Oklahoma when an accident occurs. The Ps sue the Ds in Oklahoma for their injuries, alleging that the car was defective. The Ds are the distributor of the car (a non-Oklahoma resident that distributes only in New York, New Jersey and Connecticut) and the dealer (a non-Oklahoma resident whose showroom is in New York). Neither the distributor nor the dealer has ever sold cars in Oklahoma or done any other business there. But some non-trivial number of cars sold by the Ds outside of Oklahoma eventually find their way into the state.

   Held, for the Ds — it would be a violation of the Ds' due process rights for the Oklahoma court to exercise personal jurisdiction over them. A "mere ***likelihood that a product will find its way*** into the forum State" does ***not*** suffice for jurisdiction over a defendant. The court must find that each D had enough "***conduct*** and ***connection with the forum state***" to cause him to "***reasonably anticipate being haled into court there.***" If either of the Ds had made ***efforts "to serve, directly or indirectly, the market for its products"*** in Oklahoma, it would not be unreasonable for the Oklahoma courts to subject that defendant to Oklahoma's jurisdiction. But P has not shown that about either of the Ds. *World-Wide Volkswagen Corp. v. Woodson.*

a. **An "extra" focus on the forum state's market:** However, once the defendant is shown to have been merely ***aware*** that one of its products is likely to find its way into a particular state, even a relatively ***small degree*** of voluntary ***"targeting"*** by the defendant on that particular state market will probably be ***enough*** to show that the defendant has crossed the line from mere-awareness into "purposeful availment" of that state's market.

b. **Sold via distributor:** The "purposeful availment" of the privilege of doing business in the forum state, i.e., the "targeting" of the forum state, probably need ***not*** be done ***directly*** by the defendant. Instead, if the defendant manufacturer ***selects a distributor*** — and intends that the distributor will ***attempt to make meaningful sales in the forum state*** — this act of selection probably suffices to trigger jurisdiction over the manufacturer.

   i. **Use of distributor who "targets" the forum state:** But where an out-of-forum-state defendant manufacturer relies on a distributor to make any in-forum-state sales, it's not enough for jurisdiction over the manufacturer that the *distributor* decided to "target" the forum state. The application of the "purposeful availment" requirement above means that unless the ***defendant manufacturer itself*** takes intentional steps (or directs or encourages the distributor to take steps) targeted to the forum state, the distributor's *own* conscious efforts to serve the forum state — including the distributor's sale of the injury-producing product into the forum state — *won't suffice* for forum-state jurisdiction over the manufacturer.

c. **Efforts as to U.S. as a whole:** Where D is a non-U.S.-based corporation that takes steps to sell lots of units in ***America as a whole*** — but does ***not*** take any steps to ***single out the forum state as a particular sales target*** — the absence of efforts by D to target the forum state will likely be enough to ***deprive*** the forum state of specific jurisdiction.

d. **Shipment of significant quantity of goods into the state:** Where the defendant ***knows that a substantial number of items*** it manufactures are flowing into the forum state, that known flow will likely ***suffice*** for specific jurisdiction, even if the defendant has not consciously decided to focus on the particular market represented by that state.

4. **P's claim must "arise out of" or relate to" the forum state:** Beyond the requirement that D have minimum contacts with the forum state, there's an important second requirement for specific jurisdiction: the plaintiff's claim "must ***arise out of or relate to"*** the forum state. [*Volkswagen*]

   a. **What does this "arise out of" or "/ relate to" requirement mean?** In product liability cases where the defective product is made and sold outside the forum state, the requirement does ***not*** mean that the defendant's in-state contacts or activities must have had anything to do with the accident. All that's required is that there be "an ***affiliation*** between the forum and the underlying controversy, [usually an] ***activity or occurrence that takes place in the forum State[.]"*** See the Example based on *Ford Motor Co.*, immediately below.

i. Accident occurs in state: Furthermore, the "activity or occurrence that takes place in the forum State" ***need <u>not</u> be an act committed by the defendant.*** So, for instance, the fact that the accident ***occurred in the forum state*** is, by itself, ***sufficient for specific jurisdiction.***

Example: Edison Motors, a large car manufacturer, designs and manufactures all of its vehicles in Georgia. Edison has a nationwide network of dealers each of whom markets, sells and repairs Edison to their local community. Edison makes a particular 2015 Model V sedan in Georgia, and sells that car through a dealer in Ohio. The buyer is Able (from Ohio), who 2 years later sells the Model V to Pete in Ohio. Pete then moves the car to his home state, Wyoming. While Pete is driving the car in Wyoming, the steering wheel comes loose, the car crashes, and Pete is injured. Pete sues Edison in Wyoming state court. Edison concedes that it has minimum contacts with Wyoming. But the company points out (correctly) that for specific jurisdiction, the claim must "arise out of or relate to" the forum state (Wyoming). And Edison asserts that the phrase "arose out of or related to" covers only scenarios where D's *voluntary in-state activities* were a *but-for cause* of each accident; since nothing D voluntarily did in Wyoming was a but-for cause of Pete's accident, Edison says that the "arise out of" test is not satisfied.

Pete would win. To satisfy the "arise out of" test, all that's required is "an ***affiliation*** between the forum and the underlying controversy," which is usually an ***"activity or occurrence that takes place in the forum State[.]"*** And the "activity or occurrence" that takes place in the forum State ***need not be an act committed by the defendant.*** So it doesn't matter that nothing Edison did in Wyoming had any causal connection with the accident. Rather, the fact that the accident took place in Wyoming is enough to meet the "arise out of" requirement, and the Wyoming courts have specific jurisdiction over Pete's case. Cf. *Ford Motor Co. v. Montana Eighth Judicial Dist. Court,* on similar facts.

E. P's injury occurs outside of the forum state: Now, suppose that P's injury from the defective product occurs ***outside of the forum state.*** The same general principles discussed above in Pars. (B) and (C) as applied to the injury-*in*-the-forum-state scenario will still apply here on the question of whether D had the requisite minimum contacts with the forum state.

But P will have to work hard to surmount the ***second*** major hurdle to the forum state's power to exercise jurisdiction over D: because P's suit against the non-forum-based D will have to qualify for "specific" (not general) jurisdiction, P will still have to show (as she would in the in-forum-state-injury scenario) that her suit ***"arises from" (or "relates to") some voluntary connection between D and the forum state.*** And given that the injury or harm forming the basis for P's claim occurred outside the forum state, P will usually have a hard time making this showing.

1. **Presence of co-plaintiffs won't help:** One factor that we now know *won't* help a plaintiff injured outside of the forum state to meet the "claim arose from a forum-state connection" requirement is the fact that P is joined in her suit by ***other plaintiffs*** who have virtually identical claims, but whose harm occurred in the forum state. Cf. *Bristol-Myers Squibb v. Sup. Ct.* (discussed at length *infra*, p. 50).
2. **P's in-state residence won't suffice:** Similarly, even the fact that P is herself a ***resident of the forum state***, standing alone, will probably ***not*** suffice to let P meet the "claim arose from a forum-state connection" requirement in her product-liability suit against the out-of-state D.

F. **Operation of an Internet Website that reaches in-staters:** A hot issue today is whether the operation of an ***Internet Website*** that's hosted outside the forum state, but that's accessed by some in-staters, constitutes minimum contacts with the state. The main issue is, did the Website operator ***intended to "target" residents*** of the forum state? If yes, there are probably minimum contacts; if no, there probably aren't.

1. **Passive site that just posts information:** So if an out-of-state local business just passively ***posts info*** on the Web, and doesn't especially want to reach in-staters or conduct transactions with them, this probably doesn't amount to minimum contacts, even if some in-staters happen to access the site.

   Example: D operates a local jazz cafe in a small town in Kansas. He puts up a Website with a schedule of upcoming events, and uses a trademark belonging to P on the site. P, based in New York, sues D in N.Y. federal court for trademark infringement. Even though a few New Yorkers may have accessed D's site, this won't be enough to constitute minimum contacts with N.Y., because D wasn't trying to attract business from N.Y.

2. **Conducting transactions with in-staters:** But if D runs an ***"e-commerce"*** site that actively ***tries to get in-staters to buy stuff*** from the site, and a significant number do, that probably ***will*** be enough to constitute minimum contacts with the state, at least where the suit ***relates to the in-staters' transactions*** (i.e., the suit is based on ***specific*** jurisdiction).

   a. **Rationale:** The court would likely conclude that D, by hosting an out-of-state site that tries to get business from in-state customers, has ***purposely availed itself of the opportunity*** to do business in the forum state (i.e., has ***"targeted"*** the forum state for business opportunities).

b. General jurisdiction: But now, let's consider a suit brought against a defendant who uses the Internet to target customers in the forum state, but where the suit ***does not arise out of any in-forum-state contacts*** between that defendant and the forum state (i.e., the case involves ***general*** rather than specific jurisdiction). Here, unless the defendant is ***incorporated in or headquartered in*** the forum state, ***no amount*** of forum-state-targeted Internet activity (or for that matter in-forum-state sales) will be enough for the state to exercise for jurisdiction over the defendant. [*Daimler AG v. Bauman*]

i. Possible workaround based on registration: The above rule that general jurisdiction applies only where the corporation is "at home" in the forum state, and no amount of in-state business can suffice — is subject to one important ***exception:*** If a state (1) requires that an out-of-state corporation ***register*** in order to ***do business in the stat***e; and (2) provides that such registration amounts to consent to general jurisdiction, this scheme ***does not violate*** the corporation's due process rights, that suffices for general jurisdiction. So in theory, any state can make mandatory registration by a corporation a form of consent to general jurisdiction — and that scheme will yield general jurisdiction over the corporation. [*Mallory v. Norfolk Southern Ry*]

G. Suits based on contractual relationship: The requisite "minimum contacts" are more likely to be found where one party to a ***contract*** is a resident of the forum state. But the fact that one party to a contract is a resident does not by itself automatically mean that the other party has "minimum contacts" — the existence of a contract is just one factor to look at.

1. Contractual relationship involving the state: Where the contract itself somehow ties the parties' business activities into the forum state, this will be an important factor tending to show the existence of minimum contacts. For instance, if one party is to make payments to the other, and the latter will be receiving the payments in the forum state, this stream of payments coming into the state is likely to establish minimum contacts and thus to permit suit against the payor.

Example: D runs a fast food restaurant in Michigan under franchise from P, which has its headquarters in Florida. The contract requires D to make royalty payments to P in Florida.

Held, P may sue D in Florida. The fact that the payment stream comes into Florida is an important factor, though not by itself dispositive, in the court's conclusion that there were minimum contacts with Florida. [*Burger King Corp. v. Rudzewicz*]

2. Choice-of-law clause: Where there is a contract between the parties to the suit, the fact that the contract contains a ***choice of law clause*** requiring use of the forum state's law will also be a factor (though not a dispositive one) tending towards a finding of minimum contacts. (*Example:* On the facts of the above example, the franchise contract stated that Florida law would be used.

This was a factor helping lead the court to conclude that D had minimum contacts with Florida.)

3. **"Reasonable anticipation" of defendant:** In suits relating to a contract, as with any other kind of suit, the minimum contacts issue always boils down to this: ***Could the defendant have reasonably anticipated being required to litigate in the forum state?*** The fact that the other party was a resident of the forum state, the fact that a stream of payments went into the forum state, and the fact that the forum state's law was to be used in the contract, are all non-dispositive, but important, factors tending towards the conclusion that the out-of-stater had minimum contacts with the forum state.

H. **Irrelevance of D's non-claim-related contacts with forum-state (*Bristol-Myers*):** Recall (see p. 37) that the key requirement for specific jurisdiction is that P's claim must ***"arise out of"*** or ***"relate to"*** the defendant's contacts with the forum. But what happens when a suit in State *A* involves ***multiple plaintiffs who join together*** in a single action against out-of-state corporate defendant D, where all the Ps assert ***virtually identical claims*** arising from a single type of behavior by D, but only *some* of the Ps assert claims that arise out of events that ***occurred in State A?*** Can the State *A* court exercise personal jurisdiction over D to hear the claims by the other Ps, the ones whose claims have ***no connection to anything that happened in the forum state?*** The answer is ***"no."*** [***Bristol-Myers Squibb Co. v. Superior Court*** (2017)]

1. **Facts of *Bristol-Myers*:** In *Bristol-Myers*, more than 600 plaintiffs brought various suits in California state court against D (a drug manufacturer) alleging that they had been injured by Plavix, a prescription blood-thinning drug. Eighty-six of the Ps were California residents (the "resident Ps"), but the other 592 Ps resided in other states (the ***"nonresident Ps"***).

   a. **Nature of nonresident Ps' claims:** The nonresident Ps did not allege that their *own* injury claims had any real connection with California. For instance, these Ps did not claim that they had obtained Plavix from a California physician or any other California source; nor did they claim that their injury occurred in California.

   b. **The nonresident Ps' claims:** But these nonresident Ps asserted that California had personal jurisdiction over D — of the "specific jurisdiction" variety — to hear the nonresidents' claims. These Ps argued that because D had ***extensive contacts with California***, relating to that same drug, and the same sales-and-marketing practices for that drug, as were involved in the *resident* Ps' claims that were already before the court; and

2. **Supreme Court answers "no":** But the Supreme Court, by an 8-1 vote, ***rejected*** the nonresident Ps' argument, and found that the California courts ***did not have specific jurisdiction*** to hear these nonresident Ps' claims even though the court was already hearing claims by the resident Ps that were virtually identical, except for the lack of a California nexus for the nonresident Ps' claims.

I. **Minimum contacts in intentional-tort cases:** What kind of contacts with the forum state are required when the plaintiff's claim is for an ***intentional tort?***

1. **Intent to produce significant effects in the forum state:** The main rule is that D, the intentional tortfeasor, will be deemed to have minimum contacts with the forum state as long as D ***intended*** that the tort would ***produce significant effects in the forum state,*** even if all of D's relevant conduct took place ***outside*** of the forum state.

   Example: Law professors like to pose this example: D stands in State *A* near the border with State *B*, and throws a rock at P, who is standing in State *B*. P can sue D in State *B* for either assault (if P sees the rock coming) or for battery (if the rock hits P), *even though D did not set foot in State* B — D will be deemed to have the constitutionally-required minimum contacts with State *B* by virtue of the fact that he intended his act to produce its main *effect* (injury) in that state.

2. **Defamation case:** The Supreme Court has applied this type of analysis to the ***defamation*** context. That is, suppose that D, while sitting in State *A*, makes a statement that defames P, a resident of State *B*. At least when D *knows* that P will suffer significant reputational injury in State *B*, D will be deemed to ***have minimum contacts with State B*** sufficient to allow P to sue D in that state. [*Calder v. Jones*]

   a. **Requirements for minimum contacts:** So for minimum contacts to exist in an intentional-tort context, there seem to be ***three requirements:***

      [1] An ***intentional act*** by D;

      [2] ***expressly aimed at the forum state,*** that

      [3] ***caused harm*** that was ***felt in the forum state*** (as D knew it would be.)

J. **Class action plaintiffs:** An "absent" plaintiff in a class action that takes place in the forum state may be ***bound*** by the decision in the case, even if that plaintiff ***did not have minimum contacts with the forum state*** (and therefore couldn't be sued as a defendant). [*Phillips Petroleum Co. v. Shutts*]

K. **Plaintiff's lack of contacts:** The fact that the ***plaintiff has no contacts*** with the forum state will ***not block*** jurisdiction.

V. "GENERAL" JURISDICTION

A. **Where we are now:** So far, most of the cases we've covered involved "*specific* jurisdiction." That is, the claim against the defendant ***arose out of the defendant's contacts with the forum state***. But it's now time to take a look at ***"general jurisdiction."*** That is, we're going to look at the rules governing when personal jurisdiction may be exercised with respect to a claim that does ***not*** arise out of the defendant's contacts with the forum state.

1. **Individuals:** Where the defendant is an ***individual***, general jurisdiction over her will exist if she is ***"domiciled"*** in the forum state. In fact, it seems probable that for individuals, ***nothing less*** than domicile in the forum state (or, perhaps, residence there) will suffice for general jurisdiction. [*Goodyear Dunlop Tires Operations, S.A. v. Brown*]

2. **Corporations:** Where the defendant is a ***corporation***, the defendant must have such extensive contacts with the forum state that the defendant can be said to be ***"essentially at home"*** in that state. *Goodyear, supra.* And to be "essentially at home" in the forum state, the corporation must — except in exceptional cases — either:

   [1] be ***incorporated*** in the forum state, or

   [2] have its ***principal place of business*** in that state.

   Daimler AG v. Bauman.

   Example: P, a resident of North Carolina, is riding in a bus in Paris when a tire blowout causes the bus to crash, injuring P. The bus was made by X, a French company. The tire was made by D, a corporation headquartered in Paris, incorporated in France and with all operations in France. About 10% of D's worldwide sales are made to U.S.-based customers (mainly vehicle manufacturers). As D knows, about one-half of 1% of D's annual worldwide sales (worth about $3 million per year) are made by D to North Carolina-based customers. The particular tire that blew out was not one of these — it was sold to by D's sales staff directly to X in France. P sues D in North Carolina state court based on product liability. D asserts that the North Carolina courts cannot constitutionally assert personal jurisdiction over it.

   D is correct — it would violate D's federal constitutional rights for the court to exercise general jurisdiction over D. D's knowingly making of $3 million of annual sales into the forum state would probably be enough for *specific* jurisdiction (i.e., jurisdiction in a suit arising out of D's North Carolina-related activities), since all that's required for specific jurisdiction is that D have "targeted" the forum state. But except in exceptional circumstances, a U.S. court may not constitutionally exercise *general* jurisdiction over a corporate defendant unless that corporation is either incorporated in the forum state or has its principal place of business there. And we know that neither of these things is true of D, since both of these elements are located in France. [Cf. *Daimler AG v. Bauman*; *Goodyear Dunlop Tires Operations, S.A. v. Brown.*] (Note that these facts are a modified version of the facts in *Goodyear.*)

VI. FEDERAL JURISDICTION OVER THE PARTIES

A. **General principles:** To determine whether a ***federal*** court has personal jurisdiction over the defendant, you must check ***three things***:

   1. **Territory for service:** Whether service took place within the appropriate ***territory***;

   2. **Manner of service:** Whether the service was carried out in the correct ***manner***; and

   3. **Amenability:** Whether the defendant was ***"amenable"*** to the federal suit.

Note: For an overview of federal jurisdiction over the parties (as well as how it fits together with federal subject-matter jurisdiction), see the Flow Charts printed as Figures 2-2 and 2-3.

B. Territory for service: Here are the rules about the territory in which service may be made on the defendant in a federal action:

1. **General rule:** As a general rule, in both diversity actions and federal question cases, ***service of process*** may be made only:

   [1] ***within the territorial limits*** of the ***state in which the District Court sits***; or

   [2] ***anywhere else permitted by the state law*** of the ***state where the District Court sits.***

   FRCP 4(k)(1)(A); 4(k)(2).

   Example (within the territorial limits of state): P sues D in a federal action in the Northern District of Ohio. Whether the suit is based on diversity or federal question, service will be territorially valid if D is served with process anywhere within the state of Ohio, since this is the state where the district court sits. This is true even if service is physically made in the Southern District of Ohio.

   Example (out-of-state service based on state law): Under the New Jersey long-arm statute, if a non-resident is involved in a motor vehicle accident inside New Jersey with a New Jersey resident, the New Jersey resident may serve the non-resident outside New Jersey, and the New Jersey courts may then exercise personal jurisdiction. P, a New Jersey resident, and D, a California resident, have an accident in New Jersey. P may sue D in diversity in federal District Court for New Jersey; P may serve D with process in California, because the long-arm of the state where the district court sits (New Jersey) would allow such service. FRCP 4(k)(1)(A).

2. **100-mile bulge:** A special ***100-mile bulge*** provision (FRCP 4(k)(1)(B)) allows for out-of-state service sometimes, even if local law does not permit it. When the provision applies, it allows service anywhere (even across a state boundary) within a 100-mile radius of the federal courthouse where suit is pending. The bulge provision applies only where out-of-staters will be brought in as ***additional parties*** to an ***already pending*** action. There are two types of parties against whom it can be used:

   a. **Third-party defendants:** ***Third-party defendants*** (FRCP 14) may be served within the bulge.

   Example: P sues D in a New Jersey federal district court diversity action. D claims that if D is liable to P, X is liable to D as an indemnitor. The suit is pending in Newark, less than 100 miles from New York City. The "100 mile bulge" provision means that D may serve X in New York City, even if no New Jersey long-arm statute would allow the suit.

b. **Indispensable parties:** So-called ***"indispensable parties"*** — that is, persons who are needed in the action for just adjudication, and whose joinder will not involve subject-matter jurisdiction problems — may also be served if they are within the bulge.

Example: P sues D for copyright infringement in federal district court for the Eastern District of Kentucky, located in Lexington. D files a counterclaim against P. D wants to join X as a co-defendant to this counterclaim, arguing that P and X conspired to violate D's copyrights. X resides in Cincinnati, Ohio, located 78 miles from Lexington. If the court agrees that X is required for just adjudication of D's counterclaim, service on X in Cincinnati is valid, even if the Kentucky long-arm would not allow service there.

3. **Nationwide service of process:** In several kinds of cases, Congress has provided for ***nationwide*** service of process. Suits against ***federal officials and agencies***, and suits based on ***statutory interpleader***, are examples of nationwide service.

4. **Foreign defendant not servable in any state:** Rule 4(k)(2) allows a ***federal question*** suit to be brought against any person or organization who cannot be sued in ***any state*** court (almost always because they are a ***foreigner***).

C. **Manner of service:** Once you determine that the party to be served lies within the territory described above, you must determine if the service was carried out in the correct ***manner***.

1. **Individual:** Service on an ***individual*** (Rule 4(e)) may be made in any of several ways:

a. **Personal:** By serving him ***personally***;

b. **Substitute:** By handing the summons and complaint to a person of ***"suitable age and discretion"*** residing at D's residence;

c. **Agent:** By serving an ***agent*** appointed or designated by law to receive process. (*Example:* Many states designate the Director of Motor Vehicles as the agent to receive process in suits involving car accidents);

d. **Local state law:** By serving D in the manner provided by either: (1) the ***law of the state where the district court sits***, if that state has such a provision, or (2) the ***law of the state where the person is being served.*** (*Example*: P brings an action against D, a resident of California, in New Jersey federal court, and wishes to serve him by certified mail. Service will be possible if ***either*** the courts of New Jersey ***or*** California allow certified-mail service.)

2. **Corporation:** Service on a ***corporation*** may be made by leaving the papers with an ***officer***, a managing or general ***agent***, or any other agent authorized by appointment or by law to receive process for the corporation. FRCP 4(h)(1).

a. **Local state law:** As with individuals, service on a corporation may also be made in the manner provided by the local law of (i) the state where the

action is pending or (ii) the state where the ***service is made***. FRCP 4(h)(1)(A).

3. **Waiver of service:** Rule 4(d) allows plaintiff to in effect serve the summons and complaint by ***mail***, provided that the ***defendant cooperates***. P mails to D a ***"request for waiver of service";*** if D agrees, no actual in-person service is needed.

   a. **Incentives:** D is free to refuse to grant the waiver, in which case P must serve the summons by the in-person methods described above. But, if D refuses the waiver, the court will impose the ***costs*** subsequently incurred by P in effecting service on D unless "good cause" is shown for D's refusal. (FRCP 4(d)(2).)

D. **Amenability to suit:** If D was served in an appropriate territory, and in an appropriate manner, you still have to determine whether D is closely-enough linked to the state where the federal district court sits to make him ***"amenable to suit"*** in that court.

1. **Federal question:** In ***federal question*** cases, most courts hold that D is amenable to suit in their court if jurisdiction could ***constitutionally be exercised*** over him in the ***state courts*** of the state where the federal court is sitting, even if the state court itself would not (because of a limited long-arm) have jurisdiction.

   Example: P sues D for copyright infringement. The suit is brought in the Northern District of Ohio. D's only contact with Ohio is that he sold 100 copies of the allegedly infringing book in Ohio. The state courts of Ohio, although they could constitutionally take personal jurisdiction over D in a similar state-created claim — libel, for instance — would not do so because the Ohio long-arm is very limited and would not cover any action growing out of these facts. However, the federal district court will hear the federal question copyright claim against D, because P has minimum contacts with the state where the federal court sits.

   a. **Foreign defendants:** In general, if the defendant is a ***foreign*** corporation or resident, most federal courts will exercise jurisdiction over the defendant only if that defendant has minimum contacts with the state where the federal court sits, not merely minimum contacts with the United States as a whole. (Again, as with an out-of-state but not foreign defendant, the federal court will hear the federal question claim even though the state courts might not exercise jurisdiction over the defendant due to a limited state long-arm.)

      i. **Narrow exception:** If a foreign defendant could not be sued in ***any state***, he may be sued on a federal question claim in any federal judicial district, assuming that he has minimum contacts with the U.S. as a whole. (FRCP 4(k)(2).) But assuming that the foreign defendant could be sued in at least some state court, the general rule described in the prior paragraph (D must have minimum contacts with the state where the federal court sits, not just with the U.S. as a whole) continues to apply.

2. **Diversity:** In ***diversity*** cases, as a matter of practice the federal courts exercise only the jurisdiction that is allowed ***by the statutory law of the state in which they sit***. So if the state statutory law does not go to the limits of due process, the federal court will follow suit.

VII. JURISDICTION OVER THINGS

A. **Two types of actions:** There are two types of actions that relate primarily to ***"things"*** rather than to people: (1) ***in rem*** actions; and (2) ***quasi in rem*** actions.

1. ***In rem* actions:** ***In rem*** actions are ones which do not seek to impose personal liability on anyone, but instead seek to affect the interests of persons in a specific thing (or *res*). (*Examples:* Probate court actions; admiralty actions concerning title to a ship; actions to quiet title to real estate or to foreclose a lien upon it; actions for divorce.)

2. ***Quasi in rem* actions:** ***Quasi in rem*** actions are actions that would have been *in personam* if jurisdiction over D's person had been attainable. Instead, property or intangibles are seized not as the object of the litigation, but merely as a ***means of satisfying a possible judgment*** against D.

B. ***In rem* jurisdiction:**

1. **No personal liability:** In *in rem* actions, ***no*** judgment imposing ***personal liability*** on anyone results — all that happens is that the ***status of a thing*** is adjudicated.

Example: In a quiet title action, a determination is reached that A, rather than B, is the owner of Blackacre. This is an *in rem* action, and does not result in the imposition of personal liability on anyone.

C. ***Quasi in rem* jurisdiction:** As noted, a *quasi in rem* action is one that would have been *in personam* if jurisdiction over D's person had been attainable. Instead, property or intangibles are seized not as the ***object*** of the litigation, but merely as a means of satisfying a possible judgment against D. D has ***no liability beyond the value of the property or intangibles seized***.

Example: P wants to sue D on a contract claim in California state court. The contract has no connection with California, nor does D himself have sufficient contacts with California to allow that state to exericise personal jurisdiction over him. D does, however, own a bank account in California. Putting aside constitutional due process problems, P could attach that bank account as a basis of jurisdiction, and bring a *quasi in rem* action on the contract claim. If P wins, he will be able to collect only the value of the bank account, and D will not be personally liable for the remainder if the damages exceed the value of the account.

1. **Requirement of minimum contacts (*Shaffer*):** *Quasi in rem* jurisdiction over D cannot be exercised unless D had such ***"minimum contacts"*** with the forum state that ***in personam jurisdiction could be exercised over him***. *Shaffer v. Heitner*.

a. **Utility wiped out:** Generally speaking, *Shaffer* means that *quasi in rem* jurisdiction has ***very little value today***. Given *Shaffer*, holding that *quasi in rem* jurisdiction can only be exercised where the defendant had minimum contacts with the forum state, *quasi in rem* could rarely do anything that *in personam* jurisdiction couldn't do better.

D. **Limited appearance:** Some states allow a ***"limited appearance."*** Under a limited appearance, D appears in an *in rem* or *quasi in rem* suit, contests the case on its merits, but is subjected to liability ***only to the extent of the property attached*** by the court.

1. **Distinguished from special appearance:** Distinguish limited appearances from special appearances — in the latter, a defendant against whom personal jurisdiction is asserted is allowed to argue the invalidity of that jurisdiction without having this argument, or his presence in the court, itself constitute a submission to the court's jurisdiction.

2. **Federal limited appearances:** Federal courts usually follow the rule of the ***state in which they are sitting*** in determining whether to allow a limited appearance.

VIII. NOTICE AND OPPORTUNITY TO BE HEARD

A. **Notice generally:** Even if the court has authority to judge the dispute between the parties or over the property before it (covered in the above sections), the court may not proceed unless D received ***adequate notice*** of the case against him.

1. **Reasonableness test:** In order for D to have received adequate notice, it is not necessary that he ***actually*** have learned of the suit. Rather, the procedures used to alert him must have been ***reasonably likely to inform him***, even if they actually failed to do so.

Example: P's process server leaves the summons and complaint at D's house, with D's wife. D's wife throws it in the garbage, and D never learns of it. D has received adequate notice, so the court can exercise jurisdiction over him. Conversely, if P's process server had left the papers on the sidewalk outside the house, and D had happened to pick them up, this would ***not*** be adequate notice to D — the procedures used were not reasonably likely to give D notice, and they are not saved by the fact that D in fact learned of the suit.

2. **Substitute service:** Personal service — handing the papers to D himself — will always suffice as adequate notice. But all states, and the federal system, also allow ***"substitute service"*** in most instances. "Substitute service" means some form of service other than directly handing the papers to the defendant.

a. **Leave at dwelling:** The most common substitute service provision allows the process papers to be left at D's ***dwelling*** within the state, if D is not at home. These provisions usually require the papers to be left with an adult who is reasonably likely to give them to D. (*Example:* FRCP 4(e)(2) allows the papers to be left with a person of "suitable age and discretion who resides there.")

b. **Mail:** Some states, and the federal system, allow service to be made by ordinary ***first class mail***. However, usually this method is allowable only if D returns an acknowledgement or waiver form to P's lawyer. If D does not return the form, some other method of service must then be used. See FRCP 4(e)(1).

3. **Service on out-of-staters:** Where D is not present in the forum state, he must somehow be served ***out of state***. Remember that in a state court suit, this can only be done if the state has a long-arm statute covering the type of case and defendant in question. Once the long-arm covers the situation, the out-of-state defendant must still be given some sort of notice.

   a. **Mail notice:** Many states provide for notice by ***registered or certified mail*** on the out-of-state defendant.

   b. **Public official:** Sometimes, service may be made by serving a ***state official***, plus giving notice by mail to D. (*Example:* Many non-resident motorist statutes allow P to serve the state Director of Motor Vehicles with a matching mailing to the out-of-state defendant.)

   c. **Newspaper publication:** If D's identity or residence are unknown, some states allow service by ***newspaper publication***. But this may only be used where D truly cannot be found by reasonable effort.

4. **Corporations:** Several means are commonly allowed for giving notice of suit to ***corporations***.

   a. **Corporate officer:** Many states require that a corporation, if it wishes to be incorporated in the state or to do business in the state, must ***designate a corporate official*** to receive process for suits against the company. Service on this designated official is, of course, deemed to be adequate notice.

   b. **Federal Rule:** The Federal Rules, and the rules of many states, are more liberal, in that they allow service on any person associated with the corporation who is of sufficiently high placement. Thus FRCP 4(h)(1) provides that service on a corporation may be made by giving the papers to "an officer, a managing or general agent, or to any other agent authorized by appointment or by law to receive service of process."

B. **Constitutional due process:** Just as the Fourteenth Amendment's Due Process Clause prohibits jurisdiction over a defendant who lacks minimum contacts with the forum state (*International Shoe*), so that clause prohibits the exercise of jurisdiction over a defendant who has not been given ***"reasonable notice"*** of the suit. [*Mullane v. Central Hanover Bank*]

1. **Mail notice to all the identifiable parties:** For instance, if a party's name and address are "reasonably ascertainable," publication notice will not be sufficient, and instead notice by ***mail*** (or other means equally likely to ensure actual notice) must be used. [*Mennonite Board of Missions v. Adams*]

2. **Actual receipt doesn't count:** Remember that what matters is the ***appropriateness*** of the notice prescribed by statute and employed, ***not*** whether D actually ***got*** the notice.

C. Opportunity to be heard: D must not only be notified of the suit against him, but must also be given an ***opportunity to be heard.*** That is, before his property may be taken, he must be given a chance to defend against the claim. This "opportunity to be heard" must be given to D not only when his property will be taken forever, but even before there is any ***significant interference*** with his property rights.

1. **Pre-judgment remedy:** Opportunity-to-be-heard questions arise most frequently in the context of ***pre-judgment remedies***, which protect plaintiff against the defendant's hiding or squandering his assets during litigation. Two common forms of pre-judgment remedies are the ***attachment*** of D's ***bank account*** and the placing of a ***lis pendens*** against her ***real estate.***

   a. **Due process right:** Before the plaintiff is allowed to attach the defendant's property, the defendant's right to due process must be respected.

   Example: Suppose a state allows pre-judgment attachment of real estate without a prior hearing, without a bond and without a showing of exigent circumstances.

   These three procedures, taken together, violate the property owner's 14th Amendment due process rights. [*Connecticut v. Doehr*]

IX. DEFENSES TO CLAIMS OF JURISDICTION

A. Special appearance: In a ***"special appearance,"*** D appears in the action with the express purpose of making a jurisdictional objection. By making a special appearance, D has ***not consented*** to the exercise of jurisdiction.

1. **Appeal:** Most courts allow a defendant who has unsuccessfully made a special appearance to then defend on the merits, without losing his right to appeal the jurisdictional issue.

2. **Federal substitute for special appearance:** The federal courts (and the many state courts with rules patterned after the Federal Rules) have ***abolished*** the special appearance. Instead, D makes a ***motion*** to dismiss for lack of jurisdiction over the parties; making this motion does not subject D to the jurisdiction that he is protesting. FRCP 12(b)(2).

   a. **Waiver:** The right to make a motion to dismiss for lack of personal jurisdiction is ***waived*** in the federal system if: (1) D makes a motion raising any of the defenses listed in Rule 12, and the personal jurisdiction defense is not included; or (2) D neither makes a Rule 12 motion nor raises the defense in his answer.

B. Collateral attack:

1. **General enforcement of judgments:** A judgment entered in one jurisdiction may generally be ***enforced*** in another. That is, if State 1 enters a judgment against D, D's property in State 2 (or wages owed him in State 2) may be seized to satisfy the earlier State 1 judgment.

2. **Collateral attack on default judgment:** If D ***defaults*** in an action in State 1, she may ***collaterally attack*** the default judgment when it is sued upon in

State 2. Most commonly, D collaterally attacks the earlier judgment on the grounds that State 1 did not have personal jurisdiction over her, or did not have valid subject-matter jurisdiction.

Example: D has no contacts with Iowa. P, an Iowa resident, sues D in Iowa court. D never appears in the action, and a default judgment is entered against him for $100,000. P then brings a suit in D's home state of New Jersey to enforce the earlier Iowa judgment. D will be permitted to collaterally attack the Iowa judgment, by arguing that Iowa lacked personal jurisdiction over him. The New Jersey court will undoubtedly agree with D that, because D did not have minimum contacts with Iowa, Iowa could not constitutionally take jurisdiction over him. Therefore, the New Jersey court will decline to enforce the Iowa judgment.

3. **Waiver by D:** A defendant who ***appeared in the original action*** without objecting to jurisdiction, or one who unsuccessfully litigated the jurisdictional issue in the first action, may ***not*** collaterally attack the judgment. (Instead, a defendant who unsuccessfully litigates jurisdiction in the first action must appeal to the first state's system, rather than later making a collateral attack.)

C. **Defense of fraud or duress:** A court may constitutionally exercise jurisdiction over a defendant found within the forum state, even if D's presence was the result of ***fraud*** or ***duress*** on the part of the plaintiff. But the court may exercise its ***discretion*** not to exercise jurisdiction. (*Example:* P entices D into the jurisdiction with a false love letter and a false statement that she is leaving the country forever and wants to see D once more. When D arrives at the airport in the forum state, P serves him with papers. *Held*, the forum state will decline to exercise its jurisdiction because of P's fraud. [*Wyman v. Newhouse*])

D. **Immunity:** Most jurisdictions give to non-residents of the forum state an ***immunity*** from service of process while they are in state to ***attend a trial***. This is true whether the person is a ***witness***, a ***party***, or an ***attorney***. Most states also grant the immunity for related proceedings such as depositions.

1. **Federal suits:** Out-of-state parties, witnesses, and attorneys also generally receive immunity from ***federal*** court suits (whether diversity or federal question).

X. VENUE

A. **Definition:** ***"Venue"*** refers to the ***place within a sovereign jurisdiction*** in which a given action is to be brought. It matters only if jurisdiction over the parties has been established. (*Example:* State X is found to have jurisdiction over the person of B, in a suit against him by A. Venue determines in which ***county*** or ***district*** of State X the case should be tried.)

B. **State action:** In state trials, venue is determined by statute. The states are free to set up virtually any venue rules they wish, without worrying about the federal constitution.

1. **Basis for:** Most commonly, venue is authorized based on the county or city where the ***defendant resides***. Many states also allow venue based on where the cause of action arose, where the defendant does business, etc.

2. ***Forum non conveniens:*** Under the doctrine of ***forum non conveniens***, the state may use its discretion not to hear the case in a county where there is statutory venue. Sometimes, this involves shifting the case to a different place within the state. At other times, it involves the state not having the case take place in-state at all. Usually, it is the defendant who moves to have the case dismissed or transferred for *forum non conveniens*.

   a. **Factors:** Three factors that state courts often consider in deciding whether to dismiss for *forum non conveniens* are: (1) whether the plaintiff is a state ***resident*** (if so, he has a stronger claim to be able to have his case heard in his home state); (2) whether the witnesses and sources of proof are more available in a different state or county; and (3) whether the forum's own state laws will govern the action (transfer is more likely if a different state's law controls).

C. **Venue in federal actions:** In ***federal*** actions, the venue question is, ***"Which federal district court shall try the action?"*** Venue is controlled by 28 U.S.C. §1391.

1. **Still need personal jurisdiction:** When you consider a venue problem, remember that venue is ***not a substitute*** for personal jurisdiction: the fact that venue lies in a particular judicial district does not automatically mean that suit can be brought there. Suit can be brought only in a district that satisfies ***both*** the venue requirements and the personal jurisdiction requirements as to all defendants.

2. **Three methods:** There are three basic ways by which there might be venue in a particular judicial district:

   [1] if ***any*** defendant ***resides*** in that district, and ***all defendants reside in the state*** containing that district;

   [2] if a "***substantial part of the events***...giving rise to the claim ***occurred***, or a substantial part of property that is the subject of the action is situated," in the district; or

   [3] if at ***least one defendant*** can be subjected to ***personal jurisdiction*** in the district, and ***no other district qualifies*** under either of the above two provisions (i.e., the all-defendants-reside and the where-events-occurred provisions).

   We consider each of these separately below, as Paragraphs 3, 4 and 5.

3. **"Defendant's residence" venue:** For both diversity and federal question cases, venue lies in any district where ***any defendant resides***, so long as, if there is more than one defendant, ***all the defendants*** reside in the ***state*** containing that district. 28 U.S.C. §1391(b)(1).

   Example: P, from Massachusetts, brings a diversity suit against D1, from the Southern District of New York, and D2, from the Eastern District of New York. Venue will lie in either the Southern District of New

York or the Eastern District of New York — each of these is home to at least one defendant, and each of these two districts is in a state that is home to all the defendants. But if D2 had been a resident of the District of Connecticut instead of any New York district, there would not be any "defendant's residence" venue anywhere.

4. **"Place of events or property" venue:** For both diversity and federal question cases, venue lies in any district "in which a ***substantial part*** of the ***events*** or omissions giving rise to the claim ***occurred***, or a substantial part of ***property*** that is the subject of the action is ***situated***...." This is "place of events" venue.

   a. **Multiple districts:** There can be ***multiple*** districts qualifying for "place of events" venue, as long as each district was the locus for a "substantial part" of the events relating to the claim.

      Example: P, from Massachusetts, sues D, a car dealer from Connecticut. P alleges that D sold P a car in Connecticut, that P drove the car to Massachusetts, and that a defect in the car caused P to be injured in Massachusetts. Probably venue in either the District of Massachusetts or the District of Connecticut would be allowed under the "place of events" provision, since probably both the selling of the defective car and the incurring of the accident were a "substantial part" of the events.

5. **"Escape hatch" provision:** Finally, for both diversity and federal question cases, there is an ***"escape hatch,"*** by which venue may be founded in a district with which some or all defendants have close ties, if there is ***no district in which the action may otherwise be brought***. This escape hatch is used mainly for cases in which nearly all the ***events occurred abroad***. §28 U.S.C. §1391(b)(3).

   a. **Diversity and federal question cases:** The escape hatch provision gives venue, for both diversity and federal-question suits, in any judicial district as to which ***two things*** are true:

      [1] there is ***no district*** in which the action may ***otherwise be brought*** (i.e., there is no district meeting either the "all defendants reside in the state" or the "substantial part of the events occurred" requirements described above);

      and

      [2] at least one defendant is ***"subject to the court's personal jurisdiction"*** with respect to the suit.

6. **No "plaintiff's residence" venue:** There is ***no*** venue based on ***plaintiff's residence***.

7. **Corporation:** The residence of a ***corporation*** for venue purposes matters only if the corporation is a defendant.

   a. **Three locations:** In the typical case involving ***specific*** jurisdiction (i.e., the suit relates to the corporation's in-state activities; see *supra*, p. 37), a corporation will be deemed to be a resident of at least:

[1] the district where it has its ***principal place of business***;

[2] any district where it has ***substantial operations***; and

[3] (probably) ***any district*** in its ***state of incorporation.***

(These categories aren't explicitly stated anywhere in the statute, but can be inferred from 28 U.S.C. §1391(d).)

On the other hand, it is no longer the case, as it once was, that if a corporation does business anywhere in a state, it is deemed to reside in ***all districts*** of that state.

Example: D, a one-store jewelry-retailing corporation, is incorporated in Delaware (which has only one federal judicial district). D's only store is in New York City (in the Southern District of New York), and the corporation makes sales only to people who visit the store. P, a New Jersey resident, buys an expensive diamond ring at D's store, later finds that it's fake, and wants to sue D in diversity for breach of warranty.

For venue purposes, D is a resident of the District of Delaware and the Southern District of New York. Therefore P may bring suit either in the District of Delaware (based on district-where-all-defendants-reside venue, coupled with an inference based on 28 U.S.C. §1391(d) that a corporation is a resident of any district in its state of incorporation) or the Southern District of New York (based on district-where-all-defendants-reside venue, coupled with an inference from §1391(d) that a corporation is a resident of the district in which the defendant has its principal place of business).

But P may *not* sue D in, say, the Northern District of New York. The fact that D conducts substantial business operations in one part of New York state (Southern District) does not mean that venue is proper in another part of that state (Northern District).

8. **Removal:** In some situations, the defendant may be entitled to ***remove*** a case from state to federal court. (See *infra*, p. 75.) A case ***removed*** from state to federal court passes to "the district court of the U.S. for the district and division embracing the place ***where such action is pending***." 28 U.S.C. §1441(a).

9. **Transfers for convenience in federal courts:** In the federal system, when a defendant successfully moves for *forum non conveniens*, the original court ***transfers*** the case to another district, rather than dismissing it. Under 28 U.S.C. §1404(a), "for the convenience of parties and witnesses … a district court may transfer any civil action to any other district or division where it might have been brought."

   a. **Defendant's motion:** Usually, it is the defendant who moves for *forum non conveniens*. When this happens, the case may be transferred only to a district where P would have had the right, ***independent of the wishes of D***, to bring the action.

Example: Suppose that suit in a particular district would *not* have been possible, as an initial matter, either because one or more of the Ds could not be personally served there, or because venue would not have been proper there. The Ds do not have the right to move to have the case transferred to that not-initially-proper district by saying, in effect, "We consent to this transfer." (*Rationale:* Allowing the Ds to do this would disturb P's right to choose from among the eligible locations for the suit.)

i. **Consent of all parties:** But if *all* parties, including P, consented, then the case *could* be transferred even to a district where it could not have originally been brought.

b. **Discretion of judge:** The decision whether to transfer the action is left to the ***discretion*** of the judge where the action is pending, based on the judge's analysis of the convenience of the parties and witnesses.

CHAPTER 3

SUBJECT-MATTER JURISDICTION

I. GENERAL PRINCIPLES

A. **Diversity vs. federal question:** In the federal courts, there are two basic kinds of controversies over which the federal judiciary has subject-matter jurisdiction: (1) suits between ***citizens of different states*** (so-called ***diversity*** jurisdiction); and (2) suits involving a ***"federal question."***

1. **Other cases:** Certain other kinds of cases specified in the constitution also fall under the federal judicial power. These are cases involving ***ambassadors***, cases involving ***admiralty***, and cases in which the ***United States*** is a party. But except in these very unusual cases, when you are considering a case that is brought in the federal courts, you must ask: Does it fall within the diversity jurisdiction or federal question jurisdiction? If it does not fall within either of these, probably it cannot be heard by the federal courts.

B. **Amount in controversy:** In federal suits based on diversity, an amount in excess of ***$75,000*** must be in dispute. This is the ***"amount in controversy"*** requirement. In federal question cases, there is no amount in controversy requirement.

C. **Burden:** The party seeking to ***invoke the jurisdiction*** of a federal court must make an ***affirmative showing*** that the case is within the court's subject-matter jurisdiction. (*Example:* If P wants to invoke diversity jurisdiction, in her pleading she must allege the relevant facts about the citizenship of the parties.)

D. **Dismissal at any time:** ***No matter when*** a deficiency in the subject-matter jurisdiction of a federal court is noticed, the suit must be stopped, and ***dismissed*** for lack of jurisdiction. See FRCP 12(h)(3), requiring the court to dismiss the action at any time if it appears that the court lacks subject-matter jurisdiction.

> **Example:** A case brought under federal question jurisdiction goes through trial and through one level of appeals, and is then heard by the Supreme Court. The Supreme Court decides that there was no federal question in the first place. *Held*, the entire case must be dismissed for lack of federal subject-matter jurisdiction. [*Louisville & Nashville Railroad v. Mottley*]

II. DIVERSITY JURISDICTION

A. Definition: The Constitution gives the federal courts jurisdiction over "***controversies ... between the citizens of different states....***" This is the grant of "diversity jurisdiction."

> **Example:** P, a citizen of California, wants to sue D, a citizen of Oregon, for hitting P with D's car. Assuming that P's damages exceed $75,000, P can bring her negligence suit against D in federal court, because it is between citizens of different states.

1. **Date for determining:** A party's citizenship for diversity purposes is determined ***as of the commencement of the action***.

   a. **Later change doesn't defeat diversity:** This means that if diversity ***existed*** between the parties on the filing date, diversity is ***not defeated*** because one of the parties ***later became a citizen of the same state*** as his opponent.

   b. **Later change can't create diversity:** Conversely, if parties on opposite sides are citizens of the same state when the action is commenced, there is ***no diversity*** (and the case must be dismissed), even if by the time of trial the citizenship of one party has changed in such a way that diversity is now present.

2. **Domicile:** What controls for citizenship is ***domicile***, not residence. A person's domicile is where she has her true, fixed and permanent home. (*Example:* P has his main home in New York, but has an expensive second home in Florida. D has her only home in Florida. P can bring a diversity action against D, because P is deemed a citizen only of New York, not Florida, even though P has a "residence" in Florida.)

   a. **Resident alien:** A ***resident alien*** (an alien who lives in the United States permanently) is deemed a citizen of the state in which he is domiciled.

   b. **Presence of foreigner:** In a suit between citizens of different states, the fact that a ***foreign*** citizen (or foreign country) is a party does ***not destroy*** diversity. (*Example:* P, a citizen of Ohio, sues D1, a citizen of Michigan, and D2, a citizen of Canada. Diversity jurisdiction exists.) (In situations where one side consists *solely* of foreign citizens or foreign countries, "alienage" jurisdiction applies. See below.)

3. **Complete diversity:** The single most important principle to remember in connection with diversity jurisdiction is that ***"complete diversity" is***

required. That is, it must be the case that ***no plaintiff is a citizen of the same state as any defendant***.

Example: P, a citizen of New York, brings a suit against D1, a citizen of New York, and D2, a citizen of New Jersey. We ask, "Is there any plaintiff who is a citizen of the same state as any defendant?" Since the answer is "yes," the requirement of complete diversity is not satisfied, and there is no diversity jurisdiction.

4. **Pleading not dispositive:** In order to determine whether diversity exists, the pleadings do not settle the question of who are adverse parties. Instead, the court looks beyond the pleadings, and arranges the parties according to their real interests in the litigation.

   a. **Nominal parties ignored:** In determining the existence of diversity, ***nominal*** or purely ***formal*** parties are ignored. (*Example:* Where a guardian of an infant sues, the guardian is deemed to be a citizen only of the same state as the infant. See 28 U.S.C. §1332(c)(2).)

B. **Alienage jurisdiction:** Related to diversity jurisdiction, but analytically distinct, is ***"alienage"*** jurisdiction. Alienage jurisdiction exists where there is a suit between citizens of a state, on one side, and foreign states or citizens thereof, on the other.

Example: P, a citizen of Mexico, sues D, a citizen of Illinois. Even if there is no federal question issue, there will be federal subject-matter jurisdiction of the "alienage" variety, assuming that the amount in controversy requirement is satisfied.

1. **Suit solely between or among foreign citizens:** But a suit solely between or among citizens of ***two or more foreign countries*** does ***not*** fall within the alienage jurisdiction.

   Example: If P, a citizen of Canada, sues D, a citizen of Mexico, there is no alienage (or other diversity) jurisdiction.

   a. **Resident alien:** A foreigner ***living in the U.S.*** — i.e., a ***resident alien*** — is deemed to be a ***citizen of the state where she permanently resides***, for diversity purposes.

   Example: P, a citizen of Illinois, sues D, a Canadian living permanently in Illinois. D will be deemed to be a citizen of Illinois. Therefore, there's no diversity (of either the regular or alienage variety), so the suit can't go forward without a federal question.

   b. **Resident alien vs. non-resident alien:** Courts are ***split*** about whether there's diversity in a suit by a ***resident alien*** against a ***non-resident alien*** (or against a resident alien who lives in a different state).

   Example: P, a Spaniard living in Florida, sues D, a Canadian living in Canada. Courts are split about whether there's diversity. If the same P sued D, a Canadian living permanently in Michigan, courts are similarly split about whether there's diversity.

2. **Aliens and U.S. citizens on same side:** Jurisdiction is not destroyed by the fact that one or more non-resident foreigners ***and*** one or more U.S. citizens are ***each present*** on each side of the litigation. Here, the jurisdiction is deemed to be conventional diversity, rather than alienage jurisdiction.

   Example: P1, a citizen of Ohio, and P2, a citizen of Canada (living in Canada), sue D1, a citizen of New Jersey, and D2, a citizen of Canada (living in Canada). The configuration is analyzed as if the foreigners were not present; therefore, the requirements for conventional diversity jurisdiction are satisfied, and the suit may proceed.

C. **Diversity involving partnerships and corporations:** Often, it will be necessary to determine the citizenship status of non-human entities like ***partnerships*** and ***corporations***.

1. **Partnerships:** ***Partnerships*** do ***not*** have a single state of citizenship. Instead, the citizenship of ***each member counts***.

   Example: In a diversity suit where one of the parties is a limited partnership, *every member of the partnership* (even the limited partners, who have no say in how the partnership is run) must be diverse with each opposing party.

2. **Corporations:** A ***corporation*** is deemed a citizen both of ***any state where it is incorporated*** *and* of the state where it has its ***"principal place of business."*** In other words, for diversity to exist, no adversary of the corporation may be a citizen of *either* the state in which the corporation is incorporated, or of the state in which it has its principal place of business.

   Example: XYZ Corp., a corporation which is incorporated in Delaware, has its principal place of business in New York. In order for there to be diversity, no adverse party may be a citizen of *either* Delaware or New York.

   a. **Principal place of business:** What's the test for determining where a corporation's ***"principal place of business"*** is? The hard case is where the corporation's top managers direct the company from a ***headquarters location*** that is in ***one*** state, but where the bulk of the corporation's daily ***business activities*** take place in a ***different*** state.

      i. **"Nerve center" test:** In this situation, courts use the ***"nerve center"*** test, under which the principal place of business will normally be the ***headquarters*** location. [*Hertz Corp. v. Friend* (2010)] Under the nerve center test, a corporation's principal place of business refers to "the place where the corporation's ***high level officers direct, control, and coordinate*** the corporation's activities." *Id.* That place will usually turn out to be the corporate headquarters.

      Example: The Ps, California citizens, work for D (a rental-car chain) in California. They sue D in the California state courts on a state-law claim. D, seeking to remove the case to federal district court (see p. 75), argues that there is diversity because D's "principal place of business" is New Jersey, where D has its corporate headquarters at which its top management works. The Ps retort that D conducts more of its daily business activities in California than in any other single state, so D's principal place of business should be considered to be California.

Held, for D: The phrase "principal place of business" is "the place where the corporation's officers direct, control, and coordinate the corporation's activities." This "nerve center" will normally be the place where the corporation has its ***headquarters,*** and that's the case here. Therefore, D is a citizen of New Jersey, not California, and there is diversity, so D can remove to federal court. [*Hertz Corp. v. Friend, supra*]

D. **Devices to create or destroy diversity:** The federal courts will not take jurisdiction of a suit in which any party has been ***"improperly or collusively joined"*** to obtain jurisdiction. 28 U.S.C. §1359.

1. **Assignment:** This means that a claimant may ***not assign her claim*** in order to create diversity. (*Example:* Alex and Dennis are both citizens of Florida. Alex wants to bring a diversity action against Dennis. Alex assigns his claim to Barbara, a Massachusetts citizen, with the understanding that Barbara will remit to Alex 80% of any recovery. The court will not take diversity jurisdiction over the Barbara-vs.-Dennis action, because Barbara's presence in the suit was an improper or collusive joinder. [*Kramer v. Caribbean Mills*])

2. **Devices to defeat removal:** A plaintiff suing in state court may sometimes seek to defeat her adversary's potential right to ***remove to federal court***. There is no federal statute prohibiting "improper or collusive" joinder for the purpose of defeating jurisdiction. However, as a matter of judge-made law, courts will often ***disregard*** obvious removal-defeating tactics (e.g., joinder of a defendant who has nothing to do with the underlying dispute, but who is a citizen of the same state as a plaintiff.)

   a. **Low dollar claim:** But the state-court plaintiff is always free to make a claim for ***less than the amount in controversy*** ($75,000), in order to defeat removal, even if P has really suffered a loss greater than this amount. (But the less-than-$75,000 amount must be named *before* D removes.)

E. **Date of determination:** A party's citizenship for diversity purposes is determined ***as of the commencement of the action***. If diversity existed between the parties at that date, it is ***not defeated*** because one of the parties ***later became a citizen of the same state*** as his opponent.

   a. **No diversity:** Conversely, if parties on opposite sides are citizens of the same state when the action is commenced, there is ***no diversity*** (and the case must be dismissed), even if by the time of trial the citizenship of one party has changed in such a way that diversity is now present.

1. **Motive for moving irrelevant:** A person's ***motive for changing her state of citizenship*** is ***irrelevant***. So if a person, by moving, meets the test of domicile in his new state of residence, it is immaterial for diversity purposes that

he moved in order to create or destroy diversity. However, the move must be made *before* the commencement of the action.

III. FEDERAL QUESTION JURISDICTION

A. **Generally:** The Constitution gives the federal courts authority to hear ***"federal question"*** cases. More precisely, under 28 U.S.C. §1331, the federal courts have jurisdiction over "all civil actions ***arising under the Constitution, laws, or treaties of the United States***."

1. **Federal claim:** There is no precise definition of a case "arising under" the Constitution or laws of the United States. But in the vast majority of cases, the reason there is a federal question is that federal law is the ***source of the plaintiff's claim***.

   Examples: A claim of copyright infringement, trademark infringement or patent infringement raises a federal question, because in each of these situations, a federal statute — the federal copyright statute, trademark statute or patent statute — is the source of the right the plaintiff is asserting.

   a. **Interpretation of federal law:** It is normally ***not*** enough that P is asserting a ***state-created*** claim that requires ***interpretation*** of federal law. [*Merrell Dow Pharmaceuticals, Inc. v. Thompson*]

   b. **Anticipation of defense:** Similarly, the federal question must be ***integral*** to P's cause of action, as revealed by P's complaint. It normally does ***not*** suffice for federal question jurisdiction that P ***anticipates a defense*** based on a federal statute, or even that ***D's answer*** does in fact raise a federal question. Thus the federal question must be part of a "well pleaded complaint."

   Example: P claims that D Railroad has breached its agreement to give P free railroad passes. A recently-passed federal statute prohibits the giving of such passes. In P's complaint, he anticipates the railroad's federal statutory defense, claiming that the statute violates the Fifth Amendment.

   Held, since P's claim was merely a breach of contract claim, and the federal statute was not essential to that claim, there was no federal question — the fact that federal law was an integral part of D's anticipated defense is irrelevant. [*Louisville & Nashville RR v. Mottley*]

IV. AMOUNT IN CONTROVERSY

A. **Diversity only:** In ***diversity*** cases, but ***not*** in federal question cases, plaintiff must satisfy an ***"amount in controversy"*** requirement. In all diversity cases, the amount in controversy must exceed ***$75,000***.

1. **Interest not included:** The $75,000 figure does not include interest or court costs.

B. Standard of proof: The party seeking to invoke federal diversity jurisdiction does not have to ***prove*** that the amount in controversy exceeds $75,000. All she has to show is that there is ***some possibility*** that that much is in question.

1. **"Legal certainty" test:** To put it another way, the claim cannot be dismissed for failing to meet the $75,000 requirement unless it appears to a ***legal certainty*** that the claim is really for less than the jurisdictional amount. [*St. Paul Mercury Indemnity Co. v. Red Cab*]

2. **Eventual recovery irrelevant:** The fact that P ***eventually recovers*** far ***less*** than the jurisdictional amount does ***not*** by itself render the verdict subject to reversal and dismissal on appeal for lack of jurisdiction.

   a. **Discretion to deny costs:** But the federal court has discretion to ***deny costs*** to P, and even to impose costs on him, if he recovers less than $75,000. 28 U.S.C. §1332(b).

C. Whose point of view followed: The courts are split as to ***which party's*** point of view is to be considered in calculating the amount at stake. Most courts hold that the controversy must be worth $75,000 to the ***plaintiff*** in order to satisfy the jurisdictional amount.

D. Aggregation of claims: In multi-plaintiff or multi-claim litigation, you must understand the rules governing when ***aggregation*** of claims is permissible for meeting the jurisdictional amount:

1. **Aggregation by single plaintiff:** If a single plaintiff has a claim in excess of $75,000, he may add to it ***any other claim of his against the same defendant***, even though these other claims are for less than the jurisdictional amount. This is done by the doctrine of supplemental jurisdiction.

   a. **No claim exceeds $75,000:** Even if a plaintiff does ***not*** have any single claim worth more than $75,000, he may add together all of his claims against a single defendant. So long as these claims against a single defendant ***total*** more than $75,000, the amount in controversy requirement is satisfied.

   b. **Additional defendants:** But a plaintiff who has aggregated his claim against a particular defendant, usually may ***not*** join claims against ***other*** defendants for less than the jurisdictional amount.

   Example: P has two claims, each for $40,000, against D1. P will be deemed to meet the amount in controversy requirement as to these claims, because they aggregate more than $75,000. But if P tries to bring D2 into the lawsuit, and has a single claim worth $40,000 against D2, most courts will not allow this claim, because P's total claims against D2 do not exceed $75,000, and the doctrine of supplemental jurisdiction does not apply.

2. **Aggregation by multiple plaintiffs:** In suits involving ***multiple plaintiffs***, where not all plaintiffs meet the jurisdictional amount, there are two analytically different cases: (1) ***at least one*** of the plaintiffs meets the amount, but others do not; (2) ***none*** of the plaintiffs singly meets the amount, but their claims when ***aggregated*** exceed the amount.

total $1,000. Y is from New Jersey. D may bring Y in as a Rule 13(h) additional defendant to D's compulsory counterclaim against P, even though D and Y are both from New Jersey, and even though D's claim does not total $75,000 — supplemental jurisdiction applies, and obviates the need for D-Y diversity or for D to meet the amount in controversy requirement.

iii. Rule 13(g) ***cross-claims***, i.e., claims by one defendant against another.

Example: P, from Ohio, brings a diversity suit against D1 and D2, both from Kentucky. D1 brings a Rule 13(g) cross-claim against D2 — since it is a cross-claim, it necessarily relates to the same subject matter as P's claim. Even though there is no diversity as between D1 and D2, the cross-claim may be heard by the federal court.

iv. Rule 14 ***impleader*** of third-party defendants, for claims ***by and against third-party plaintiffs***, and claims ***by third-party defendants***, but ***not*** claims by the ***original plaintiff*** against third-party defendants.

Example: P, from California, sues D, a retailer from Arizona, claiming that a product D sold P was defective and injured P. The suit is based solely on diversity. D brings a Rule 14 impleader claim against X, the manufacturer of the item, claiming that if D owes P, X must indemnify D. X is a citizen of Arizona. Because D's suit against X falls within the court's supplemental jurisdiction, the lack of diversity as between D and X makes no difference. Supplemental jurisdiction would also cover any claim by X against P. But any claim by P against X would *not* be within the court's supplemental jurisdiction, so P and X must be diverse and the claim must meet the amount in controversy requirement.

v. ***Multiple plaintiffs*** who join together under Rule 20's ***"permissive joinder"*** provision. (More precisely, supplemental jurisdiction applies for ***amount-in-controversy*** purposes, but does ***not*** apply so as to remove the requirement of ***complete diversity***.)

Example: P1 and P2, both citizens of New York, bring a diversity-only suit against D, a citizen of New Jersey. P1's claim is worth $100,000, and P2's claim is worth no more than $50,000. The two claims arise out of the same transaction or occurrence. The action may proceed — supplemental jurisdiction allows P2 to ride P1's coattails, for amount-in-controversy purposes. (But supplemental jurisdiction does *not* remove the need for *complete diversity.* So P3, a citizen of New Jersey, would not be permitted to join the action, because she's a citizen of the same state as D.) [*Exxon Mobil Corp. v. Allapattah Services*]

vi. ***Joinder of plaintiffs*** for Rule 23 ***class actions based on diversity.*** (If one or more named plaintiffs meet diversity and amount in controversy requirements, the unnamed plaintiffs ***don't*** need to meet the amount, because they fall within the court's supplemental jurisdiction.)

Example: In a Rule 23 diversity-only class action, the named plaintiff class members are P1, a citizen of New York with a claim for $100,000 and P2, a citizen of Pennsylvania with a claim for $90,000. The defendants are D1 (a citizen of New Jersey) and D2 (a citizen of California). Because all named plaintiffs (a) meet the amount in controversy requirement and (b) are diverse with all defendants, the class action may go forward even though it includes unnamed class members whose claims are not individually worth in excess of $75,000, and who are citizens of New Jersey and/or California. [*Exxon Mobil Corp. v. Allapattah Services, Inc.*]

b. **Claims not covered:** Where the core claim is based solely on diversity, some important types of claims do ***not*** get the benefit of supplemental jurisdiction:

i. **Claims against third-party defendants:** Claims made by an original plaintiff against a ***third-party defendant***, pursuant to Rule 14(a), are ***excluded***.

Example: P sues D, and D brings a third-party claim against X, asserting that if D is liable to P, X is liable to D. P and X are citizens of the same state. P does not get supplemental jurisdiction for her claim against X, so the P-vs.-X claim must be dismissed.

ii. **Compulsory joinder:** When a person is joined under Rule 19(a) as a person to be "joined if feasible" (***"compulsory joinder"***), neither a claim ***against*** such a person, nor a claim ***by*** that person, comes within the supplemental jurisdiction in a diversity-only case.

iii. **Rule 20 joinder of defendants:** When a plaintiff sues multiple defendants in the same action on common law and facts (Rule 20 ***"permissive joinder"*** of defendants), supplemental jurisdiction does not apply.

Example: P is hit by D1's car, then negligently ministered to by D2. P is from New York, D1 is from Connecticut, and D2 is from New Jersey. P's claim against D2 is for $20,000. The federal court cannot hear the P-D2 claim, because it does not meet the amount in controversy and does not fall within supplemental jurisdiction.

iv. **Intervention:** Claims by prospective plaintiffs who try to ***intervene*** under Rule 24 do not get the benefit of supplemental jurisdiction. This is true whether the intervention is permissive or of right.

Example: P1 sues D in diversity. P2, on her own motion, moves for permission to intervene under Rule 24(b), because her claim against D has a question of law or fact in common with P1's claim. P1 is a citizen of Indiana, P2 of Illinois, and D of Illinois. Because there is no supplemental jurisdiction over intervention, the fact that P2 and D are citizens of the same state means that the court may not hear P2's claim. The same result would occur even if P2's claim was so closely related to the main action that P2 would otherwise be entitled to "intervention of right" under Rule 24(a).

c. **Defensive posture required:** If you look at the situations where supplemental jurisdiction is allowed in diversity-only cases, and those where it is not allowed, you will see that basically, additional claims asserted by ***defendants*** fall within the court's supplemental jurisdiction, but additional claims (or the addition of new parties) by ***plaintiffs*** are generally not included. So expect supplemental jurisdiction only in cases where the claimant who is trying to benefit from it is in a ***"defensive posture."***

4. **Discretion to reject exercise:** Merely because a claim is within the court's supplemental jurisdiction, this does not mean that the court ***must*** hear that claim. Section 1367(c) gives four reasons for which a court may ***decline to exercise*** supplemental jurisdiction that exists. Most importantly, the court may abstain if it has already ***dismissed all claims*** over which it has original jurisdiction. This discretion is especially likely to be used where the case is in its early stages.

   Example: P sues D1 (the U.S.) under a federal statute, then adds state-law claims against D2 and D3, as to which there is neither diversity nor federal question jurisdiction. Soon after the pleadings are filed, the court dismisses P's claim against D1 under FRCP 12(b)(6). Probably the court will then exercise its discretion to decline to hear the supplemental claims against D2 and D3.

5. **No effect on personal jurisdiction:** The application of the supplemental jurisdiction doctrine does ***not*** eliminate the requirement of ***jurisdiction over the parties***, nor does it eliminate the requirement of ***service of process***. It speaks solely to the question of subject-matter jurisdiction. (But often in the supplemental jurisdiction situation, service in the ***100-mile bulge*** area will be available.)

   a. **Venue:** Where supplemental jurisdiction applies, probably ***venue*** requirements do not have to be satisfied with respect to the new party. But usually, venue will not be a problem anyway in these kinds of situations.

VI. REMOVAL TO THE FEDERAL COURTS

A. **Removal generally:** Generally, any action brought in ***state court*** that the plaintiff could have brought in federal court may be ***removed*** by the defendant to federal district court.

   Example: P, from New Jersey, sues D, from New York, in New Jersey state court. The suit is a garden-variety automobile negligence case. The amount at issue is $100,000. D may remove the case to federal district court for the District of New Jersey.

1. **Diversity limitation:** The most important single thing to remember about removal jurisdiction is this: In ***diversity*** cases, the action may be removed only if ***no defendant is a citizen of the state in which the action is pending***.

   Example: P, from New Jersey, brings a negligence action against D, from New York, in the New York state court system. D may not remove the case to federal court for New York, because he is a citizen of the state (New York) in which the action is pending. (But if P's suit was for trademark infringement — a kind of suit that raises a federal question but may be brought in either state or federal court — D would be able to remove, because the "not a citizen of the state where the action is pending" requirement does not apply in suits raising a federal question.)

   a. **Exception:** There is an ***exception*** to this general "no removal allowed if any D is a citizen of the state where the action is pending" rule: most state-court ***class actions*** can be removed even though one or more defendants are citizens of the forum state.

2. **Where suit goes:** When a case is removed, it passes to the federal district court for the district and division embracing the place where the state cause of action is pending. (*Example:* If a suit is brought in the branch of the California state court system located in Sacramento, removal would be to the federal district court in the Eastern District of California encompassing Sacramento.)

B. **Diversity and amount in controversy rules applicable:** In removal cases, the usual rules governing existence of a federal question or of diversity, and those governing the jurisdictional amount, apply. (*Example:* If there is no federal question, diversity must be "complete.")

C. **No plaintiff removal:** Only a ***defendant*** may remove. A plaintiff defending a counterclaim may not remove. (*Example:* P brings a suit for product liability against D. D counterclaims for libel in an amount of $100,000. P is from Ohio; D is from Indiana. The suit is pending in Michigan state court. Even though P is not a resident of the state where the action is pending, P may not remove, because the right of removal is limited to defendants.)

D. **Look only at plaintiff's complaint:** The right of removal is generally decided from the face of the pleadings. The jurisdictional allegations of plaintiff's complaint control.

   Example: P is badly injured in an automobile accident caused by D's negligence. P's medical bills total $80,000, but P sues only for $60,000, for the express purpose of thwarting D's right to remove. The jurisdictional allegations of P's complaint control, so that D may not remove even though more than $75,000 is "really" at stake.

1. **Plaintiff controls her claim:** The above rule (that removability is decided based on the complaint) has an important consequence: Plaintiff is "***master of his (or her) claim***"; if he/she chooses not to assert a federal claim, even though one is available to him/her, the defendant may not remove.

Example: P and D are both citizens of Kentucky. P brings an action in Kentucky state court, asserting that D has acted in a way that violates Kentucky unfair competition laws. P also has a valid claim that these same actions by D violate *federal antitrust laws* (which under federal law can be asserted in state, not just federal, court). But P wants to be sure that the case remains in state court, i.e., that D can't remove it. Therefore, P can decline to add the (valid) federal antitrust claim to her state-court action. This will have the effect P desires — *D can't remove* to federal court. In other words, the rule that "P is master of her claim" *applies* here — she is able to defeat removal by *omitting a valid federal claim* from her state-court suit.

a. **P's right to drop federal claim after removal:** Furthermore, even if P *initially* asserts both state and federal claims in state court (where the two are based on the same facts) and D removes to federal court, P can get the case ***returned*** to state court by ***amending her complaint*** so that it drops the federal claim. [*Royal Canin U.S.A., Inc. v. Wullschleger*]

E. **Removal of multiple claims:** Where P asserts against D in state court two claims, one of which could be removed if sued upon alone, and the other of which could not, removability depends on whether one of the claims raises a federal question.

1. **Diversity:** If the claim for which there is federal jurisdiction is a ***diversity*** claim, the presence of the second claim (for which there is no original federal jurisdiction) ***defeats*** the defendant's right of removal entirely — the whole case must stay in state court.

2. **Federal question case:** Where the claim for which there is original federal jurisdiction is a ***federal question*** claim, and there is another, "separate and independent," claim for which there is no original federal jurisdiction, D may remove the whole case. 28 U.S.C. §1441(c).

Example: P and D1 are both citizens of Kentucky. P brings an action in Kentucky state court alleging federal antitrust violations by D1. P adds to that claim a claim against D1 and D2, also from Kentucky, asserting that the two Ds have violated Kentucky state unfair competition laws. Section 1441(c) will allow D1 and D2 to remove to federal court, if the antitrust claim is "separate and independent" from the state unfair competition claim.

a. **Remand:** If §1441(c) applies, and the entire case is removed to federal court, the federal judge need not hear the entire matter. The court may instead remand all matters in which state law predominates.

i. **Remand even the federal claim:** In fact, the federal court, after determining that removal is proper, may remand ***all claims*** — even the properly-removed federal claim — if state law predominates in the whole controversy.

F. **Compulsory remand:** If the federal judge concludes that the removal did not satisfy the statutory requirements, she ***must remand*** the case to the state court from which it came. (*Example:* If in a diversity case it turns out that one or more of the Ds was a citizen of the state in which the state suit was commenced, the federal judge must send the case back to the state court where it began.)

G. Mechanics of removal:

1. **Time:** D must usually file for removal within ***30 days*** of the time he receives service of the state-court complaint. (See Par. H)(1) below.)

2. **All defendants joined:** ***All defendants*** (except purely nominal ones) must ***join*** in the notice of removal.

H. Time limits: There are time limits on the defendant's right to remove the case.

1. **Original complaint makes case removable:** In the usual case where the plaintiff's ***original*** state-court complaint makes it clear that the case ***is removable*** — whether based on a federal question or diversity — the defendant must file the notice of removal ***within 30 days*** after the defendant received the complaint.

2. **Original action not removable, but P amends:** But it sometimes happens that the original state-court complaint shows that the action is ***not removable.*** For instance, consider the common scenario where the complaint does not include a federal issue — so that the case would be removable only if ***based on diversity*** — and according to the complaint the requirements for diversity are not satisfied. But a ***later amendment*** by the plaintiff to ***drop one of the defendants*** from the complaint may ***remove the block*** to diversity. If that happens, what is the time limit on the defendant(s)' right to remove?

   a. **30 days after diversity block removed:** Normally, the defendant has ***30 days*** — starting with the moment when "it may ***first be ascertained"*** that the case is one that has ***become removable*** — to file her petition for removal. So as soon as the defendant is or should be aware of the amendment dropping the non-diverse defendant(s), the defendant has 30 days to remove.

   b. **Special one-year rule:** But there is a special ***exception*** to this rule giving D 30 days to remove after the amendment dropping defendant(s) made the case now removable based on diversity: as a general rule, the defendant(s) may not remove ***more than one year*** after ***P began the action***. 28 U.S.C. §1446(c)(1).

      i. **Exception for bad-faith removals:** But this exception — no removal allowed more than one year after the plaintiff's original state-court filing regardless of how recently the plaintiff's amendment made the case removable — is itself subject to its own ***exception:*** removal more than one year after plaintiff originally commenced the action in state court (but no more than 30 days after the case became removable due to plaintiff's amendment) is allowed if the district court finds that the plaintiff has ***"acted in bad faith*** in order to ***prevent a defendant from removing the action."*** *Id.*

CHAPTER 4

PLEADINGS

I. FEDERAL PLEADING GENERALLY

A. Approach generally:

1. **Two types:** In most instances, there are only two types of pleadings in a federal action. These are the ***complaint*** and the ***answer***. The complaint is the document by which the plaintiff begins the case. The answer is the defendant's response to the complaint.

   a. **Reply:** In two circumstances, there will be a third document, called the ***reply***. The reply is, in effect, an "answer to the answer." A reply is allowable: (1) if the answer contains a ***counterclaim*** (in which case a reply is ***required***); and (2) at plaintiff's option, if plaintiff obtains a court order allowing the reply.

2. **No verification generally:** Pleadings in a federal action normally need not be ***"verified,"*** i.e., sworn to by the litigant. However, there are a couple of exceptions, two of which are: (1) the complaint in a stockholders' derivative action (see FRCP 23.1); and (2) when the complaint is seeking a ***temporary restraining order*** (FRCP 65(b)).

3. **Attorney must sign:** The pleader's ***lawyer*** must ***sign*** the pleadings. This is true for both the complaint and the answer. By signing, the lawyer indicates that to the best of her belief, formed after reasonable inquiry, the pleading is not interposed for any ***improper purpose*** (e.g., harassing or causing unnecessary delays), the claims and defenses are warranted by existing law or a non-frivolous argument for changing existing law, and (in general) the allegations or denials have evidentiary support. FRCP 11.

   a. **Sanctions:** If Rule 11 is violated (e.g., the complaint, as the lawyer knows, is not well grounded in fact, or supported by any plausible legal argument), the court must impose an ***appropriate sanction*** on either the signing lawyer, the client, or both. The most common sanction is the award of ***attorneys' fees*** to the other side.

   b. **Safe harbor:** A party against whom a Rule 11 motion is made has a 21-day ***"safe harbor"*** period in which she can withdraw or modify the challenged pleading and thereby avoid any sanction.

4. **Pleading in the alternative:** The pleader, whether plaintiff or defendant, may plead ***"in the alternative."*** "A party may set forth two or more statements of a claim or defense alternately or hypothetically." FRCP 8(e). (*Example:* In count 1, P claims that work done for D was done under a valid written contract. In count 2, P claims that if the contract was not valid, P rendered value to D and can recover in *quantum meruit* for the value. Such alternative pleading is allowed by Rule 8(e).)

II. THE COMPLAINT

A. Complaint generally: The complaint is the initial pleading in a lawsuit, and is filed by the plaintiff.

1. **Commences action:** The filing of the complaint is deemed to "commence" the action. The date of filing of the complaint is what counts for statute of limitation purposes in federal question suits (though in diversity suits, "commencement" for statute-of-limitations purposes depends on how state law defines commencement).

2. **Elements of complaint:** There are three essential elements that a complaint must have (FRCP 8(a)):

   a. **Jurisdiction:** A short and plain statement of the grounds upon which the court's ***jurisdiction*** depends;

   b. **Statement of the claim:** A short and plain ***statement of the claim*** showing that the pleader is entitled to relief; and

   c. **Relief:** A demand for judgment for the ***relief*** (e.g., money damages, injunction, etc.) which the pleader seeks.

B. Specificity: Plaintiff must make a ***"short and plain statement"*** of the claim showing that she is entitled to relief. The level of factual detail required is not high — gaps in the facts are usually remedied through discovery. Plaintiff needs to state only the facts, not the legal theory she is relying upon.

1. **Dismissal:** Even though the level of factual detail required is not high, the complaint may contain such ***sparse*** factual allegations that the defendant may successfully move to have it dismissed for "failure to state a claim on which relief may be granted" (Rule 12(b)(6)). It's relatively difficult for the defendant to satisfy this standard. But if the court, after assuming that all factual allegations in the complaint are true, cannot ***"plausibly infer"*** that the defendant is liable, the court will dismiss the complaint for failure to state a claim. See *infra*, p. 81.

C. Special matters: Certain ***"special matters"*** must be pleaded with ***particularity*** if they are to be raised at trial.

1. **Catalog:** The special matters (listed in FRCP 9) include: (1) denial of a party's legal ***capacity to sue*** or be sued; (2) the circumstances giving rise to any allegation of ***fraud*** or ***mistake***; (3) any denial of performance or occurrence of a ***condition precedent***; (4) the existence of ***judgments*** or ***official documents*** on which the pleader plans to rely; (5) material facts of ***time and place***; (6) ***special damages***; and (7) certain aspects of admiralty and maritime jurisdiction.

   a. **Note:** The above matters requiring special pleading apply to the ***answer*** as well as to the complaint.

2. **Effect of failure to plead:** The pleader takes the full risk of failure to plead any special matter.

   Example: P brings a diversity claim for breach of contract against D. P has suffered certain unusual consequential damages, but fails to plead these special damages as required by FRCP 9(g). Even if P proves these items at trial, P may not recover these damages, unless the court agrees to specially permit this "variance" between proof and pleadings.

III. MOTIONS AGAINST THE COMPLAINT

A. **Defenses against validity of complaint:** Either in the ***answer***, or by separate ***motion***, defendant may attack the validity of the complaint in a number of respects. Rule 12(b) lists the following such defenses:

1. Lack of ***jurisdiction over the subject matter;***
2. Lack of ***jurisdiction over the person***;
3. Improper ***venue***;
4. Insufficiency of ***process***;
5. Insufficiency of ***service of process***;
6. Failure to ***state a claim upon which relief may be granted***; and
7. Failure to ***join a necessary party*** under Rule 19.

B. **12(b)(6) motion to dismiss for failure to state a claim:** Defense (6) above is especially important: if D believes that P's complaint does not state a legally sufficient claim, he can make a Rule 12(b)(6) motion to dismiss for ***"failure to state a claim upon which relief can be granted."*** The motion asserts that on the facts as pleaded by P, no recovery is possible under ***any legal theory***.

Example: If P's complaint is barred by the statute of limitations, D should move under 12(b)(6) for failure to state a valid claim. If the court is convinced that under the facts alleged by P, any cause of action would be time-barred, the court will dismiss.

1. **"Plausibility" standard:** Under recent Supreme Court decisions, the 12(b)(6) motion to dismiss for failure to state a claim can succeed by demonstrating that even if every fact asserted in the complaint is taken as true, no recovery is ***"plausible"*** under ***any legal theory.*** This standard is ***easier for the defendant to satisfy*** than the standard that applied before 2007.

   a. **Assumption of truth:** When the court is deciding whether the complaint should be dismissed for failure to state a claim, all truly ***"factual"*** allegations in the complaint are to be ***assumed to be true***.

   b. **Pure legal conclusions:** But ***pure "legal conclusions" don't qualify*** for this assumed-to-be-true treatment.

   Example: P is a Pakistani Muslim who was imprisoned by federal authorities after 9/11. He brings a federal civil-rights action against D1 (the U.S. Attorney General) and D2 (the FBI Director). He alleges that the two Ds knew and approved of their subordinates' plan to imprison P and hundreds of other Muslim men in extra-harsh conditions solely on account of the men's race, religion or national origin, thus violating their constitutional rights. The two Ds move for dismissal under Rule 12(b)(6), alleging that even if the subordinates intentionally violated P's rights, P has not sufficiently alleged facts showing that the two Ds acted with a discriminatory purpose (as is required by the substantive rules for supervisor liability in such cases).

Held, for the Ds: complaint dismissed. It's true that factual allegations in the complaint must be taken as true. But pure ***"legal conclusions" don't qualify*** for this "taken as true" treatment. And those allegations that *are* truly factual must ***"plausibly suggest"*** that P is entitled to relief. In determining whether the complaint meets this "plausible suggestion of entitlement to relief" standard, the trial judge is to draw on his ***"judicial experience and common sense."*** Here, the complaint does not satisfy the plausibility standard, because even taking P's truly-factual allegations as true, the "more likely explanation" of the Ds' motives is that they were making a *bona fide* pursuit of national security, not acting for forbidden discriminatory purposes. [***Ashcroft v. Iqbal*** (2009), a 5-4 vote]

c. **Where P lacks personal knowledge:** The "plausibility" standard will generally make the most difference where the plaintiff alleges facts as to which he ***doesn't have personal knowledge***, and as to which the defendants are in ***sole control*** of the ***relevant records or testimony***. Cases trying to hold ***supervisors*** liable for violations of ***civil rights laws*** (as in *Iqbal*, *supra*) or ***employment discrimination laws*** are good illustrations.

d. **D is relieved from discovery:** When the plausibility requirement makes a difference, the main way it will do so is that D gets ***spared from having to undergo discovery.*** That is, P's case gets dismissed before he gets to examine D's files or take depositions.

C. **Amendment:** If the complaint is dismissed in response to D's dismissal motion, P will almost always have the opportunity to ***amend*** the complaint. (See *infra*, p. 85.)

D. **Motion for more definite statement:** If the complaint is so "vague or ambiguous that [the defendant] cannot reasonably prepare a response," D may move for a ***more definite statement*** under Rule 12(e).

E. **Motion to strike:** If P has included "redundant, immaterial, impertinent or scandalous" material in the complaint, D may move to have this material ***stricken*** from the pleading. Rule 12(f).

F. **Waiver of defense:** Certain defenses that can be raised by a 12(b) motion will be ***waived*** if they are not included in a 12(b) motion that is made based on other defenses. For instance, the defenses of ***lack of personal jurisdiction, improper service*** and ***improper venue*** are all waived if D makes a 12(b) motion of some sort and fails to include these, providing that these omitted defenses were "available" to him at the time of the 12(b) motion. See FRCP 12(g) and 12(h)(1).

Example: D is sued by P in Texas federal district court in a diversity action. D has no connections whatsoever with Texas. D brings a 12(b)(6) motion to have the complaint dismissed for failure to state a claim on which relief can be granted. By bringing this 12(b) motion and not including a 12(b)(2) motion for lack of personal jurisdiction, D has waived his right to have the case dismissed for lack of personal jurisdiction, because that defense was "available" to him (i.e., he knew the relevant facts) at the time he brought the 12(b)(6) motion.

IV. THE ANSWER

A. **The answer generally:** The defendant's response to the plaintiff's complaint is called an ***"answer."*** In the answer, D states in short and plain terms his ***defenses*** to each claim asserted, and admits or denies each count of plaintiff's complaint. Rule 8(b).

1. **Alternative pleading:** Defenses, like claims, may be pleaded in the ***alternative***. (*Example:* In a breach of contract suit brought by P, D can in count 1 of his answer state that no contract ever existed, and in count 2 state that if such a contract did exist, it was breached by P, not D.)

B. **Signed by defendant's attorney:** The answer must be ***signed*** by the defendant's lawyer. As with the complaint, the attorney's signature constitutes a certificate that the signer has read the pleading, believes it is well founded, and that it is not interposed for delay. Rule 11.

C. **Denials:** The defendant may make various kinds of ***denials*** of the truth of plaintiff's allegations.

1. **Where not denied:** Averments in a complaint, other than those concerning the amount of damages, are deemed admitted if the allegation is not denied in the answer. Rule 8(b)(6).

2. **Kinds of denials:** There are five kinds of denials in federal practice:

   a. **General denial:** D may make a ***"general"*** denial, by which he denies each and every allegation in P's complaint. (But D must then contest all of P's allegations, or face sanctions.)

   b. **Specific denial:** D may make a ***"specific"*** denial, which denies all of the allegations of a particular paragraph or count of the complaint.

   c. **Qualified denial:** D may make a ***"qualified"*** denial, i.e., a denial of a particular ***portion*** of a particular allegation.

   d. **Denial of knowledge or information (DKI):** D may make a denial of ***knowledge or information*** (DKI), by which he says that he does not have enough knowledge or information sufficient to form a belief as to the truth of P's complaint (but D must do this in good faith).

   e. **Denial based on information and belief:** D may deny ***"based on information and belief."*** By this, D effectively says, "I don't know for sure, but I reasonably believe that P's allegation is false." This kind of denial is often used by large corporate defendants.

D. **Affirmative defenses:** There are certain defenses which must be ***explicitly pleaded*** in the answer, if D is to raise them at trial. These are so-called ***"affirmative defenses."***

1. **Listing:** Rule 8(c) lists 19 specific affirmative defenses, of which the most important are ***contributory negligence***, ***fraud***, ***res judicata***, ***statute of limitations***, and ***illegality***.

2. **General formulation:** Also, Rule 8(c) contains a more general requirement, by which D must plead affirmatively "any avoidance or affirmative defense." Any defense which relies on facts ***particularly within the defendant's knowledge*** is likely to be found to be an affirmative defense.

E. **Counterclaim:** In addition to defenses, if D has a claim against P, he may (in all cases) and must (in some cases) plead that claim as a ***counterclaim***. If the counterclaim is one which D is ***required*** to plead, it is called a ***compulsory*** counterclaim. If it is one which D has the option of pleading or not, it is called a ***permissive*** counterclaim. A counterclaim is compulsory if it "arises out of the transaction or occurrence that is the subject matter of the [plaintiff's] claim...." Rule 13(a).

V. TIME FOR VARIOUS PLEADINGS; ELECTRONIC FILING OF PLEADINGS

A. **Time table:** Here is the time table for various pleading steps (see Rule 12(a)):

1. **Complaint:** Filing of the complaint usually occurs before it is served. Service must then normally occur within 120 days. Rule 4(m).

2. **Answer:** The ***answer*** must be served within ***21 days*** after service of the complaint, except that

   a. **Different state rule:** If P has served D ***out of state***, by using the state long-arm (see Rule 4(k)(1)(A)), the time to answer allowed under that state rule (typically longer) controls.

   b. **Rule 12 motion:** If D makes a Rule 12 motion against the complaint and loses, D has 10 days after the court denies the motion to answer.

   c. **Waiver of formal service:** If D ***waives*** formal service pursuant to Rule 4(d), then he gets ***60 days*** to answer running from the date the request for waiver was sent by P. Rule 12(a)(1)(A)(ii).

3. **Reply to counterclaim:** If the answer contains a ***counterclaim***, P must serve his ***reply*** within ***21 days*** after service of the answer. Rule 12(a)(1)(B).

B. **Electronic filing of pleadings:** Increasingly, state and federal courts throughout the U.S. encourage, or even in some cases require, the ***electronic filing and service*** of answers, other post-complaint pleadings, and non-pleading papers exchanged in a case (e.g., motions, discovery requests, discovery disclosures, etc.).

1. **Mandatory e-filing:** In a federal-court case, service of any document ***on any "registered user"*** of a federal court's ***e-filing system*** may be made by ***filing the document with that system.*** (The federal e-filing system is known as "PACER"; see Par. 2 below.) And if the filer is herself a "registered user" of the e-filing system (as all attorneys practicing in a local federal court system will be), the filer ***must*** use the e-filing system rather than paper-filing as the means of *filing* the document with the court. See Rules 5(b)(2)(E) (covering electronic *service* on a recipient) and Rule 5(d)(3)(A) (covering electronic *filing* with the court).

2. **PACER system:** The federal e-filing system is embodied in a website known as ***"PACER"*** ("Public Access to Court Electronic Records"). See https://www.pacer.gov. ***Nearly all post-complaint service and filing of pleadings and other papers*** in federal cases occurs ***via PACER.***

VI. AMENDMENT OF THE PLEADINGS

A. **Liberal policy:** The Federal Rules are extremely ***liberal*** in allowing amendment of the pleadings.

B. **Amendment:** Here is a general summary of the rules on when federal pleadings may be amended:

1. **Amendment as of right:** A pleading may be amended once ***as a matter of course*** (i.e., ***without leave*** of court) in the following circumstances:

   [1] Amendment of right is ***always*** allowed if it occurs within ***21 days*** after the pleader ***served the original pleading***. Rule 15(a)(1)(A).

   [2] In those cases in which a ***responsive pleading*** is required, amendment of right is *also* allowed even if it happens *more* than 21 days after the original pleading was served, as long as the amendment happens within 21 days following the earlier of (a) service of the ***responsive pleading*** or (b) service of the other side's ***motion*** under Rule 12(b), (e), or (f). Rule 15(a)(1)(B).

   a. **More time:** Point [2] above means that in the case of a ***complaint*** (which requires a "responsive pleading"), the plaintiff can amend of right at any time until 21 days after the defendant has served *either* an ***answer*** or a 12(b), (e) or (f) ***motion, no matter how much time has elapsed*** since the plaintiff served the original complaint.

2. **Amendment by leave of court:** If the situation does not fall into one of the above "amendment as of right" categories, then P may amend only by getting ***leave of court*** (i.e., permission). But Rule 15(a)(2) says "the court should ***freely*** give leave [to amend] when ***justice so requires***."

   a. **"Actual prejudice" usually required:** Normally, leave to amend should be denied only if it would cause ***actual prejudice*** to the other party.

   b. **Amendment after dismissal:** And in the case where D has succeeded with a ***motion to dismiss*** the original complaint, the court will almost always give P leave to amend, on the theory that justice so requires.

C. **Relation back:** When a pleading has been amended, the amendment will ***relate back*** to the date of the original pleading, if the claim or defenses asserted in the amended pleading "arose out of the conduct, transaction or occurrence set out — or attempted to be set out — in the original pleading." Rule 15(c)(1)(B). This "relation back" doctrine is mainly useful in meeting statutes of limitations that have run between filing of the original complaint and the amendment.

   Example: On Jan. 1, P files a complaint against D for negligently manufacturing a product that has injured P. The case is brought in diversity in

Ohio federal district court. On Feb. 1, the Ohio statute of limitations (which controls in a diversity case) on both negligence and product liability claims arising out of this episode runs. On March 1, P amends to add a count alleging strict products liability. Because the products liability claim arises out of the same conduct or transaction as set forth in the original negligence complaint, the amendment will relate back to Jan. 1, and P will be deemed to have met the statute of limitations for his products liability claim.

1. **A single "conduct, transaction or occurrence":** Courts take a fairly ***narrow*** view of when the amendment and the original pleading involve the same "conduct, transaction or occurrence" (the requirement for relation-back). If what's amended is simply P's ***claim or theory***, the court will typically find that the "same conduct" test ***is*** satisfied. But where the ***underlying facts*** needed to sustain the new pleading are ***materially different*** from those alleged in the original complaint, the court is likely to find that the "same conduct" standard is ***not*** met.

2. **When action is deemed "commenced":** According to Rule 3, an action is deemed "commenced" as of the ***date on which the complaint is filed***. In federal question cases, it is to this date that the amendment relates back. In diversity cases, by contrast, it is the date that state law regards as the date of commencement which controls.

   Example: In a diversity case, assume that state law regards the date on which the complaint is served, not the filing date, as being the commencement. In a diversity action in that state, any relation back will be to the date the complaint was served, not to the filing date. (This follows from the *Erie* doctrine, p. 101.)

3. **Change of party:** Where the amendment to a pleading ***changes the party*** against whom the claim is asserted, the amendment "relates back" only if, in addition to the "same transaction or occurrence" rule discussed above, it is the case that "within the [120-day] period provided by Rule 4(m) for serving the summons and complaint, the party to be brought in by amendment:

   (i) received such notice of the action that it will ***not be prejudiced in defending*** on the merits; and

   (ii) ***knew*** or ***should have known*** that the action would have been ***brought against it***, but for a ***mistake*** concerning the ***proper party's identity***."

   Rule 15(c)(1)(C).

VII. VARIANCE OF PROOF FROM PLEADINGS

A. **Federal practice:** The Federal Rules allow substantial ***deviation*** of the proof at trial from the pleadings, so long as the variance does not seriously prejudice the other side. Rule 15(b). Unless omission of the issue from the pleading was intentional, and was designed to lead the objecting party into wasted preparation, the court will almost certainly allow amendment at trial.

Example: P brings a diversity action for breach of contract against D. P's complaint does not allege any special damages. At trial, P shows that P lost considerable business and profits. D objects that special damages were not pleaded. Since D probably cannot show the court that D has wasted preparation, the court will almost certainly allow P to amend his pleadings to allege the special damages. If necessary, the court will give D extra time to develop evidence to rebut P's newly-claimed special damages.

CHAPTER 5

DISCOVERY AND PRETRIAL CONFERENCE

I. GENERAL PRINCIPLES

A. Forms of discovery: Discovery under the Federal Rules includes six main types:

1. Automatic disclosure;
2. ***Depositions***, taken from both written and oral questions;
3. ***Interrogatories*** addressed to a party;
4. Requests to ***inspect documents*** or property;
5. Requests for ***admission*** of facts;
6. Requests for physical or mental ***examination***.

II. SCOPE OF DISCOVERY

A. Scope generally: Rule 26(b), which applies to all forms of discovery, provides that the parties "may obtain discovery regarding ***any nonprivileged matter that is relevant to any party's claim or defense.***" So the two principal requirements for discoverability of material are that it is: (1) ***not privileged***; and (2) ***relevant*** to some claim or defense in the suit.

B. Relevant but inadmissible: To be discoverable, it is ***not required*** that the information necessarily be ***admissible***. For example, inadmissible material may be relevant, and thus discoverable, if it: (1) is likely to serve as a ***lead*** to admissible evidence; or (2) relates to the identity and whereabouts of any ***witness*** who is thought to have discoverable information.

C. "Proportional to the needs of the case": Rule 26(b)(1) also requires that the discovery sought be ***"proportional to the needs of the case[.]"***

1. Six factors to consider: 26(b)(1) lists ***six factors*** that are to be considered in determining whether the proposed discovery meets the "proportional to the needs of the case" requirement:

[1] "the ***importance of the issues*** at stake in the action";

[2] "the ***amount in controversy";***

[3] "the parties' ***relative access to relevant information";***

[4] "the parties' ***resources***";

[5] "the ***importance of the discovery*** in ***resolving the issues";*** and

[6] "whether the ***burden or expense*** of the proposed discovery ***outweighs its likely benefit."***

2. **In addition to relevance:** The "proportionality" analysis is to be done ***in addition to the relevance analysis:*** even if the material would be unquestionably relevant to some issue that is certain to emerge in the case, the material won't be discoverable if, say, the ***issue is a minor one,*** and the ***cost*** to the discoveree of locating and assembling the material would be large.

3. **Use in context of electronically-stored information ("ESI"):** Proportionality analysis is especially likely to come into play in connection with ***electronically stored information ("ESI")***, i.e., information ***stored on computer systems.*** And, in fact, Rule 26(b)(2)(B) contains a special proportionality standard, and procedures for applying the standard, directed to the ESI situation.

D. **Privilege:** Only material which is ***not privileged*** may be discovered.

1. **Who may assert:** Only the ***person who could assert the privilege at trial*** may resist discovery on the grounds of privilege. (*Example:* P sues D1 and D2 for conversion. At P's deposition of D1, P asks D1 questions relating to the facts. D1 knows the answer and is willing to respond, but D2's lawyer objects on the grounds that the questions may violate D1's privilege against self incrimination. D2's objection is without substance, because only D1 — the person who could assert the privilege at trial — may assert the privilege during discovery proceedings.)

2. **Determining existence of privilege:** Generally, in ***diversity cases***, ***state law of privilege applies***. See Federal Rule of Evidence 501. (*Example:* P brings a diversity action against D, asserting that D intentionally inflicted emotional distress on him. D seeks to depose P's psychotherapist, to determine the extent of P's anguish. The suit is brought in Ohio Federal District Court. The privilege laws of the state of Ohio, not general federal principles, are looked to to determine whether patient-psychotherapist confidences are privileged.)

E. **Trial preparation immunity:** Certain immunity from discovery is given to the ***materials prepared by counsel for trial purposes***, and to the ***opinions of experts*** that counsel has consulted in trial preparation. This immunity is often referred to as ***"work-product"*** immunity.

1. **Qualified immunity:** ***"Qualified"*** immunity is given to documents prepared ***"in anticipation of litigation"*** or for trial, by a party or that party's ***representative***.

   a. **"Representative" defined:** A party's "representatives" include his ***attorney***, consultant, insurance company, and anybody working for any of these people (e.g., a private investigator hired by the attorney).

b. Hardship: The privilege is "qualified" rather than "absolute." This means that the other side might be able to get discovery of the materials, but only by showing (i) that it has "***substantial need*** for the materials to prepare its case" and (ii) that it "cannot without ***undue hardship***" obtain the "***substantial equivalent***" by other means. Rule 26(b)(3)(A)(ii).

Example: A car driven by D runs over P. D's insurance company interviews X, a non-party witness to the accident. The insurer then prepares a transcript of the statement. This transcript was prepared "in anticipation of litigation," so it is protected by the qualified work-product immunity. Therefore, P will be able to obtain discovery of it only if he can show substantial need, and the inability without undue hardship to obtain the substantial equivalent by other means. Since P could conduct his own interview of the witness, the court will probably find that the qualified immunity is not overcome.

2. **Absolute immunity:** In addition to the qualified work-product immunity discussed above, there is also ***"absolute"*** immunity. Rule 26(b)(3) provides that even where a party has substantial need for materials (in other words, the showing for qualified immunity has been made), the court "***must protect*** against disclosure of the ***mental impressions***, ***conclusions***, ***opinions***, or ***legal theories*** of a party's attorney or other representative concerning the litigation."

Example: Same facts as above example. Now, D's lawyer reads X's statement, and writes a memo to the file stating "X appears to be lying for the following three reasons...." This lawyer memo, since it reflects the mental impressions and conclusions of an attorney or other representative of a party, will receive absolute immunity, and no showing by P will entitle him to get the memo.

F. **Statements by witnesses:** A person who makes a ***statement*** to a party or the party's lawyer may obtain a ***copy*** of that statement without any special showing. Rule 26(b)(3)(C). This is true whether the person making the statement is a party or a non-party.

Example: In an accident suit, D's insurance company takes P's statement about the accident, and transcribes it. D must give P a copy of P's statement, without any special showing of need by P.

G. **Names of witnesses:** The ***"identity and location of persons who know of any discoverable matter"*** (so-called "occurrence witnesses") are discoverable. Rule 26(b)(1). This means, for instance, that each party must upon request disclose to the other the identity and whereabouts of any ***eyewitness*** to the events of the lawsuit. (*Example:* In an accident case, D's lawyer and investigator locate all eight people who saw the accident. D must on request furnish this list to P.)

1. **Some disclosure is automatic:** If a person has discoverable information that a party plans to ***use in its case,*** then that party must ***automatically*** disclose the person's name and address (even without a specific request from the adversary), early on in the litigation. See Rule 26(a)(1)(A).

H. **Discovery concerning experts:**

1. **Experts to be called at trial:** Where one side expects to call an expert ***at trial***, the other side gets extensive discovery:

   a. **Identity:** First, a party must automatically (without a request) give the other side a list ***identifying*** each expert who will be called at trial.

   b. **Report:** Second, the party who intends to call an expert at trial must have the expert prepare and sign a ***report*** containing, among other things: (i) the expert's ***opinions***, and the basis for them; (ii) the ***data*** considered by the expert; (iii) any ***exhibits*** to be used by the expert at trial; (iv) the expert's ***qualifications***; (v) her ***compensation***, and (vi) the names of all ***other cases*** in which she testified as an expert in the preceding 4 years.

   c. **Deposition:** The expert who will be called at trial must also be made available for ***deposition*** by the other side.

   See Rule 26(a)(2)(A); 26(a)(2)(B); 26(b)(4)(A).

2. **Experts retained by counsel, but not to be called at trial:** Where an expert has been retained by a party, but will ***not*** be called at trial, discovery concerning that expert (her identity, knowledge and opinions) may be discovered only upon a showing of ***exceptional circumstances*** making it impractical for the party seeking discovery to obtain the information by other means. Rule 26(b)(4)(B).

3. **Unretained experts not to be called at trial:** Where an expert is ***consulted*** by a party, but ***not retained***, and not to be called at trial, there is virtually no way the other side can discover the identity or opinions of that expert.

4. **Participant experts:** A ***participant*** expert — one who actually took part in the transactions or occurrences that are part of the subject matter of the lawsuit — is treated like an ***ordinary witness***. (*Example:* P's estate sues to compel D, an insurance company, to pay off on a policy covering P's life. D claims that it was a suicide, based on the results of an autopsy conducted by X, a pathologist. P may depose X, even though X is an expert — because X participated in the events, he is treated like an ordinary witness for purposes of discovery.)

   a. **Expert is a party:** Similarly, a ***party*** who is herself an expert (e.g., a doctor who is a defendant in a malpractice suit) is treated like an ordinary witness for discovery purposes, not like an expert.

   Note: See also the Flow Chart on experts, printed as Figure 5-3.

I. **Insurance:** A party may obtain discovery of the existence and contents of any ***insurance agreement*** under which any insurer will be liable to satisfy any judgment that may result. (*Example:* P brings an automobile negligence suit against D in diversity. P may ask D, in an interrogatory, whether D has insurance, and in what amount by what insurer. P may do this without any special showing of need.)

J. **Mandatory disclosure:** Certain types of disclosure are now (since 1993) ***automatic*** and ***mandatory***.

1. **All witnesses with discoverable information:** First, each party must disclose the name, address and phone number of ***each individual*** likely to have ***discoverable information*** that the party plans to ***use in its case.***

   Example: P sues D concerning a car accident in which P and D drove cars that collided. D plans to call W, who saw the accident, as a trial witness. Early in the case, D must automatically disclose W's name and address to P, even without a request from P for this information. (But if D didn't plan to call W, perhaps because W's story favors P, then D would *not* have to disclose W's name unless P specifically asked for this type of information in discovery.)

2. **Documents:** Second, a party must furnish a ***copy***, or else a ***description*** by category and location, of all ***documents*** and ***tangible*** things in that party's possession, that the party plans to ***use in its case***.

   Note: See the Flow Chart on automatic disclosure, Figure 5-2.

3. **Other:** Later in the litigation, each party must automatically disclose to the other the details of expert testimony (as discussed above) and witnesses and exhibits to be used at trial.

K. **Privilege log:** If a party is declining to furnish documents or information because of a claim of ***privilege*** or ***work product*** immunity, the party must make the claim ***expressly***, and must describe the nature of the documents or communications. (Thus the party can't keep silent about the fact that such a claim is being made or about the nature of the documents/communications as to which it is being made). Rule 26(b)(5).

L. **Duty to supplement:** A party who makes a disclosure during discovery now normally has a duty to ***supplement*** that response if the party then learns that the disclosed information is incomplete or incorrect.

1. **How it applies:** This "duty to supplement" applies to any ***automatic pre-discovery disclosure*** (mainly witness names and documents); to any disclosure regarding ***experts*** to be called at trial; and to any responses to an ***interrogatory***, a request for production, or request for admission. Rule 26(e)(1); 26(e)(2).

   Example: P is suing D regarding a car accident in which P was injured. Early in the litigation, P gives D a list of all witnesses to the accident that P knows of, as required by Rule 26(a)(1)(A). If P later learns of another person who saw the accident, P must "supplement" her earlier disclosure by telling D about the new witness.

III. METHODS OF DISCOVERY

A. **Characteristics:** The various forms of discovery (depositions, interrogatories, requests to produce, requests for admission and requests for examination) have several common characteristics:

1. **Extrajudicial:** Each of these methods (except requests for physical examination) operates ***without intervention of the court.*** Only where one party refuses to comply with the other's discovery request will the court intervene.

2. **Scope:** The scope of discovery is the same for all of these forms: the material sought must be relevant to the subject matter for the suit, and unprivileged.

3. **Signature required:** Every request for discovery of each of these types, and any response or objection to discovery, must be ***signed*** by the lawyer preparing it. Rule 26(g).

4. **Only parties:** Each of these types — except for depositions — may only be addressed to a ***party***. Depositions (whether upon oral or written questions) may be addressed to either a party or to a non-party who possesses relevant information.

B. **Times usable:** There are some "presumptive limits" on the ***number of times*** a particular method of discovery may be used, and on the number of times discovery may be demanded from a given person. That is, unless the court orders otherwise, or the parties so stipulate:

1. **Total number:** Each side is limited to ***10 depositions*** and ***25 interrogatories*** (not ***sets*** of interrogatories, but individual interrogatory questions). Rules 30(a)(2)(A) and 33(a).

C. **Oral depositions:** After the beginning of an action, any party may take the ***oral testimony*** of any person thought to have information within the scope of discovery. This is known as an ***oral deposition***. Rule 30.

1. **Usable against non-party:** Not only parties, but any non-party with relevant information, may be deposed.

2. **Subpoena:** If a non-party is to be deposed, then the discovering party can only force the deponent to attend by issuing a ***subpoena***. This subpoena must require the deposition to be held no more than ***100 miles*** from the place where the deponent resides, is employed, or regularly transacts business in person. Rule 45(c)(3)(A)(ii).

   a. **No subpoena for party:** If a ***party*** is to be deposed, a subpoena is not used. Instead, non-compliance with the notice can be followed up by a motion to compel discovery or to impose sanctions under Rule 37.

3. **Limits on deposition of any given person:** A particular person's ***deposition*** may be taken ***only once,*** and for a ***maximum of 7 hours.*** Rule 30(d)(1).

4. **Limited to ten:** Each side is limited to a total of ***ten oral depositions***, unless the adversary agrees to more or the court issues an order allowing more. Rule 30(a)(2)(A)(i).

5. **Request to produce:** The person seeking discovery will often also want documents held by the deponent. If the deponent is a party, the discovering party may attach a Rule 34 ***request to produce*** to the notice to the party. But if the deponent is a non-party, the discovering party must use a subpoena *duces tecum*.

6. **"Meet and confer" requirement:** When the upcoming deposition is of a person who will be deposed on behalf of a ***corporation or other organization***, disputes about what will be covered in the deposition are common. To reduce the need to have the court resolve the dispute, Rule 30(b)(6) says that "Before or promptly after the notice [of deposition] or subpoena is served, the serving party and the organization ***must confer in good faith*** about the matters for examination."

7. **Method of recording:** The party ordering the deposition can arrange to have it recorded by stenography (court reporter), by ***audio tape recorder***, or by ***video recorder***. Rule 30(b)(3)(A).

D. **Depositions upon written questions:** Any party may take the oral responses to ***written questions***, from ***any person*** (party or non-party) thought to have discoverable information. Rule 31. This is called a "deposition on written questions."

1. **Distant non-party witnesses:** Depositions on written questions are mainly used for deposing ***distant non-party witnesses***. Such witnesses cannot be served with interrogatories (since these are limited to parties), and cannot be compelled to travel more than 100 miles from their home or business.

E. **Interrogatories to the parties:** An ***interrogatory*** is a set of ***written questions*** to be ***answered in writing*** by the person to whom they are addressed. Interrogatories may be addressed ***only to a party***. Rule 33(a).

1. **Limit of 25 questions:** Each party is limited to ***25 interrogatory questions*** directed to any other party, unless the parties stipulate otherwise or the court orders otherwise. Rule 33(a).

F. **Requests for admission:** One party may serve upon another party a written request for the ***admission, for the purposes of the pending action only, of the truth of any discoverable matters***. Rule 36. This is a ***"request for admission."***

1. **Coverage:** The statements whose genuineness may be requested include statements or opinions of fact, the application of law to fact, and the genuineness of any documents. (*Example:* P, in a breach of contract action, may request that D admit that the attached document is a contract signed by both P and D.)

2. **Expenses for failure to admit:** If a party fails to admit the truth of any matter requested for admission under Rule 36(a), and the party making the request ***proves*** the truth of the matter at trial, the court may then require the party who refused to admit to pay ***reasonable expenses*** sustained by the movant in proving the matter. Rule 37(c). (But no expenses may be charged in several situations, including where the party who failed to admit had reasonable grounds to think he might prevail on the issue at trial.)

3. **Effect at trial:** If a party makes an admission under Rule 36, the matter is normally ***conclusively established at trial***. (However, the court may grant a motion to withdraw or amend the admission, if this would help the action to be presented on its merits, and would not prejudice the other side.)

G. **Request to produce documents, ESI and tangible things:** A party may require any other party to ***produce documents, electronically stored information***

("ESI"), and ***tangible things***. Rule 34. Thus any papers, photos or objects relevant to the subject matter of the case may be obtained from any other party, but not from a non-party.

> **Example:** P sues D1 and D2 for antitrust and price fixing. P believes that the records of both Ds will show that they set prices in concert. P may require D1 and D2 to produce any documents in their control relating to the setting of prices.

1. **Only to parties:** A request to produce can only be addressed to ***parties***. If documents in the possession of a non-party are desired, a subpoena *duces tecum* must be used.
2. **Party's control:** A party may be required to produce only those documents or other objects which are in her ***"possession, custody or control."*** Rule 34(a).
3. **"Electronically stored information" or "ESI" (i.e., computer files):** Rule 34's reference to ***"electronically stored information"*** (***"ESI"***) means that ***computer files*** are discoverable on the same basis as paper documents.
   a. **Right to specify form for the data:** The requesting party can specify the ***"form or forms"*** in which the ESI is to be produced. Rule 34(b)(1)(C).

      Example: The requesting party might ask for certain "email and word-processed files, supplied in the original electronic format as created by the application that produced the file."

   b. **Social media records:** The types of ESI sought by a party may include records of the other party's postings on ***social media outlets*** like ***TikTok, X, YouTube,*** etc. Such postings are often voluminous, and frequently touch on relatively private matters that the poster would not want to be disclosed to the general public. Therefore, a demand for, say, "All of your social media postings from Jan. 1, 2015 to the present" might result in public disclosure of massive amounts of personal data that have nothing to do with the controversy. Courts have therefore sometimes held that demands for social-media records are to be restricted to certain categories and time periods that are especially ***relevant*** to issues in the case.
4. **Land:** Rule 34 also allows a party to demand the right to inspect, photograph and survey any ***land*** within the control of another party. (*Example:* P sues D, a merchant, for negligence, because P fell on D's slippery floor. P may require D to open the premises so that P may inspect and photograph them.)

H. Physical and mental examination: When the mental or physical condition of a ***party*** is ***in controversy***, the court may order the party to submit to a ***physical or mental examination*** by a suitably licensed or certified examiner. Rule 35.

1. **Motion and good cause:** Unlike all other forms of discovery, Rule 35 operates only by ***court order***. The discovering party must make a ***motion*** upon notice to the party to be examined, and must show ***good cause*** why the examination is needed.

2. **Controversy:** The physical or mental condition of the party must be ***in controversy***. In other words, it is not enough (as it is for other forms of discovery) that the condition would be somehow relevant. (*Example:* If P is suing D for medical malpractice arising out of an operation, P's condition would obviously be in controversy, and D would be entitled to have a physician conduct a physical examination of P. But if P were suing D for breach of contract, and D had some suspicion that P was fabricating the whole incident, a mental examination of P to find evidence of delusional behavior would probably not be found to be supported by good cause, so the court order granting the exam would probably not be made.)

3. **Reports from examiner:** The ***actual medical report*** produced through a Rule 35 examination is discoverable (in contrast to the usual non-discoverability of experts' reports).

   a. **Who may receive:** A ***person examined*** (typically the opposing party) may request, from the party causing the exam to be made, a copy of the examiner's written report.

   b. **Other examinations:** Once the examined party asks for and receives this report, then the other party is entitled to reports of any ***other*** examinations made at the request of the examinee for the same condition. (*Example:* P sues D for automobile negligence. D causes P to be examined by a doctor retained by D, to measure the extent of P's injuries. P asks for a copy of the report, and D complies. Now, D is entitled to receive from P copies of any other reports of examinations made of P at P's request. In other words, by asking D for the report, P is deemed to have waived the physician-patient privilege as to exams conducted at P's request.)

IV. ORDERS AND SANCTIONS

A. **Two types:** Discovery normally proceeds without court intervention. But the court where the action is pending may intercede in two main ways, by issuing orders and by awarding sanctions. The court may order abuse of discovery stopped (a protective order) or may order a recalcitrant party to furnish discovery (order compelling discovery). Sanctions can be awarded for failing to handle discovery properly.

B. **Abuse of discovery:** One party sometimes tries to use discovery to harass her adversary. (*Example:* P requests that D reveal trade secrets, or schedules 10 repetitive depositions of D.) The discoveree may fight back in two ways: (1) by simply ***objecting*** to a particular request; or (2) by seeking a Rule 26 ***protective order***.

   1. **Objection:** A party may ***object*** to a discovery request the same way a question at trial may be objected to. Typical grounds are that the matter sought is

not within the scope of discovery (i.e., not ***relevant*** to the subject matter) or that it is privileged.

a. **Form of objection:** The form depends on the type of discovery. An objection to an ***interrogatory*** question is written down as part of the set of answers. Similarly, an objection to a request to admit is made in writing. An objection to a ***deposition*** question, by contrast, is raised as an oral objection by the lawyer representing the deponent or the party opposing the deposition. The deposition then continues, and the objections are later dealt with en masse by the judge.

2. **Protective order:** Where more than a few questions are at stake, the party opposing discovery may seek a ***"protective order."*** Rule 26(c)(1) allows the judge to make "an order to protect a party or person from ***annoyance***, ***embarrassment***, ***oppression***, or undue ***burden*** or expense[.]"

Example 1: In a simple automobile negligence case brought under diversity, D schedules P for ten different depositions, and asks substantially the same questions each time. P may seek a protective order in which the judge orders that no further depositions of P may take place at all. The court will probably grant this request.

Example 2: P sues D for patent infringement, alleging that D's manufacturing methods violate P's patents. In a deposition of D's vice president, P asks the details of D's secret manufacturing processes. D may seek a protective order preventing P from learning these trade secrets, perhaps on the grounds that P does not need to know these secrets in order to pursue his patent case.

a. **Prohibition of public disclosure:** One common type of protective order allows trade secrets or other information to be discovered, but then ***bars the public disclosure*** of the information by the discovering litigant. (*Example:* On the facts of the above example, the judge might allow P to get discovery of D's trade secrets, but prevent P from disclosing that information to any third party.)

C. **Compelling discovery:** Conversely, if one party refuses to cooperate in the other's discovery attempts, the aggrieved party may seek an ***order compelling discovery*** under Rule 37(a).

1. **When available:** An order to compel discovery may be granted if the discoveree fails to: (1) answer a written or oral deposition question; (2) answer an interrogatory; (3) produce documents, or allow an inspection; (4) designate an officer to answer deposition questions, if the discoveree is a corporation.

D. **Sanctions for failing to furnish discovery:** The court may order a number of ***sanctions*** against parties who behave unreasonably during discovery. Principally, these sanctions are used against a party who fails to cooperate in the other party's discovery efforts.

1. **Financial sanctions:** If a discovering party seeks an order compelling discovery, and the court grants the order, the court may require the discoveree to

pay the ***reasonable expenses*** the other party incurred in obtaining the order. These may include attorney's fees for procuring the order. Rule 37(b)(2)(C).

2. **Other sanctions:** Once one party obtains an order compelling the other to submit to discovery, and the latter ***persists in her refusal*** to grant discovery, then the court may (in addition to the financial sanctions mentioned above) impose additional sanctions:

   a. **Facts established:** The court may order that the matters involved in the discovery be taken to be ***established***. (*Example:* In a product liability suit, P wants discovery of D's records, to show that D made the product that injured P. If D refuses to cooperate even after the court issues an order compelling discovery, then the court may treat as established D's having manufactured the item.)

   b. **Claims or defenses barred:** The court may prevent the disobedient party from making certain claims or defenses, or introducing certain matters in evidence.

   c. **Entry of judgment:** The court may also ***dismiss*** the action, or enter a default judgment.

   d. **Contempt:** Finally, the court may hold the disobedient party in ***contempt*** of court.

3. **Failure to preserve ESI:** Rule 37 contains a special provision, 37(e), that covers remedies for a party's ***failure to preserve "electronically stored information" ("ESI").*** These special remedies apply only when ***three initial requirements*** concerning the ESI are all met (specified in Rule 37(e)(1)):

   [1] The ESI "should have been ***preserved*** in the ***anticipation*** or ***conduct of litigation***";

   [2] The ESI was "***lost*** because a party ***failed to take reasonable steps to preserve it***"; and

   [3] The ESI "cannot be ***restored or replaced through additional discovery.***"

   a. **Consequence:** If these 3 requirements of 37(e)(1) are met, and the failure to preserve the ESI ***causes prejudice*** to the other party, the court may "order measures ***no greater than necessary to cure the prejudice.***" Typically, the court would do this by awarding the ***money*** needed to ***re-create the missing materials***, if such a recreation can be done by the expenditure of money.

   b. **Intent to deprive other party of ESI's use in the litigation:** But the ***most severe*** sanctions under Rule 37(e) are available only if the court finds not only that the three above requirements are met, but *also* finds that the party that had custody of the ESI "acted with the ***intent to deprive [the other] party of the information's use in the litigation.***" In that event, Rule 37(e)(2) allows the court to impose greater punishment on the wrongdoer. Among other things, the court may:

   [1] instruct the jury that it "***may or must presume that the information***

was unfavorable" to the wrongdoing party; and

[2] ***"dismiss the action*** or ***enter a default judgment.***"

Example (37(e) applies): Suppose that D, a business, follows a self-imposed standard practice of making daily backup tapes of all emails from its computer servers, deleting the online copies after one year, and then doing weekly destruction of any backup tapes that have just turned two years old. Assume that there is no law or regulation requiring D to preserve emails longer than this. P and D enter into a contract that was completed in late 2022. In December 2023, P's lawyer sends D a letter saying, "P believes that you have breached the P-D contract, and unless this matter is resolved to P's satisfaction, you are on notice that P will institute legal action." P doesn't actually bring suit until early 2025 (still within the statute of limitations for a claim on this contract). After getting the Dec. 2023 letter, D does nothing to reverse its usual practice of destroying two-year-old backup tapes, so that all copies of the relevant emails from 2022 are destroyed at the end of 2024, and can no longer be restored or replaced.

37(e) ***will apply***. That's because as soon as D got the Dec. 2023 letter, (i) the relevant emails "should have been preserved in the anticipation … of litigation"; and (ii) it's clear that D is a "party [who] ***failed to take reasonable steps to preserve"*** the emails, given that the emails were already contained in backup tapes and all D had to do was to refrain from destroying them. (The remedies available to the court for the destruction will depend on what the court concludes about D's intent, as we'll see below.)

i. **Intent to deprive other party:** As to sanctions for breaching Rule 37(e), the most severe ones are available when there has been ***intentional wrongdoing*** by the discoveree. That scenario is governed by Rule 37(e)(2). So assuming that the core requirements for any application of Rule 37(e) are met (i.e., the discoveree failed to take reasonable preservation steps in anticipation of litigation, leading to irretrievable loss of the data), 37(e)(2) says:

> "(2) ***only*** upon finding that the party acted ***with the intent to deprive another party of the information's use in the litigation*** [the court] may:
>
> (A) ***presume*** that the lost information was ***unfavorable to the party;***
>
> (B) instruct the jury that it may or must ***presume the information was unfavorable*** to the party; or
>
> (C) ***dismiss*** the action or enter a ***default*** judgment."

V. USE OF DISCOVERY RESULTS AT TRIAL

A. **Use at same trial:** The rules for determining whether the fruits of discovery can be ***introduced at trial*** vary depending on the type of discovery.

B. **Request to produce:** The admissibility of ***documents*** and ***reports*** that were obtained through a Rule 34 ***request to produce*** is determined ***without regard*** to the fact that these items were obtained through discovery. These documents will thus be admissible unless their contents constitute prejudicial, hearsay, or other inadmissible material.

C. **Depositions:** The admissibility of ***depositions*** is determined through a two-part test. Both parts must be satisfied:

1. **Test 1:** First, determine whether the deposition statement sought to be introduced would be admissible ***if the deponent were giving live testimony***. If not, the statement is automatically inadmissible.

   Example: Deponent says, "X told me that he committed the murder." If the hearsay rule would prevent deponent from making this statement live at trial, it will also prevent the deposition statement from coming in.

2. **Test 2:** Second, apply the ***"four categories"*** test. Since the use of a deposition statement rather than live testimony is itself a form of hearsay, the deposition statement must fall within one of the four following categories, which are in effect exceptions to the hearsay rule:

   a. **Adverse party:** The deposition of an ***adverse party***, or of a ***director or officer*** of an adverse ***corporate*** party, may be admitted for ***any purpose at all***. See Rule 32(a)(3).

   b. **Impeachment:** The deposition of any witness, ***party or non-party***, may be used to ***impeach the witness' credibility***. See Rule 32(a)(2).

   c. **Adverse witness' deposition for substantive purposes:** A party may use a deposition of an ***adverse witness*** for ***substantive*** purposes, if the deposition conflicts with that witness' trial testimony.

      Example: In a suit by P versus D, W, a witness favorable to D and called by D, states at trial, "The light was red when P drove through it." P may introduce W's statement in a deposition, "The light was green when P drove through," not just for impeachment but to prove the substantive fact that the light was green.

   d. **Other circumstances:** The deposition of any person (party or non-party) can be used for any purpose if one of the following conditions, all relating to the witness' ***unavailability***, exists: (1) the deponent is ***dead***; (2) the deponent is located ***100 or more miles*** from the trial; (3) the deponent is ***too ill*** to testify; (4) the deponent is ***not obtainable by subpoena***; or (5) there are ***exceptional circumstances*** that make it desirable to dispense with the deponent's live testimony. See Rule 32(a)(4).

3. **Partial offering:** If only ***part*** of a deposition is offered into evidence by one party, an ***adverse*** party may introduce ***any other parts*** of the deposition which in ***fairness*** ought to be considered with the part introduced. Rule

32(a)(6). (*Example:* If one side reads part of an answer, the other side may almost always read the rest of the answer.)

D. Interrogatories: The ***interrogatory answer*** of a party can be used by an ***adverse party*** for ***any purpose***.

1. **Not binding:** Statements made in interrogatories, like statements made in depositions, are ***not binding*** upon the maker — he may contradict them in court. (Obviously the witness' credibility will suffer, but the witness is not legally bound to the prior statement.)

E. Admissions: ***Admissions*** obtained under Rule 36 ***conclusively establish*** the matter admitted.

F. Physical and mental examinations: The results of ***physical and mental examinations*** made under Rule 35 are almost always ***admissible at trial***. (Also, remember that if the examined party requests and obtains a report of the examiner, the examinee is held to waive any privilege associated with the report, such as the doctor/patient privilege.)

> **Note:** All of the above discussion of use at trial assumes that the use takes place during the very proceeding that gave rise to the discovery itself. Where the fruits of discovery in Action 1 are sought to be used in Action 2, different, more complicated, rules apply.

VI. PRETRIAL CONFERENCE

A. Generally: Many states, and the federal system, give the judge the authority to conduct a ***pretrial conference***. The judge may use such a conference to simplify or formulate the issues for trial, and to facilitate a settlement. See Rule 16(a) and 16(c).

1. **Scheduling:** The federal judge must issue a ***"scheduling order"*** within 90 days after any defendant has been served with the complaint. This order sets a time limit for filing of motions, completion of discovery, etc. Rule 16(b). The trial judge may, but need not, conduct a pretrial conference.

2. **Pretrial order:** If the judge does hold a pretrial conference, she then must enter a ***pretrial order*** reciting the actions taken in the conference (e.g., narrowing the issues to be litigated, and summarizing the admissions of fact made by the lawyers).

CHAPTER 6

ASCERTAINING APPLICABLE LAW

I. NATURE OF PROBLEM

A. Generally: A particular controversy that is litigable in federal court may also, in most situations, be brought in state court. This chapter is about which law — federal law or state law — should be applied in cases brought in federal court.

1. **Forum shopping:** A key concept to keep in sight is the federal courts' desire to ***discourage "forum shopping."*** If a particular case could be brought in either state or federal court, and the state courts would apply rules of law different from those that would be applied by the federal court, the plaintiff (and in situations where removal is possible, the defendant) will have an incentive to ***choose the court more favorable to her case***. To prevent forum shopping of this sort, the courts ***generally apply state law*** in diversity cases.

2. **Rules of Decision Act:** The Rules of Decision Act (RDA), 28 U.S.C. §1652, based upon the Supremacy Clause of the Constitution, is the main statute stating when the federal court should apply federal law, and when it should apply state law.

   a. **Federal law applied:** According to the clear language of the RDA, the federal Constitution, treaties, and constitutional ***statutes*** enacted by Congress, always take precedence, where relevant, over all ***state*** provisions. (In fact, this rule applies not only to federal proceedings but also to state court proceedings.)

   b. **State statutes:** The RDA also clearly provides that in the absence of a federal constitutional or statutory provision on point, the federal courts must follow ***state constitutions and statutes***.

   c. **Dispute about common law:** The interesting question, and one on which the RDA is silent, is what the federal court should do where there is ***no controlling constitutional or statutory provision***, federal ***or*** state. In other words, the key question is, what law should the federal court follow where what is at issue is ***"common,"*** or ***judge-made***, law.

      Example: P sues D in a diversity action arising out of an automobile accident that took place in Kansas. The Kansas courts apply common-law contributory negligence. Must the federal judge hearing the case apply Kansas' common-law contributory negligence, or is the court free to make its own determination that comparative negligence is a sounder principle? The answer, as set forth in *Erie v. Tompkins* (discussed below), is that Kansas common law must be followed.

B. ***Erie v. Tompkins:*** The most important Supreme Court case in all of Civil Procedure is ***Erie Railroad v. Tompkins***. That case holds that when the Rules of Decision Act says that the federal courts must apply the "law of the several states, except where the Constitution or ... acts of Congress otherwise require...," this language applies to state ***common law*** as well as state statutory law. The net result is that ***in diversity cases, the federal courts must apply state judge-made law on any substantive issue***.

1. **Discrimination against citizens:** The contrary rule that had been followed before *Erie* — *Swift v. Tyson*'s holding that federal judges could ignore state common law in diversity cases — allowed non-citizens to ***discriminate against citizens of the state where the federal court sat***.

   Example: P, an Ohio resident, sues D, a Kansas resident, in federal district court for the District of Kansas. Kansas law would be favorable to D. *Swift v. Tyson*, which would allow P to choose federal or state court in

Kansas, whichever was more favorable to him, would thus allow P to profit at D's expense. *Erie v. Tompkins*, by forcing the federal court to apply Kansas law, guarantees D, the Kansas citizen, the benefits of his own state's law.

2. **Facts of *Erie*:** The facts of *Erie* remain a good illustration of the case's principle, that state rather than federal common law is to be followed on substantive matters in diversity cases. P, a Pennsylvania citizen, was injured while walking on the right of way maintained by D, a New York railroad. Under Pennsylvania judge-made law, P would probably have lost his negligence suit, because P was a trespasser, to whom D would be liable only for gross, not ordinary, negligence. P instead sued in New York federal district court, expecting the federal court to follow *Swift v. Tyson* and make its own "federal common law" which P hoped would make the railroad liable to him for ordinary negligence.

   a. **Holding:** But the Supreme Court held that the federal court must follow state law on substantive issues, and that "state law" included judge-made (common) law as well as state statutes. So Pennsylvania law on the railroad's duty of care was to be followed (though the Court did not specify why Pennsylvania rather than New York law was what should be followed).

   Note: For an overview of how to analyze an *Erie* problem, see the Flow Chart printed as Figure 6-1.

II. *ERIE* PROBLEMS

A. **Ascertaining state law:** Several problems arise when the federal court tries to determine what *is* the "state law," when there is no state statute on point. Obviously if the highest court of the state where the federal court sits has recently spoken on the issue, the problem is easy. But where this is not the case, life gets trickier. The general principle is that the federal court must try to determine ***how the state's highest court would determine the issue if the case arose before it today***.

   1. **Intermediate-court decisions:** If there is no holding by the highest state court, the federal court looking for state law to apply ***considers intermediate-court*** decisions. These intermediate-court decisions will normally be followed, unless there are other reasons to believe that the state's highest court would not follow them.

   2. **Where no state court has spoken:** If no court in the state has ever considered the issue in question, then the court can look to other sources. One important source is decisions in ***prior federal diversity cases*** which have attempted to predict and apply the law of the same state. Similarly, the federal court may look at the practice of other states, other authorities (e.g., Restatements), etc. But the issue is always: What would the highest state court decide today?

3. **State decision obsolete:** Where there is an ***old*** determination of state law by the highest state court, the federal court hearing the present case is always free to conclude that the state court would decide the issue differently if confronted with the present case. In that situation, the old ruling is not binding.

4. **Certification to state court:** Where the federal district court is ***uncertain*** about how the highest state court would decide an unresolved issue of state law, a procedure called ***"certification"*** lets the federal court simply ***ask that state court to explain*** how it would decide that issue. 49 states (all but North Carolina) now allow their highest court to respond to a certification request from a federal court.

   a. **Sometimes mandatory (*McKesson*):** In fact, sometimes it can be ***reversible error*** for the district court ***not*** to certify the unresolved question to the highest court of the state whose law applies. This can happen, for instance, where one interpretation of an unresolved state-law issue would require the federal court to decide an issue of federal constitutional law, whereas the alternative interpretation of that issue would make it *unnecessary* for the federal court to decide that constitutional issue. [*McKesson v. Doe*]

5. **Change to conform with new state decision:** The federal court (even an appellate court) must give effect to a ***new*** decision of a state's highest court, even if the state court decision was handed down ***after*** the federal district court action was completed.

B. **Conflict of laws:** The federal court must also apply state law governing ***conflict of laws***. In other words, the conflict of laws rules of the state ***where the federal court sits*** must be followed. [*Klaxon Co. v. Stentor Electric Mfg. Co.*]

   Example: P, a soldier, is injured in the state of Alpha by an explosion of a shell manufactured by D. The Ps sue D in a federal diversity action in the district of Beta. Assume that Alpha tort law allows strict liability and that Beta tort law does not allow strict liability. Assume also that in tort actions, Beta's conflict-of-laws rules say that the court must apply the tort law of the state in which the accident occurred.

   The federal court must apply Beta conflict-of-laws principles. Since the Beta courts would apply the tort law of the place where the accident occurred — Alpha — so must the federal court. Therefore, strict liability will not be applied, and the Ps will lose.

C. **Burden of proof:** The federal court must also follow the rules governing the ***allocation of the burden of proof*** in force in the state where the federal court is sitting.

D. **Statute of limitations:** Where a state-law claim is being litigated in a federal diversity action, *Erie* principles require that the federal courts ***obey the statute of limitations of the state under which the state-law claim arose.*** [*Guaranty Trust Co. v. York*]

E. **Procedure/substance distinction:** *Erie v. Tompkins* says that state common law controls in "substantive" matters. But federal rules and policies control on matters that are essentially "procedural." Here are some guidelines for handling the ***procedure/substance distinction***:

1. **Federal Rules take precedence:** *Erie* is only applicable where there is no controlling federal statute. Since the Federal Rules of Civil Procedure are adopted pursuant to a congressional statute (the Rules Enabling Act), ***the FRCP, when applicable, take precedence over state policy***. So if a Federal Rule arguably applies to the situation at hand, ask two questions: (1) Does the Rule in fact apply to the issue at hand? and (2) Is the Rule valid under the Rules Enabling Act? If the answer to both questions is "yes," then the Federal Rule takes precedence.

   a. **Does Rule apply:** The mere fact that a Federal Rule seems to have something to do with the issue at hand does not mean that the Rule applies — the Rules are ***construed narrowly***, to cover just those situations that Congress intended them to cover. If the federal court decides that the Rule in question was not designed to answer the situation at issue, the federal court should apply state law covering that issue.

      Example: The issue in a diversity case is not whether the statute of limitations is applicable at all, but whether it is satisfied by the mere filing of the complaint with the court within the designated period, or instead requires service on the defendant within the period. The state law holds the latter, but Federal Rule 3 says that "a civil action is ***commenced by filing a complaint*** with the court." *Held* (by the Supreme Court), Rule 3 was not designed to determine under what circumstances the statute of limitations will be deemed satisfied. Therefore, the state rule is controlling and must be followed. [Cf. *Ragan v. Merchants Transfer*]

   b. **Is Rule valid:** If you conclude that the Rule applies to the issue at hand, the next question is, "Is the Rule valid?" The Rules Enabling Act provides that to be valid, a Rule must not "abridge, enlarge, [or] modify the substantive rights of any litigant." But as long as the Rule is arguably "procedural," it will be found to satisfy this test. ***No Federal Rule has ever been found to violate*** the "no abridgement, enlargement or modification of substantive rights" test of the Rules Enabling Act.

   c. **Illustration:** To see how this "arguably procedural" test works, consider the following example taken from the important case of *Hanna v. Plumer* (immediately *infra*). There, the Court concluded that (1) the relevant Federal Rule was intended to govern the situation at hand; (2) the Rule was "arguably procedural"; (3) the Rule was valid under the Enabling Act; and therefore (4) the Rule had to be applied, thereby displacing the relevant state principle, even though this result might be somewhat outcome-determinative.

      Example: P sues D in diversity in Massachusetts federal court. D is the executor of an estate. P causes process to be served on D's wife, by leaving copies of the summons and complaint with her at D's dwelling place. Federal Rule 4(d)(1) (now Rule 4(e)(2)) allows service on a defendant by leaving copies of the summons and complaint at the defendant's dwelling place with a person of suitable age and discretion, a standard met here. But a Massachusetts statute sets special standards for service on an executor of an estate, which were not complied with here.

Held, the Federal Rule applies. 4(d)(1) is in harmony with the Enabling Act, since it is arguably procedural. Second, the Rule clearly applies to the issue here, since it specifies the allowable method of service in a federal action. Therefore, the Rule takes priority over any contrary state policy or statute, even if applying the Rule might help produce a different outcome than had the state rule been applied. [*Hanna v. Plumer*]

2. **Case not covered by a Federal Rule:** If the issue at hand is ***not*** covered by anything in the FRCP, but is nonetheless arguably "procedural," the situation is more complicated:

   a. **Rejection of "outcome determination":** At one time, the test was whether the choice between state and federal policy was ***"outcome determinative"*** — if the choice was at all likely to influence who won the lawsuit, then the litigants' substantive rights would be affected by the choice, and the state policy must be followed. But the Supreme Court has ***rejected outcome-determinativeness as the standard.*** [*Byrd v. Blue Ridge*]

   b. **Balance state and federal policies:** Today, the federal court ***balances*** the state and federal policies against each other. ***Where the state interest in having its policy followed is fairly weak, and the federal interest strong, the court is likely to hold that the federal procedural policy should be followed.*** Here are some illustrations of how this balancing works out:

      i. **Judge/Jury allocation:** Where the question is, "Who decides a certain factual issue, judge or jury?" ***federal*** policies are to be followed.

      Example: Whether P was an employee rather than an independent contractor is to be determined by following the federal policy of having factual matters determined by a jury, not the state policy of having such an issue decided by the judge, because the federal policy on judge-jury allocation is strong, the state policy is not tightly bound up with the rights of the parties, and the choice is not very outcome determinative. [*Byrd v. Blue Ridge*]

      ii. **Unanimity for jury trials:** Federal policy requiring a ***unanimous jury verdict*** will be applied in diversity suits, at the expense of the state policy allowing a verdict based on a less-than-unanimous majority. The state's policy (reducing hung juries) has little weight here, since the case is not taking place in the state system; the federal policy is strong, supported by tradition; the choice is not heavily outcome-determinative.

      iii. **Statute of limitations:** But a state ***statute of limitations*** must be followed in a diversity case. Here, the state's interest is heavily outcome-determinative, and deeply bound up with the rights of the parties. The federal interest is relatively weak, and there is little to be gained from district-to-district uniformity. [*Guaranty Trust Co. v. York*, an older case that is still valid.]

3. **Federal statute (not Rule) on point:** Where there is a federal procedural ***statute*** (as distinct from a Federal Rule) that is directly on point, it will control over any state law or policy, even though this may promote forum shopping.

III. FEDERAL COMMON LAW

A. **Federal common law still exists:** Even though *Erie* makes it clear that there is no ***general*** federal common law, there are still ***particular instances*** in which federal common law is applied. That is, the federal court is occasionally free to disregard state law in deciding the case.

B. **Federal question cases:** Most importantly, in ***federal question*** cases, ***federal common law, not state common law, usually applies.***

Example: P sues D, the United States, in federal district court for the Northern District of Texas. This suit raises a federal question, since it involves the U.S. as a party. Even if there is no federal statute on point, and even if it is clear that under Texas law the U.S. would not be negligent, the federal court may and should apply general federal common law principles in deciding whether the U.S. was negligent and is thus liable.

C. **Diversity cases:** Occasionally, federal common law may even be applied where the basis for federal jurisdiction is diversity. For instance, if P's claim does not raise issues of federal law, but a defense asserted by D does raise federal law, the validity of that defense will be determined under federal common law principles.

D. **Federal common law in state courts:** Conversely, the *states* are occasionally required to apply *federal* common law. If concurrent jurisdiction (state and federal) exists concerning a particular claim, and the suit is brought in state court, federal common law applies there if it would apply in federal court.

Example: P brings a state-court action against D, a city, under a federal statute giving a cause of action for deprivation of civil rights. The statute has a one-year statute of limitations. On the other hand, state law requires that P give notice to D within 120 days of injury before suing a municipal government. The state court ***may not*** impose this state-created procedural rule, since it would abridge federally-granted rights.

CHAPTER 7
TRIAL PROCEDURE

I. BURDEN OF PROOF

A. **Two meanings of "burden of proof":** There are two kinds of "burden of proof" which a party may have to bear. Assuming that the issue is called *A*:

1. **Burden of production:** The party bears the "burden of ***production***" if the following is true: unless the party produces ***some*** evidence that *A* exists, the judge must direct the jury to find that *A* does not exist.

2. **Burden of persuasion:** The party bears the "burden of ***persuasion***" if the following is true: at the close of the evidence, if the jury cannot decide whether *A* exists or not, the jury must find that *A* does not exist.

    Example of two burdens: P sues D, arguing that D failed to use reasonable care in driving his car, and therefore hit P, a pedestrian. P bears both the burden of production and the burden of persuasion as to D's negligence. To meet the burden of production, P will have to come up with at least some evidence that D was careless; if P does not do so, the judge will not let the jury decide the issue of negligence, and will instead direct the jury to find that there was no negligence. If P comes up with some evidence of negligence, and the case goes to the jury, the fact that P also bears the burden of persuasion means that the judge will tell the jury, "In order to find that D was negligent, you must find it more likely than not that D was negligent. If you find exactly a 50-50 chance that D was negligent, you must find non-negligence."

II. PRESUMPTIONS

A. **Definition:** A ***presumption*** is a convention that when a designated ***basic fact*** exists (call the designated basic fact *B*), another fact, called the ***presumed fact*** (call it *P*) ***must*** be taken to exist unless there is rebuttal evidence to show that *P* does not exist.

B. **Effect of presumption:** The existence of a presumption always has an effect on the burden of production, and sometimes has an effect on the burden of persuasion. (In the following discussion, assume that there is a legal presumption that if *B*, then *P*. Assume also that plaintiff is trying to prove *P*. Also assume that if there were no presumption, plaintiff would bear the burden of persuasion as to *P*.)

1. **Effect on burden of production:** The party against whom the presumption is directed bears the initial burden of ***producing*** evidence of non-*P*. If he produces no evidence, he ***suffers a directed verdict***.

    Example: A statute establishes a presumption that when a railroad locomotive causes damage, the railroad was negligent. P proves that D's locomotive caused damage to him. Neither party puts on any evidence about D's actual negligence. Assume that if there were no presumption, P would have the burden of production on negligence. By showing damage, P has carried his burden of production; if D does not come up with any rebutting evidence of non-negligence, the judge will direct the jury to find for P on the negligence issue.

2. **Burden of persuasion:** If the defendant offers enough evidence of non-*P* that a reasonable jury might find non-*P*, it is clear that defendant has met his production burden, and that the case will go to the jury. But courts are ***split*** as to who bears the burden of ***persuasion***.

a. **Federal Rules of Evidence:** Most states, and federal courts in federal-question cases, follow the approach set out in the Federal Rules of Evidence. Under this approach, the presumption has ***no*** effect on the burden of persuasion, merely on the burden of production. This approach is sometimes called the ***"bursting bubble"*** approach — ***once evidence tending to show the non-existence of the presumed fact is introduced, the presumption bursts like a bubble.*** See FRE 301 ("A presumption imposes on the party against whom it is directed the burden of going forward with evidence to rebut or meet the presumption, but does not shift to such party the burden of proof in the sense of the risk of non-persuasion...").

Example: Same facts as above example. After P shows evidence of damage by the locomotive, D comes forward with evidence that it was not negligent. This is enough to send the case to the jury. Now, under the FRE "bursting bubble" approach, P will still bear the burden of persuasion — unless P convinces the jury that it is more likely than not that D was negligent, D will win on the issue of negligence. This is because the presumption — that where there is locomotive damage, there is railroad negligence — has no effect on the burden of persuasion.

b. **State law in diversity cases:** But in ***diversity*** cases, the federal courts must defer to any contrary state rule concerning the effect of a presumption on the burden of persuasion. See FRE 302. In other words, FRE 301, applying the bursting bubble approach, applies only where a federal claim or defense is at issue, or state law is silent.

III. PREPONDERANCE OF THE EVIDENCE

A. **"Preponderance" standard generally:** The usual standard of proof in civil actions is the ***"preponderance of the evidence"*** standard. A proposition is proved by a preponderance of the evidence if the jury is convinced that it is ***"more likely than not"*** that the proposition is true.

B. **Adversary's denials:** A party who has the burden of proving a fact by a preponderance of the evidence may ***not rely solely on the jury's disbelief of his adversary's denials of that fact.***

Example: P asserts that D behaved negligently by driving through a red light. P produces no affirmative evidence of this allegation. D takes the stand, and says, "The light was green when I drove through." P does not cross-examine D on this point. There is no other relevant evidence. The court must hold that P could not possibly have satisfied the "preponderance of the evidence" standard as to D's negligence — the fact that the jury might possibly disbelieve D's denials of negligence is not enough, and the court must enter a directed verdict for D on this point.

IV. ADJUDICATION WITHOUT TRIAL

A. **Voluntary dismissal by plaintiff:** A plaintiff in federal court may ***voluntarily dismiss*** her complaint ***without prejudice*** any time before the defendant serves an answer or moves for summary judgment. The fact that the dismissal is "without prejudice" means that she may ***bring the suit again***. See Rule 41(a)(1).

1. **Only one dismissal:** Only the ***first*** dismissal of the claim is without prejudice.

2. **After answer or motion:** After D has answered or moved for summary judgment, P may no longer automatically make a voluntary dismissal. Instead, P must get the court's approval. FRCP 41(a)(2).

B. **Involuntary dismissal:** P's claim may also be ***involuntarily*** dismissed by court order.

1. **Examples:** Some of the grounds for which, under FRCP 41(b), the court may grant an involuntary dismissal, are: (1) P's failure to ***prosecute***; (2) P's failure to ***obey court orders***; (3) lack of ***jurisdiction*** or ***venue***; or (4) P's failure to join an ***indispensable party***.

2. **Prejudice:** Normally an involuntary dismissal is ***with prejudice***. FRCP 41(b). But some kinds of dismissals are ***not*** with prejudice (and thus the action may be brought anew): (1) dismissal for ***lack of jurisdiction***, of both parties and subject matter, or for insufficient service; (2) improper ***venue***; and (3) failure to ***join*** an indispensable party under Rule 19. *Id.* Also, the court may specify that a dismissal not falling into one of these 3 categories is nonetheless without prejudice. *Id.*

C. **Summary judgment:** If one party can show that there is ***no "genuine dispute of material fact"*** in the lawsuit, and that she is "entitled to judgment as a matter of law," she can win the case without going to trial. Such a victory without trial is called a ***"summary judgment."*** See FRCP 56.

1. **Court goes behind pleadings:** The court will go ***"behind the pleadings"*** in deciding a summary judgment motion — even if it appears from the pleadings that the parties are in dispute, the motion may be granted if the movant can show that the disputed factual issues presented by the pleadings are ***illusory***.

2. **How shown:** The movant can show the lack of a genuine dispute by a number of means. For example, the movant may produce ***affidavits***, or use the fruits of ***discovery*** (e.g., depositions and interrogatory answers) to show that there is no genuine issue of material fact.

   a. **Burden of production:** The person moving for summary judgment bears the initial burden of production in the summary judgment motion — that is, the movant must come up with at least some affirmative evidence that there is no genuine issue of material fact.

3. **Opposition:** The party ***opposing*** the summary judgment usually also submits affidavits, depositions and other materials.

   a. **Opponent can't rest on pleadings:** If the materials from the record submitted by the movant show that there is no genuine material dispute for trial, the party opposing the motion can't avoid summary judgment merely by ***repeating his pleadings' denial*** of the allegations of the movant's affidavits. Instead, the non-movant who wants to claim that what the movant says is a non-disputed fact really *is* disputed will have to either:

[1] ***point to specific places in the record*** (such as depositions, documents, admissions, etc.) showing that the fact in question is disputed, or else

[2] demonstrate that the movant won't be able to produce ***admissible evidence*** to establish the fact.

Rule 56(c)(1)(A) and (B).

Example: P sues D on a promissory note. P's claim states that the note was validly executed by D. D's answer denies that D signed the note. P moves for a Rule 56 summary judgment, and submits an affidavit by X stating that X saw D sign the note.

D cannot avoid summary judgment by merely repeating his answer's general denial of the signature. He must do something more. For instance, D can point to something in the record that establishes a genuine dispute about whether he signed (e.g., an affidavit or deposition testimony — even if only his own — asserting that the signature is a forgery, or that it was obtained by duress, etc.). Or, he can show that P won't be able to come up with any admissible evidence at trial that D really signed. But D can't just rest on his own answer, in which he denied ever signing. Cf. Rule 56(c)(1)(A) and (B).

4. **Partial summary judgment:** Summary judgment may be granted with respect to ***certain claims*** in a lawsuit even when it is not granted with respect to all claims. This is called ***partial summary judgment***. See Rule 54(b).

   Example: P sues D for breach of contract. The court might grant P partial summary judgment on the issue of liability, on the grounds that there is no genuine dispute about whether a breach occurred. If so, the court would then probably conduct a trial limited to the remaining issue, damages.

V. TRIALS WITHOUT A JURY

A. **When tried to court:** A case will be tried without a jury if ***either*** of the two following conditions exists:

   1. **No right to a jury trial** exists; or
   2. **All parties** have **waived** the right to a jury trial.

      a. **When waived:** A party who wants a jury trial on a particular issue must file a ***demand*** for jury trial to the other parties within ***10 days*** after the service of the ***last pleading*** directed to that issue. FRCP 38(b). Otherwise, the party is deemed to have waived her right to jury trial.

B. **Effect:** If there is no jury, the trial judge serves as both the ***finder of fact*** and the decider of law.

C. **Evidence rules:** The rules of evidence followed by the judge (in federal trials, these are the Federal Rules of Evidence) are officially the ***same*** in non-jury trials as in jury trials. However, in practice, judges tend to ***relax the rules*** when there is no jury present.

D. Findings of fact: If an action is tried without a jury, FRCP 52 requires the trial court to "***find the facts*** specially and [to] state its conclusions of law separately[.]" So the trial judge must set forth the facts with ***particularity***, and must in a separate section of her opinion state the law which she believes applies to those facts.

1. **Where separate findings required:** The federal judge must make separate findings of fact and conclusions of law not only in cases that are fully tried, but also:

   a. Where requests for interlocutory ***injunctions*** are made (whether granted or denied); and

   b. Where ***"judgment on partial findings"*** is given pursuant to Rule 52(c).

2. **Separate findings not required:** The trial judge is ***not*** obligated to make separate findings of fact and conclusions of law when disposing of a ***motion***, except a Rule 52(c) motion for judgment on partial findings. (*Examples:* If the judge denies a motion for summary judgment, or grants a 12(b)(6) motion to dismiss for failure to state a claim, the judge need not make detailed findings of fact.)

3. **Judgment on partial findings:** The judge can conduct a ***"mini trial"*** of just one issue, if the judge thinks that this will dispose of the case. If the judge then finds against the party bearing the burden of proof on that issue, the judge issues a "judgment on partial findings." See FRCP 52(c). (*Example:* In an auto accident case, D pleads the three-year statute of limitations. The judge can conduct a mini trial concerning only the date of the accident; if the date is more than three years before P started the action, the judge can issue a judgment in D's favor based on the partial finding that the action is time-barred.)

4. **Appellate review of factual findings from bench trials:** If the loser of a non-jury trial ***appeals***, the appellate court will be ***reluctant to second-guess*** the trial judge's findings of fact. In the federal system, the trial judge's findings of fact will be set aside only if they are ***"clearly erroneous."*** See FRCP 52(a). Appellate review of findings of fact in bench trials is covered later as part of our general discussion of appeals; see p. 121, *infra*.

VI. THE JURY

A. Seventh Amendment generally: The Seventh Amendment to the U.S. Constitution says that "in suits at ***common law ... the right of trial by jury shall be preserved....***" This Amendment applies to ***federal trials***, but does ***not*** apply to ***state*** trials.

B. Number of jurors: Traditionally, juries have been composed of 12 members. But this is breaking down today.

1. **Federal:** Even in federal civil cases, the Seventh Amendment does ***not*** require a 12-member jury. FRCP 48 provides that a jury of at least ***six*** members will be seated.

   a. **Too few remaining:** Normally the federal court seats more than six jurors, so that if some have to leave the panel, there will be at least six at the time of verdict. If there are fewer than six at the time of verdict, the court must declare a mistrial unless both parties agree to continue.

2. **State trials:** The number of jurors in ***state trials*** varies from state to state.

C. **Unanimity:**

1. **Federal:** The verdict of a ***federal*** civil jury must be ***unanimous***, unless the parties stipulate otherwise. FRCP 48.

2. **States:** Most states allow a ***less-than-unanimous*** civil verdict.

D. **Jury selection:** The process by which the jury is selected is called the ***"voir dire."*** In most states, the *voir dire* consists of oral questions by both sides' counsel to the prospective jurors. These questions are designed to discover whether a juror would be biased, or has connections with a party or prospective witness.

1. **Dismissal for cause:** Any juror who is shown through the *voir dire* to be biased or connected to the case must be dismissed upon motion by a party (dismissal ***"for cause"***). There is no limit to the number of for-cause challenges by either party.

2. **Challenges without cause:** In addition to the jurors dismissed for cause, each party may dismiss a certain number of other prospective jurors ***without showing cause*** for their dismissal (***"peremptory challenges"***).

   a. **Federal practice:** In federal civil trials, each party receives ***three*** peremptory challenges.

3. **Balanced pool:** The Seventh Amendment requires that the jury, and the pool from which it is drawn, be roughly ***representative of the overall community***.

4. **Alternates:** In most states, the court orders the selection of up to six ***alternates*** after the "regular" members of the jury have been selected. But under federal practice, alternates are no longer used (FRCP 48).

E. **Instructions:** The judge must ***instruct*** the jury as to the ***relevant law***. (*Example:* If P sues D for negligence, the judge must instruct the jury about the "reasonable person" standard, and the requirement of proximate cause.)

1. **Objections:** A party who wants to raise the inadequacy of the instructions on appeal must ***object*** to those instructions ***before the jury retires***. (Sometimes courts make an exception to this rule for "plain error.")

F. **Juror misconduct:** A jury verdict may be set aside, and a ***new trial*** ordered, for certain types of ***jury misconduct***. (*Examples:* Talking to a party, receiving a bribe, concealing a bias on voir dire.)

1. **Traditional impeachment rule:** The traditional rule, still followed in most states, is that the jury may ***not impeach its own verdict***. That is, the verdict

will not be set aside because of a juror's testimony of his own or another juror's misconduct — only evidence from a ***third party*** will suffice.

a. **Federal Rule:** But the Federal Rules of Evidence have modified this principle slightly for federal trials. The general "jury can't impeach its own verdict" rule still applies, except that a juror may testify about whether extraneous prejudicial information was improperly brought to the jury's attention, or whether any ***outside influence*** was improperly brought to bear upon a juror. FRE 606(b). (*Examples:* One juror can testify that another read a newspaper article about the case, or was bribed by one of the parties. But a juror cannot testify that the jury disregarded the judge's instructions.)

2. **Post-trial discovery of bias:** If, after the trial, it turns out that a juror ***failed to disclose*** information during voir dire that would have indicated bias, the party may move for a new trial. In federal trials, the movant must show: (1) that the juror failed to answer honestly a material question during the voir dire; and (2) that a correct response would have led to a valid challenge for cause. [*McDonough Power Equipment Inc. v. Greenwood*] (*Example:* A party can get a new trial if he proves that a juror lied about knowing one of the parties, but not if the juror honestly gave a mistaken answer in voir dire because of confusion about the question.)

VII. CHALLENGING THE JUDGE FOR BIAS

A. **Judicial bias generally:** Both federal and state systems try to protect the litigants against ***judicial bias***. In general, systems do this by giving a litigant a chance to ask the judge to ***"recuse" (i.e., disqualify) herself*** from the case where there is a danger of bias.

B. **The federal recusal statute:** In federal litigation, a litigant may challenge a judge only for ***cause.*** That is, unlike some states, the federal system does ***not*** give litigants any ***"peremptory"*** challenges analogous to those given as to jurors.

1. **Grounds for recusal:** 28 U.S.C. §455 specifies the circumstances under which there is cause for a judge to recuse herself. Section 455 recognizes ***two main categories*** in which recusal is required:

a. **Broad provision:** The first is a ***broad***, but ***vague***, "***appearance***-of-bias" category — if the facts are such that it would ***look to an observer*** as though the judge might well be biased for or against one party, the judge must recuse himself even if he ***subjectively*** (and reasonably) ***believes*** that he can in fact be perfectly fair to both sides. 28 U.S.C. §455(a). (But the parties may agree to ***waive*** any danger of bias under this general provision.)

b. **Narrow provisions:** Second is a set of narrow, ***specific*** categories requiring recusal. 28 U.S.C. §455(b). Unlike the above "appearance of bias" category, the parties are ***not free to waive*** the conflict in a situation covered by §455(b). The specific categories requiring recusal under §455(b) include:

[1] that the judge has "***personal knowledge*** of disputed ***evidentiary facts***" that will be involved in the suit;

[2] that the judge served as a "***lawyer*** in the ***matter in controversy***" when he was in private practice, or was ***associated*** with a lawyer who served in that matter while the two practiced law together;

[3] that when the judge "served in ***governmental employment,***" he "***expressed an opinion*** concerning the ***merits*** of the ***particular case***";

[4] that the judge or a member of his immediate family "has a ***financial interest*** in the ***subject matter*** in controversy or in a ***party*** to the proceeding." (*Example:* If the judge owns even ***$1 of stock*** in a company that is a party, the judge must recuse himself.)

c. **Rule 7.1 requires disclosure:** As you can see from [4] above, one of the specific categories requiring recusal under 28 U.S.C. §455(b) is when the judge or the judge's immediate family member "has a ***financial interest in . . . a party to the proceeding."*** Where the party is a publicly traded corporation, it will be easy for the judge to determine — just from the case caption — whether she or her family have a financial interest in that party. But what if the party is ***not publicly traded***, but is instead a ***subsidiary or affiliate*** of a different publicly traded company?

Hypo: To see the problem, let's imagine that the defendant in the case is X Corp, and that X is wholly owned by Y Corp, a publicly traded company. The judge presumably knows that he or she has a financial interest in Y Corp, but if so, how is the judge to know that one of the parties — X Corp — is controlled by Y?

i. **Disclosure statement under Rule 7.1:** To assist the judge with this subsidiary/affiliate recusal problem, FRCP 7.1 requires each party to ***file a "disclosure statement"*** at the beginning of the case. And that statement must identify ***"any parent corporation*** [of that party] and any ***publicly held corporation owning 10% or more*** of [that party's] stock." So in our hypo above, the defendant X Corp will have to say in a Rule 7.1 disclosure that Corp Y is its parent company.

C. **Bias great enough to violate due process:** In extreme circumstances, a judge's ***refusal*** to recuse himself for bias, or apparent bias, may constitute a violation of a litigant's ***federal constitutional right to due process.***

1. **Judicial campaigns:** For instance, recusal may be required where one litigant makes large ***campaign expenditures*** on behalf of a candidate for a judgeship — the opposing litigant's due process rights may be violated by the judge's post-election refusal to recuse himself from hearing the case. [*Caperton v. A.T. Massey Coal Co., Inc.* (2009)]

Example: The Ps are small mining companies who claim that D, a much larger mining company, has improperly driven them out of business. The Ps obtain a $50 million damage award from a West Virginia jury. D appeals to the West Virginia Supreme Court. While the appeal is pending, the CEO of D spends $3 million in independent campaign expenditures in a successful attempt to have a sitting justice of that court replaced by Brent Benjamin. When the appeal comes before the court, Benjamin refuses to recuse himself; he then votes with a 3-2 majority that throws out the $50 million verdict against D. The Ps now claim that Benjamin's refusal to recuse himself violated their federal constitutional due process rights.

Held, by the U.S. Supreme Court on a 5-4 vote, for the Ps. Benjamin's refusal to recuse himself violated the Ps' constitutional due process rights. Due process can be violated not just by proof of "actual bias," but also by a "serious risk of actual bias ... based on objective and reasonable perceptions[.]" That risk of serious bias exists where "a person with a personal stake in a particular case had a significant and disproportionate influence in placing the judge on the case by raising funds or directing the judge's election campaign when the case was pending or imminent." [*Caperton v. A.T. Massey Coal Co., Inc., supra*]

VIII. DIRECTED VERDICT

A. Defined: In both state and federal trials, either party may move for a ***directed verdict***. Such a verdict ***takes the case away from the jury, and determines the outcome as a matter of law***.

1. **Federal trials:** In federal trials, the phrase "directed verdict" is no longer used — instead, a party moves for "judgment as a matter of law."
2. **When made:** Motions for directed verdict or judgment as a matter of law are made when the opposing party has been ***fully heard*** on the relevant issues. Thus D can move for directed verdict at the close of P's case, and either party may move for directed verdict after both sides have rested.

B. Standard for granting: Generally, the court will direct a verdict if the evidence is such that ***reasonable people could not differ*** as to the result.

1. **Federal standard:** In federal trials, the standard is that the judge may enter judgment as a matter of law "[i]f a party has been fully heard on an issue during a jury trial and the court finds that ***a reasonable jury would not have a legally sufficient evidentiary basis to find for the party on that issue***[.]" FRCP 50(a)(1).

IX. SPECIAL VERDICT AND INTERROGATORIES

A. Special verdict defined: A "special verdict" is a ***specific finding of fact***, as opposed to a general verdict (which merely grants victory to one side or the other). (*Example:* In a contract case, the jury might be asked to render a special verdict as to whether a valid contract existed between the parties.)

B. General verdict with interrogatories: The judge may, instead of requiring a special verdict, require a general verdict, supported by ***interrogatories*** as to specific findings of fact. See FRCP 49(b). This "general verdict with interrogatories" approach is more common than the specific verdict approach.

X. NEW TRIAL

A. Generally: The trial court, in both state and federal courts, usually has wider discretion to grant a ***new trial*** motion than to direct a verdict or disregard the jury's verdict (JNOV). The reason is that the grant of a new trial interferes less with the verdict winner's right to jury trial.

B. Federal rules for granting: Here is a summary of the rules on grants of new trials. We concentrate here on federal civil cases, but also sometimes mention state-court rules:

1. **Harmless error:** A new trial may not be granted except for errors in the trial which are serious enough that they affect the substantial rights of the parties. FRCP 61. This is the so-called ***"harmless error"*** doctrine. Basically, unless the trial judge believes that the error ***might have made the case come out differently***, she cannot grant a new trial motion.

2. **Evidence error:** One common ground for granting a new trial is that the trial judge ***erroneously admitted or excluded evidence.***

3. **Objection:** For most types of error at the trial court level, the party injured by the error must make a ***timely objection***, in order to preserve the right to cite that error on appeal as a ground for a new trial. (For more about this, see the discussion of appeals on p. 121.)

4. **Improper conduct:** A new trial may be granted because of ***improper conduct*** by a ***party***, ***witness*** or ***lawyer***, posing a substantial risk that an unfair verdict will result. Similarly, a new trial may be granted where there is evidence that the ***jury*** behaved improperly (e.g., a juror was bribed or was contacted by a party).

5. **Verdict against weight of evidence:** The trial judge (or the appeals court) may set aside a verdict as ***"against the weight of the evidence."***

   a. **Federal standard:** In federal courts, a verdict must be against the ***clear weight*** of the evidence, be based upon evidence which is ***false***, or result in a miscarriage of justice. It is not enough that there is substantial evidence against the verdict, or that the trial judge disagrees with the verdict and would vote otherwise if he were a juror. (But it is still easier to get a federal judge to grant a new trial as against the weight of the evidence than to get the trial judge to direct judgment as a matter of law.)

6. **Verdict excessive or inadequate:** A new trial may be granted where a verdict is ***excessive*** or ***inadequate***.

   a. ***Remittitur*** **and** ***additur:*** Where the verdict is excessive or inadequate, the judge may grant a ***conditional*** new trial order — the new trial will occur unless the plaintiff agrees to a reduction of the damages to a specified amount (called "*remittitur*") or the new trial to occur unless the defendant consents to a ***raising*** of the damages (called "*additur*"). Most state courts allow both *additur* and *remittitur*. In federal practice, only *remittitur* is allowed. If a party accepts the *remittitur/additur*, he may not thereafter ***appeal***.

7. **Partial new trial:** The trial judge may grant a ***partial*** new trial, i.e., a retrial limited to a particular issue. Most typically, this occurs when the trial judge feels that the jury's conclusion that D is liable is reasonable, but feels that the damages awarded are inadequate or excessive — the judge can grant a new trial limited to the issue of damages.

8. **Newly-discovered evidence:** The trial judge may grant a new trial because of ***newly-discovered evidence***. The person seeking the new trial must show that: (1) the evidence was discovered since the end of the trial; (2) the movant was ***"reasonably diligent"*** in his search for the evidence before and during the trial, and could not reasonably have found the evidence before the end of the trial; (3) the evidence was ***material***, and in fact likely to produce a different result; and (4) injustice would otherwise result.

XI. JUDGMENT NOT WITHSTANDING VERDICT / JUDGMENT AS A MATTER OF LAW

A. **Definition:** Most states allow the judge to set aside the jury's verdict, and enter judgment for the verdict-loser. This is called a Judgment Notwithstanding Verdict, or ***JNOV***. In federal practice, the device is called ***"judgment as a matter of law"*** (JML).

1. **Usefulness:** Judges like the JNOV procedure better than directed verdicts, because it allows the jury to reach a verdict — then, if the judge is reversed on appeal, a new trial is not necessary (as would be the case if the trial judge erroneously directed a verdict).

B. **Federal practice:** Federal practice for "judgment as a matter of law" is spelled out in FRCP 50:

1. **Motion before jury retires:** The most important thing to remember about JML in federal practice is that the party seeking the JML must make a ***motion*** for that judgment ***before the case is submitted to the jury***. The movant also specifies why (in terms of law and facts) she thinks she is entitled to the JML. The judge reserves decision on the motion, then submits the case to the jury. If the verdict goes against the movant, and the judge agrees that no reasonable jury could have found against the movant, then the judge may effectively overturn the verdict by granting JML.

Example: P brings an employment discrimination action against his former employer, D, alleging racial discrimination. The suit is brought in federal court. After both sides have presented their evidence, D believes that P has not made an evidentiary showing that would enable a reasonable jury to find that D discriminated against P on the basis of race. Before the case goes to the jury, D should make a "motion for judgment as a matter of law," pursuant to FRCP 50(a).

Even if the judge agrees that no jury could find in P's favor on the core issue of whether there was racial discrimination against P, the judge will probably ***reserve decision*** on D's motion, and submit the case to the jury anyway. If the jury finds in favor of P, and the judge believes that the jury could not reasonably have done so, then the judge will belatedly grant judgment as a matter of law (or, alternatively, order a new trial). See FRCP 50(b). But if D ***failed to make the judgment-as-a-matter-of-law motion before the case went to the jury,*** then the judge would ***not be authorized*** to grant the judgment as a matter of law. See FRCP 50(b). (The reason for requiring a motion before the case is sent to the jury is to give the opponent an opportunity to cure any deficiency in that opponent's proof that may have been overlooked.)

2. **Appeal:** Appellate courts frequently reverse both grants and denials of JML. Since a JML is granted based on the legal sufficiency of the parties' cases, not a detailed consideration of the evidence, the appellate court is quicker to second-guess the trial judge than in the case of a motion for a new trial.

XII. CONSTITUTIONAL RIGHT TO JURY TRIAL

A. **Seventh Amendment:** The Seventh Amendment provides that "in suits at ***common law***...the right of trial by jury shall be preserved...."

1. **No state application:** The Seventh Amendment has never been applicable to ***state*** trials, only federal ones.

2. **Federal Rule:** The Seventh Amendment does apply to all federal civil jury trials, and is incorporated in Rule 38(a).

a. **Party must demand:** The right to a jury trial in federal practice is ***not*** self-executing. A party who wishes a jury trial on a particular issue must file a ***demand*** for that jury trial to the other parties within ***14 days*** after the service of the last pleading directed to that issue. (Rule 38(b).)

b. **Equitable claim:** There is no jury trial right as to ***"equitable"*** claims (e.g., a claim for injunction). The distinction between legal and equitable claims is very important, and is discussed further below.

B. **Suits with both legal and equitable claims:** If a case presents both ***legal*** and ***equitable*** claims, and one party wants a jury trial on the legal claims, the court must normally ***try the legal claims first***. [*Beacon Theatres v. Westover*] If the court allowed the equitable claims to be tried first, without a jury, this might effectively dispose of some of the legal issues as well, thus thwarting the party's right of jury trial on the legal claims.

> **Example:** P sues D for an injunction against certain contract violations. D counterclaims for damages for breach of contract. D demands a jury trial on its counterclaim. Assuming, as seems likely, the injunction claim is equitable and the damages counterclaim is legal, the judge must try the counterclaim to a jury ***before*** it conducts a bench trial of the injunction claim, as long as there may be some issues common to both claims.

C. **Distinguishing "legal" vs. "equitable" claims:** In deciding whether a claim is "legal" rather than "equitable," the issue is whether the claim is a claim "at common law." The main test is whether the claim is one which the courts of law (as opposed to equity) would have recognized prior to the 1791 adoption of the Seventh Amendment. The problem usually arises in the case of a modern statute that has no precise pre-1791 analogue.

1. **Two-part test:** The Supreme Court has articulated a ***two-part test*** for deciding whether a claim based on a modern statute is legal or equitable:

   ❑ First, the court must compare the ***statutory action*** to the actions available in the courts of England in 1791. If the most similar action available then was legal, that's a factor in favor of the modern action's being considered legal.

   ❑ Second, the court examines the ***remedy*** sought, and determines whether it would have been considered legal or equitable in nature in 1791.

   [*Tull v. U.S.*] The second of these inquiries — concerning the nature of the ***remedy sought*** — is the ***more important***.

2. **Examples:** Here's how some particular types of claims are treated:

   a. **Damages:** Claims that basically involve ***money damages*** are almost always ***legal***. (The one exception is a claim for ***restitution*** of a benefit unfairly kept by D, such as a suit for backpay against an employer — such a claim is equitable, even though it in a sense involves damages.) [*Chauffeurs, Teamsters and Helpers Local 391 v. Terry*]

   b. **Injunctions are equitable:** An action where the principal relief sought is an ***injunction*** will almost always be ***equitable***.

   c. **Declaratory judgment:** A ***declaratory judgment*** suit can be either legal or equitable, depending on the underlying issues in the suit.

XIII. REMEDIES

A. **Damages generally:** The primary form of judicial relief is ***money damages***. We consider here the two major types of damages, compensatory and punitive.

   1. **Compensatory damages:** The usual form of money damages is ***"compensatory"*** damages. Compensatory damages attempt to make the plaintiff ***"whole"*** for the damage she has suffered as the result of the defendant's wrongdoing. For instance, in a contract action, the usual form of damages for breach is a form of compensatory damages called "expectation" damages — the sum of money needed to put the plaintiff in the position she would have been in had the contract been fulfilled.

   2. **Punitive damages:** A second form of damages is ***"punitive"*** damages. Punitive damages, as the name implies, are used to ***"punish"*** the defendant for extreme wrongdoing. Punitive damages are rare in contract suits, but are somewhat common in tort suits, especially those involving serious personal injuries.

      a. **Due process limits:** The ***due process clause*** of the 5th and 14th Amendments puts real ***limits*** on the extent to which federal and state courts can award punitive damages.

i. **"Grossly excessive" standard:** An award will violate due process if it is ***"grossly excessive."*** [*BMW of North America v. Gore*]

ii. **Ratio of actual to punitive:** One of the most important factors in whether an award of punitive damages is grossly excessive and thus violates due process is the ***ratio*** of the ***punitive damages*** to the ***actual damages.*** As a rule of thumb, the Court will view suspiciously any award that ***exceeds*** "a ***single-digit ratio*** between punitive and compensatory damages." [*State Farm Mut. Automobile Insur. Co. v. Campbell*]

Examples: The Court has struck down awards that were 500 times the amount of compensatory damages [$2 million punitive vs. $4,000 compensatory — *BMW of North America, supra*] and 145 times that amount [$145 million punitive vs. $1 million compensatory —*State Farm v. Campbell, supra*].

iii. **Reprehensibility:** The more ***reprehensible*** D's conduct, the higher the punitive award (and the ratio between the punitive and the compensatory damages) can be without a due process violation. (*Example:* Where D's conduct involves non-disclosure but not trickery or deceit, it's less reprehensible, and a lower amount of punitive damages will nonetheless constitute a violation of due process. [*BMW v. Gore*]

B. **Equitable remedies:** Money damages are the usual form of relief in civil actions. But occasionally, the appropriate form of relief is ***"equitable"*** rather than "legal."

1. **Two forms of equitable relief:** There are two main types of equitable relief: (1) ***injunctions***; and (2) ***orders of specific performance***.

a. **Injunctions:** An ***injunction*** is an order of the court ***prohibiting*** a party from doing something.

Example: P, an author, claims that D, a publisher, is distributing a book that violates P's copyrights. If P can establish that this is true, the court will "enjoin" D from making any further distribution of the book. That is, the court will issue an order telling D not to distribute. If D violates the order, D will be in contempt of court, and can be fined or sent to prison.

b. **Specific performance:** A decree of ***specific performance*** is a decree ordering a party to ***do something*** affirmative, typically, to ***comply with a contract.***

Example: P and D have a contract under which D is to supply all of P's requirements for uranium to be used in P's nuclear power generation plant for a 10-year period. D violates the contract by refusing to deliver. The court may well issue a decree of specific performance against D, ordering that D comply with the contract by delivering the required amount of uranium (as opposed to just paying damages for uranium not delivered). If D doesn't comply, D will be in contempt of court, and can be fined or (if an individual) sent to jail.

c. **Legal remedy inadequate:** The most important single principle about equitable relief is this: the court may only award equitable relief ***if legal relief*** (i.e., an award of money damages) is ***inadequate in the circumstances***.

Example: Return to the prior example, about uranium supplies. If the court can compute with reasonable precision how much uranium P will need over the remainder of the contract, and what the market price will be over that period, the court can (and will) make P whole by awarding him damages. But if (as is probable) P doesn't know exactly what his requirements for uranium will be (because he doesn't know how much power he'll need to generate), and/or it isn't knowable what the market price of uranium will be during the future course of the contract, then an award of damages ***isn't "adequate,"*** in which case the court will probably issue a decree of specific performance.

XIV. APPEALS

A. **Appeals generally:** In both federal and state litigation, the party who loses at trial generally has the right to ***appeal*** the adverse judgment.

B. **The scope of appellate review:** Both federal and state systems have various procedural rules that significantly limit ***what issues*** may be grounds for reversal.

1. **Objection:** Generally, the party who hopes to raise issue X on appeal must promptly make an ***"objection"*** to the trial court's handling of X, and must state on the record her ***grounds*** for that objection.

a. **FRCP 46:** Thus in federal trials, FRCP 46 says that for any ruling or order that's made or denied, the party must "***state*** the action that it wants the court to take or ***objects*** to, along with the ***grounds*** for the request or objection." If the party doesn't do this, that contention is deemed ***waived*** on appeal.

b. **Deference to trial court:** The appellate court will usually make a closer scrutiny of decisions of ***law*** than of findings of ***fact***.

i. **Questions of law:** If the issue is a ***pure question of law***, the appeals court typically decides the issue ***from scratch*** — it ***does not give deference*** to the trial court's ruling.

ii. **Facts found by judge in bench trial:** Appellate courts conduct a somewhat ***more probing review*** of factfinding by ***judges*** in ***bench*** trials, i.e., ones conducted ***without a jury,*** than of factfinding in ***jury trials***. But even in reviewing bench trials, appeals courts typically give ***significant deference*** to the trial court.

(1) **FRCP 52(a)(6) for federal practice:** FRCP 52(a)(6) expressly ***requires*** this deference in federal trials. That Rule says that, in appeals from bench trials, "Findings of fact, whether based on

oral or other evidence, must ***not be set aside*** unless ***clearly erroneous***, and the reviewing court must give ***due regard*** to the ***trial court's opportunity to judge the witnesses' credibility.***"

c. **"Harmless error" doctrine:** All appellate courts apply some version of the ***"harmless error"*** doctrine. Under this doctrine, the results in the trial court will be reversed only if the appeals court believes that there is a substantial chance that the error ***made a difference to the outcome***.

i. **Federal standard:** In federal cases, the harmless error doctrine is imposed by statute, 28 U.S.C. §2111. That provision says that the appellate court must conduct its review of the record "without regard to errors or defects which ***do not affect the substantial rights*** of the parties."

Example: P brings a federal diversity action against D for making what P claims was a defective product that injured P. In a jury trial, P puts on no proof that the product was defective. D offers testimony from Expert 1, which is properly admitted, that the product was not defective. D also offers an affidavit to the same effect from Expert 2, which the trial court allows, but which is in fact inadmissible because it is hearsay not within any exception. The jury finds for D. P appeals.

If, as seems likely, the appeals court concludes that even without considering the inadmissible affidavit D has offered so much unrebutted evidence of the product's non-defectiveness that a rational jury could not have found for P, the appeals court will affirm. That is, the appeals court will conclude that the trial judge's error of law in admitting the affidavit was "harmless error," because P was extremely unlikely to win the case even if the affidavit had been excluded.

C. **The "final judgment" rule, and exceptions to it:** The federal system, and the vast majority of state systems, apply some form of the ***final judgment rule.*** The basic concept behind the rule is that an appeal is allowed only after ***all the issues*** involved in the suit have been ***finally determined by the trial court.***

1. **Suit, not just issue, must be finally determined:** So even if a particular ***issue*** in the case has been finally determined, the loser on that issue cannot generally take an immediate appeal. At least in the standard two-party scenario, the final judgment rule means that ordinarily the loser on one or more issues cannot take an appeal until the ***entire case has been finished at the trial-court level***, and a judgment in the case has been entered.

a. **"Interlocutory" appeals:** As a matter of nomenclature, an appeal that is taken when no final judgment has yet been entered is called an ***"interlocutory"*** appeal.

b. **Federal statute:** The ***federal*** court system ***applies*** the final judgment rule in a fairly rigorous way. 28 U.S.C. §1291 says that except in a few special situations covered by other statutory provisions, the U.S. Courts of Appeal shall only have jurisdiction over "***final decisions*** of the district courts."

c. **State-court exceptions:** The ***states*** are, whenever they wish, free to decide not to impose the final judgment rule. A few states in fact allow interlocutory appeals where the federal system would not. Most famously, in ***New York***, a very broad range of interlocutory appeals is allowed.

2. **Certifying the issue:** In the federal courts, one path by which an appeal may be taken before the entire case has been concluded is the ***"certification"*** method. 28 U.S.C. §1292(b) sometimes allows an interlocutory appeal of an otherwise-unappealable district court order if the judge who rendered the order certifies that order for an immediate appeal. But this certification method requires that ***both*** the trial court and the court of appeals ***approve*** the interlocutory appeal.

3. **The "collateral order" exception:** The most important exception to the final judgment rule in federal litigation is the so-called ***"collateral order"*** doctrine. This doctrine holds that even where some part of the case remains unresolved, an order may be immediately appealed if that order ***finally determines an important right that is "collateral to" the main issue*** in the case, and a delay on the appeal would ***seriously impair the value of that collateral right.***

   a. **Three requirements:** The Supreme Court has held that the collateral order doctrine allows for an immediate appeal only if the order satisfies ***three requirements***:

      [1] the order must ***"conclusively determine*** the disputed question";

      [2] the order must "resolve an ***important issue completely separate from the merits*** of the action"; and

      [3] the order must "be ***effectively unreviewable*** on appeal from a final judgment."

      [*Lauro Lines s.r.l. v. Chasser*]

   b. **Categories that don't qualify:** Here are some examples of categories where the court has ruled that an interlocutory appeal is ***not*** permitted:

      [1] Orders ***denying or allowing*** the ***introduction of evidence.***

      [2] Orders compelling ***disclosure of materials*** that a party claims are ***privileged*** (e.g. the attorney-client privilege).

      [3] Orders denying a party's attempt to have the case ***tried somewhere else*** on the basis of a ***forum-selection clause*** in a contract.

      [4] Orders granting or denying a party's attempt to have the other party's ***lawyer disqualified on account of a conflict.***

      [5] Orders ***denying class action status*** (see *infra*, p. 137).

   c. **Categories that qualify:** There are only a very ***small number of categories*** that the Supreme Court has found to ***qualify*** for immediate appeal under the collateral order doctrine. Here are the two most important ones:

      [1] Rulings where a ***government official*** asserts a ***qualified or absolute immunity*** from suit, and the trial court denies the motion as

a ***matter of law***. [*Nixon v. Fitzgerald*]

[2] Rulings where the court ***refuses to dismiss*** an action against a ***governmental entity*** which has asserted ***Eleventh Amendment immunity*** from federal-court suit.

4. **Orders involving the grant or denial of an injunction:** In federal litigation, there is a special provision making it easy to take an interlocutory appeal from a decision granting or denying an ***injunction***. 28 U.S.C. §1292(a)(1) allows for an immediate appeal of a federal district court order "***granting***, continuing, ***modifying***, ***refusing*** or dissolving ***injunctions***, or ***refusing to dissolve or modify*** injunctions."

   Example: The Ps claim that D is running an intentionally-segregated school system in violation of the Ps' constitutional rights. The Ps seek both damages and an injunction against continuation of the segregation. If the court *denies* the injunction, the Ps may take an immediate appeal from this denial, even though D's liability, and the Ps' right to damages, have not yet been resolved. Similarly, if the court *grants* the injunction, D may take an immediate appeal (even though here, too, liability and damages have not yet been decided).

CHAPTER 8

MULTI-PARTY AND MULTI-CLAIM LITIGATION

I. COUNTERCLAIMS

A. **Federal Rules generally:** A "counterclaim" is a claim ***by a defendant against a plaintiff***. The Federal Rules provide for both ***"permissive"*** and ***"compulsory"*** counterclaims. FRCP 13.

1. **Compulsory counterclaim:** If a claim arises "out of the ***transaction or occurrence that is the subject matter of the opposing party's claim…,"*** it is a ***"compulsory"*** counterclaim. See Rule 13(a).

   a. **Failure to state compulsory counterclaim:** If D does not assert her compulsory counterclaim, she will ***lose*** that claim in any future litigation.

   Example: P and D make a contract. P sues D in diversity, claiming that D breached. D believes that not only did he not breach, but that P breached.

   D ***must assert*** his claim that P breached as a compulsory counterclaim, since it arose from the same "transaction or occurrence" as P's claim (the performance of the contract). If D doesn't make the counterclaim, he won't be able to assert P's breach in a separate diversity suit.

2. **Permissive counterclaim:** A defendant has ***discretion*** to assert as a counterclaim "any claim that is ***not compulsory.***" This means that ***no claim is too far removed from the subject of the plaintiff's claim to be allowed as a***

counterclaim. A counterclaim that is not compulsory is known as a "***permissive***" counterclaim.

Example: P sues D in diversity for a 2007 car accident. D counterclaims for breach of a 2008 contract having nothing to do with the auto accident. D's counterclaim is allowed, and is a "permissive" one because it has nothing to do with the subject matter of P's claim against D.

3. **Default by plaintiff:** If D asserts a counterclaim (whether compulsory or permissive), and P neglects to either serve a reply or make a motion against the counterclaim, a ***default judgment*** may be entered against P on the counterclaim. Rule 55(a).

B. **Claims by third parties:** A counterclaim may be made by ***any party*** against ***"an opposing party."*** Rule 13(a), Rule 13(b).

1. **By third-party defendant:** Thus a ***third-party defendant*** may counterclaim against either the original defendant, or against the original plaintiff. (In the latter case, a claim by the plaintiff against the third-party defendant must first have been made.)

2. **By plaintiff:** If D has counterclaimed against P, P may then assert a "counterclaim" against D, even though P has already asserted "regular" claims against D. In fact, P's "counter-counterclaim" will be compulsory if it relates to the same subject matter as D's counterclaim.

Example: P sues D about a car accident. D sues P for breach of an unrelated contract. Any claims P might have against D relating to that same contract are now compulsory counterclaims.

3. **New parties:** ***New parties*** to a counterclaim can be brought into a suit. Rule 13(h).

Example: P sues D for an auto accident. D believes that P and X conspired to ruin D's business, in an unrelated action. D may not only counterclaim against P for this conspiracy — a permissive counterclaim — but D may bring in X as a new party to D's counterclaim.

C. **Subject-matter jurisdiction:** The ***subject-matter jurisdiction*** treatment of counterclaims depends on whether the counterclaim is compulsory or permissive:

1. **Compulsory counterclaim:** A ***compulsory*** counterclaim in a federal action is within the federal courts' ***supplemental jurisdiction***. Therefore, it requires ***no independent subject-matter jurisdictional grounds***.

Example: A, a N.Y. resident, sues B, a Massachusetts resident, in a federal-court diversity case arising out of a car accident; P seeks $100,00 in damages. The accident involved three motorists, A, B and C, each of whom drove a car involved in the accident. (A does not make a claim against C.) B counterclaims against A for $20,000, saying A proximately caused the accident. B also joins C to B's counterclaim, seeking $25,000 damages (not overlapping with the $20,000 B is claiming against A). C is a Massachusetts resident not yet in the action.

B's counterclaim against A is compulsory (because it arises out of the same transaction or occurrence — the accident — as A's claim against B). Since B's counterclaim against A is compulsory, it falls within the court's supplemental jurisdiction. Therefore, the presence of C (who is from the same state as B) doesn't disturb the required complete diversity. Also, the jurisdictional amount does not have to be satisfied by B's counterclaim.

2. **Permissive counterclaims:** A ***permissive*** counterclaim is ***not*** within the court's supplemental jurisdiction, and must therefore independently satisfy the requirements of federal subject matter jurisdiction.

Example: Same facts as above example, except that now, B's claim against A and C does not relate to the same transaction as A's claim against B. This makes B's counterclaim permissive. Since supplemental jurisdiction doesn't apply to permissive counterclaims, the absence of diversity as between B and C, and the fact that B's claim does not meet the jurisdictional amount, are both fatal, so B's permissive counterclaim may not go forward against either A or C.

II. JOINDER OF CLAIMS

A. **Joinder of claims generally:** ***Once a party has made a claim against some other party***, he may then make ***any other claim he wishes against that party***. Rule 18(a).

Example: P sues D, claiming that D intentionally assaulted and battered him. P may join to this claim a claim that D owes P money on a contract entirely unrelated to the tort.

1. **Never required:** Joinder of claims is ***never required*** by Rule 18(a), but is left at the claimant's option. (However, the rules on former adjudication, especially the rule against splitting a cause of action, may cause a claimant to lose the ability to bring the unasserted claim in a later suit.)

2. **Subject-matter jurisdiction not affected:** ***Supplemental*** jurisdiction probably does ***not*** apply to a claim joined with another under Rule 18(a). Thus the requirements of subject-matter jurisdiction must be ***independently satisfied*** by the joined claim. However, usually there will not be a subject-matter jurisdiction problem for joinder of claims (since diversity will not be affected, and since P may add all claims together for purposes of meeting the $75,000 requirement, under the aggregation doctrine).

III. JOINDER OF PARTIES

A. **Permissive joinder:** Joinder under Rule 20, done at the discretion of the plaintiffs, is called ***"permissive"*** joinder. ("Compulsory" joinder under Rule 19 is described below.) FRCP 20 allows two types of permissive joinder of parties: (1) the right of ***multiple plaintiffs*** to join together; and (2) a plaintiff's right to make several parties ***co-defendants*** to her claim.

1. **Joinder of plaintiffs:** Multiple ***plaintiffs*** may voluntarily join together in an action if they satisfy two tests:
   a. **Single transaction or occurrence:** Their claims for relief must arise from a ***single "transaction, occurrence, or series of transactions or occurrences,"*** and
   b. **Common questions:** There must be a ***question of law or fact common to all plaintiffs*** which will arise in the action.
2. **Joinder of defendants:** If one or more plaintiffs have a claim against ***multiple defendants***, these defendants may be joined based on the same two tests as plaintiff-joinder. That is, claims against the co-defendants must: (a) arise from a ***single "transaction***, occurrence, or series of transactions or occurrences"; and (b) contain a ***common question*** of law or fact.
   a. **At plaintiff's option:** Joinder of multiple defendants is at the ***option of the plaintiff*** or plaintiffs.

B. **Jurisdiction in permissive joinder cases:** Here's a summary of how personal and subject-matter jurisdiction work in permissive joinder cases:

1. **Personal jurisdiction:** Where joinder of multiple ***defendants*** is involved, the requirements of personal jurisdiction must be met with regard to ***each defendant individually***. That is:
   a. **Service:** Each D must be ***personally served***;
   b. **Contacts:** Each D must individually fall within the ***in personam jurisdiction*** of the court (by having "minimum contacts"); and
   c. **Long-arm limits:** Each D must be ***"amenable"*** to suit. Since federal courts in diversity suits follow the long-arm of the state where they sit, if a potential co-defendant cannot be reached by the state long-arm, he cannot be part of the federal diversity action even if he has the requisite minimum contacts. (But in federal question suits, it doesn't matter that the state long-arm can't reach D.)
2. **Subject-matter jurisdiction:** All parties (whether plaintiffs or defendants) joined under Rule 20 must meet federal ***subject-matter jurisdiction*** requirements. ***Supplemental jurisdiction generally does not apply*** to Rule 20 joinder of ***multiple defendants***; it only partially applies to Rule 20 joinder of ***multiple plaintiffs***.
   a. **Complete diversity:** If the action is brought as a diversity action, the diversity must be ***complete***. That is, ***no state may be represented on both sides of an action.***

      Example: In an action where no federal question is present, there are 12 plaintiffs, 11 from Connecticut and one from New York, and 12 defendants, 11 from New Jersey and one from New York. On these facts there is no diversity, because complete diversity is required. Thus one of the New Yorkers must be dropped if the action is to proceed in federal court. And supplemental jurisdiction does not apply so as to remove the complete-diversity requirement.

b. **Aggregation where one P meets the amount:** ***Multiple plaintiffs*** are ***permitted*** to ***aggregate*** their claims to meet the amount in controversy requirement, ***if at least one plaintiff meets the amount. Supplemental jurisdiction applies*** to this situation. [*Exxon Mobil Corp. v. Allapattah Services, Inc.*]

Example: P1 is a nine-year-old girl who has been severely injured when she sliced her finger on a tuna can made by D; her claim is for more than $75,000. P2, P3, etc. are members of P1's immediate family, who have claims for less than $75,000 for items like emotional distress and medical expenses.

Held, P2, P3, etc., may join with P1 as co-plaintiffs under FRCP 20. As long as one plaintiff meets the jurisdictional amounts, additional co-plaintiffs may join the suit under Rule 20 even though their individual claims don't meet the amount, because supplemental jurisdiction applies. [*Exxon Mobil Corp. v. Allapattah Services, Inc.*]

Note: But remember that in the Rule 20 scenario, supplemental jurisdiction applies only to the amount in controversy, ***not the requirement of complete diversity.*** So if, on the facts of the above Example, any one of the Ps was a citizen of the same state as D, the suit could not go forward.

i. **Each defendant must meet:** Where the Rule 20 joinder involves ***multiple defendants***, supplemental jurisdiction does ***not*** apply even for amount-in-controversy purposes, so ***each defendant*** must have claims against him equal to the jurisdictional amount.

Example: P1 has a diversity claim for $80,000 against D1, and a diversity claim for $15,000 against D2 that is closely related to the claim against D1. Supplemental jurisdiction does not apply. Therefore, P1's claim against D2 must be dropped from the suit, since it does not independently meet the amount-in-controversy requirement.

C. **Compulsory joinder (Rule 19):** There are certain situations in which additional parties ***must*** be joined, assuming the requirements of jurisdiction can be met. Such joinder, specified by Rule 19, is called ***"compulsory"*** joinder. The basic idea is that a party must be joined if it would be uneconomical or unfair to litigate a claim without her.

1. **Two categories:** There are two categories of parties who must be joined where possible:

a. **"Necessary" parties:** The "less vital" group consists of parties: (1) who must be joined if this can be done; but (2) in whose absence because of jurisdictional problems the action will nonetheless be permitted to go forward. See Rule 19(a). These parties are called ***"necessary"*** parties (though 19(a) doesn't use this term).

b. **"Indispensable" parties:** The second, "more vital" group consists of parties who are so vital that if their joinder is impossible for jurisdictional reasons, the whole action must be ***dropped***. They are covered in Rule 19(b). Such vital parties are often called ***"indispensable"*** parties (though 19(b) doesn't use this term).

2. **"Necessary" defined:** A party is "necessary" — and must be joined if jurisdictionally possible — if the party is not "indispensable" (defined below) ***and either*** of the two following tests is met:

   a. **Incomplete relief:** In the person's absence, ***complete relief*** cannot be accorded among those already parties; or

   b. **Impaired interest:** The absentee has an interest relating to the action, and trying the case without the absentee will either ***impair the absentee's interest*** or leave one of the people already parties subject to ***multiple or inconsistent obligations***.

3. **"Indispensable" defined:** If a party meets the test for "necessary" given in paragraph (2) above, but the party's joinder is ***impossible*** because of jurisdictional problems, the court has to decide whether the party is ***"indispensable."***

   a. **Consequence of indispensability:** If the party is "indispensable," then the action must be ***dismissed*** in that party's absence.

   b. **Factors:** When the court decides whether a party is "indispensable," the factors are: (1) the extent of ***prejudice*** to the absentee, or to those already parties; (2) the possibility of framing the judgment so as to ***mitigate*** such prejudice; (3) the ***adequacy*** of a ***remedy*** that can be granted in the party's absence; and (4) whether the plaintiff will have an adequate remedy if the action is dismissed. Rule 19(b).

   Example: P sues D, a bank holding some stock. P alleges that although the stock is registered solely in the name of X, P and X in fact co-own the stock. P and D are citizens of different states, but X is a citizen of the same state as P. X thus cannot be joined as a co-defendant, because his presence would destroy diversity. The issue is whether X is "necessary" or "indispensable."

   Held: (1) X is definitely a person who must be joined if feasible under Rule 19(a), because his absence will expose D to the risk of double obligation — a judgment that P owns the stock will not bind X, who can later sue D for the whole value of the stock; (2) X is in fact "indispensable" — his presence is so important that the suit must be dismissed rather than proceed in X's absence. [*Haas v. Jefferson Bank*]

4. **Jurisdiction:** Where a non-party is one who must be "joined if feasible," the doctrine of ***supplemental jurisdiction*** does ***not*** apply to overcome any jurisdictional problems. So if the person who is sought to be joined as a defendant is not diverse with all plaintiffs, or if the claim against that would-be defendant does not meet the amount-in-controversy requirement in a diversity case, the joinder may not take place.

IV. CLASS ACTIONS

A. **Definition:** The class action is a procedure whereby a single person or small group of co-parties may ***represent*** a larger group, or ***"class,"*** of persons sharing a ***common interest.***

1. **Jurisdiction:** In the class action, ***only the representatives*** must satisfy the requirements of personal jurisdiction, subject-matter jurisdiction, and venue. (*Example:* P1 and P2 are the named co-plaintiffs who bring a diversity class action against D. There are 2,000 non-named class members. Only P1 and P2 must meet the requirements of diversity vis-a-vis D, so the fact that many non-named plaintiffs are citizens of the same state as D is irrelevant.)

2. **Binding on absentees:** The results of a class action are generally ***binding on the absent members***. Therefore, all kinds of procedural rules (discussed below) exist to make sure that these absentees receive ***due process*** (e.g., they must receive notice of the action, and notice of any proposed settlement).

3. **Defendant class:** In federal practice, as well as in states permitting class actions, the class may be composed ***either*** of plaintiffs or defendants. The vast majority of the time, the class will be composed of plaintiffs.

4. **Certification as class:** At some point before trial, a federal court must ***"certify"*** the action, i.e., affirmatively determine that it meets the requirements of FRCP 23. If the judge rejects certification, the action must proceed as a normal action involving only the named parties, or not proceed at all.

   a. **"Putative" designation:** Until certification has occurred, the action is called a ***"putative"*** class action.

   b. **Usually desired by plaintiffs:** Normally, it is the named ***plaintiffs*** (or at least their lawyer(s)) that wish to proceed as a class action, and the defendant(s) typically oppose class certification. But sometimes the reverse is true — the defendant(s) want to turn one or more individual suits into a class action in which absent plaintiff class members will be bound.

B. **Rule 23 generally:** The federal procedures for ***class actions*** are spelled out in FRCP 23.

1. **Four prerequisites:** ***Four prerequisites*** (discussed below) must be met before there is any possibility of a class action.

2. **Three categories:** Once these prerequisites are met, a class action will still not be allowed unless the action fits into one of ***three categories***, represented by Rule 23(b)(1), 23(b)(2), and 23(b)(3). (See Table 8-2, "Class Actions.")

C. **Prerequisites:** Here are the four prerequisites which must be met before any federal class action is allowed:

1. **Size:** The class must be ***so large*** that joinder of all members is impractical. Nearly all class actions involve a class of at least 25 members, and most involve substantially more (potentially tens of thousands).

2. **Common questions:** There must be ***"questions of law or fact common to the class."***

3. **Typical claims:** The claims or defenses of the representatives must be ***"typical"*** of those of the class.

4. **Fair representation:** Finally, the representatives must show that they can ***"fairly and adequately protect the interests of the class."*** Thus the representatives must not have any ***conflict of interest*** with the absent class members, and they must furnish ***competent legal counsel*** to fight the suit.

D. **Detail on the prerequisites:** Here is some further detail on these prerequisites that all federal class actions must satisfy:

1. **Common questions:** Of the four Rule 23 prerequisites, the one that is most likely to be in dispute is 23(a)(2)'s requirement that there be ***"questions of law or fact common to the class."*** In the 2014 case of ***Wal-Mart Stores, Inc. v. Duke***, a majority of the Supreme Court held that the common-questions requirement means that before a federal trial judge may certify a class action, the judge must be satisfied, after ***"rigorous analysis,"*** that the plaintiffs are prepared to demonstrate affirmatively at trial ***all*** of the following:

   [1] that there is at least one ***"common contention"*** of law or fact ...

   [2] whose ***"truth or falsity"*** will ...

   [3] resolve ***"in one stroke"*** ...

   [4] an ***issue*** that is ***"central to the validity of each one of the claims."***

   This is a new and ***much tougher standard*** for commonality than the Court had ever previously applied.

   Example: The named Ps are three female employees of D (the Wal-Mart store chain) who have worked in various local stores owned by D. These named Ps bring a class-action for employment discrimination on behalf of a class of all 1.5 million female employees of 3,500 Wal-Mart stores located in all 50 states. The suit claims that D has given each store manager in the U.S. (nearly all of them male) wide discretion over pay and promotion practices at the manager's local store, and that these individual managers have exercised that discretion in a way that has had a disparate impact on women. The Ps claim that this system of giving discretion to individual store managers itself violates the federal statute barring gender discrimination in employment. D opposes certification on the grounds that there is no common question of law or fact.

   Held, for D. The commonality requirement is ***not*** satisfied merely by the fact that all of the class members (i.e., all of the 1.5 million female employees) claim to have suffered a ***violation of the same law*** (the statute barring employment discrimination based on gender). There must be a common contention that is "capable of classwide resolution." And this "capable of claswide resolution" requirement means in turn that the determination of the supposedly-common contention's truth or falsity must ***resolve an issue*** that is "central to the validity of each one of the claims ***in one stroke.***"

   Here, for each class member, the central issue is "the ***reason*** for a particular employment decision" (e.g., a particular promotion or firing decision).

The 1.5 million class members are thus purporting to sue about "literally millions of employment decisions at once." But there is no single common contention (of either law or fact) whose resolution will resolve all of these claims. Therefore, the case does not meet the commonality prerequisite of Rule 23(a), and cannot proceed as a class action of any sort. [*Wal-Mart Stores, Inc. v. Duke*]

2. **"Fair and adequate" representation of class:** Recall that one of the four requirements imposed by Rule 23(a) is ***adequacy of representation"*** — the court must be satisfied that the representatives "will ***fairly and adequately protect the interests*** of the class." Rule 23(a)(4).

   a. **Class members versus lawyers for class:** Courts differ as to *which* participants should be most closely scrutinized for adequacy of representation: some look mostly at the adequacy of the ***named class members***, and others at the adequacy of the ***lawyers*** representing the class.

   b. **Avoidance of conflicts:** The main function of the adequacy requirement is to ensure that there are no major ***conflicts*** between the interests of the representatives and the interests of the unnamed class members.

      i. **Reps have separate lawsuits:** A key reason why the trial court might find an inadequacy of representation is that some of the named representatives have ***separate individual pending or potential lawsuits*** against the defendant, and the court believes that the representatives' ***real reason*** for pursuing the class action is to ***gain leverage for their own case.***

   c. **Separate sub-classes:** Adequate-representation problems in which different groups of plaintiffs have different incentives can sometimes be overcome if the suit designates ***multiple "sub-classes" of plaintiffs,*** and has ***separate named representatives and lawyers*** for each sub-class.

E. **Three categories:** As noted, there are three categories of class actions, all of which must meet the four prerequisites listed above. They are covered in Rules 23(b)(1), 23(b)(2) and 23(b)(3).

1. **23(b)(1) actions:** The first of the three categories, ***23(b)(1)***, applies to situations similar to the circumstances requiring the ***joinder of necessary parties*** under Rule 19.

   a. **Test:** A class action is allowed under 23(b)(1) if individual actions by or against members of the class would create a ***risk*** of either: (a) ***inconsistent decisions*** forcing an opponent of the class to observe ***incompatible standards of conduct*** (Rule 23(b)(1)(A)); or (b) the ***impairment of the interests*** of the members of the class who are not actually parties to the individual actions (23(b)(1)(B)).

   Example: Taxpayers residing in City XYZ are unhappy with a municipal bond issue by XYZ. Some taxpayers want the issue declared invalid; others want merely to have the terms of the issue changed. If each taxpayer brought his own action, as the result of one suit XYZ might have to refrain from floating the issue altogether, but as the result of the other suit might just be forced to limit the size of the issue. XYZ thus faces a risk of incompatible standards of conduct. Therefore, a Rule 23(b)(1) action would be suitable on these facts.

b. **No opting out:** Members of the 23(b)(1) class ***may not "opt out" of the class***. Any absentee will therefore ***necessarily be bound*** by the decision in the suit.

c. **Mass tort claims:** Courts are increasingly allowing use of the 23(b)(1) class action in ***mass tort cases***, where there are so many claims that D may be ***insolvent*** before later claimants can collect.

Example: Tens of thousands of women may have been injured by breast implants manufactured by D. If each brings an individual suit, D's financial resources may be exhausted, leaving nothing for those who bring suit later. A federal court might therefore hold that a 23(b)(1) action is suitable for determining, once and for all, whether D sold a defective device and whether it typically caused a certain type of medical injury. Each P would then have a separate claim on causation and damages only.

2. **23(b)(2) actions:** The second category, 23(b)(2), allows use of a class action if "the party opposing the class has acted or refused to act on ***grounds that apply generally to the class***, so that final injunctive relief or corresponding declaratory relief is appropriate respecting the class as a whole." In other words, if the suit is for an ***injunction*** or declaration that would affect all class members, (b)(2) is probably the right category.

a. **Civil rights case:** The main use of 23(b)(2) is for ***civil rights cases***, where the class says that it has been discriminated against, and seeks an ***injunction*** prohibiting further discrimination.

Example: A class action is brought on behalf of all black employees of XYZ Corp., alleging that executives of XYZ have as a matter of company-wide policy paid them less money and given them fewer promotions than white employees. The suit seeks an injunction against further discrimination, as well as money damages. This would likely be an appropriate suit for a 23(b)(2) class action.

b. **Equitable relief:** Notice that 23(b)(2) requires, in essence, that the wrong of which the defendant is accused have been a ***class-wide*** wrong, and that "final ***injunctive*** relief or corresponding ***declaratory*** relief" must be "appropriate respecting the ***class as a whole***." So it's clear that a b(2) claim must not only allege a class-wide wrong, but seek a ***class-wide equitable remedy*** (an injunction and/or declaratory judgment that would run in favor of the entire class).

c. **Seeking of back pay:** Suppose an employment discrimination suit seeks not only an injunction against further discrimination against plaintiff class members, but also an award of ***back pay*** to restore each class member to the financial position he or she would have been in had there been no discrimination. (Such an award of back pay is authorized by Title VII, the federal anti-employment-discrimination statute.) Notice that since the appropriate amount of back pay depends on when (or even whether) the discriminatory action occurred (longer-ago discrimination requires more back pay to make P whole now), the back-pay aspect will require a ***separate, individualized, determination*** for each class member. Does this need for individualized back-pay findings automatically make the action ***unsuitable*** for (b)(2) certification?

i. ***Wal-Mart* rejects (b)(2) suits for back-pay:** The Supreme Court, in *Wal-Mart Stores, Inc. v. Duke* (see p. 132), has answered ***"yes."*** So if the amount of ***back pay*** would ***vary*** from member to member, the mere ***request*** for it ***rules out (b)(2) certification***, even if the back-pay being sought is viewed as ***"subordinate"*** to the class members' main goal of getting an injunction against further discrimination.

(1) **Significance:** So *Wal-Mart* means that in ***mass employment-discrimination cases***, plaintiffs lawyers will have to choose between bringing a (b)(2) action that seeks only injunctive and declaratory relief (in which case any court-awarded ***attorneys fees*** are likely to be ***small***, and the plaintiffs' lawyers' bargaining position in post-certification settlement negotiations likely to be weak), and ***not bringing a federal class action at all*** (since bringing a (b)(3) action, discussed below, requires that the (b)(3) format be a "superior" method, and in mass-employment-discrimination suits the (b)(3) format will usually *not* be superior).

d. **No opt-out:** Members of a 23(b)(2) class may not ***"opt out"*** of the class. See Rule 23(c)(3).

3. **23(b)(3) actions:** The final type of class action is given in Rule ***23(b)(3)***. This is the ***most common*** type of class action.

a. **Two requirements:** The court must make ***two findings*** for a (b)(3) class action:

i. **Common questions:** The court must find that the "questions of law or fact ***common*** to class members ***predominate*** over any questions affecting only individual members..."; and

ii. **Superior method:** The court must also find that "a class action is ***superior to other available methods***" for deciding the controversy. In deciding "superiority," the court will consider four factors listed in 23(b)(3), including:

[1] the interest of class members in ***individually controlling*** their separate actions;

[2] the presence of any suits that have ***already been commenced*** involving class members;

[3] the desirability of ***concentrating the litigation*** of the claims in a ***particular forum***; and

[4] any difficulties likely to be encountered in the ***management*** of a class action.

b. **Securities cases:** (b)(3) class actions are especially common in ***securities fraud*** cases, and in ***antitrust*** cases.

c. **Mass torts:** (b)(3) actions are sometimes brought in ***mass tort*** cases (e.g., airline crashes) and mass ***product liability*** cases (e.g., mass pharmaceutical cases). But many courts still frown on (b)(3) class action status for such suits, because individual elements typically predominate. See *supra*, p. 133.

F. **Requirement of notice:** Absent class members (i.e., those other than the representatives) must almost always be given ***notice*** of the fact that the suit is pending.

1. **When required:** The Federal Rules explicitly require notice only in ***(b)(3)*** actions. But courts generally hold that notice is required in (b)(1) and (b)(2) actions as well.

a. **Individual notice:** ***Individual*** notice, almost always ***by mail***, must be given to all those class members whose names and addresses can be obtained with ***reasonable effort***. This is true even if there are millions of class members, each with only small amounts at stake. [*Eisen v. Carlisle & Jacquelin*]

b. **Publication notice:** For those class members whose names and addresses cannot be obtained with reasonable effort, ***publication*** notice will usually be sufficient.

2. **Contents:** The most important things notice does is to tell the claimant that he may ***opt out*** of the class if he wishes (in a (b)(3), but not (b)(1) or (b)(2), action); and that the judgment will affect him, favorably or unfavorably, unless he opts out.

3. **Cost:** The cost of both ***identifying*** and ***notifying*** each class member must normally be borne by the ***representative plaintiffs***. If the plaintiff side is unwilling to bear this cost, the case must be ***dismissed***. [*Eisen v. Carlisle*; *Oppenheimer Fund v. Sanders*]

G. **Binding effect:** Judgment in a class action is ***binding***, whether it is ***for or against the class***, on all those whom the court finds to be members of the class.

1. **Exclusion:** In the case of a (b)(3) action, a person may ***opt out***, i.e., exclude himself, from the action, by notifying the court to that effect prior to a date specified in the notice of the action sent to him. A person who opts out of the action will not be bound by an adverse judgment, but conversely may not assert collateral estoppel to take advantage of a judgment favorable to the class. (Absent class members in (b)(1) and (b)(2) actions do ***not*** have the right to opt out and thereafter bring their own suit.)

H. **Subject-matter jurisdiction issues:** In the federal courts, class actions can occasionally raise questions of ***subject-matter jurisdiction***.

1. **Federal question cases:** Where the plaintiffs' claims are based on a ***federal question***, there are no significant subject-matter jurisdiction issues. Diversity of citizenship, of course, does not matter. And there is no amount in controversy requirement. So nationwide class actions based upon federal causes of action are quite easy to bring, even where each claim is for a small amount.

2. **Diversity cases:** On the other hand, a federal class action in which all claims are based ***solely on diversity*** *does* face subject-matter jurisdiction problems, principally related to amount in controversy.

   a. **Diversity:** In determining whether the required ***"complete diversity"*** exists, there will rarely be a problem. That's because of the Supreme Court has long held that ***only the citizenship of the class representatives***, not the citizenship of the unnamed class members, counts. So as long as none of the named representatives is a citizen of the same state as any defendant, there is no diversity problem. And, since the lawyer for the plaintiff class gets to decide who the named representatives will be, the lawyer can easily assure that no representative is a citizen of the same state as any defendant.

   b. **Amount in controversy:** By contrast, diversity class actions raise issues regarding the ***amount in controversy*** requirement.

      i. **At least one named member meets amount:** If ***at least one named class member satisfies*** the jurisdictional amount, other class members ***can*** be part of the action even though their claim is for ***less than this amount.*** This result is due to the doctrine of ***"supplemental jurisdiction."*** [*Exxon Mobil Corp. v. Allapattah Services, Inc.*]

      Example: 10,000 Exxon dealers bring a diversity-only class action against Exxon, claiming that Exxon has overcharged them for fuel. Some named members of the class have a claim for the jurisdictional amount ($75,000), but many other class members' claims are for less than the $75,000 amount. *Held*, the dealers whose claims do not meet this amount may remain part of the class — as long as at least one named class member meets the jurisdictional amount, supplemental jurisdiction applies to the claims of the other class members, no matter how small those claims. [*Exxon Mobil Corp. v. Allapattah Services, Inc.*]

      ii. **Named members can't aggregate:** On the other hand, ***at least one named class member must independently meet the jurisdictional amount.*** So unless the plaintiff's lawyer can find at least one named claimant with $75,000 at stake, the diversity class action cannot go forward. In other words, several named class members, each having a claim of less than $75,000, ***cannot "aggregate" their claims*** to get over the $75,000 minimum. (There's an exception if the action involves at least $5 million in total, discussed immediately below.)

      iii. **$5 million at stake:** Under the ***Class Action Fairness Act of 2005*** ("CAFA"), a class action can go forward if: (a) there is minimal diversity (at least one plaintiff is diverse with at least one defendant); and (b) there is ***at least $5 million in controversy in the aggregate,*** even if ***no class member's claim is for more than $75,000.***

I. **Certification and denial of class status:** Soon after an action purporting to be a class action is brought, the court must decide whether to ***"certify"*** the action. By certifying, the court agrees that the class action requirements have been met, and allows the suit to go forward as a class action. If the court refuses to certify the action:

1. **Continued by representative:** The suit may still be continued by the "representatives," but with no *res judicata* effect for or against the absent would-be class members. Usually, the representatives will not want to proceed on this non-class action basis.

2. **Sub-class:** Alternatively, the suit may be continued by a ***sub-class*** of the original class. If so, *res judicata* extends to the members of the sub-class, but not to the other members of the original class.

3. **No appeal:** The denial of class action status may ***not*** be immediately appealed, because it is not deemed to be a ***"final order."***

J. **Waiver of the right to bring class action:** An increasingly important issue is whether a party to a contract may agree in advance to ***waive*** her right to bring a class action if litigation should ensue. The issue typically arises where the contract contains a boilerplate clause stating that all disputes will be subject to one-plaintiff-at-a-time ***arbitration***.

   1. **Waivers are valid:** The general principle is that such waivers are ***valid***, and will be ***enforced***. In fact, a federal statute — the ***Federal Arbitration Act (FAA)*** —essentially ***compels*** both state and federal courts to ***enforce as drafted any arbitration*** clause.

      a. **Unconscionability doesn't avoid the waiver:** The FAA will usually require judicial enforcement of an agreement to arbitrate even if the court believes that the contract's arbitration clause would be otherwise be ***unenforceable*** due to the state-law doctrine of ***unconscionability***. [*AT&T Mobility LLC v. Concepcion*]

      b. **Same rule for employment contracts:** Similarly, the FAA is now interpreted to require state and federal courts to enforce any clause in an ***employment agreement*** in which the employee waives the right to assert either a class-action suit or a class-action arbitration in the event a dispute about the employment arises. [*Epic Systems Corp. v. Lewis*]

K. **Settlements:** Any proposed ***settlement*** of the class action must be ***approved by the court***. FRCP 23(e). The court will approve the settlement only if it is convinced that the interests of the absent class members have been adequately protected (e.g., that settlement is not being urged by greedy contingent-fee lawyers who will pocket most of the settlement money).

   1. **Notice requirement:** If the class has already been certified, ***notice*** of any proposed settlement must be given to ***each class member***.

   2. **Settlement-only class actions:** Sometimes, a class is certified ***"for settlement purposes only."*** That is, certification approving the settlement occurs before the court has ever concluded that the case meets the requirements for a valid class action.

      a. **Purpose:** A settlement-only class action is a way of giving the parties — especially the defendants — a method of ***disposing of all claims on a par-***

ticular subject, even claims that have ***not yet ripened,*** held by persons who may not yet even have been injured.

b. **Notice:** Prior to certifying a class action "for settlement only," the court must (as in the case where an already-certified class action is proposed to be settled) direct to class members ***"the best notice that is practicable*** under the circumstances, including individual notice to all members who can be identified through reasonable effort." Rule 23(c)(2)(B).

c. **Must meet regular rules:** Settlement-only classes must ***meet the same basic requirements*** (e.g., numerosity) as class actions that will be tried. Thus the trial court cannot certify the class (a prerequisite to approving the settlement) unless the requirements are all satisfied.

L. **Attorneys' fees:** The court may award ***reasonable attorneys fees*** to the lawyers for the class. These fees are generally in rough proportion to the size of the recovery on behalf of the class.

1. **Federal statute requires:** In the usual case of a class action brought under a ***federal statute***, attorneys fees may be awarded ***only if a federal statute so provides***. [*Alyeska Pipeline Service Co. v. Wilderness Society*.] Congress has authorized attorneys fees for many important federal statutes that are frequently the subject of class action suits (e.g., civil rights and securities law).

M. **Mass tort cases:** Class actions have begun to be used increasingly in ***"mass tort"*** cases.

1. **Definition of "mass tort":** Mass torts fall into two categories. In a ***"mass accident,"*** a large number of persons are injured as a result of a single accident. (*Examples:* an airplane crash, the collapse of a building, or the explosion of a factory accompanied by the release of toxic substances.) In a ***"mass product liability"*** case, a ***defective product*** is sold to thousands of buyers, who are thereby injured.

2. **Single-accident cases:** In mass-tort cases involving a ***single "mass accident,"*** or a single "course of conduct" by one defendant, many courts allow class certification. Cases involving a single explosion, or a single toxic dumping by one defendant on one occasion, are examples.

3. **Product liability cases:** In mass-tort cases involving ***product liability***, by contrast, most federal courts have held that the federal class action is ***not suitable***. Usually courts don't allow it to be used even for the limited purpose of deciding core "all or nothing" issues like D's negligence, or the product's defectiveness.

a. **Class action difficult to maintain.** All in all, it's very hard to get (and keep on appeal) federal class action status for a mass-tort suit, where the suit relates not to a single "accident" but to people who are exposed to a faulty product at different times and different circumstances.

i. **State-by-state law variations:** A big factor cutting against class action status in a mass-tort case tends to be the problem that ***multiple states' laws*** must be applied. In the typical diversity case in which there are class members from every or nearly every state, the fact that the federal court would somehow have to come to grips with the ***differing laws of 50 states*** weighs heavily ***against*** class status.

V. INTERVENTION

A. Intervention generally: By the doctrine of ***"intervention,"*** certain persons who are not initially part of a lawsuit may enter the suit ***on their own initiative***. The person who intervenes is called an "intervenor."

1. **Two forms:** In federal suits, FRCP 24 creates two forms of intervention:
   a. ***"Intervention of right"*** (Rule 24(a)); and
   b. ***"Permissive intervention"*** (Rule 24(b)).
2. **Distinction:** Where the intervention is "of right," ***no leave of court*** is required for the party's entry into the case. Where the facts are such that only "permissive" intervention is possible, it is up to the court's ***discretion*** whether to allow intervention.

B. Intervention of right:

1. **Three tests:** A stranger to an existing action may intervene ***"of right,"*** under Rule 24(a), if she meets ***all*** of the three following criteria:
   a. **Interest in subject-matter:** She must "claim[] an interest relating to the ***property or transaction*** that is the ***subject*** of the action";
   b. **Impaired interest:** She must be "so situated that disposing of the action may as a ***practical matter impair or impede [her] ability to protect [that] interest***"; and
   c. **Inadequate representation:** She must show that this interest is ***not "adequately represented" by existing parties***.

   Note: Even if the outsider cannot meet one or more of these criteria, she may nonetheless automatically intervene under Rule 24(a) if a federal ***statute*** gives her such a right. (*Example:* The U.S. may intervene in any action involving the constitutionality of an act of Congress.)

   Example: P (the U.S. government) sues D, a local Board of Education, charging that D has drawn school boundaries on racially-discriminatory lines. X, the parent of a black public school student attending D's schools, wants to intervene. Probably X's intervention will be of right, since X has an interest in the subject-matter, and his ability to bring his own action in the future will be compromised if the U.S. loses the case. X will have to show that the U.S. may not adequately represent X's interest, which he can do by showing that the U.S. may be pursuing other objectives, such as settling a lot of suits quickly.
2. **Jurisdiction:** ***Independent subject-matter*** jurisdictional grounds are ***required*** for intervention of right in a diversity case. In other words, such intervention does not fall within the court's ***supplemental*** jurisdiction.

   Example: P, from California, sues D, from New York, in a diversity suit. X, from New York, would like to intervene. Even if the court concludes that the requirements of intervention of right are met by X, X cannot intervene because there is no supplemental jurisdiction for intervention of right; after X's intervention there would have to be complete diversity, and this would not be the case since X and D are both citizens of New York.

C. Permissive intervention: For a person to seek ***"permissive intervention,"*** she merely has to have a "claim or defense" that involves a ***"common question of law or fact" with the pending action.***

1. **Discretion:** Where the outsider seeks permissive intervention, it is up to the trial court's ***discretion*** whether to allow the intervention. The trial court's decision — whichever way it goes — is rarely reversed on appeal.

2. **Jurisdiction:** Like any intervenor of right, a permissive intervenor in a diversity case must independently meet federal subject-matter jurisdictional requirements. (*Example:* There must be diversity between the intervenor and all defendants.)

VI. INTERPLEADER

A. Definition: Interpleader allows a party who owes something to one of two or more other persons, but is not sure whom, to force the other parties to argue out their claims among themselves. The technique is designed to allow the "stakeholder" to avoid being made to pay the same claim twice.

Example: X and Y both claim a bank account at Bank. Y demands the money from Bank. If Bank had to litigate against Y, and then possibly defend a second suit brought by X, Bank might have to pay the amount of the account twice. By using the interpleader doctrine, Bank can force X and Y to litigate between themselves as to the ownership of the account, with Bank paying only the winner.

1. **Federal practice:** In federal practice, ***two*** kinds of interpleader are allowed:

   a. ***"Statutory interpleader"*** under 28 U.S.C. §1335; and

   b. ***"Rule interpleader"*** under FRCP 22.

   Note: See Table 8-3, "Comparison: Statutory and Rule Interpleader."

B. Federal statutory interpleader: 28 U.S.C. §1335 allows a person holding property which ***is*** or ***may be*** claimed by two or more "adverse claimants" to interplead those claimants.

1. **Jurisdictional benefits:** The main benefits to the stakeholder from using statutory interpleader instead of Rule interpleader relate to ***jurisdiction*** and ***service***:

   a. **Nationwide service:** ***Nationwide service of process*** is allowed in statutory interpleader actions. See 28 U.S.C. §2361. Thus the court where the stakeholder files a statutory interpleader suit may serve its process on any claimant, ***no matter where in the U.S. that claimant resides or is found.***

b. **Diversity:** Diversity is satisfied as long as ***any two claimants are citizens of different states.***

Example: Two New York residents and a Californian all claim the proceeds of a particular insurance policy. Since either of the New Yorkers and the Californian form a diverse pair, the diversity requirement for statutory interpleader is satisfied. The citizenship of the insurance company is irrelevant.

c. **Amount in controversy:** The property which is the subject of the suit must merely exceed ***$500*** in value, in contrast to the usual $75,000.

2. **How commenced:** A statutory interpleader suit is commenced by the ***stakeholder***. The stakeholder must, to begin the suit, ***deposit into court*** the amount of the property in question, or post a ***bond*** for that amount.

   a. **Right to deny debt:** Even though the stakeholder must deposit the amount of the property with the court, he is not estopped from claiming at trial that he does ***not owe the money to any claimant at all.***

3. **Restraint on other suits:** Once the statutory interpleader suit is begun, the court may ***restrain all claimants*** from starting or continuing any other action, in any state or federal suit, which would affect the property. (*Example:* On the facts of the above example, the court could prevent the two New Yorkers and the Californian from starting any state action to collect on the policy.)

C. **Rule interpleader:** FRCP 22 provides an interpleader remedy for any person who "is or may be exposed to double or multiple liability." This is so-called ***"Rule interpleader."*** The stakeholder may invoke interpleader by coming into court on his own initiative (i.e., as plaintiff), or by counterclaiming or cross-claiming as ***defendant*** in an action already commenced against him by one claimant.

1. **Jurisdiction:** The main difference between statutory interpleader and Rule interpleader is that ***Rule 22 interpleader has no effect on ordinary jurisdictional and venue requirements.***

   a. **Complete diversity:** Thus ***diversity*** must be ***complete*** between the stakeholder on one hand and all claimants on the other (assuming there is no federal question). (*Example:* Two New Yorkers and a Californian all claim a particular insurance policy, which is issued by a California-based insurer. Rule 22 interpleader cannot be used, because it is not the case that all claimants are of different citizenship than the insurer.)

   b. **Service:** Service of process must be carried out as in any other diversity action — that is, within the state where the district court sits, or pursuant to the long-arm of the state. There is ***no "nationwide service of process"*** as in statutory interpleader.

   c. **Amount in controversy:** The ***$75,000*** amount in controversy requirement must be met.

2. **No deposit:** The stakeholder is ***not required*** to ***deposit*** the property or money into the court (as she is in statutory interpleader).

3. **Denial of liability:** The stakeholder may "aver that the plaintiff is not liable in whole or in part to any or all of the claimants." FRCP 22(1). In other words, the stakeholder may ***deny liability***.

VII. THIRD-PARTY PRACTICE (IMPLEADER)

A. **Impleader right generally:** A defendant who believes that a third person is ***liable to him*** "for all or part of the claim against [the defendant]" may ***implead*** such a person as a ***"third party defendant."*** FRCP 14(a).

> **Example:** Victim is injured when a van driven by Employee and owned by Employer runs her over. Victim brings a diversity action against Employer, on a *respondeat superior* theory. Employer believes that if Employer is required to pay a judgment to Victim, Employee, under common law indemnity rules, will be required to reimburse Employer.
>
> Instead of waiting until the end of the Victim-Employer suit, Employer may instead "implead" Employee. That is, Employer (the third-party plaintiff or TPP) brings Employee into the action as a "third party defendant" (TPD), so that in a single action, the court may conclude that Employer owes Victim, and that Employee owes indemnity to Employer.

B. **Claim must be derivative:** For a third-party claim to be valid, the TPP may not claim that the TPD is the ***only*** one liable to the plaintiff, and that he himself is not liable at all.

> **Examples:** Impleader works for claims for ***indemnity***, ***subrogation***, ***contribution*** and ***breach of warranty***, since as to each of these, the TPD is liable only if the TPP is liable.

1. **Alternative pleading:** However, the TPP is not precluded from claiming in an ***alternative*** pleading that neither she nor the TPD is liable.
2. **Partial claim:** Also, the TPP may allege that only a ***portion*** of the recovery is due from the TPD. (*Example:* If TPP claims that TPD is liable for "contribution" rather than "indemnity," TPP will recover from TPD at most only part of any judgment that TPP owes to P.)

C. **Leave of court:** Leave of court is ***not*** necessary for impleader, as long as the TPP serves a summons and complaint on a TPD within ***14 days*** after the time the TPP served his answer to P's claim. FRCP 14(a)(1). After this 14-day period, however, the court's permission to implead is necessary.

D. **Impleader by plaintiff:** Just as the defendant may implead a TPD, so a ***plaintiff*** against whom a ***counterclaim*** is filed may implead a third person who is liable to him for any judgment on the counterclaim. FRCP 14(b).

E. **Jurisdictional requirements relaxed:** Both personal and subject-matter ***jurisdictional*** requirements are ***relaxed*** with respect to the third-party claim:

1. **100-mile bulge:** Service of the third-party complaint may be made anywhere within the ***100-mile bulge*** surrounding the courthouse, even if the

place of service is outside the state and is beyond the scope of the local long-arm. FRCP 4(k)(1)(B).

Example: In the above Victim/Employer/Employee example on p. 142 *supra*, if the suit is pending in the Southern District of New York (Manhattan), Employee could be served in Newark, New Jersey, even if the New York State long-arm would not reach him.

2. **Supplemental jurisdiction:** A third-party claim generally falls within the court's ***supplemental jurisdiction***. Thus the TPD's citizenship is unimportant, and no amount-in-controversy requirement must be satisfied.

   Example: In the previous example, suppose that Victim (original plaintiff) is a citizen of Kansas, and that Employer (TPP) and Employee (TPD) are both citizens of Missouri. Supplemental jurisdiction applies to the third-party indemnification claim by Employer against Employee. Therefore, the fact that there is no diversity between Employer and Employee doesn't matter — the third-party claim can be heard as part of the Victim-Employer "original" suit.

3. **Venue:** If ***venue*** is proper between the original parties, it remains valid regardless of the residence of the TPD.

F. Additional claims involving the TPD:

1. **Claim by TPD:** Once a TPD has been impleaded, she may make ***claims of her own***, including: (1) counterclaims against the TPP (either permissive or compulsory); (2) cross-claims against any other TPDs; (3) any claim against the original plaintiff, but only if it arises out of the same transaction or occurrence that is the subject of the plaintiff's claim against the TPP; (4) any counterclaim against the original plaintiff, if the original plaintiff has made a claim against the TPD; and (5) impleader claims against persons not previously part of the suit, if these persons may be liable to the TPD for all or part of the TPP's claim against the TPD.

   a. **Supplemental jurisdiction:** All of the above kinds of claims, except permissive counterclaims, fall within the court's ***supplemental jurisdiction***, and thus need no independent federal subject-matter jurisdictional grounds.

   b. **Defenses:** A TPD may also raise against the original plaintiff the same ***defenses*** that the original defendant could have raised.

2. **Claims by original plaintiff:** The original plaintiff may assert any claims against the TPD arising out of the transaction or occurrence that is the subject-matter of that plaintiff's claim against the TPP.

   a. **Jurisdiction:** But a claim by a plaintiff against the TPD must ***independently satisfy jurisdictional requirements*** — supplemental jurisdiction does not apply in this situation.

   Example: In a diversity case, the original plaintiff's claim against the TPD must be supported by diversity between the plaintiff and the TPD, and that claim must satisfy the $75,000 amount in controversy.

G. Dismissal of main claim: If the main claim is ***dismissed*** before or during trial, the court has ***discretion*** whether to hear the third-party claims relating to it (assuming that these are within the court's supplemental jurisdiction, as they will be in the case of an ordinary impleader claim).

VIII. CROSS-CLAIMS

A. Definition: A claim by a party against a ***co-party*** is called a ***"cross-claim."*** A cross-claim is made only against a party who is on the ***same side*** of an already-existing claim (e.g., a claim by one co-defendant against another, or by one co-plaintiff against another).

B. Requirements: A cross-claim must meet two main requirements:

1. **Transaction requirements:** It must have arisen out of the ***"transaction or occurrence"*** that is the subject of the original action or the subject of a counterclaim. FRCP 13(g). (A cross-claim is thus comparable to a compulsory counterclaim, in terms of how closely related it must be to the original claim.)

2. **Actual relief:** The cross-claim must ask for ***actual relief*** from the co-party against whom it is directed. (*Example:* D1 claims that he is blameless, and that D2 is the one who should be liable for all of P's claims. This is not a cross-claim, since D1 is not asking for actual relief from D2 — instead, D1 is merely asserting a defense.)

C. Not compulsory: A cross-claim, no matter how closely related it is to the subject of the existing action, is ***never compulsory***.

D. Jurisdiction: Cross-claims are within the ***supplemental jurisdiction*** of the court, and thus need no independent jurisdictional grounds.

CHAPTER 9

FORMER ADJUDICATION

I. GENERAL PRINCIPLES

A. Former adjudication generally: There is a set of rules that prevents re-litigation of claims and issues; the set is sometimes collectively called the doctrine of ***"res judicata"*** (Latin for "things which have been decided").

1. **Two categories:** There are two main categories of rules governing re-litigation:

   a. **Merger and bar:** One set of rules prevents a ***claim*** (or "cause of action") from being re-litigated. These rules are collectively called the rules of ***claim preclusion***. They break down into two sub-rules:

      i. **Merger:** Under the rule of ***"merger,"*** if P ***wins*** the first action, his claim is "merged" into his judgment. He cannot later sue the same D on the same cause of action for higher damages.

ii. **Bar:** Under the doctrine of ***"bar,"*** if P ***loses*** his first action, his claim is extinguished, and he is barred from suing again on that cause of action.

b. **Collateral estoppel:** The second main set of rules prevents re-litigation of a particular ***issue of fact or law***. When a particular issue of fact or law has been determined in one proceeding, then in a subsequent proceeding between the same parties, ***even on a different cause of action***, each party is ***"collaterally estopped"*** from claiming that that issue should have been decided differently than it was in the first action. This is known as the doctrine of "collateral estoppel" or ***"issue preclusion."***

i. **Use by stranger:** Today, even one who is not a party to the first action (a "***stranger*** to the first action") may in some circumstances assert in the second suit that her adversary, who was a party to the first action, is collaterally estopped from re-litigating an issue of fact or law decided in that first action.

B. **Applicable only to new actions:** The rules discussed in this "Former Adjudication" chapter apply only to ***new actions*** subsequent to the action in which the original judgment was rendered — they do not apply to ***further proceedings*** in the same action in which the original judgment was rendered. (*Examples:* These rules do not apply to a party seeking a ***new trial***, or to one seeking to have a judgment reversed on ***appeal***.)

C. **Only parties bound:** The rules of claim preclusion and collateral estoppel generally apply only to the ***parties*** to the first action, ***not to "strangers"*** to that action.

1. **Exceptions:** But there are a few situations in which someone who was not a party to the first action is ***so closely linked*** to someone who was, that the stranger ***will be bound*** by the first result, for claim preclusion and collateral estoppel purposes, as if she had been a party. For instance, a ***successor in interest*** to property (e.g., the purchaser of real estate which has been the subject of an earlier quiet-title action), would be bound by the result in the earlier action. For more about these exceptions see p. 148 (claim preclusion) and p. 150 (collateral estoppel).

II. CLAIM PRECLUSION (MERGER AND BAR)

A. **Definition:** If a judgment is rendered for the plaintiff, his claim is "merged" into the judgment — the claim is extinguished and a new claim to enforce the judgment is created. If a judgment is for the defendant on the merits, the claim is extinguished and nothing new is created; plaintiff is "barred" from raising the claim again.

> **Example 1:** P sues D for $1,000 damages resulting from an automobile accident. The verdict and judgment grant P only $500. His claim, or cause of action, is "merged," meaning that P cannot start a new suit for the other $500.

Example 2: Same as Example 1, but D is found not to be liable at all. P is now "barred" from making the same claim in a second suit against D.

B. No claim-splitting: The basic concept of claim preclusion is that a judgment is conclusive with respect to the ***entire "claim"*** which it adjudicates. Consequently, P ***may not split her claim*** — if she sues upon ***any portion*** of the claim, the other aspects of that claim are merged in her judgment if she wins, and barred if she loses.

Example: P believes that D has breached a contract with him, and that P has lost $100,000 as a result. If P sues for $25,000 and loses, P may not bring a second suit for the other $75,000. The same is true if P wins the $25,000 — the rule is "one suit per claim."

1. **Installment contracts:** Where the claim relates to payments due under a ***lease*** or ***installment contract***, generally P must sue at the same time for ***all payments*** due at the time the suit is filed. (*Example:* If Tenant is six months behind in the rent at the time Landlord brings suit, Landlord must sue for the entire six months at once — any months missed that are not sued for when the suit is brought are waived.)

2. **Personal and property damage from accident:** Today, most states hold that claims for ***personal injuries*** arising from an auto accident are part of the ***same cause of action*** as a claim for ***property damage*** sustained in the same accident. Thus generally, P must bring a single suit for property damage and personal injuries from a given accident.

3. **Multi-theory actions:** The rule against splitting a claim also applies where P has several claims, all arising from the same set of facts, but involving ***different theories*** or remedies. The modern rule is that there will be merger or bar of all of P's rights against D with respect to all or any part of the ***transaction***, or series of connected transactions, out of which the action arose.

   Example: P works for D, and is then fired. P sues D for breach of an alleged oral contract promising two years of employment. P loses. P then sues D, alleging the same facts, and asserting the right to recover in *quantum meruit* for the reasonable value of services he performed for D. A modern court would probably hold that the two suits related to a single transaction or series of transactions, and that the first judgment against P therefore barred him from bringing the second suit.

   a. **Equitable/legal distinction:** A demand for ***legal*** relief (generally, money damages) and a demand for ***equitable*** relief (e.g., an injunction) will both be deemed to be part of the same claim if they relate to the same facts — therefore, demands for both types of relief will have to be made in the same action. (*Example:* If P believes that D is violating P's copyrights, P cannot bring a suit for an injunction, followed by a separate suit for money damages.)

4. **Exceptions based on jurisdictional requirements:** There is one important ***exception*** to the rule against splitting a cause of action — if the court trying the first action would not have had ***subject-matter jurisdiction*** for a claim now asserted in the second action, there will be no bar or merger.

Example: P sues D in state court under state antitrust law, and loses on the merits. P then sues D in federal court alleging the same facts, and charging a violation of federal antitrust laws. Because the federal courts have exclusive jurisdiction of antitrust claims, the state court could not have heard the federal claim. Therefore, the second — federal court — action will not be barred.

5. **State law followed in diversity cases:** In diversity cases, the federal courts follow ***state law*** with respect to the application of the rules of claim preclusion (as well as collateral estoppel). In other words, if (and only if) the law of the state where the district court sits would have granted claim preclusion or collateral estoppel effect to an earlier state court judgment, the federal court will do the same.

C. **Adjudication on merits:** Not every loss by the plaintiff in the first action will act as a "bar" to subsequent suits on the same claim. Plaintiff will be barred only if the original adjudication in favor of the defendant was ***"on the merits."***

1. **Non-prejudicial grounds:** In other words, some of the ways that a plaintiff may "lose" the first suit are deemed to be "without prejudice" to future suits. For instance, if the first suit is brought in federal court, plaintiff will ***not*** be barred from bringing a new action if the first action is dismissed because of: (1) lack of jurisdiction; (2) improper venue; or (3) failure to join an indispensable party. See FRCP 41(b). Any other type of dismissal (e.g., dismissal for failure to state a claim under 12(b)(6)) ***does*** bar a future claim by P, unless the court granting the dismissal specifies otherwise in its order. FRCP 41(b), last sentence.

D. **Counterclaims:** A defendant who pleads a ***counterclaim*** is, in effect, a plaintiff with respect to that claim. He is bound by the outcome, just as a plaintiff is bound by the outcome of his original claim.

1. **No splitting:** Thus D may not split his counterclaim into two parts. (*Example:* P sues D for damages from an auto accident. D counterclaims for his property damage from that same accident, but not for personal injuries. Whether D wins or loses with the counterclaim, he may not bring a second suit against P for personal injury arising from that same accident.)

2. **Compulsory counterclaim:** Observe that state and federal rules making certain counterclaims "compulsory" serve a similar function to the merger or bar doctrine. (*Example:* P sues D for damages arising out of an auto accident. The rules of merger and bar do not by themselves force D to assert either his claim for property damage, or for personal injury, arising out of that same accident. But in the federal court and in most state courts, any counterclaim by D for either of these things would be "compulsory," so that D would not be able to use that claim in a subsequent suit against P.)

E. **Change of law:** Once a final judgment has been rendered (and any appeals resolved), ***not even a change in the applicable law*** will prevent claim preclusion from operating. The fact that the losing party would, because of such an overruling of legal precedent, win the lawsuit if she were allowed to start it again, is irrelevant.

F. Persons not party to first action: Normally, ***only parties*** to the initial judgment will be subject to merger or bar.

III. COLLATERAL ESTOPPEL

A. Definition: Regardless of which of the parties to an action wins, the judgment decides for all time any ***issue actually litigated*** in the suit. A party who seeks to re-litigate one of the issues disposed of in the first trial is said to be ***"collaterally estopped"*** from doing so.

> **Example:** Cars driven by A and B collide. A sues B for property damage. Assume that the jurisdiction has no rules making any counterclaim a compulsory counterclaim. B declines to assert any counterclaim in the suit brought by A. A recovers $1,000 of damages. The jurisdiction follows common-law contributory negligence, by which even a small amount of contributory negligence by A would have barred him from recovery. In a subsequent suit, B sues A for personal injuries arising out of the same accident.
>
> The court will hold that B is "collaterally estopped" from re-litigating the issue of whether A was negligent — the first judgment in A's favor amounted to a specific finding that A was not negligent, because contributory negligence would have barred recovery if he had been. Therefore, B cannot recover from A on a negligence theory. [*Little v. Blue Goose*]

1. **Distinguished from merger and bar:** There are two major differences between collateral estoppel and claim preclusion (merger and bar):

   a. **Issue vs. claim:** Whereas claim preclusion applies only where the "cause of action" or ***"claim"*** in the second action is the ***same*** as the one in the first action, collateral estoppel applies as long as any ***issue*** is the same, even though the causes of action are different.

   b. **Suit not prevented:** Whereas claim preclusion prevents the second suit altogether, collateral estoppel does not prevent suit, but merely compels the court to make the ***same finding of fact*** that the first court made on the identical issue.

2. **To whom applied:** Collateral estoppel always applies where ***both*** the parties in the second action were present in the first action. Collateral estoppel also sometimes, but not always, allows a ***stranger to the first action*** to assert, in a fresh action against that same defendant, that the defendant is estopped as to an issue decided in the first action. (See p. 150 *infra* for our discussion of "mutuality," the relevant doctrine which controls when estoppel on behalf of a stranger-to-the-first-action is or isn't allowed.)

B. Issues covered: For an issue to be subject to collateral estoppel, three requirements concerning that issue must be satisfied: (1) the issue must be the ***same*** as one that was ***fully and fairly litigated*** in the first action; (2) it must have been actually ***decided*** by the first court; and (3) the first court's decision on this issue must have been ***necessary*** to the outcome in the first suit.

1. **Same issue:** For the re-litigation of an issue to be collaterally estopped, that issue must be ***identical*** to an issue litigated in the earlier trial.

2. **Actually litigated and decided:** The issue must have been actually ***litigated*** and ***decided*** at the first trial.

   a. **Need not raise all defenses:** This means that D in the first trial is ***not obligated to raise all of his defenses***. D does not forfeit these defenses by not raising them as he would forfeit a compulsory counterclaim.

   Example: P sues D for an installment of rent under a lease, and wins. In a later suit for subsequent installments due on the same lease, D will not be collaterally estopped from denying that the lease was ever executed — since the issue of execution was not actually litigated and decided in the first action, collateral estoppel does not apply even though D *could* have raised this as a defense the first time. [*Jacobson v. Miller*]

   b. **"Full and fair" litigation:** Also, the party against whom collateral estoppel is sought to be used must have had a ***"full and fair opportunity"*** to litigate the claim.

   Example: In a negligence case by P against D, D asserts his own due care, but the trial court incorrectly excludes relevant evidence tending to prove that D was careful. In a subsequent suit by D against P for his own injuries, D will not be estopped from contending that he behaved with due care, since he lacked a full and fair opportunity to litigate the due care issue in the first suit.

3. **Issue essential to verdict:** Not only must the issue have been litigated and decided in the first action, but the finding on that issue must have been ***necessary to the judgment***.

4. **Reasonably foreseeable future litigation:** Many courts today apply collateral estoppel in a subsequent action only where that action was ***reasonably foreseeable*** at the time of the initial suit. Otherwise, "defeat in one suit might entail results beyond all calculation…; a trivial controversy might bring utter disaster in its train." [*The Evergreens v. Nunan*]

5. **Court of limited jurisdiction:** A finding made by a court of ***limited jurisdiction*** may be denied collateral estoppel effect in a subsequent suit that would have been beyond the first court's jurisdiction. This is especially true where the first court has jurisdiction limited to a dollar amount, and also has ***informal procedures***.

   Example: Suppose P's first suit against D is in a small claims court, where there are no pleadings, no rules of evidence and no lawyers. A factual finding made in the first suit (either in P's favor or D's) will generally not be held to have collateral estoppel effect in a later suit, if that later suit could not have been brought in the small claims court (e.g., because the later suit would have been beyond the maximum claim-size permitted in small-claims court).

6. **Differences in burden of proof:** If in the first action the allocation of the ***burden of proof*** was more favorable to the party now seeking to apply collat-

eral estoppel than it was in the second action, collateral estoppel will not be allowed.

7. **Settlement:** In most jurisdictions, the ***settlement*** of an action by consent of the parties has ***no*** collateral estoppel effect. (The settlement document may, of course, provide otherwise.)

8. **Findings of law:** A court's conclusion of ***law***, like a conclusion of fact, is generally given collateral estoppel effect.

   a. **Exceptions:** But a conclusion of law generally will ***not*** be given collateral estoppel effect where there has been a significant ***change in legal principles*** between the two suits. That's especially true where use of collateral estoppel would impose on one of the parties a significant disadvantage, or confer on him a significant benefit, with respect to his ***competitors***.

C. **Persons who can be estopped:** Generally, only the ***actual parties*** to the first action can be ***bound*** by the finding on an issue, i.e., by collateral estoppel. (There are a few exceptions, but these apply to so few scenarios that we won't consider them here.)

1. **Strangers to first action:** This means that a true ***stranger*** to the first action ***cannot be collaterally estopped*** by the former judgment.

Example: A bus owned by Bus Co. collides with a car driven by Driver. In a suit between these two, Bus Co. is held to have full responsibility. Passenger, who was riding in Driver's car, now sues Driver. Even though the court in the first action decided that Driver was not at all at fault, Passenger is not bound by this finding. This is because Passenger was a complete stranger to the first action, and none of the few exceptions to the "no binding of strangers" rule applies to the ordinary passenger-driver situation. Therefore, the usual rule applies that a stranger to the first action (here, Passenger) cannot be bound by any finding of fact in the first action.

D. **Persons who can benefit from estoppel:**

1. **Mutuality:** Originally, it was held that a party ***not bound*** by an earlier judgment (because not a party to it) could not use that judgment to bind his adversary who ***was*** a party to the first action. This rule prohibiting a stranger's use of collateral estoppel was known as the doctrine of ***"mutuality."***

   a. **Abandoned:** Nearly all courts have ***abandoned*** the general principle of mutuality. While many courts refuse in ***particular circumstances*** to allow the use of estoppel by one not a party to the first action, it is no longer a general rule that a stranger to the first action cannot benefit from findings of fact made against her adversary.

   Example: A bus owned by Bus Co. and a car driven by Driver collide. Also involved in the collision is Pedestrian, who is badly injured. Bus Co. sues Driver for negligence, and the court decides that Driver was totally at fault. In a separate suit, Pedestrian now sues Driver. Application of the doctrine of mutuality would prevent Pedestrian from collaterally estopping Driver on the issue of negligence. But most courts today would give Pedestrian the benefit of collateral estoppel in this situation, even though Pedestrian was a stranger to the first action.

2. **Offensive/defensive distinction:** Courts are ***more willing*** to allow the ***"defensive"*** use of collateral estoppel by a stranger than they are to allow the ***"offensive" use***.

   a. **Nature of distinction:** The defensive/offensive distinction can be summarized as follows:

      [1] Where a ***defendant*** in the second action seeks to assert estoppel against the plaintiff, this use of estoppel is said to be ***"defensive"*** — estoppel is being used as a ***"shield"*** rather than as a ***"sword."***

      [2] Where a ***plaintiff*** in the second action seeks to assert estoppel against the defendant, this use is ***"offensive."***

   b. **Rationale for allowing defensive use:** The arguments for allowing ***defensive use*** of estoppel are ***stronger*** than those for allowing offensive use. In the defensive use case, plaintiff has chosen the second forum and the adversary — plaintiff is likely to have had the prospect of the second lawsuit in mind at the time of the first lawsuit, and it is not terribly unjust to hold him to the findings of fact made in that suit.

      i. **Plaintiff in both suits:** Where the plaintiff in the second action was ***also a plaintiff in the first action***, the arguments for collaterally estopping him are very strong.

      ii. **P in second suit was D in first suit:** If the plaintiff in the second action was a ***defendant in the first action***, and is seeking to assert estoppel, this is still "offensive" estoppel, but the arguments for estoppel are less compelling. Nonetheless, many courts would allow estoppel here.

   c. **Offensive use sometimes OK:** Even ***offensive use*** is sometimes approved by the courts, just not as often as defensive use. (The above example involving BusCo is an illustration of offensive use that would probably be accepted by a court.)

      Example: The SEC sues D, a corporation, based on a false proxy statement D has issued. The trial court decides in the SEC's favor, concluding that the proxy statement contained certain falsehoods. P then brings a stockholder's derivative action against D, based on the same proxy statement. P wants to collaterally estop D from relitigating the falsity of the proxy statement.

      Held, P may use collateral estoppel. This is true even though P was a stranger to the first action, and even though P's use is offensive, in the sense that P, the person seeking collateral estoppel, is the plaintiff in the second action. [*Park Lane Hosiery Co. v. Shore*]

   d. **Factors:** Here are some of the factors courts consider in deciding whether to allow offensive non-mutual estoppel in a particular case:

i. **Alignment:** Whether the party sought to be bound (the defendant in the second suit) was a ***plaintiff*** or ***defendant*** in the ***first*** suit. (If she was a defendant, this will cut against use of estoppel.)

ii. **Incentive to litigate:** Whether the person to be estopped had a reasonable ***incentive*** to litigate the issue fully in the first suit, which will depend in part on whether the second suit was ***foreseeable*** at the time of the first suit. (The more incentive the party had to litigate the first time, the fairer it is to bind him now.)

iii. **Discouraging break-away suits:** Whether the plaintiff in the second action ***could have joined*** in the first action, but instead sat out that first action in order to derive a tactical advantage. If so, this cuts against allowing non-mutual estoppel to benefit the plaintiff.

iv. **Multiple plaintiff anomaly:** Whether permitting offensive estoppel would present a danger of the ***"multiple plaintiff anomaly."*** That is, if there were numerous potential plaintiffs ***waiting in the wings,*** the court would be ***less likely to permit offensive estoppel, than where the second suit would probably be the last.***

Example: All 200 passengers are killed when a plane owned by D crashes. If each P sues *seriatim*, and offensive estoppel is allowed, D might win the first 20 suits, lose the 21st, and then be estopped from denying liability in the next 179. This would be unfair to D, and the court will almost certainly not allow it.

v. **Issue of law:** Whether the issue is one of ***law*** or merely of "fact." (Where the issue is one of law, the court is likely to use the more flexible doctrine of *stare decisis* rather than collateral estoppel.)

vi. **Government as party:** Whether the defendant in the second action is the ***government*** — non-mutual offensive use of collateral estoppel will virtually ***never*** be allowed against the government. [*U.S. v. Mendoza*]

3. **Criminal conviction:** Courts are split as to whether a party's previous ***criminal conviction*** may serve to collaterally estop him in the subsequent civil action.

Example: D is convicted of drunk driving after getting into an accident in which V is injured. In a subsequent civil suit by V, some but not all courts will allow V to collaterally estop D from denying that he was drunk.

a. **Guilty plea:** Courts are also split about whether offensive collateral estoppel effect should be given to a ***guilty plea*** in the first proceeding.

b. **Acquittal:** ***Acquittal*** in a criminal case is ***never binding*** in a subsequent civil action. The main reason is that to grant estoppel effect to an acquittal would be to allow the criminal defendant to ***bind a non-party to the original action.***

Example: D is prosecuted by the state for drunk driving in an accident in which V was injured. D is acquitted. V now brings a civil action for negligence against D, and seeks to show that D was drunk.

D will not be able to use collateral estoppel against V (i.e., to claim that D's acquittal establishes that he was not drunk). That's because the "beyond a reasonable doubt" standard of proof necessary in a criminal case was tougher for the prosecution to meet than the "preponderance of the evidence" standard used in the later civil suit, so estopping V (preventing him from showing D was more likely than not drunk) would be highly unfair to V.

IV. FULL FAITH AND CREDIT

A. Full Faith and Credit generally: Special problems arise when two related suits occur in ***different jurisdictions***. There may be two different states involved, or a state court and a federal court. In either situation, the second court's handling of the first court's judgment is governed by a general principle called "full faith and credit."

1. **Two states:** When the courts of ***two different states*** are involved, the result is dictated by the ***Full Faith and Credit*** Clause of the U.S. Constitution (Article IV, Section 1). This clause requires each state to give to the judgment of any other state ***the same effect that that judgment would have in the state which rendered it***.

    Example: P wins a judgment against D in Connecticut, but cannot find any property in Connecticut on which to levy. P then locates property held by D in Illinois. P may collect in Illinois by bringing a suit based on the Connecticut judgment. Because of the Full Faith and Credit Clause, the courts of Illinois must accept this judgment at face value, and may not reconsider any issues which it concluded. The Illinois courts must therefore give P all the rights that a judgment creditor would have if he got an Illinois judgment, including the right to have the sheriff sell D's Illinois assets.

    a. **Misinterpretation:** The rule of full faith and credit applies even where the second court is convinced that the first court made a ***mistake*** on law or facts. Indeed, State A must give full faith and credit to an adjudication of State B even if that judgment was based on a ***misinterpretation of the laws of State A***. [*Fauntleroy v. Lum*]

    b. **Collateral attack on jurisdiction:** There is ***one exception*** to the rule that the second court may not reconsider any aspect of the original judgment: the second court may reconsider whether the first court had ***jurisdiction*** (either personal or subject-matter), provided that the jurisdictional question was ***not litigated or waived*** in the first action. This is the doctrine of ***"collateral attack."***

    Example: P sues D in Connecticut. D defaults, by never appearing in the suit at all. The Connecticut court enters a judgment in favor of P. P then sues in Illinois, having found property of D there. At D's request, the Illinois court may consider whether the Connecticut court ever had valid personal jurisdiction over D. If it concludes that Connecticut did not, the Illinois court need not enforce the judgment. (But if D had litigated the jurisdictional issue in Connecticut, Illinois could not reconsider the jurisdiction question, even if it was convinced that Connecticut wrongly determined that it had jurisdiction.)

2. **State followed by federal court:** If the first court is a state court, and the second court is a ***federal*** court, a similar full faith and credit principle applies, but this is not dictated by the Constitution. Instead a federal statute, 28 U.S.C. §1738, requires every federal court to give to the judgment of any state court the same effect that that judgment would have in the courts of the state which rendered it.

3. **Federal followed by state court:** Conversely, if the first judgment is in a federal court and the second suit is in a state court, full faith and credit again applies, though the mechanism by which this happens is not so clear. (Probably the Constitution's Supremacy Clause dictates that the state court honor a federal court judgment).

B. **Duty to follow the *res judicata* effect of first judgment:** The full faith and credit principle — that one jurisdiction's courts must honor the judgments of another jurisdiction — applies not only generally, but specifically to the issue of ***res judicata effect***. In other words, the earlier judgment must be given ***exactly the same effect***, in terms of claim preclusion and collateral estoppel, as the judgment would have in the court that rendered it.

1. **Two states:** Thus a state must give to the judgment of any other state at least the *res judicata* effect that that judgment would have in the state of its rendition.

   Example: P litigates an issue with D in State 1. The issue is decided in favor of P. X now sues D in State 2 in a suit raising the same issue. The State 2 court determines that the courts of State 1 would allow X to use offensive collateral estoppel in this situation. The courts of State 2 must follow suit, even if the State 2 courts do not themselves generally allow offensive collateral estoppel in this situation.

   a. **Greater effect:** Courts are split about whether they may or should give ***greater effect*** to another state's judgment than it would have in that other state. Probably no constitutional principle prevents the second state from giving greater effect to the first state's judgment, so it is within the second court's discretion whether to do so.

   Example: On the facts of the above example, assume that State 2 would allow offensive collateral estoppel, but State 1 would not. Probably State 2 is free to give the State 1 judgment collateral estoppel effect, but State 2 might choose not to do so.

2. **State followed by federal:** Similarly, if the first judgment is in a state court and the second suit is in a federal court, the federal court must grant the state court judgment the same *res judicata* effect that it would have in that state.

a. **Right of Congress to specify otherwise:** There is an exception to this rule: Congress is always free to provide ***otherwise***, in a specific context. If Congress does provide otherwise, then the federal court may be free to deny the earlier state court judgment the *res judicata* effect it would have in the rendering state.

Example: 42 U.S.C. §1983 gives a person the right to bring a federal suit against anyone who violates his constitutional rights "under color of" state law. Suppose Congress added a clause to §1983 saying that any state court criminal proceeding absolving an official of unconstitutional conduct should be ignored by the federal court hearing the §1983 action. If Congress did this, a federal court hearing a §1983 suit would be free to deny any state judgment the collateral estoppel effect it would have in the courts of the state that rendered it. But Congress has not in fact done this in §1983, so the federal courts must honor the collateral estoppel effect of state court judgments in §1983 suits.

b. **Can't give greater effect:** The federal court may ***not*** give ***greater*** preclusive effect to the prior state court judgment than that state would give it. [*Migra v. Warren City Board of Ed.*]

Example: If the initial state judgment comes from a state that does not allow non-mutual offensive use of collateral estoppel, the federal court hearing the second suit may not apply such collateral estoppel, even if the situation is one in which the Supreme Court allows the use of collateral estoppel.

3. **State suit follows federal suit:** Suppose now that the ***federal*** suit comes ***first***, and the ***state*** suit ***second***.

a. **First case is a diversity action:** First, let's assume that Suit 1 is a ***diversity*** action. Here, the rule is that the state court in Suit 2 must give to the earlier federal judgment ***the same preclusive effect as such a judgment would have been given by the courts of the state where the first (federal) court sat.*** [*Semtek Int'l Inc. v. Lockheed Martin Corp.*]

Example: In Suit 1, P sues on a state-law claim, in California federal court sitting in diversity. The court concludes that the claim is barred by California's statute of limitations, and therefore dismisses it. (A federal court sitting in diversity must follow the statute-of-limitations law of the state where the federal court sits, under *Erie*.) Assume that the California courts would not regard a dismissal for failure to meet the statute of limitations a dismissal "on the merits" (i.e., they would not expect that if P re-filed in some state with an unexpired statute, the case would be barred on account of the California dismissal). Now, in Suit 2, P makes the same claims in Maryland state court.

The Maryland court must give to the prior federal dismissal the same preclusive effect that California (the state where the federal diversity court sat) would expect a dismissal by it on statute-of-limitations grounds to have in another court. Since California wouldn't expect the

Maryland courts to bar the action, Maryland must allow the action. [*Semtek*]

b. **First case is a federal question case:** Now, assume that Suit 1 is based on a ***federal question***. Here, the federal courts will develop their own case-by-case policies about when their judgment should have preclusive effects. Then, a state court hearing Suit 2 will be required to give the same preclusive effect (whatever that is) when a claim that was decided in Suit 1 is brought in the state court.

EXAM TIPS

TABLE OF CONTENTS of EXAM TIPS

EXAM TIPS

General tactic: Often in Civ Pro exams, your prof will state the procedural facts of a lawsuit, then tell you that the judge reached a particular ***ruling*** on a particular procedural issue. You are then asked to say whether the ruling was correct, and why. A good general tip is that if you're in doubt, try very hard to find a reason why the judge was ***wrong***. Mistakes by judges simply tend to make better exam questions than correct rulings by judges, so you should be biased in favor of the view that the judge was wrong.

Exam Tips on ***JURISDICTION OVER THE PARTIES***

Jurisdiction generally

In any fact pattern involving the starting of a lawsuit or the service of process, you must of course be alert to issues of jurisdiction over the parties. Here are some particular things to check for:

- **Key distinction:** At the very beginning of your analysis of personal jurisdiction, always check whether ***P's claim derives*** from D's ***in-state*** activities.
  - **Specific jurisdiction:** If it ***does*** derive from in-state activities, then the forum state court needs to have only "***specific*** jurisdiction" over D, and it's enough for this that D has ***minimum contacts*** with the forum state. (For more about minimum contacts, see p. 163.)
  - **General jurisdiction:** But if P's claim does ***not*** derive from D's in-state activities, the case requires ***"general"*** jurisdiction. And it's much tougher for the court to have general jurisdiction than specific jurisdiction:
    - **D is individual:** If D is an ***individual***, for the court to assert general jurisdiction over D, D probably has to satisfy one of the following: be ***domiciled*** in the forum state (or, perhaps, be a resident there), be ***served while physically present*** in the forum state, or have ***consented*** to service.
    - **D is corporation:** If D is a ***corporation***, for the court to assert general jurisdiction over D, D has to be ***"at home"*** in the forum state. This means that D must either be ***incorporated*** in the forum state or have its ***principal place of business*** there.
  - **Two examples:** Here are two examples to illustrate the differences in treat-

ment between suits based on general jurisdiction and ones based on specific jurisdiction:

Example 1 (suit not on in-state activities, and thus requiring general jurisdiction): On his way home to Michigan from a five-day vacation in Kentucky, D is involved in a car accident in Indiana. The other car is driven by P, a resident of Kentucky. P sues D in Kentucky state court. The Kentucky courts cannot constitutionally exercise jurisdiction over D for this claim, because: (1) the claim does not relate to D's Kentucky activities; and (2) D is not domiciled in Kentucky. (For general jurisdiction over an individual defendant as opposed to a corporation, D must probably be a domiciliary of — or at least a resident of — the forum state, unless D is served while physically in the state, or consents to service.)

Example 2 (suit on in-state activities, and thus requiring merely specific jurisdiction): D, a lawyer, practices in New Illinois. P, also a lawyer, practices in South Montana. By mail, D signs a contract with P under which P agrees to give D advice about a contingent-fee case that P is handling in New Ill. for Client; in return, D agrees to pay P 1/3 of any fee that D eventually earns. P gives the advice to D over the phone from So. Mont. (At no time does D ever enter So. Mont.). D settles, collects a fee, then refuses to pay P P's agreed-upon portion. P sues D in So. Mont. state court for breach of the agreement.

Because P is suing on a cause of action arising out of her in-forum-state work (i.e., P is asserting specific jurisdiction), D will be deemed to have minimum contacts with the forum state even though he never entered the state. But if D sued P out of some claim having nothing to do with the forum state (e.g., a battery by D that occurred when P paid a purely social visit to D in D's home state), the existence minimum contacts between D and So. Montana would be irrelevant — this would be a suit in general jurisdiction, and P could not bring it unless D was a domiciliary of So. Montana (which we know he is not), consented, or was physically served while in So. Montana.

☛ **Long-arm allowing service outside the state:** In a state-court suit, if D is served ***outside*** the forum state, check whether the applicable ***long-arm*** statute was complied with. If not, service is ***invalid*** even if there are minimum contacts.

☞ **Typical long-arm statutes:** Your prof will often specify the text of the relevant long-arm provision. Read that text carefully to ***make sure it applies*** to the facts at hand — often it ***won't.***

Example: D, a corporation, puts an advertisement in a newspaper published in State A, but distributed also in State B. P, a state B resident who reads the ad there, is thereby induced into buying D corp. stock, and loses his money. He sues D in State B court. The only relevant State B long-arm gives jurisdiction over any corporation that "does business in" State B. The taking out of an ad in a State A newspaper that has incidental State B circulation probably doesn't constitute doing business in State B, so the long-arm probably doesn't apply.

☞ **Service inside the forum state:** If D was served ***inside*** the forum state (even during a brief visit), the ***long-arm is irrelevant***, and ***service is valid***. You don't even have to check for minimum contacts, since presence at the time of service is treated as the equivalent of minimum contacts. And being served in the forum state suffices for due process purposes even if the suit has nothing to do with any of D's in-state contacts (i.e., involves "general" jurisdiction).

Example: D, a pro golfer, while at his home in State Red, issues a statement endorsing Par Golf Clubs. X hears the endorsement in State Blue and buys a set of Par clubs. While X is playing in Blue with the clubs, the head flies off, injuring P. P sues D (and X) in State White state court. D is served in the suit while he's briefly in State White to play a tournament. D's physical presence in State White at the moment of service is enough for personal jurisdiction, regardless of whether the long-arm would allow out-of-state service on D, and regardless of whether D has minimum-contacts with State White.

☛ **D lured into state by trickery:** But if P lures D into the state by ***trickery***, for the purpose of serving him, the court may well decline to exercise jurisdiction even though the exercise of jurisdiction would not be unconstitutional.

☛ **Minimum contacts:** At least where D is not served inside the state, make sure each D has ***minimum contacts*** with the forum state. (Remember, such contacts are necessary in the case of claims based on ***"specific"*** jurisdiction, i.e., claims relating to D's in-forum-state activities. For claims based on "general" jurisdiction, much tougher rules have to be satisfied for jurisdiction to exist — D has to be "at home" in the forum state.)

☞ **Voluntary doing of business in-state:** See whether D ***voluntarily did business in***, or with residents of, the forum state. If so, minimum contacts probably exist. If not, D probably doesn't have minimum contacts. The issue is always whether D should reasonably have ***anticipated being haled into court*** in the forum state.

☞ **Shipment of product into the state:** If D ***made a product outside the state*** that ***caused in-state injuries***, the jurisdiction issue can go either way depending on D's actions relating to the state:

☛ **No targeting of forum state:** If D ***didn't "target"*** the forum state for sales, and the injury-causing product just ***found its way into the state***, that's ***not*** enough for minimum contacts, even if it was ***"foreseeable"*** to D that some products might end up in the forum state and cause injury there.

☛ **Targeting of forum state:** But if D ***did "target"*** the forum state for sales (e.g., took out ***ads*** specifically directed at in-state customers, or ***regularly shipped goods*** into the state, or ***opened an office*** in-state), then that targeting *does* constitute minimum contacts with the state (so the court can exercise specific jurisdiction).

☞ **Mail order:** Watch out for the targeting issue in the case of ***mail order*** operations. If D merely sells a relatively small quantity of goods into the forum state by mail order (from a nationally-distributed catalog), there's a good chance that D won't be found to have targeted the forum state, and that the small-scale shipments therefore ***don't*** rise to the level of minimum contacts.

Example: D publishes a mail-order catalog and mails it to consumers whose names are found on commercial mailing lists, which lists include consumers located in all states. Less than 1% of D's sales are made to consumers of State X, and D has no operations in X other than to ship the order to that state. P, a State X resident who has bought merchandise from D, sues D in State X when the merchandise proves shoddy. Although the case could go either way (and the main thing is to spot the minimum-contacts issue), probably D's contacts with X are too minimal and untargeted to the forum state, to give rise to personal jurisdiction for P's lawsuit.

☞ **Operation of website:** Similarly, if all D did in connection with the forum state was to ***operate an out-of-state Internet Website*** that some in-staters accessed (and there's no evidence that D wanted to ***"target"*** in-staters as customers), this probably ***won't*** constitute minimum contacts with the forum state, at least where the claim doesn't relate to the in-staters' accesses.

☛ **Signing of contract in forum state:** If D's only contact with the forum state is that D was ***physically present in the forum state when he signed a contract*** with P, a forum-state resident, this probably won't by itself be enough to generate minimum contacts, at least for a suit not involving the contract.

☞ **Fairness as additional test:** Don't forget that even if D has minimum contacts with the forum state, D won't be required to defend suit if to do so would be ***unfair*** because of the great burden this would impose on D. In other words, ***fundamental fairness*** is a ***second condition*** (in addition to minimum-contacts) that must be satisfied before D will be forced to defend in the forum state, even where the suit is based on relatively easy-to-establish "specific" jurisdiction.

☛ **Foreign defendant:** Think hard about the possibility that it's not "fundamentally fair" for the court to exercise specific jurisdiction if D is a ***for-***

eign corporation, with no offices in the U.S., and D ***doesn't target its business at the forum state***, and merely makes some products that are brought by others into the forum state.

☛ **Claim must "relate to" forum state:** Also, keep in mind that in addition to the "minimum contacts" requirement, a second requirement for specific jurisdiction is that the claim must ***"arise out of or relate to"*** the forum state.

Example: P buys a car manufactured by D. The sale takes place in P's home state of Rhode Island, and the car was made in Michigan. P is injured in Rhode Island when the car crashes due to a defective steering wheel. Because the statute of limitations on a Rhode Island claim has already run, P sues in Maine state court, where the action is timely. D targets Maine (and every other state) with marketing efforts, and maintains a network of local dealership network there, thus giving D minimum contacts with Maine. But the accident has nothing to do with Maine.

P's claim cannot be said to have "arisen out of" or been "related to" Maine. Therefore, the Maine court can't exercise specific jurisdiction over D, and the suit can't go forward.

☛ **Sufficiency of notice:** For suits against both in-state and out-of-state defendants, make sure that the constitutional requirements of notice are satisfied: the method used must be one ***reasonably calculated to apprise D*** of the lawsuit.

☞ **Actual receipt not dispositive:** Actual receipt of the notice by D is ***not*** very important. The constitutional test is whether the method used, viewed in advance, was reasonably likely to give actual notice. So a good method that doesn't give actual notice will be permissible, and a bad method that does happen to give actual notice won't be permissible.

☞ **Service solely by mail:** Beware of service by ***mail***. A common fact pattern is that D, a corporation, is served by mail (without a prior attempt to make in-person service), and the wrong person — or no one — at D gets the document. Typically, you should express doubts in your essay about whether the method is constitutionally sufficient.

Jurisdiction in federal suits

☛ **Place for service:** Check that service took place in the correct ***place.*** This is either: (1) within the ***territorial limits*** of the state where the District Court sits; or (2) somewhere else ***permitted by the state law*** (i.e., the long-arm) of the state where the District Court sits.

☞ **100-mile bulge:** But if D is a ***third-party defendant*** or ***indispensable party,*** think ***"100-mile bulge."*** Rule 4(k)(1)(B) allows service within a 100-mile bulge around the federal courthouse.

☛ **Manner of service:** Check that service took place in the correct ***manner.*** This is either: (1) a method specified in the Federal Rules (e.g., delivery of summons and complaint to a person of "suitable age and discretion" at D's residence), or else (2) a method allowed by the ***local law*** of either (a) the state where service is made or (b) the state where the District Court sits.

Example 1 (adequate service): P sues D, an individual, in federal court for Massachusetts. Service is made by mailing a certified letter containing a copy of the summons and complaint to D's office in Illinois, where D's secretary signs for it and gives the contents to him. Assume that this procedure is a *valid* method of service under Mass. law. The service is valid for the federal action even though it was not made by the method specifically allowed for service on individuals in FRCP 4(e)(2), since FRCP 4(e)(1) allows any service method allowable in the state courts where the federal court sits.

Example 2 (inadequate service): P sues D in federal district court for State X. P serves D, an individual, by going to D's house in State X, ringing the bell, getting no answer, and sliding the summons and complaint under the front door. D actually finds the documents when he returns home that night. The relevant State X statute contains service provisions that are identical to those of FRCP 4(e)(2).

Service was *not valid.* FRCP 4(e)(2) allows service on an individual by (i) delivery to D personally; (ii) leaving a copy at D's dwelling "with someone of suitable age and discretion who resides there"; or (iii) delivering a copy to an agent authorized to receive service. Sliding a copy under the door of D's home does not meet any of these provisions, so it's invalid (since State X's statute doesn't allow any additional methods not listed in 4(e)(2)). The fact that D in fact got the papers in a timely way does not save the service from invalidity.

☛ **Amenability to service:** Check that D is ***"amenable"*** to service. This means that:

☞ if the case involves a ***federal question***, it's enough that D has minimum contacts with the forum state (even if the long-arm of the state where the federal court sits wouldn't allow the state courts to exercise jurisdiction);

☞ if the case is a ***diversity*** case, the long-arm of the ***state*** where the federal court sits ***must*** allow jurisdiction, or the federal court can't exercise jurisdiction.

☛ **State your assumption:** In a diversity situation, if your fact pattern doesn't mention the long-arm of the state where the federal court sits, state that you are ***assuming*** that the state long-arm would allow service on the type of defendant, in the type of case, in question. Also state that if this assumption is wrong, the federal court won't be able to properly exercise jurisdiction.

☛ **Quasi in rem:** If P is trying to get jurisdiction based on D's ***assets*** in the forum state (***quasi in rem*** jurisdiction), remember that P can't go forward unless D has

minimum contacts with the forum state, just as if this were an *in personam* suit.

- **Venue:** In federal suits, check for ***venue***. Venue will lie only in the following places:
  - ❑ **Defendants' residence:** in any district where ***any defendant resides***, if all defendants reside in the ***state*** containing that district; or
  - ❑ **Substantial-part-of-events:** in any district where a ***"substantial part of the events"*** giving rise to the claim occurred; or
  - ❑ **Catch-all:** in unusual cases where there is ***no district*** satisfying either of the two prior tests, in any district where ***any*** D could be ***subject to personal jurisdiction.***
  - **Corporation:** A corporation "resides" (for venue purposes) in any district with which it has ***minimum contacts.*** This means at least that there is venue in the district where the corporation has its ***principal place of business***, and also in any district where it has ***substantial operations.***
  - **Venue in removal cases:** Venue in ***removal*** cases is sometimes tested. Remember that in a removal case, the action goes to "the district court of the U.S. for the district and division ***embracing the place where such action is pending.***")
  - **Forum *non conveniens*:** Forum *non conveniens* is sometimes tested, if the fact pattern involves a federal suit. Generally, the question will have to explicitly mention the D's request for a forum-non-conveniens transfer if this is to be an issue in the case.
    - **"Where action might have been brought":** Remember that the court may, in its discretion, transfer the action to any district "where [the action] ***might have been brought.***" This mainly means that you must make sure that the transferee district is one in which ***venue*** would have been proper. Also, remember that if defendant is the one seeking the change, the defendant ***can't waive*** the lack of venue in the transferee district.
    - **Convenience of parties:** You'll need to analyze whether the transfer would be "for the ***convenience*** of the parties," and whether the ***"interests of justice"*** would thereby be served. P's choice of forum will normally be respected, so the burden is on D to show that convenience/justice require a transfer.
      - **Exception:** But if all events occurred in, and all witnesses are in or near, the transferee district, and P chose the transferor district for forum-shopping reasons, a strong case for transfer will be made. (But even so, the choice-of-law rules of the transfer<u>or</u>, not transferee, court will apply.)

Exam Tips on ***SUBJECT-MATTER JURISDICTION***

Subject-matter jurisdiction generally

In any fact pattern involving a federal suit, you must check to make sure that the requirements of subject-matter jurisdiction are satisfied. Here are some particular things to do and to check for:

Diversity

☛ **Diversity:** Always check to see whether ***diversity*** can serve as the basis for subject-matter jurisdiction.

> ☞ **Diversity must be complete:** Most important of all, make sure diversity is ***complete.*** Professors love to make fact patterns that include "incomplete" diversity (e.g., P1 from NY, P2 from CA, D1 from MA and D2 from CA). Remember that the requirement of complete diversity means that ***no plaintiff may be a citizen of the same state as any defendant.***
>
> > ☛ **Corporation:** Also, remember that a ***corporation*** is deemed to be a citizen of ***both*** the state where it is ***incorporated***, and the state where it has its ***principal place of business***, so no opposing party can be a citizen of *either* of these states.
> >
> > > ☞ **"Nerve center" test:** Keep in mind that a corporation's "principal place of business" is determined by the ***"nerve center"*** test: it's generally the ***corporate headquarters*** (not the place where the corporation does the most daily business).
> > >
> > > **Example:** P, a citizen of Arizona, is suing D, an airline, for injuries he sustained. D is incorporated in Massachusetts and has its corporate headquarters there, but has its main booking terminal, reservation center and most of its employees in Arizona. In your answer, say that since the "nerve center" test is used, there's diversity (since D is a citizen only of Massachusetts, its principal place of business as well as its state of incorporation). The fact that Arizona is the locus of most assets, activities and employees doesn't make Arizona D's principal place of business.
> > >
> > > ☞ **Removal:** Also, be especially alert to diversity issues where D is a corporation that seeks to ***remove*** a case to federal court — remember

that if the claim is not based on a federal question, ***complete diversity is required for removal***, just as if the case had been started in federal court.

☞ **Diversity tested at time complaint is filed:** Remember that the test is done ***as of the time the complaint is filed***, not the earlier time when the events at issue occurred. Profs love to try to trip you up with fact patterns involving a party who changes her domicile after the events in the suit, but before commencing the suit.

Example: P is domiciled in Ohio at the time he's involved in an auto accident with D, who's also a citizen of Ohio. After the accident and before filing suit, P moves to Michigan. He then starts a diversity suit against D. There's diversity, because P is deemed to be a citizen of Michigan (his domicile at the time suit was filed), not Ohio.

☛ **Joinder after suit starts:** But watch for ***joinder*** of an additional plaintiff or defendant that occurs after the main suit has already commenced. Diversity is tested again as the new party is added, and if that joinder destroys the diversity the new party will have to be dropped.

Example: P, a citizen of N.J., bring a diversity action against C Corp., a citizen of N.Y., for fraud. P later moves to have Dave, a stockbroker from N.J. who was involved in the alleged fraud, joined as a co-defendant. The claim against Dave can't go ahead, because Dave's presence would destroy diversity; therefore, Dave must be dropped.

☞ **Amount in controversy:** In diversity situations, make sure the ***amount in controversy*** requirement is satisfied. More than ***$75,000*** must be at stake.

☛ **"Legal certainty" standard:** Remember that the standard is whether it can be said "to a ***legal certainty***" that the amount at stake is less than $75,000 — the mere fact that it is possible or even likely that less than $75,000 will ultimately be recovered by P ***won't be enough*** to induce the court to dismiss for lack of subject-matter jurisdiction (nor will the fact that P eventually *does* recover less than $75,000.)

☛ **Aggregation:** Professors frequently test ***aggregation*** issues relating to amount-in-controversy. You can spot such an issue when you see either: (1) several claims totalling more than $75,000, with no single claim equalling $75,000; or (2) one (or more) claims exceeding $75,000, plus one (or more) claims for less than $75,000.

The rules on aggregation are too tricky to summarize here, but in general:

[1] a P may combine several claims against a single D to get to $75,000;

[2] a P who sues D1 may not bring in an additional D (D2) against whom all claims total no more than $75,000;

[3] multiple P's can't combine their claims against a single D if no P has a claim for more than $75,000;

[4] but if one of multiple Ps *does* have a claim for more than $75,000, under supplemental jurisdiction other Ps whose claims are for less than $75,000 *can* join under Rule 20, because of *Exxon Mobil v. Allapattah.*

☞ **Class actions:** Pay attention when the fact pattern presents a ***class action*** based on diversity. Because of supplemental jurisdiction as interpreted by *Exxon Mobil v. Allapattah*, ***only a single named member*** needs to have a claim exceeding $75,000.

Example: P1, the only named class member in a diversity class action, has a claim against D for $80,000. All other (unnamed) class members have claims ranging from $2,000 to $30,000. The amount in controversy requirement is satisfied, because each named member(s)' claims exceed $75,000, and the unnamed class members get to join by means of supplemental jurisdiction under *Allapattah.*

Federal question

☛ **Federal question:** Whether there's diversity or not, check on whether there's a ***federal question*** present. The existence of a federal question means, of course, that the case can go forward even if there's no diversity.

☞ **Definition:** Remember that a "federal question" is one "arising under the Constitution, laws or treaties of the United States." Usually, your fact pattern will involve a constitutional issue or a federal statute if the professor is trying to see whether you can spot a federal question.

☞ **Look to P's claim only:** In general, look ***only to P's claim***, not to D's possible ***defenses***, to determine whether there's a federal question.

☛ **Exception:** But in rare cases where resolving P's state-law claim requires ***interpreting federal law***, and there is a strong federal interest in having a ***uniform interpretation*** of that federal law (e.g., interpretation of an IRS statute), then the case might be found to raise a federal question anyway.

☞ **Amount in controversy:** You don't have to worry about the amount in controversy if a federal question is present.

Supplemental jurisdiction

☛ **SJ generally:** Once you've determined that your fact pattern contains a valid diversity claim between two or more parties, or a valid federal question claim, be on the lookout for applications of ***supplemental jurisdiction*** ("SJ"). Professors love to create patterns that have SJ lurking in them, because SJ can be well hidden.

☞ **Federal question claim at core:** If the "core" (basic) claim in your fact pattern involves a ***federal question***, remember that SJ lets ***state-law claims*** be added to the suit. So anytime a P wants to assert both a federal-law-based claim and a state-law (perhaps common-law) claim, and there is not diversity between P and D, "Think SJ".

- **Additional parties to state-law claim:** Also, recall that SJ lets ***additional parties*** be added to the state-law claim. So look for patterns where P has a federal claim against D1, and related state-law-only claims against D2; if P is a citizen of the same state as D2, SJ is the way that the state-law claim against D2 can go forward.

  Example: Borrow, an Ohio citizen, gets a car loan from Finco, an Ohio finance company. Borrow then sues Finco in Ohio state court, claiming that the terms of the loan violated the federal Truth in Lending statute. Finco timely removes to federal court for the appropriate district in Ohio. Borrow then amends his suit to add an additional defendant, Dealer, the company that sold Borrow the car — this claim says that Dealer violated Ohio law by giving him wrong information about the terms of the loan, and seeks damages of $20,000. Dealer is a citizen of Ohio.

  Without SJ, Borrow's state-law claim against Dealer would have to be dismissed, since: (1) there's no diversity between Borrow and Dealer; and (2) the $75,000 amount-in-controversy requirement applicable to state-law claims is not satisfied. But SJ applies not only to state-law claims that are transactionally related to a valid federal-law claim, but also to a ***new party*** who is brought in to defend against the state-law claim. So the lack of diversity and amount-in-controversy don't matter. (But this works only because the state-law claim against Dealer arises out of the ***same basic transaction*** as the federal-law claim against Finco.)

☞ **Diversity claim at core:** If the "core" claim is state-law-only, but is supported by ***diversity***, look to see whether SJ is available to cover ***new claims*** or ***new parties*** that would otherwise destroy diversity or would fail to satisfy amount-in-controversy.

- **Covered by SJ:** These types of situations are ***covered*** by SJ:

  - ❑ ***compulsory counterclaims***;
  - ❑ joinder of ***additional parties*** to ***compulsory counterclaims***;
  - ❑ ***cross-claims***;
  - ❑ ***impleader claims*** by ***third-party plaintiffs*** (TPPs) against third-party defendants (TPDs);

- ❑ any claims by TPP's or TPD's against anyone else.

  Example: While Bobb, a police officer with the Ames, Texas, Police Department (APD), is trying to arrest Paul, a private citizen, Bobb chokes Paul. Paul sues Bobb for assault, in a diversity action. Paul, Bobb and the APD are all citizens of Texas. Bobb then makes an impleader (third-party) claim against the APD, saying that under the APD officers' union contract, the APD is liable to pay Bobb's legal-defense costs.

  Even though Bobb and the APD are both citizens of Texas, the lack of diversity doesn't matter because third-party claims by a third-party plaintiff (Bobb) against a third-party defendant (APD) fall within the court's supplemental jurisdiction.

☛ **Not covered by SJ:** These types of situations are ***not covered*** by SJ:

- ❑ claims by a ***P against a TPD***.

  Example: Same facts as above example. Now, Paul sues the APD, making a state-law claim that the APD is liable for his injuries. Since Paul and the APD are both citizens of Texas, there's no diversity between them. Since supplemental jurisdiction doesn't apply to a suit by an original plaintiff (Paul) against a third-party defendant, the lack of Paul/APD diversity means that the court does not have jurisdiction over the Paul/APD suit.

- ❑ claims by a ***P*** against a person who is to be ***"joined if feasible."***
- ❑ claims by a ***P*** against ***multiple Ds***; and
- ❑ claims by ***would-be intervenors*** who want to enter on the Plaintiff side of the suit.

☛ **Defensive posture:** If you can't remember all this, just remember the rule of ***"defensive posture"***: in a diversity case, SJ ***helps only those in a defensive posture.*** So, for instance, SJ applies to additional claims by defendants (including TPDs and TPPs), but ***not*** to additional claims asserted by original plaintiffs against TPDs.

☛ **No help on personal jurisdiction:** Remember that SJ ***never affects*** the requirements of ***personal*** jurisdiction. So if a D (even a TPD) does not have minimum contacts with the forum state, the fact that the claim is of a type to which SJ applies is not enough to allow D to be joined.

Waiver

☛ **Waiver never occurs:** Remember that lack of subject-matter jurisdiction may be raised at any time, and therefore is not capable of being waived.

Example: P, a New York Corp., sues D, an individual domiciled in New York, in a diversity action. D files an answer that doesn't mention subject-matter jurisdiction, and also a dismissal motion on non-jurisdictional grounds. D has not waived its right to argue that the case must be dismissed for lack of diversity — a lack of subject-matter jurisdiction is a defense that can never be waived, and can even be raised by the court on its own at any time.

Removal

☛ **Generally:** Whenever your pattern involves a D who is sued in ***state*** court, and you're asked about the options available to D, consider ***removal*** of the suit to the federal courts. In general, any action brought in state court which P could have brought in federal court may be removed.

☞ **No D is citizen of state where action is pending:** But remember that in a ***diversity*** case (not in federal question cases), there's a key additional requirement: the case may be removed only if ***no D is a citizen of the state in which the action is pending.*** Professors love to test on this exception, because it's easy to slip into the fact pattern and easy for the student to miss.

☛ **Corporate citizenship:** Any time a ***corporate*** defendant is trying to remove, be especially suspicious of the D-not-a-citizen-of-the-state-where-the-action's-pending requirement. Remember that a corporation can be a citizen of two states simultaneously (state of ***incorporation***, plus state of ***principal place of business***) — if ***either*** of these states matches the state where the action is pending, there can be no removal.

☞ **"Nerve center" test:** And remember that a corporation's ***principal place of business*** is judged by the "nerve center" test — so the state where the company's ***headquarters*** is located (not the state where it has the most activities or employees) is the principal place of business. [*Hertz Corp. v. Friend*]

Example: P sues D Corp. in state court for the State of Green, in a contract action. (P is a citizen of the State of Blue.) D Corp. is incorporated in, and has its headquarters in, State Red, but it has its major manufacturing facility in State Green. D Corp. removes to federal court for the district of Green. Since no federal question is present, removal can occur only if D Corp. is not a citizen of State Green. Since the "nerve center" test for D's principal place of business is used, the action can proceed, since D is a citizen only of Red. The fact that Green is the location of main productive assets doesn't make Green D's principal place of business, so the fact that P is a citizen of Green doesn't destroy complete diversity and thus doesn't block D's right to remove.

- ☞ **Diversity requirements apply:** Also, remember that in removal of an action where there's no federal question, you must check that ***every requirement for diversity*** is satisfied, as if the case had originally been brought by P in federal court. This means that: (1) the Ps must be completely diverse with the Ds; and (2) the amount in controversy requirement (> $75,000 at stake) must be satisfied. Again, profs. love to test this, since they figure that you might miss these requirements given that the case started out in state court.

Exam Tips on PLEADING

Pleading generally

Be alert to Pleadings issues whenever the fact pattern gives you information about either (1) ***when*** a pleading was served or filed (whether it's a complaint, answer or reply), or (2) the ***contents*** of the pleading. Here are some particular things to check for:[1]

The complaint

- **Jurisdictional allegations:** If the pleading you are given is a federal complaint, make sure that it contains the requisite ***jurisdictional*** allegations. Professors sometimes give you the text of a complaint, and expect you to notice that the jurisdictional allegations are missing. If so, state that D can move to dismiss for lack of jurisdiction (since the burden is on P to make the jurisdictional allegations explicitly).

- **Statement of claim:** Check whether the complaint meets the requirements of a ***"short and plain statement*** of the claim showing that the pleader is entitled to relief."

- **Special matter:** On the other hand, make sure that any ***"special matter"*** is pleaded with ***particularity***. If it is not, have the defendant make a motion for a more definite statement.

  - ☞ **Illustrations:** Thus be on the lookout for allegations of ***fraud***, ***mistake***, etc., that are stated conclusorally.

---

1. We'll assume in this whole discussion of Pleading that the FRCP's pleading rules apply to the suit.

Example: P brings a class action suit on behalf of himself and 300 other people against C Corp., a mail-order company. In the complaint, P alleges fraud and misrepresentation in the sale of certain high-tech alarm clocks to 300 people, and claims that each person was damaged in the sum of $250. The complaint refers to alleged misrepresentations, but does not contain a description of the fraudulent statements. C Corp. can probably successfully move for a more definite statement.

☞ **Special damages:** Also, if the complaint claims damages that are in fact ***"special" damages*** (i.e., ones which would not normally be expected to flow from the kind of injury P is claiming), make sure these special damages are pleaded in detail. For instance, damages for intangible torts like slander and false imprisonment, or consequential damages in contracts cases, will often be "special."

☛ **Pleading in the alternative:** Remember that pleading in the ***alternative*** is ***allowable*** under the FRCP (and in most states), so don't fall for assertions that a complaint should be dismissed because the allegations are inconsistent or mutually exclusive.

The answer, and motions by D

☛ **The answer:** Remember that D will be deemed to have ***admitted*** any allegation that is not specifically denied in the answer, unless the allegation relates to damages. (FRCP 8(b)(6).)

☞ **P's answer to D's counterclaim:** Remember that this principle also applies to P's answer to any counterclaim by D. So if D makes a counterclaim and P doesn't deny the allegations of the counterclaim, P will be deemed to have admitted the counterclaim's non-damage-related allegations.

☛ **No answer needed to affirmative defense:** But also remember that this principle doesn't apply to D's assertion of an ***affirmative defense*** (since no responsive pleading is required to respond to an affirmative defense). FRCP 8(b)(6). In other words, if D raises an affirmative defense, P can remain silent, and will be deemed to have denied the allegation.

Example: P sues D for breach of a contract between P and D, under which P licensed D a game that P invented and D agreed to pay royalties. The suit says that D failed to pay the agreed-upon royalties. D answers by stating that D owes nothing because P breached the contract; D says that P didn't really invent the game as he represented he had, and that he had in fact stolen the game from X. P fails to respond to this statement in the answer. D asserts that P's silence in the face of D's answer must be taken as an admission.

D will lose on this point — since D was asserting an affirmative defense (not a counterclaim seeking affirmative relief), P was not required to serve a responsive pleading. P's silence will therefore not be deemed to be an admission of anything. (See FRCP 8((b)(6).)

☛ **Motions:** Scrutinize any ***motions*** made by D, to determine whether the rules governing motions have been satisfied. For instance, a Rule 12(b)(6) motion for "failure to state a claim upon which relief can be granted" must be made ***before*** D answers (though after the answer, D can move under 12(c) for "judgment on the pleadings.")

- ☞ Keep in mind that in deciding a 12(b)(6) motion, the court must ***assume*** that all factual allegations are ***true***. If, when the court does this, the court thinks it's not ***"plausible"*** for P to recover under any theory, the complaint should be dismissed for failure to state a claim. (So it's not enough that the judge thinks that P is very unlikely to be able to *prove* the allegations contained in the complaint; the question is whether liability is legally plausible *assuming* that the alleged facts are all true.) Cite to *Ashcroft v. Iqbal* on this point.

  - ☛ But also remember that statements in the complaint that just recite ***"legal conclusions"*** rather than factual allegations *aren't* assumed to be true, and get disregarded when the court is deciding the 12(b)(6) motion. (Again, cite to *Ashcroft v. Iqbal.*)

- ☞ **Waiver:** Remember that if D brings a 12(b) motion of any sort, and doesn't include the defenses of ***lack of personal jurisdiction***, ***improper service,*** or ***improper venue***, he ***waives*** these defenses if they were ***"available"*** at the time he brought the 12(b) motion. FRCP 12(g)(2); 12(h)(1).

  Example: P serves D, an individual, in a federal action based on a federal statute. P makes service by slipping the summons and complaint under D's door. D brings a 12(b)(6) motion to dismiss on the grounds that the statute does not allow recovery on the facts as pleaded by P. The court denies the motion. Next, P brings a motion under 12(b)(5) alleging that service was improper.

  D will ***lose*** on the motion, because he ***waived*** the right to bring it. At the time D made his 12(b)(6) motion, the 12(b)(5) insufficient-service motion was "available" to him (i.e., he knew all the facts that would tell him he had grounds for the motion), and he failed to include it with the 12(b)(6) motion. See FRCP 12(g)(2) and 12(h)(1).

Time limits; Amendments

☛ **Time limits generally:** Be alert to whether pleadings are served and filed in a ***timely*** manner. In a federal suit:

- ❑ D has ***21 days*** after service to answer, but if he has been served out of state by use of the state's long-arm, any ***longer*** period to answer allowed by that long-arm controls.

- ❑ If D ***waives*** formal service, then he gets ***60 days*** from the date the request for waiver was sent to him by P.

- ❑ If the answer contains a ***counterclaim***, P gets ***21 days*** after service to reply.

☛ **Amendments:** Know when ***amendment*** is allowed ***of right***, and when it must instead be allowed by leave of court.

☞ **Amendment of complaint by P as of right:** For instance, P gets to amend once ***by right*** prior to D's service of "responsive pleading" (i.e., an answer). FRCP 15(a)(1)(A). Note that D's service of a motion (as opposed to an answer) does not terminate P's right to amend.

Example: P sues D on March 1. On March 15, D makes a 12(b)(6) motion to dismiss. The court denies the motion on April 1. On April 5, P amends the complaint. On April 6, D answers the original complaint. P's amendment is of right — it occurred before D served any "responsive pleading," since D's 12(b)(6) motion was not a responsive pleading (as an answer would be). But if P sought to amend for the first time after the April 6 service of D's answer, P would need court approval.

☞ **Statute of limitations:** If there seems to be a question whether a ***statute of limitations*** (S/L) is satisfied, and the complaint was originally served before expiration of the S/L, but amended after expiration, look for a ***"relation back"*** issue. In general, the amended complaint "relates back" to the date the action was originally commenced

☛ If the amendment ***changes the identity of the defendant***, then be sure that during the original time for service under the statute of limitations, the newly-named defendant ***knew or should have known*** that it (not the originally-named defendant) was the party P would have sued but for P's mistake about who was the proper party.

☞ **Variance of proof from pleadings:** Remember that the FRCP are very tolerant of ***variance*** between proof and pleadings.

Exam Tips on DISCOVERY

Discovery generally

The good news about Discovery on exams is that you'll almost always be able to recognize that you are indeed dealing with a discovery issue — you'll be told about a deposition, a request for document production, etc. The bad news is that discovery issues are extremely technical and based on the precise working of the FRCP — you can't rely on general reasoning or on "On the one hand, on the other hand …" analysis. Here are some particular things to check for:[2]

Procedures

- **Procedures:** Make sure that the detailed ***procedures*** governing discovery are followed. Three examples:

  - **Automatic discovery:** Don't forget that some discovery is ***automatic*** — i.e., due without a request from the other side. If the party doesn't perform the required automatic disclosure, then unless the party has "substantial justification" for the failure or the failure is harmless, the material that should have been disclosed ***may not be used*** by that party at trial. FRCP 37(c)(1).

    - ❑ Most important: If a party will use particular discoverable information to ***"support its claims or defenses,"*** the party must automatically disclose, early in the lawsuit, the ***name, address and phone number*** of anyone who possesses that information, along with a list of the "subjects of that information" (FRCP 26(a)(1)(A)(i).) (*Exception:* No disclosure is required if the individual's info will be used solely for impeachment, not substantively.)

    - ❑ Ditto for ***documents***: If a party plans to use a document (or other tangible thing) as part of her substantive case at trial, that party must ***give a copy or description*** to the other party early in the case, without a request. 26(a)(1)(A)(ii).

      Example: P is injured while riding a bus operated by D. P sues D in federal court. D supplies no documents to P during discovery, and P asks for none. At trial, D offers a ticket stub like the one sold to P for the ride; this stub has a "waiver of liability" printed on the back purporting to absolve D of tort liability in the absence of gross negligence. P objects to the stub's admission. How should the court rule?

      The court must ***exclude*** the stub. FRCP 26(a)(1)(A)(ii) requires a party to automatically (i.e., even without a request) furnish to the other a copy or description of all "documents ... that the disclosing party ... may use to support its claims or defenses, unless the use would be solely for impeachment." The ticket stub falls within this description, so D was required to give P a copy or description of it. FRCP 37(c)(1) says that D is therefore "not allowed to use that information ... to supply evidence ... at a trial," unless the failure to disclose "was substan-

---

2. In most of this discussion, we're assuming that your exam question is to be answered by reference to the FRCP.

tially justified or is harmless." Neither of these exceptions applies here, so the stub must be excluded.

☞ **Document production:** Look out for a party's attempt to ***get documents*** from the other party. The discovering party ***can't use interrogatories*** for this purpose — instead, a Rule 34 Request to Produce Documents must be used.

☞ **Sanctions:** Normally, before a court orders ***sanctions***, the party seeking documents must first obtain an FRCP 37(a) ***order compelling discovery***. If the opposing party still persists in her refusal to produce the documents, only then may sanctions be imposed.

  ☛ **Automatic discovery:** But note that this no-sanctions-without-prior-order principle does ***not*** apply to a party's failure to provide automatic discovery — here, even without a prior order compelling discovery, the court ***must*** prohibit the party from ***using the discoverable information at trial,*** unless the failure was either "substantially justified" or "harmless." 37(c)(1).

Privileges

☛ **Privileges:** Be alert to ***privileges.*** Remember that information protected by a privilege may not be subjected to discovery. Also, remember that on federal question issues, federal common law determines what is privileged, but on ***state-law issues, state law of privilege controls.***

Work-product immunity

☛ **Work-product immunity generally:** Be alert to ***work-product immunity*** issues. Any time one litigant seeks from the other information that was prepared in anticipation of litigation, either the qualified or the absolute work product ("w.p.") immunity will apply. So be on the lookout for attempts to get a lawyer's notes or memos, an investigator's report, etc.

  ☞ **Qualified vs. absolute:** Be sure to distinguish between ***qualified*** and ***absolute*** immunity. The latter applies only to ***"mental impressions, conclusions, opinions or legal theories."*** So documents that are entirely fact-based (e.g., what caused the accident?) will generally get merely qualified protection. If the immunity is qualified, it can be overcome by a showing of "substantial need" and an inability to obtain the equivalent materials without "undue hardship."

  ☞ **"Prepared in anticipation of litigation":** Before you conclude that something is w.p., make sure it was ***"prepared in anticipation of litigation."*** Even a document written by or to a lawyer won't be w.p. if it wasn't prepared at least partly in anticipation of litigation (so that, for instance, a document prepared to comply with a statute or government regulation won't be covered, though it might be covered by attorney-client privilege).

☞ **Non-lawyer documents:** Remember that documents prepared by a ***non-lawyer*** (e.g., a private investigator) who is assisting in preparing for litigation can be covered.

☞ **Substantial need for materials:** Once you have determined that a document *is* covered by the qualified work product privilege, apply the standard that the document can be discovered only if the party seeking it shows a ***"substantial need"*** for it, and shows that the equivalent info is ***otherwise unobtainable*** without "undue hardship." FRCP 26(b)(3)(A)(ii). Argue both sides.

> **Example:** A truck owned by Corp., while driven by Corp's employee Emp, strikes and injures Pam. Pam sues Corp. and serves Corp. with notice to produce a written statement made and signed by Zed, a coworker of Emp who was in the truck at the time of the accident. The statement was made to an adjuster for Corp's insurance carrier.
>
> The statement is clearly qualified w.p. (prepared in anticipation of litigation). Pam could argue that she has substantial need of the statement, because it was probably taken soon after the accident and would therefore be the most reliable version of the accident. But Corp. can argue that Pam should instead get the same info by deposing Z. However, Pam can probably successfully respond that a deposition is not likely to be the substantial equivalent of the report — Zed's likely to be a hostile witness in deposition because he'd be reluctant to make a statement harmful to his employer. So Pam will probably win on "substantial need," in which case she'd get the report.

☞ **Experts:** If the document in question was prepared by an ***expert***, special rules governing experts (discussed below), not the w.p. immunity rules, apply.

☛ **Copy to maker of statement:** Remember that if a person (whether party or non-party) makes a statement concerning the litigation to a party, the maker of the ***statement*** is automatically entitled to a copy. This rule overrides any work product immunity.

Experts

☛ **Special rules for experts:** Keep in mind that special rules apply to ***experts.*** Professors love to test this area. If a party plans to call an expert at trial, the party must have the expert prepare and sign a ***report*** containing his opinions and other information; the report is automatically given to the other side.

Party/non-party distinction

☛ **Distinction generally:** Always keep in mind the distinction between ***parties*** and ***non-parties***. For instance, an ***interrogatory*** can only be addressed to a ***party***; disclosure relating to non-parties must occur through ***depositions***.

☞ **Subpoenas on non-parties:** Also, beware of the limits on the use of subpoenas for depositions. A subpoena to force a non-party to be deposed must set the deposition for no more than ***100 miles*** from the deponent's residence or place of business.

☞ **No subpoena needed for party:** Conversely, remember that ***no subpoena*** is needed to take the deposition of a ***party***.

☛ **Medical exams:** Remember that ***medical exams*** are especially limited: ***only a party*** may be forced to undergo an exam, and then only if the party's condition is ***in controversy*** and the discovering party convinces the court that there is ***good cause*** for the exam.

Example: D, a pilot, has to make an emergency landing of his plane at night on a highway. When he does so, he hits a car driven by P, injuring P. P sues D for negligence, claiming that D carelessly failed to use carburetor heat, causing the engine to fail. P then seeks a court order that D be examined to determine whether his eyesight, hearing and physical dexterity were adequate for piloting a plane.

D can at least make a strong argument that no good cause for the exam has been established — if P's theory of the case is that carburetor heat was omitted, D's eyesight, hearing, etc. would be irrelevant. (But if P can show a colorable claim that such impairments by D might have been additional contributing causes, then he may be able to show good cause and get the order for an exam. So argue both sides.)

Settlements and pre-trial conferences

☛ **Court's right to order settlement discussions:** Remember that under Rule 16(c), the court may "if appropriate" require a party or its representative to ***attend a pretrial conference*** and to "***consider possible settlement***" of the dispute. So if a party refuses to attend the pretrial conference or to discuss settlement, this refusal can be punished by various sanctions, including a contempt-of-court citation. 16(f).

Admissibility of discovery results

☛ **Deposition admissibility:** Professors like to test the ***admissibility*** of discovery results at trial. Use of ***deposition*** transcripts is the most-frequently-tested area. Use the two-part test:

☞ **Live-testimony test:** First, ask whether the deposition statement would be admissible if the deponent were giving ***live testimony***.

☞ **Four categories:** Second, make sure the statement falls into one of these ***four categories***:

[1] it was made by an ***adverse party***, or by an officer or director of an adverse

corporate party (in which case it is admissible for *any* purpose);

[2] it is used to ***impeach*** the deponent's credibility while the deponent is testifying (in which case it doesn't matter whether the deponent is a party);

[3] it ***conflicts*** with the deponent's trial testimony, if the interests of the deponent and the questioner are adverse (in which case it may even be used for *substantive* purposes); or

[4] various circumstances make the deponent ***unavailable*** to testify at trial (e.g., she is dead, or is located 100 or miles from the trial site).

Exam Tips on *ASCERTAINING APPLICABLE LAW*

Erie problems generally

Whenever your facts involve a ***diversity*** suit, you must be alert to *Erie* problems. Look for any suggestion that there is (or may be) a conflict between federal law and state law. Here are some particular things to check for:

- **Categorize the problem:** The most important thing is to ***categorize*** the problem accurately. Decide which of the following 3 categories the facts belong to:
  - Category **1**: A ***conflict*** between state law (whether embodied in a statute, court rule or judge-made, i.e., common, law) and a federal policy ***not embodied in the FRCP***. In this instance, ***use Erie analysis***: If the state law is basically ***substantive***, *Erie* dictates that the state law must be followed. If the state law is basically ***procedural***, balance the strength of the state and federal policies (considering outcome-determinativeness and the likelihood of forum-shopping as factors).
  - Category **2**: A ***direct conflict*** between state law (statute, court rule or judge-made law) and a federal policy ***embodied in a Federal Rule***. Here, under the Supremacy Clause, the ***Federal Rule must be followed*** no matter how "substantive" the state law is (and no matter how outcome-determinative the issue is), and *Erie* principles ***never come into play***. (This assumes, of course, that the Federal Rule is valid, which every FRCP has always been found to be, and which you should assume to be the case in your answer.) If you find that the fact pattern fits into this "direct conflict" category, you should cite to *Hanna v. Plumer* and *Shady Grove Orthopedic*.

    Example 1: P sues D in a State X state court for $700 in property damage to

P's car arising out of a car collision with D. D files an answer that denies negligence and alleges contributory negligence of P, but that makes no counterclaim. State X does not make any counterclaims compulsory ones. A default judgment for $700 is entered against D when he refuses to comply with a discovery order. D does not appeal the judgment. Then P sues D in federal district court in State X for $78,000 in personal injuries suffered from the accident. D files an answer denying negligence, and counterclaims for his own personal injuries resulting from the accident.

Under the FRCP, D's counterclaim would be considered compulsory (because it arose out of the same transaction or occurrence as the main claim), and would therefore be deemed forfeited because it was not asserted in the first action. Since the FRCP are directly on point, *Hanna v. Plumer* says that the federal rule (counterclaim was compulsory and was lost if not asserted in first action) must prevail over the countervailing state rule, no matter how outcome-determinative the state's choice of rule might be and no matter how strong the state policy is in favor of not making any counterclaims compulsory.

Example 2: P, an individual, brings a diversity suit against D, the manufacturer of a machine that P says D manufactured negligently. The accident occurred in State Red, and the action is pending in State Red federal court. P's complaint does not assert that P was free from contributory negligence. D makes no affirmative defenses. At trial, D tries to introduce evidence of contributory negligence by P. P objects, correctly pointing out that under FRCP 8(c) contributory negligence is an affirmative defense that must therefore be pleaded by D. D asserts (also correctly) that under State Red law, absence of contributory negligence must be pleaded by the plaintiff.

Because there is a direct conflict between an applicable federal rule provision (requiring D to plead) and the state-law provision (requiring P to plead), the federal rule applies. Therefore, D was required to plead contributory negligence. (On the other hand, if the issue was who should bear the *burden of persuasion* on the issue of contributory negligence, that's an issue on which the FRCP are silent, so the court would conduct a Category 1 traditional *Erie* analysis. The court would then probably apply state law, on the grounds that the choice of burden of persuasion is heavily outcome-determinative and does not implicate any strong federal interest.)

☞ Category **3**: An ***overlap*** (i.e., coverage of the same subject area), but ***not direct conflict***, between state law (statute, court rule or judge-made law) and a Federal Rule. Here, if the state policy can be followed without violating the federal statute/rule, ***follow the state policy***.

☛ **What gets tested:** Most exam questions involve Categories 2 and 3 above, not 1. That is, the professor wants to see that you can recognize that ***not every federal-***

state choice-of-law problem involves Erie. So anytime the federal law that governs the precise issue before you is spelled out by a Federal Rule, be sure *not* to use *Erie*. And before you select Category 1 (true *Erie*), be sure that the point in question really *is* one on which the FRCP are silent.

Balancing the state and federal interests

- **Handling true *Erie* problems:** If you have what you decide is a true *Erie* (Category 1) problem, ***balance*** between the state and federal interests by giving heavy weight to:
  - whether the choice of which policy to follow is heavily ***outcome-determinative***. (If so, lean towards choosing the state rule).
  - whether using the federal policy is likely to induce the plaintiff to ***forum-shop,*** i.e., to choose between state and federal court based on whose law is more favorable to her. (If so, lean towards choosing the state rule).
  - whether using the state rule is likely to ***thwart an important federal policy*** governing the procedures to be used in federal trials. (If so, lean towards choosing the federal rule).

Illustrative *Erie* problems

- Some of the common situations in diversity-only suits that *are* true *Erie* problems are:
  - whether to follow the state ***statute of limitations*** where there is no applicable Congressionally-enacted S/L. (*Yes*, because the choice of S/L is heavily outcome-determinative, and important federal procedural policies aren't implicated)
  - whether to follow the state ***conflict-of-law***s provision (*yes*, for the same reason)
  - whether to follow the state allocation of the ***burden of proof*** (*yes*)

    Example: See the parenthetical remark at the end of Example 2 under Category 2, *supra*, pp. 183-183.
  - whether to follow a state ***cap on damages*** for the type of claim in question (*yes*)
  - whether to follow the state rules allocating issues between ***judge and jury*** (*no*, because this is not heavily outcome-determinative, and will not induce forum shopping)
  - **What highest state court would do:** If you do decide that *Erie* applies, remember that the issue is ***what the state's highest court would do now*** if it heard the issue fresh.

- **Old precedent:** Thus the fact that there is a precedent on the books from ***some time ago*** does not bind the federal court, if it thinks that the state's highest court would overrule that precedent ***today***.

- **Not federal court's own judgment:** Also, remember that the federal court's sole job is to rule the way it thinks the state's highest court would rule — the federal court is ***not entitled to apply its own judgment about what state law is.*** Be especially on the lookout for cases requiring the federal court to construe a ***state statute*** — these statutory-construction scenarios can obscure the reality that what matters is what the state high court thinks the statute means, not what the federal court thinks it means.

  - **Certification to state court:** Where the federal district court is ***uncertain*** about how the highest state court would decide an unresolved issue of state law, remember that a procedure called ***"certification"*** lets the federal court simply ***ask that state court to explain*** how it would decide that issue. Virtually all states now allow their highest court to respond to a certification request from a federal court.

Exam Tips on TRIAL PROCEDURE

Trial procedure generally

Trial Procedure covers a welter of disparate issues. The professor will often be able to hide the issues from you by having the litigants state their requests and objectives cursorily and without much reasoning (e.g., "D moves for summary judgment"). Because you have to figure out what the reasoning could have been, issue-spotting can be unusually difficult in the trial context.

- **Burdens of production and persuasion:** Keep in mind the distinction between the burden of ***"production"*** and the burden of ***"persuasion,"*** — don't use the ambiguous phrase "burden of proof."

  - **Presumptions:** If the facts involve a ***presumption***, remember these rules: the party against whom the presumption is directed bears the burden of ***production*** (if he produces no evidence to rebut the presumption, he suffers a directed verdict or judgment as a matter of law). But in the federal system and most states, the presumption has no effect on the burden of ***persuasion*** — once the production burden is met, the presumption disappears (***"bursting bubble"***). This is the most frequently-tested aspect of burden of proof / presumptions.

- ☛ **Summary judgment:** Where a party moves for ***summary judgment*** (s.j.), remember the applicable standard: the movant wins only if there is ***no "genuine dispute of material fact."*** Typically, the facts will ***not satisfy*** this requirement, and you should conclude that s.j. is not appropriate. For instance, often there will be a genuine dispute of material fact remaining either because:

  - ❑ there is a dispositive issue as to which you may feel that one party is highly likely to prevail at trial, but the issue still turns on the ***credibility*** of the witnesses, or

  - ❑ there are ***multiple*** sub-issues (one of which may be non-obvious), and although there's no genuine factual question as to some part(s), there *is* an issue as to one (probably a non-obvious) part.

    Example: A truck owned by C Corp., while driven by E (C's employee), strikes and injures P. P sues C and deposes E. E testifies that P was crossing with the light at the pedestrian crosswalk, and that E ran into P because the truck's brakes failed. P moves for summary judgment.

    The motion should be denied, because the fact the brakes failed does not in itself prove C's negligence (sometimes such failures just happen without negligence). Also, even if there was further evidence in E's deposition that the truck had not been properly maintained by C, there still remains the issue of whether E was acting within the scope of his employment.

- ☛ **Appeal; the clearly-erroneous standard:** If the case is ***tried to a judge***, and is then ***appealed***, be careful to distinguish between fact-based arguments for reversal and law-based ones. Remember that on appeal, the court is extremely ***limited*** in its ability to reverse for ***fact-finding*** errors: "Findings of fact, whether based on oral or other evidence, must not be set aside unless ***clearly erroneous***, and the reviewing court must give due regard to the trial court's opportunity to judge the witnesses' ***credibility***." FRCP 52(a)(6). Normally you should conclude that the appeals court can't reverse for fact-finding error, since the prof. probably can't make a fact-finding error seem egregious in a brief question without tipping off the "clearly erroneous" issue.

- ☛ **Unanimity of jury:** When the case is tried to a jury, be on the lookout for non-unanimity. In the federal system, the verdict must be ***unanimous*** unless the parties stipulate otherwise (and in the typical fact-pattern, they don't so stipulate).

<u>Judgment as a matter of law or JNOV</u>

- ☛ **Two things to remember:** If a party moves for ***judgment as a matter of law*** (in the federal system) or directed verdict / JNOV (some states), two points are most vital to remember:

  - ☞ **Reasonable-jury standard:** The standard is essentially ***whether reasonable***

jurors could differ as to the result — if they could, the court shouldn't grant JML/directed verdict/JNOV. So don't be too quick to agree that the judge was right to grant a JML or equivalent. For instance, if the case turns on credibility of witnesses, JML will almost never be appropriate.

Example: A contract for the sale of land provides for a purchase price of $85,000. The buyer, B, does not make payment and sues for reformation of the contract to reflect the alleged agreed-upon price of $37,500, claiming that a typographical error was made. The seller, S, files an answer asserting that the written contract accurately states the agreed-upon price. At a jury trial, an appraiser testifies on behalf of B that, at the time of the signing of the contract, the land was worth, at the most, $42,200. S testifies (unconvincingly in the judge's opinion) that the agreed price was $85,000. The jury renders a verdict for S. B moves for Judgment as a Matter of Law. The court grants the motion, and enters judgment for B.

The court's ruling is erroneous. It's not enough that the judge thought the jury reached the wrong factual conclusion about what happened. It's simply not the case that *no reasonable jury could have found* for S. For instance, a reasonable jury could have discounted the testimony of the expert witness testimony and instead could have found S's testimony to be more credible. Similarly, a reasonable jury could have accepted the expert's appraisal as true, but could still have believed that B agreed to a bad deal because of poor business judgment.

☞ **Time for motion:** The motion (whatever it's called) must be made ***before the jury retires***, at least under the FRCP. Profs. frequently have the jury retire without either party's making a directed verdict motion, then have the verdict loser move for JML — it's too late by then. See FRCP 50(a)(2); 50(b). This "must move for JML before case goes to jury" is the single most frequently-tested aspect of JNOV/JML practice.

Example: P brings an employment discrimination action against his former employer, D, alleging racial discrimination. The suit is brought in federal court. After both sides have presented their evidence, D believes that P has not made an evidentiary showing that would enable a reasonable jury to find that D discriminated against P on the basis of race. Before the case goes to the jury, D should make a "motion for judgment as a matter of law," pursuant to FRCP 50(a).

If D fails to make the judgment-as-a-matter-of-law motion ***before the case goes to the jury,*** then the judge is ***not authorized*** to grant the judgment as a matter of law. See FRCP 50(b). (That's so because it gives P an opportunity to cure any deficiency in P's proof that P may have overlooked.)

Juror misconduct

- ☛ **No impeachment of own verdict:** Professors frequently test on ***juror misconduct***. The most important rule to remember is that generally, "the jury ***may not impeach its own verdict***." That is, the verdict won't be set aside because of a juror's testimony about his own or another juror's misconduct — only evidence from a ***third party*** will suffice.
  - ☞ **Exception:** But under the FRCP, there is a limited ***exception*** — a juror may testify about whether ***extraneous prejudicial information*** was brought to the jury's attention, or whether any ***outside influence*** was improperly brought to bear. But a juror can't testify about how the jury conducted its deliberations, so that testimony that, say, the jurors ignored the judge's instructions will still not be allowed under the FRCP.

New-trial motions

- ☛ **New-trial grounds:** Fact patterns often involve a party's efforts to obtain a ***new trial***, either from the trial judge or on appeal. Some of the reasons for which the court (either the trial judge or the appellate court) can grant a new trial are:
  - ☞ Improper conduct by a ***party***, ***witness*** or ***counsel***
  - ☞ ***Jury*** misconduct (see above)
  - ☞ ***Judicial error*** (e.g., the judge charges the jury incorrectly)
  - ☞ ***Verdict against the weight of the evidence***. (In the federal system, the verdict must be against the "***clear*** weight" of the evidence, but a new trial can be granted even if there is substantial evidence supporting the verdict, which would be enough to prevent the issuance of Judgment as a Matter of Law.)
  - ☞ Verdict ***excessive*** or ***inadequate***
  - ☞ ***Note:*** Remember that to be grounds for a new trial, the error must "affect [some] party's substantial rights." FRCP 61. This is the ***"harmless error"*** doctrine. Whenever your fact pattern suggests to you that one of the above grounds for new trial exists, be sure to mention the possibility that the error might be "harmless" unless it's clear that it's not.
- ☛ **Remittitur and additur:** Instead of a new trial, state courts usually allow the judge to order a ***remittitur*** (new trial to occur unless the victorious plaintiff accepts a lower amount specified by the judge) or ***additur*** (new trial to occur unless the defendant agrees to pay a higher amount). But in federal trials, only remittitur is allowed — ***additur has been held to violate the constitutional right to jury trial.*** This last point is frequently tested.

  Example: In a federal personal injury case based on diversity, the jury awards the P $85,000. P moves for a new trial solely on the issue of damages. The judge orders the motion granted unless D consents to an increase in the judgment. This order is *prohibited* by the Seventh Amendment. [*Dimick v. Schiedt*] The trial court could grant a new trial solely on the issue of damages, but may not condition her new-trial order on D's agreement to an increased verdict.

Right to jury trial

- ☛ **Constitutional issue:** Many essay questions involve the ***constitutional right to jury trial***. Here are the most important (and frequently-tested) points:
  - ☞ **Federal vs. state trials:** The 7th Amendment (right to jury trial in civil cases) applies only to ***federal***, not state, trials.
  - ☞ **Legal vs. equitable:** The 7th Amendment applies only to ***"legal,"*** not ***"equitable,"*** issues.
    - ☛ **Equitable actions:** Therefore, you must be on the lookout for claims or defenses that are equitable in nature, so you can point out that there's no right to jury trial on these. Thus attempts to procure an ***injunction***, to ***rescind*** a contract, to receive an ***accounting***, to get an order of ***specific performance***, or to ***reform*** a contract for ***mistake***, would all be claims for which there is no right to jury trial.
    - ☛ **Legal actions:** A suit for ***money damages*** will almost always be ***"legal."*** The one exception is where the suit seeks money as ***restitution*** for a benefit unjustly held by the defendant (e.g., suit against an employer for back-pay which P says he would have earned had the employer not discriminated).
  - ☞ **Legal and equitable both present:** If a case contains ***both*** legal and equitable claims, and there is an issue of fact common to both, the court must usually allow the ***legal claims to be tried first*** (to the jury). This is the single most frequently-tested aspect of right-to-jury-trial. You should cite to *Beacon Theatres v. Westover* if this "which claims to try first" issue arises.
  - ☞ **Parties' labels not dispositive:** Also, remember that the ***labels*** used by the parties to describe the relief they seek are ***not dispositive*** — the court will look beneath the labels to determine whether the relief being sought is really equitable or really legal.
- ☛ **Final judgment rule for appeals:** If the exam facts involve a suit that is being ***appealed***, make sure that any applicable ***final judgment*** rule was obeyed. So in *federal* litigation, for instance, if at the time of the loser's appeal the ***entire case*** hadn't yet been resolved at the trial level, the court of appeals ***won't have jurisdiction*** unless some exception to the final judgment rule (e.g., the ***"collateral order"*** doctrine) applies.

  Example: If the judge in a federal suit gives partial summary judgment to P on liability but hasn't decided the damages so far, D can't yet appeal.

Exam Tips on MULTI-PARTY AND MULTI-CLAIM LITIGATION

Multi-party/Multi-claim suits generally

This area is a welter of individual procedural devices, and is usually tested from a federal perspective. The one overarching principle is that you must always worry about subject-matter jurisdiction and personal jurisdiction; remember that the need for the former will often be eliminated by supplemental jurisdiction. Be sure to consult the Flowchart on Supplemental Jurisdiction, Figure 3-2, *supra*. Here are some particular things to watch for:

Counterclaims

- **Permissive vs. compulsory:** If the facts involve a ***counterclaim*** ("cc"), be sure to distinguish between permissive cc's and compulsory ones. Remember that a compulsory cc is one that arises out of the ***same "transaction or occurrence"*** that is the subject matter of the opposing party's claim. Rule 13(a)(1).
  - **Consequence:** The need to distinguish between the two types of cc arises most often because you have to decide whether a claim that could have been asserted as a cc in an earlier action is now barred. Remember that a litigant ***loses*** an unasserted compulsory cc but not an unasserted permissive cc.

    Example: P and D make a contract. P sues D in diversity, claiming that D breached. D believes that not only did he not breach, but that P breached.

    D ***must assert*** his claim that P breached as a compulsory counterclaim, since it arose from the same "transaction or occurrence" as P's claim (the performance of the contract). If D doesn't make the counterclaim, he won't be able to assert P's breach in a separate diversity suit.

  - **Supplemental jurisdiction:** Remember that a ***compulsory*** cc falls within ***supplemental jurisdiction*** ("SJ"). Therefore, it does not need to independently involve $75,000. Furthermore, SJ means that D can bring in additional parties to the compulsory cc with whom D is not diverse. But there probably is ***not*** SJ for ***permissive*** cc's, so these must meet the amount-in-controversy and complete-diversity requirements.

Joinder of claims

☛ **Joinder of claims:** ***Joinder of claims*** raises few testable issues. Just remember that once P has a valid claim against a particular D, he can add as many additional claims as he wishes against that D. These do not have to independently meet the amount in controversy requirement (since "aggregation" of all claims by one P against one D is allowed).

Joinder of parties

☛ **Joinder of parties:** For ***joinder of parties,*** here are the most testable issues:

- ☞ **2 tests:** For both plaintiff-joinder and defendant-joinder, you'll need to know the two requirements imposed by FRCP 20(a):

  [1] the claims must arise from the same ***"transaction, occurrence,*** or series of transactions or occurrences"; and

  [2] there must be a ***question*** of ***law or fact common*** to ***all*** Ps or ***all*** Ds.

- ☞ **Subject-matter and personal jurisdiction:** Remember that the requirements of ***subject matter*** and ***personal jurisdiction*** must be met as to ***each D.*** So check that:

  - ❑ each D was properly served;
  - ❑ each D has minimum contacts with the forum state; and
  - ❑ no D is a citizen of the same state as any P (if it's a diversity case).

    - ☞ **Supplemental jurisdiction:** However, keep in mind that ***supplemental jurisdiction*** is available in a multi-plaintiff diversity scenario for purposes of the ***amount in controversy*** requirement. So if one P has more than $75,000 at stake against a given D, other Ps whose claims against that same D are each for less than $75,000 may "piggyback." (Cite to *Exxon Mobil v. Allapattah* on this point.)

- ☞ **"Necessary" vs. "Indispensable" parties:** ***Compulsory*** joinder is often tested. Distinguish between "necessary" parties and "indispensable" ones.

  - ❑ A party who is ***"necessary"*** (the "weaker" case for joinder) must be joined if jurisdictionally possible, but the action may go on without him if there are jurisdiction problems.

  - ❑ A party who is ***"indispensable"*** (the stronger case for joinder) not only must be joined if jurisdictionally possible, but the action must be dismissed if she cannot be joined.

  ☛ **Tests for each:** Consult the text of FRCP 19 for detailed analysis of the standards for these two classifications. Here's a brief, approximate, recap of the rules for each:

- ❑ A party is ***necessary*** if (1) in the person's absence, ***complete relief cannot be accorded*** among those already parties; or (2) trying the case without the absentee will either ***impair the absentee's interest*** or leave one of the people already parties subject to ***multiple or inconsistent obligations.***

- ❑ For a finding of ***indispensability***, the key factors are the degree of ***prejudice to the absentee*** from proceeding without him, and the ***adequacy of P's remedies*** (e.g., state court ones) if the federal action is dismissed.

☛ **No supplemental jurisdiction:** Where there's a "necessary" or "indispensable" party (as with any other type of multi-defendant joinder), ***supplemental jurisdiction does not apply***, so ordinary requirements of subject-matter jurisdiction apply.

Example: Dan (a citizen of State X) makes a forced landing of his small airplane on a highway at night and hits a truck and its driver, Pound (a citizen of State Y), causing personal injury to Pound and property damage to the truck. The truck is owned by Trucko Corp., a citizen only of State X. The truck's headlights were not on at the time of the accident (as required by state statute), and Dan did not see the truck. Pound brings a diversity action against Dan in State Z federal court. Dan files a motion claiming that Trucko Corp. should be joined as a co-defendant because it is indispensable to the full resolution of the dispute.

If the court agrees that Trucko is either a *necessary* or an *indispensable* party, its joinder as a co-defendant would destroy diversity, since Dan and Trucko are both citizens of X. There is no supplemental jurisdiction over claims by the original plaintiff against persons joined as co-defendants. And if Trucko Corp's is held to be "indispensable," the lack of diversity will mean that the action must be dismissed for lack of subject-matter jurisdiction.

☛ **Align the parties properly:** When you analyze a case of possible indispensability, make sure you ***align the parties*** (especially the absent party) ***according to their real interests.*** For instance, in the above example, Trucko should be classified as a co-defendant, since Pound is alleging that Trucko was negligent towards Pound.

Class actions

☛ **Class actions generally:** Here's what to look for if your fact pattern involves a ***class action***:

☞ **Hidden issue:** Sometimes the whole idea of a class action will be hidden. Anytime you see multiple (at least 15) people with similar "injuries," you should consider whether they might bring a plaintiff class action.

☞ **Amount in controversy:** The ***amount in controversy*** for a diversity class action is one of the most frequently-tested issues in all of Civil Procedure.

- **Supplemental jurisdiction:** If at least one named class member has a claim exceeding $75,000, but other class members (named or unnamed) don't, ***supplemental jurisdiction*** will apply to take care of amount in controversy for these less-than-$75,000 claimants. (Cite to *Exxon Mobil v. Allapattah.*)

- **Nature of showing:** A sub-issue is often what kind of a showing each P must make to satisfy the $75,000 requirement. Remember that as long as it's not a "legal certainty" that some P can't meet the requirement, the requirement will be deemed met. This essentially means that if each P has suffered some sort of ***physical injuries***, the amount requirement will usually be deemed satisfied. Another sub-issue is whether the possibility of ***punitive*** damages may be considered — the answer is unclear, but probably little weight should be given to this possibility.

☞ **Numerosity & fair representation:** ***"Numerosity"*** and ***"fair representation"*** are frequently-tested elements. If there are more than 25 claimants, "numerosity" is probably satisfied, and if less than 15, it's probably not. To decide "fair representation," look to how much the named Ps have in common with the unnamed Ps.

☞ **b(3) actions:** The majority of the time, if there is to be a class action, it will be a ***b(3)*** action, not a b(1) or b(2) action. In the garden-variety situation of multiple claimants seeking money damages from a solvent defendant, the action will proceed under b(3) or not at all.

- **Requirements for b(3):** For a b(3) action, make sure that (1) ***common issues*** of law or fact ***predominate***; and (2) the class action is ***superior*** to other methods (e.g., individual actions). Thus if there are important issues on which each P varies (e.g., each claimant has a unique set of physical injuries), the class action is probably not superior.

- **Mass torts:** You'll often have a ***mass tort*** fact pattern (e.g., an airplane crash or a toxic gas leak/explosion). Here, know that courts often ***refuse*** to allow b(3) class actions (and to require individual actions instead) because of causation issues and the variety of damages suffered. Cite to *Amchem* on this point.

  Example: For one hour on each of three successive days, a nuclear power plant emits heavy radiation over the surrounding area, which has a population of 10,000. A few people injured by radiation emitted on the third day bring a federal class action diversity suit on behalf of all those injured on any of the three days.

If the emissions on all three days were from the same source, then the question of liability would be common to the class. On the other hand, ***damages*** would probably ***vary materially*** from person to person, and this variance might be held by the court to "predominate" over the issue of liability. If so, the suit cannot be a b(3) action. Nor is it clear that the class action is "superior to other methods," such as separate actions because of this varying-damages problem, so that fact alone would rule out proceeding as a class action.

☞ **Notice:** Remember that absent class members must always be given ***notice*** of the action's existence (individual notice, where possible, as least in b(3) actions), and that this notice must be paid for by the named plaintiffs. Cite to *Eisen v. Carlisle* on this point.

☞ **Who is bound:** Class actions questions often require you to say who is ***bound*** by the judgment. In the usual b(3) action, each class member must be given a chance to ***opt out***; if she does so, she's not bound by an adverse judgment or settlement (and can bring her own suit), but conversely, she doesn't get any benefit (including collateral estoppel) from any favorable judgment. ***One who doesn't opt out (even if she never got notice) is bound by the judgment.***

- There's no right to opt out in b(1) or b(2) actions.

☞ **Certification:** Before a c.a. can go to trial, it must be "certified" as a c.a. by the court — i.e., the court declares that the requirements for a c.a. have been satisfied.

- **Sub-class:** If on particular facts you conclude that the entire proposed class does not satisfy the requirements (e.g., the named Ps' claims aren't typical, or the named Ps can't fairly represent everyone), consider the possibility that the court could certify a ***sub-class*** (just one group of Ps), which could go forward.

☞ **Settlements:** Remember that any proposed ***settlement*** must be approved by the court, and, if the action has been certified, ***notice*** of the proposed settlement must be given to absent class members, at least for b(3) actions.

- If the case is proposed to be settled ***before certification*** (a ***"settlement only"*** class action), then: (1) notice must nonetheless be given to all persons proposed to be bound by the settlement; and (2) the action must meet all of the requirements for a b(3) action, even though it hasn't already been certified as a b(3) action.

Intervention

☛ **Intervention generally:** For ***intervention***, here are the key points:

☞ **Hidden issue:** Sometimes the intervention issue is hidden. Look for a fact pattern in which persons who are not parties might be affected by the outcome, and you're asked how they can protect their interests. For instance, questions sometimes involve a non-party who might someday face a similar lawsuit, and would like to help prevent an adverse precedent that would pose *stare decisis* problems. (See "Avoidance of unfavorable precedent," below.)

☞ **Permissive vs. of-right:** Always distinguish between ***permissive*** intervention (FRCP 24(b)) and intervention of ***right*** (24(a)). Of-right requires much tighter ties to the subject matter of the litigation, among other things.

☛ **Consequence:** The main consequence of the distinction is that a trial court's denial of permissive intervention is almost never ***reversed on appeal***, but a denial of intervention of right will often be reversed.

☛ **Avoidance of unfavorable precedent:** The intervenors sometimes want to intervene in order to help ***avoid*** a ***negative precedent*** that would have some ***stare decisis effect*** on them in other litigations. When this happens, the court is very unlikely to find that the case qualifies for intervention of right, but might well allow permissive intervention if this would not make the trial unwieldy.

Example: In response to the shout of "Stop thief!" Otto, a police officer working for the Ames, Texas Police Dept. (APD), tackles and applies a chokehold to Pete as he leaves a store, seriously injuring Pete. Pete sues Otto and the APD, for $85,000 for violation of a federal civil rights statute. The APD contends that it cannot be vicariously liable for Otto's actions unless it authorized the chokehold. Numerous police departments around the country request to intervene because of a concern that if the claim is successful, similar claims will be made against them. Pete opposes this intervention.

Pete can point out that collateral estoppel certainly wouldn't apply in a later suit brought by a different plaintiff against a police department that was not present in the Pete-APD action. He can also point out that even the *stare decisis* effect of, say, a district court decision against the APD would have only very weak effect outside the district where the action is pending. Finally, Pete can argue that there is no reason to believe that the APD would not adequately assert the pro-police-department position. So the requirements for intervention of right (absentee has an interest that may be impaired, coupled with inadequate representation of that interest by the present party) apply weakly if at all. Pete will probably win on these arguments, and defeat intervention of right.

On the other hand, the absentee departments' interest in avoiding a bad *stare decisis* effect, and the contribution these departments might make to litigating an issue of great public concern, might well be enough to induce the trial court to grant permissive intervention if such intervention wouldn't make conducting the trial cumbersome. But if the court declined to allow permissive intervention, the decision wouldn't be reversible on appeal.

☞ **No supplemental jurisdiction:** Remember that the usual requirements of ***subject-matter jurisdiction*** apply to both types of intervention, i.e., there's ***no supplemental jurisdiction.*** Be alert to diversity situations where the would-be intervenor is a citizen of the same state as an opposing party — intervention can't occur no matter how heavily implicated the intervenor's interests are. (Also, in this situation, consider whether the would-be intervenor is an "indispensable" party in whose absence the action must be dismissed.)

<u>**Interpleader**</u>

☛ **Interpleader generally:** Here's what to watch for concerning ***interpleader***:

☞ **Hidden issues:** Interpleader issues are often hidden. Look for someone in possession of a ***"stake,"*** where the stakeholder doesn't know ***which of two people is entitled*** to that stake. Examples: banks that hold bank accounts, insurance companies that hold policy proceeds, contest sponsors that hold prizes, estates that hold assets. Typically, it will be up to you to notice that the stakeholder faces the possibility of double/inconsistent adjudications, and up to you to say that the stakeholder should interplead the competing claimants.

☞ **Statutory vs. rule interpleader:** If you decide that the stakeholder should use interpleader, always specify whether he should use statutory interpleader or FRCP Rule 22 interpleader. Here are the main differences:

☛ **Jurisdiction:** Statutory interpleader (s.i.) affects ***personal jurisdiction*** and ***subject-matter jurisdiction***; Rule interpleader (r.i.) does not. So nationwide service of process in allowed for s.i. (but not for r.i.). Similarly, diversity is satisfied for s.i. as long as some two claimants are citizens of different states (whereas for r.i. the stakeholder may not be a citizen of the same state as any claimant). And the amount in controversy has to be merely $500 for s.i. (compared with the usual $75,000 for r.i.)

☛ **Deposit of property:** On the other hand, the stakeholder has to deposit the property in court (or post a bond) to use s.i., but does not for r.i.

Impleader

☛ **Impleader generally:** ***Impleader*** (third-party practice) issues are very common. Here's what to look for:

☞ **Hidden issues:** Impleader issues are sometimes hidden. Look for any situation in which an existing party may want to say, in effect, "If I'm liable to so-and-so, then you're liable to me in whole or in part for anything I have to pay to so-and-so." In general, you're looking for claims of ***"indemnity"*** (whole reimbursement) and ***"contribution"*** (partial reimbursement). This means that you should think "impleader" in these types of situations (D is the original defendant, and X is a person not yet a party, who D should consider impleading):

❑ **Insurance:** D is accused of a tort, and X is D's ***insurer***. (X has agreed by contract to indemnify D.)

❑ **Seller of defective component:** P is a tort victim, D made the ***product*** that injured P, and X made a ***component*** of that product

Example: P is killed when an aircraft made by D, and whose engine was made by X, crashes. P sues only D. If P claims that the engine was defective, D may implead X on an indemnity theory.

❑ **Upstream seller of defective product:** P is a tort victim injured by a product, D sold it to P, and X is ***"upstream" in the chain of sale.*** P sues only D, on an implied warranty theory.

Example: P sues D, the retailer of a defective product, for breach of the implied warranty of merchantability. D may implead X, the manufacturer or wholesaler, for indemnity.

❑ **Joint tortfeasors:** P is a tort victim, D and X were ***separately-acting tortfeasors*** who have potentially joint-and-several liability and P has chosen to sue only D, not X. D has a common-law right of contribution from X in this situation, and so may implead her.

Example: P is a patient injured while in D, a hospital, and while under the care of X, a doctor not employed by the hospital. P sues only D. D may implead X for indemnity.

☞ **No blame-shifting:** The third-party plaintiff, or TPP (D in the above examples) may ***not*** claim that the third-party defendant, or TPD (X above) is the ***only one*** liable to P. The TPD's liability must be "derivative" of the TPP's liability. (On the other hand, TPP doesn't have to prove at the outset that TPD definitely or even probably has derivative liability; it's enough that TPD "may be" liable to TPP if TPP is liable to P.)

☞ **Jurisdiction:** When impleader claims are part of the fact pattern, be hyper-alert to ***personal and subject-matter jurisdiction*** issues, which are very frequently present. You'll typically see a TPP and TPD who are both citizens of the same state, for instance. Remember that both types of jurisdictional requirements are relaxed in impleader cases:

- ☛ **Supplemental jurisdiction:** Most important, impleader claims come within the court's s***upplemental jurisdiction***. This means that TPP and TPD ***don't have to be diverse*** to each other (and TPD doesn't have to be diverse to P), and TPP's claim against TPD doesn't have to be worth $75,000. (The third-party claim can be a ***partial*** claim, such as a claim for contribution, so this amount-in-controversy relaxation can be important.)

  Example: Paul, a citizen of State X, brings a diversity action against Dave, a citizen of State Y, alleging that Dave drove his car negligently and thereby injured Paul, a pedestrian. Dave serves a third-party complaint against Insco, a State Y insurance company, claiming that Insco is his car insurer and therefore owes him the duty of defending him and paying any resulting judgment up to the policy limits. Dave is entitled to implead Insco, and the fact that Dave and Insco are both citizens of State Y won't matter, since supplemental jurisdiction applies.

- ☛ **100-mile bulge:** Also, ***personal jurisdiction*** can be relaxed because service of the third-party complaint can occur anywhere within a ***100-mile bulge*** of the federal courthouse, even if TPD has no contacts with the state where the federal court sits. (Therefore, be on the lookout for service on TPD that takes place in a city close to the courthouse but in another state; the facts will often state the distance between courthouse and point of service, which should tip you to the presence of a "bulge" issue.)

  - ☞ **Venue:** You don't have to worry about ***venue*** for the third-party complaint.

☞ **Additional claim involving TPD:** Remember that once a party has been impleaded, there can be additional claims involving the TPD (e.g., TPD against P, P against TPD, TPD against TPP, etc.). Generally, ***supplemental jurisdiction will apply*** to these, ***except*** for: (1) P's claim vs. TPD; and (2) TPD's permissive counterclaims against TPP or against P.

Cross claims

- ☛ **Cross claims generally:** Where two people are ***already*** parties, and are on the ***same side*** (both Ps or both Ds), one may make a ***cross-claim*** against the other. Things to remember:

  - ☞ **Same transaction:** The cross-claim must arise out of the ***same "transaction or occurrence"*** as the original action.

  - ☞ **Never compulsory:** A cross-claim is ***never compulsory*** (i.e., it's not lost if not asserted in the present action).

Example: Owner is driving, and Rider is a passenger in, Owner's car when it collides with a truck driven by Trucker. Both vehicles (and Rider's person) are damaged. Rider sues Owner and Trucker in State X state court. (State X has enacted the FRCP). At this point, Trucker would be entitled to cross-claim against Owner for Trucker's own damages (since his claim arises out of the same occurrence — the crash — as Rider's claim against Owner and Trucker). But suppose that Trucker doesn't make the cross claim. The suit is decided in the defendants' favor. Trucker then sues Owner in a new State X proceeding.

Trucker's claim may go forward — although Trucker could have cross-claimed against Owner in the first suit, he wasn't required to do so, so he doesn't lose the right to bring a new suit against Owner now.

☞ **Supplemental jurisdiction:** Cross-claims come within ***supplemental*** jurisdiction. So D1 doesn't need to be diverse with D2 to cross-claim against him.

Exam Tips on *FORMER ADJUDICATION*

Former adjudication generally

You will almost always know when you have a Former Adjudication problem, because the fact pattern will have to clue you in to the existence of two suits, one of which has already resulted in a judgment. The trick, of course, is to determine what effect the first judgment should have on the second suit.

☛ **Merger/bar vs. collateral estoppel:** Make sure to distinguish between ***claim preclusion*** (sometimes called by the ambiguous phrase "res judicata," which you should avoid unless your professor uses it, or by the preferable terms ***"merger"*** and ***"bar"***) and ***issue preclusion*** (usually called ***"collateral estoppel,"*** which is the preferable phrase to use on exams.)

☞ **Claim preclusion (merger/bar):** Where the first suit was between the ***same parties*** (or their privies) as the second suit, and involved the same ***"claim,"*** you're interested in ***claim preclusion***. If you find that the requirements for claim preclusion have been met, the case is over — the claim in the second suit is ***"merged"*** into the earlier judgment (if P in the second suit won the first suit), and it's ***"barred"*** by the earlier judgment (if P in the second suit lost the first suit).

☞ **Collateral estoppel:** Where the second suit involves at least one ***different***

party than the first suit, *or* where you conclude that the second suit involves a ***different "claim"*** than the first suit, then you're interested in issue preclusion / ***collateral estoppel*** (c.e.) If c.e. applies, it resolves a ***particular issue***, but not necessarily the whole claim.

☞ **Discuss both:** Often, you'll want to examine the possibility of claim preclusion first, then go on to issue preclusion / c.e. if the requirements for claim preclusion aren't satisfied.

Claim preclusion

☛ **Claim preclusion generally:** For ***claim preclusion***, here are the major sub-issues:

☞ **Claim splitting:** One tip-off for a claim-preclusion problem is ***"claim splitting."*** Typically, P has an accident, and sues in Suit 1 for ***property damage***, and then in Suit 2 sues the same defendant for ***personal injuries*** (or vice versa). In most states, this doesn't work — since both types of damages were suffered in the same incident, they're deemed to be a single "claim." If P won in the first suit, say his second claim is "merged" into the first; if P lost the first suit, say he's now "barred."

☞ **Compulsory counterclaim:** Another situation involving claim splitting is the compulsory counterclaim context. When D in Suit 1 fails to assert what is (under the applicable federal or state procedural rules) a compulsory counterclaim, then the mechanism by which D loses the right to bring the claim later is the doctrine of merger and bar.

☛ **Stranger to first action:** Many questions involve a person who was ***not a party*** to the first action, but is very closely related, somehow, to a person who was a party. Remember that as a general rule, someone who ***wasn't a party*** to the first suit ***can't be bound*** by the result.

☞ **No virtual representation:** And remember that at least in federal courts, there's ***no*** general doctrine of ***"virtual representation"*** by which P1 (plaintiff in the first suit) will be found to be so close to P2 (plaintiff in the second suit) that P2 will be bound because P1 "virtually represented" P2 in the first suit. So, for instance, the fact that P1 and P2 are friends, have a shared interest in the subject matter, and are represented by the same lawyer against the same defendant, won't be enough to make P2 be bound by the result in P1's suit if P2 wasn't a named party to it. (Cite to *Taylor v. Sturgell* on this point.)

☞ **Exceptions:** But there are a few ***exceptions*** to the "no binding of strangers" rule. For instance, occasionally two people will be so legally-intertwined (i.e., in ***"privity"*** with each other) that one person's presence in the first suit *will* bind the other, even though the latter wasn't a party. That's true where the two are indemnitor-and-indemnitee, or principal-and-agent.

Example: D1 is an ***employee*** charged with a tort, and D2 is D1's ***employer*** (liable for D1's torts under *respondeat superior*). Here, D1 and D2 are "in privity" (D2's liability derives from D1's), so D2 is bound if D1 loses the first suit. (But the converse probably does *not* involve privity — if the employer is sued first by P and loses, the collateral estoppel doctrine will probably not bind the employee in a later suit against him by P.)

☛ **Collateral estoppel generally:** For ***collateral estoppel*** (c.e.), here are the main things to look for:

☞ **Issues actually litigated and decided:** Remember that c.e. applies only to issues that were ***actually litigated and decided*** in the first suit. Anytime you see a fact pattern that involves two suits, look for an issue decided in the first suit that may be relevant to the second suit, and determine whether c.e. may apply to compel the second court to use the first court's finding on that issue.

☛ **Default judgments:** Because the issue must have been actually litigated and decided, if the first suit ended in a ***default judgment***, it has ***no*** c.e. effect on the absent defendant.

☛ **Necessary to outcome:** The issue must also have been ***necessary to the outcome*** of the first suit. So if the first suit would have come out the same way even if the issue had not been decided at all, or decided differently, then c.e. won't apply to that issue.

☞ **Who can be bound:** C.e. questions often involve "who can be ***bound***."

☛ **Stranger can never be bound:** A true ***stranger*** to the first action can ***never be bound*** by c.e., no matter how similar the fact issue, and even if the party who won in the first suit on the issue is now present in the second suit.

Example: Golfer swings a golf club manufactured by Birdie Corp. The head flies off, injuring Price and Pringle, who are standing nearby. Price sues Birdie in products liability, contending that the club was defectively manufactured. Birdie wins, with the jury concluding that the accident was caused by Golfer's misuse of the club, not by a defect. Pringle now sues Birdie on a similar theory.

Note that Pringle was a "stranger" to the first action. (He won't be deemed to be closely related enough to Price to have the court say that Price effectively represented Pringle's interests, which would have made them "privies," see next paragraph.) As a stranger, Pringle can't be bound by the finding of non-defectiveness in the prior action, even though it's exactly the same issue and was necessary to the first verdict.

☞ **Who can benefit:** C.e. questions also often involve "who can ***benefit***" from c.e. Of course, one who was a party to the first action can benefit from c.e. But the key issue — which seems to surface in most c.e. fact patterns —is whether a true ***stranger*** to the first action can benefit from factual findings made there. Here are the key sub-issues/rules:

- **No mutuality:** Nearly all courts today have ***abandoned*** the rule of ***mutuality***, i.e., the old blanket rule that a stranger to the first action could never benefit from c.e. So when your fact pattern involves a stranger trying to use c.e., you should preface your discussion with something like "Assuming that the jurisdiction follows the nearly universal approach of abandoning mutuality, X may be able to benefit from c.e. ..."

- **Offensive-defensive distinction:** Always distinguish between ***"offensive"*** and ***"defensive"*** use of c.e., and state which kind of use is proposed in your fact pattern. "Offensive" means use by a first-action-stranger who is the *plaintiff* in the second action; "defensive" means use by one who is a *defendant* in the second action. Remember that courts are ***more willing to allow "defensive" use*** (but they do sometimes allow offensive use as well).

- **Hanging back:** If the facts involve offensive c.e., check whether P in the second suit ***"hung back,"*** i.e., declined to join the first suit even though he had a good opportunity to do so. If so, P is less likely to be allowed to use c.e., on fairness and judicial-efficiency grounds.

  Example: Same basic facts as first example on previous page: Golfer swings a golf club manufactured by Birdie Corp. The head flies off, injuring Price and Pringle, who are standing nearby. Price sues Birdie in products liability, contending that the club was defectively manufactured. This time, however, Birdie *loses*, with the jury concluding that the accident was caused by a defect in the club. Pringle now sues Birdie on a similar theory.

  Pringle is a stranger to the first action who's trying to make *offensive* use of collateral estoppel, so his claim for using c.e. is relatively weak. Furthermore, Birdie can make a strong argument that Pringle "hung back" from the first action: he could have joined with Price, but instead waited so that he could get a second bite at the apple (if Price won, Pringle could try to use c.e.; if Birdie won, Pringle could say he was a stranger who can't be bound by the prior result). There's a good chance the court will buy this argument, in which case Pringle will have to relitigate the defectiveness issue.

☛ **Incentive to litigate:** Determine whether the person to be bound had an ***incentive to litigate*** the issue the first time. A key aspect is whether that person could reasonably have ***foreseen that the second suit would come along*** — the less foreseeable, the less incentive to litigate, and the less likely the second court is to allow c.e.

Example: The SEC sues D Corp. for putting false representations in D's prospectus for an IPO. D vigorously litigates the suit, and loses; the SEC gets a fine and an injunction against further violations. Now, P, a shareholder who bought stock in the IPO, sues D, seeking damages for the false statements. P seeks partial summary judgment on the issue of whether D made false representations in the prospectus.

The court should ***apply*** offensive c.e., and thus grant P partial summary judgment. When the SEC suit was brought, D had every incentive to vigorously litigate, and should readily have foreseen that public shareholders like P would be waiting in the wings to bring additional suits if D lost.

☞ **Limited jurisdiction:** Also, check whether the first suit was in a court of ***limited jurisdiction***. If so, this makes it ***less likely*** that the party to be bound had the requisite incentive to litigate fully.

☛ **Multiple plaintiff anomaly:** Check whether the facts involve a danger of the ***"multiple plaintiff anomaly"*** (e.g., a mass tort in which each of many Ps sues in turn; once D is found liable in one, c.e. would mean D would lose all subsequent suits.) In this m.p.a. situation, courts often hold that c.e. is unfair.

Example: Payless obtains a car loan from Finco. He then sues Finco for violating the federal Truth-in-Lending Act (TLA), by failing to accurately disclose to Payless the amount of the monthly charges. In the suit, Payless introduces evidence that in two other suits brought by people who got loans using exactly the same loan documents as Payless signed, courts held that the disclosure violated the TLA. Payless then moves for summary judgment, on the grounds that Finco is collaterally estopped from relitigating the issue of whether the loan document signed by Payless violated the TLA.

There's a good chance that the court will find it unfair to Finco to apply c.e. — application of c.e. would mean that no matter how many suits Finco won on this issue (the facts here don't tell us whether Finco won a lot of suits, only that it lost two, on which Payless is relying), after the first or second litigated loss Finco would be estopped, an arguably unfair result.

Full Faith & Credit

- ☛ **FF&C generally:** Finally, look for ***Full Faith & Credit*** (FF&C) issues:
  - ☞ **When to consider:** Any time you have a ***judgment*** in Suit 1, and Suit 2 takes place in a ***different jurisdiction*** than Suit 1, you have a potential FF&C issue. You need to ask, "Is the court in Suit 2 bound to follow the judgment issued in Suit 1?"
    - ☛ **Two state-court actions:** If Suit 1 and Suit 2 were both in ***state*** courts, the FF&C clause of the ***U.S. Constitution*** requires that the Suit 2 court give to the Suit 1 judgment the same effect that that judgment would have in the state that decided it. So State 2 can't allow re-litigation of any factual or legal issues, even if the substantive law of State 2 would have produced a completely different result. Also, State 2 must ***"enforce"*** the State 1 judgment — it must let the winner of the State 1 judgment seize the loser's State 2 assets without any re-litigation of the merits.
    - ☛ **State-and-federal:** If Suit 1 is in state court and Suit 2 in federal court (or vice versa), FF&C principles similarly require the second court to honor the first court's judgment.
    - ☛ **Jurisdiction not litigated:** The key exception — frequently tested — is that the second court can reconsider whether the first court had ***jurisdiction*** (either personal or subject matter), if the jurisdiction issue was ***not litigated or waived*** in the first suit. This is ***"collateral attack."***
    - ☛ **Res judicata effect of first judgment:** FF&C means that the ***res judicata effect*** of the earlier judgment must also be enforced by the second jurisdiction. So if State 1 would allow, say, offensive use of c.e. by a stranger, State 2 must do the same. (If Suit 1 is in federal court sitting in diversity and Suit 2 is in state court, the state court must give the first judgment the same effect it would have in the court of the state where the federal court that decided Suit 1 sat. [*Semtek v. Lockheed Martin*])

SHORT-ANSWER QUESTIONS

Note: These questions are selected from among the "Quiz Yourself" questions in the full-length *Emanuel Law Outline* on Civil Procedure *(ELO)*. We've kept the same question numbering here as in the *ELO*; since some questions that appear in the *ELO* have been omitted here, there are occasional gaps in the numbering.

CHAPTER 2

JURISDICTION OVER THE PARTIES

1. D lived in Connecticut until five years ago. His company then transferred him to California to take over a troubled operation. Even though D expected to return to Connecticut eventually, he sold his Connecticut house, figuring that when he returned there he would buy a different house. D did not know for sure how long he would be residing in California, but he did not expect to remain there for more than two or three years. After D took up residence in California, he was sued in the Connecticut state courts concerning a transaction which he had carried out in New York some years before. Can the Connecticut state courts constitutionally take jurisdiction over this suit? ________________

2. D owns and runs a small bakery in Portland, Maine. P is a truck driver who lives in South Carolina. One day, P visited D's bakery just before embarking on the long truck ride from Maine to South Carolina. He bought a dozen cream-filled doughnuts from D, and remarked, "I'm going to eat one of these every two hours, so I'll still have a couple left by the time I get home to South Carolina." P followed this plan, and ate the last two doughnuts while inside the South Carolina state limits. P then fell violently ill of food poisoning, causing him to lose control of his truck, so that it went off the road and flipped over, seriously injuring P. Later, medical evidence showed that it was one of the last two doughnuts, eaten in South Carolina, that caused the food poisoning. P sued D in the South Carolina courts. Not only was P a resident of South Carolina, but at the time of the suit he was hospitalized there, and all witnesses to the accident, as well as all witnesses to the medical findings concerning the food poisoning, resided in South Carolina. Assuming that the South Carolina long-arm statute can fairly be interpreted to give jurisdiction over D on these facts, may the courts of South Carolina constitutionally hear the suit? ________________

4. D is a corporation based in Italy, with no American subsidiaries, that manufactures drill presses in Italy and exports them throughout the world. D appoints Distrib, a corporation, to be the exclusive distributor of D's products in North

America. Distrib is owned by persons who have no ownership interest in D. Distrib is incorporated in North Carolina, and has its principal place of business in South Carolina. The distributorship agreement between D and Distrib provides that Distrib "shall use its best efforts to sell as many machines made by D in the United States and Canada as is reasonably practicable." Distrib then asks D to approve (as the distribution agreement requires) Distrib's plan to open, at Distrib's expense, a sales office in New Jersey. Distrib points out to D that New Jersey has many potential customers for the type of drill presses made by D, and that these customers will be more likely to buy if Distrib has a local office. D agrees, and Distrib opens the office. From that N.J. office, Distrib sells a drill press made by D to Cust, a machine shop located in New Jersey. P, an employee of Cust, is injured when the drill press pierces the palm of P's hand. P sues D in tort in New Jersey state court, alleging that the absence of a guard on the press made the product dangerously defective. The New Jersey long-arm allows service on "any defendant, wherever based, who makes a product that causes physical injury within this state." P makes service on D as authorized by the statute. D moves for dismissal, asserting that the New Jersey courts cannot constitutionally exercise personal jurisdiction over D in this case. Should the court grant D's motion? ________________

5. D is a corporation that manufactures valves to be used in various heating devices. D is incorporated in Germany, and has its only offices there. D sells many valves to Boiler Co., a Spanish manufacturer of boilers. A boiler made by Boiler Co. and with a valve made by D is installed in a hotel in Amsterdam, Holland. While P, a Texas resident, is visiting that hotel, the boiler explodes, causing P to be burned in the ensuing fire. D has a wholly-owned U.S. subsidiary, D-Sub, that is incorporated in Delaware, and that has its principal place of business in Virginia. From the Virginia office, D-Sub makes sales of D's products throughout the U.S.; these sales collectively represent 12% of D's worldwide sales. About 8% of D-Sub's sales (and thus less than 1% of D's worldwide sales) are made to customers located in Texas. In reliance on D-Sub's sales in Texas, P brings a product liability suit against D and D-Sub in Texas state court, claiming that a defect in the valve that was sold by D to Boiler Co. and incorporated by the latter into the boiler installed in Amsterdam was the cause of P's injuries. D and D-Sub both move to dismiss the suit on grounds that personal jurisdiction may not constitutionally be exercised against either by the Texas court. How should the Texas court rule on the motions? (Answer separately with respect to D and D-Sub.) ________________

6. Big Motors Corp. ("Big"), despite its name, is a relatively small "niche" maker of all-electric vehicles. Big makes all its vehicles in two U.S. plants, and in the U.S. sells them only through five authorized dealers, each authorized to sell only in the dealer's home state. Of the states mentioned in this question, the only one with an authorized Big dealer is Montana. Owner, a retiree, owned a sedan (the "Sedan") made by Big. Owner lived (and still lives) in Texas. Owner lent the Sedan to Drive, a friend, who as Owner knew planned to drive the Sedan cross country. Drive set off on the trip accompanied by Pass, a friend and passenger. While Drive was driving the Sedan in Kentucky, the steering wheel suddenly locked due to a defective design, causing the Sedan to veer and to hit both a pedestrian, Ped, as well as a 4x4 truck owned and driven by Truck.

At all relevant times: Drive lived in South Dakota; Pass lived in North Dakota; Ped lived in Ohio; and Truck lived in Kentucky. Big Motors has its principal place of business in Tennessee, and is incorporated in Delaware. The Sedan was built by Big in its Nebraska plant, which annually produces vehicles with a wholesale value exceeding $10 million. Big also has a vehicle-manufacturing plant in Ohio, which produces wholesale revenues of $20 million, and which has 50 employees. Big has no direct operations or employees in any state mentioned here except Tennessee, Nebraska and Ohio. Big leaves all marketing and sales efforts to its authorized dealers, each of which is told by Big to confine those efforts to the dealer's home state. Fewer than ten vehicles made by Big have ever ended up "in residence" in either North Dakota or Kentucky, and in those cases the cars were purchased out-of-state and brought to the state when the owner moved there.

Two years before the accident involving the Sedan, Owner bought that vehicle in person from Deal, an authorized Big dealer whose only showroom was in Helena, Montana. Deal's dealership agreement with Big specifies that Deal is to actively market Big's entire line of vehicles within, and only within, a 25-mile radius of Deal's Helena showroom (a radius that falls entirely within Montana).

The parties have instituted various suits against Big, in various states, for physical injuries or property damage arising out of the accident involving the Sedan. All suits have been brought in state rather than federal court. All suits allege that the steering wheel of the Sedan had a dangerously defective design, which caused the accident in question. In each case, Big has moved to dismiss for lack of jurisdiction, and you are to say whether the motion should be granted. Also, if your answer is that the motion should be denied because there is personal jurisdiction over Big, you should state whether the jurisdiction is general, specific or both.

(A) Drive has sued Big in Montana. Should Big's dismissal motion be granted?

____

(B) Pass has sued Big in North Dakota. Should Big's dismissal motion be granted?

____

(C) Ped has sued Big in Kentucky. Should Big's dismissal motion be granted?

____

(D) Owner has sued Big in Tennessee. Should Big's dismissal motion be granted?

____

(E) Truck has sued Big in Ohio. Should Big's dismissal motion be granted?

____

7. StentCo, a manufacturer of medical devices, manufactured the iStent, a device designed to be implanted by a heart surgeon in the patient's coronary arteries to prevent blockage. StentCo marketed the iStent to cardiac surgeons as part of a single advertising campaign conducted from the company's New Jersey headquarters; neither this marketing campaign, nor the actual packaging of the product, contained any warning about the tendency of the iStent to rust inside patients' arteries, although StentCo was in possession of clinical information that this tendency existed. After hundreds of the devices had been implanted, they started to rust inside some patients; StentCo issued a recall, advising all patients with the device to have it surgically removed. Six plaintiffs, P1 through P6, all had an iStent placed in them in the same hospital in Minnesota, and then had it removed at that hospital in response to the recall. They all filed individual claims against StentCo as part of a single suit in Minnesota state court. (They did this pursuant to the Minnesota state-law equivalent of Federal Rule 20 allowing joinder of parties, see *supra*, p. 132, under which multiple plaintiffs may join together their claims against one or more defendants provided that all claims arise out of a single "transaction, occurrence, or series of transactions or occurrences." Assume that these plaintiffs' invocation of this rule was correct under local-state law.) Each suit alleged essentially the same facts, i.e., that each had had an iStent implanted, that StentCo had failed to include adequate warnings, that the lack of appropriate warning made the product dangerously defective, and that the defect had caused physical injury to each plaintiff.

Shortly after the suit was filed, P7, who had arranged to be represented by the same lawyer as P1-P6, sought to join their suit as an additional co-plaintiff with a similar claim against StentCo. P7 had received her iStent at a hospital in Kansas (to which StentCo had shipped the stent), and had then had it removed at that same hospital, P7 has never been to Minnesota, and her claim has no connection to Minnesota. However, P7's suit alleges exactly the same behavior by StentCo regarding warning, and the same resulting injury, as are alleged in the claims of P1 through P6.

StentCo has no offices or employees in Minnesota. Its principal place of business and state of incorporation are both New Jersey. Each year at issue in the suit, StentCo shipped at least two million dollars worth of stents and other devices to doctors in Minnesota for implantation to patients there.

(A) StentCo has moved to dismiss the claims of P1-P6, alleging that the court has no personal jurisdiction over the company to hear these claims. Should the court grant the motion? ____________

(B) StentCo has also moved to dismiss the claim of P7, on the same basis that the court has no jurisdiction over the company to hear that claim. Should the court grant the motion?

____

8. The state of Caledonia has a statute (the "Jurisdiction Act") that has two relevant provisions: (1) every corporation that does not have either its principal place of business or its state of incorporation in Caledonia (i.e., any corporation that is not "at home" in Caledonia — we'll call this a "foreign corporation," even if it's American), must, if it wishes to do business in the state, register with the state; and (2) any such registration by a foreign corporation shall be deemed to mean that the corporation "consents to defend 'any cause of action' brought against it' " in the state.

D, a foreign corporation, has never targeted the Caledonia market for its products, and has shipped virtually no products into the state. P sues D in the state courts of Caledonia for breach of contract. The suit alleges that D breached a contract with P that was signed in New Mexico and involved only acts in New Mexico. D moves to dismiss, asserting that being required to defend this suit violates its Fourteenth Amendment right to due process. Should the court dismiss the action for the reasons cited by D? ________________

11. Software Co. is a Washington-based publisher of computer software, particularly a program called "3-2-1." Clone Co., which is also a software publisher, has come out with a competing program called "4-3-2." Clone Co. has sold over 1,000 copies of 4-3-2 in the state of Washington. Software Co. has sued Clone Co. for federal copyright infringement in U.S. District Court for the Western District of Washington. The complaint alleges that 4-3-2 is so similar to 3-2-1 that it has the same "look and feel," and is therefore a violation of Software Co.'s copyrights. Assume that Clone Co., by selling over 1,000 copies in Washington, has the constitutionally-required minimum contacts with Washington to make it not violative of due process for Clone Co. to have to defend a suit there. Assume further, however, that due to the Washington courts' desire to cut down on the "litigation explosion," those courts would not exercise jurisdiction over any suit against a company which, like Clone Co., has no contacts with the state except for selling 1,000 copies of a product in the state. May the federal court for the Western District of Washington take personal jurisdiction over Clone Co. for purposes of the Software Co. copyright suit? (Assume that the method by which service is made on Clone Co. is satisfactory.)

____

12. Driver borrowed a car owned by Owner (a New Mexico resident), with Owner's permission. While Driver was driving the car in Arizona, he hit and injured Pedestrian, an Arizona resident. Pedestrian, realizing that Driver is so poor as to be judgment-proof, has brought a diversity action against Owner in Arizona Federal District Court. Applicable Supreme Court decisions indicate that Owner, by permitting his car to be driven into Arizona, has such minimum contacts with Arizona that it is not a violation of due process for him to be required to defend a suit brought in the Arizona state courts arising out of the accident. However, Arizona's non-resident motorist statute is relatively restrictive; it allows suit against one who is the driver in an Arizona-based accident, but not against one who owns a car (which he is not driving) that is involved in an Arizona accident. Therefore, Pedestrian would not have been permitted to sue Owner in the Arizona courts unless Owner was served while in Arizona. Pedestrian instituted his federal court suit by making personal service on Owner in New Mexico. May the Arizona district court hear the suit against Owner? ________________

13. Congress has just passed a statute (the "Redress for Terrorism" Act, or "RTA"). The RTA provides that if a non-governmental entity located anywhere in the world carries out a terrorist attack that kills or severely injures an American citizen, that citizen may bring a tort suit against the entity in any American federal district court. Vic is seriously injured in a terrorist attack in Somalia carried out by a group of private citizens calling themselves "Free Somalia." Vic sues the group and its members for civil damages in a single federal suit based on the RTA; the suit is brought in federal district court for the Southern District of the state of Tanzan. Assume that the means of service conformed to the requirements of the FRCP.

The Ds assert that if the federal court were to exercise personal jurisdiction over them, their Fourteenth Amendment due process rights would be violated because they lack minimum contacts with Tanzan. (Assume that the Ds indeed lack minimum contacts with Tanzan, or any other American state.) Should the court find in favor of the Ds, and therefore dismiss the action for lack of minimum contacts with Tanzan (where the federal court sits)? ___________________

14. D is a resident of Pennsylvania. While driving one day in Pennsylvania, D collided with P, a pedestrian, who is an Ohio resident who happened to be visiting his sister in Pennsylvania. D has no contacts with Ohio except for the fact that D works in Pennsylvania for a corporation whose state of incorporation and principal place of business are Ohio. P commenced an action for negligence against D in the Ohio state courts. P obtained from the Ohio state courts an order of pre-judgment garnishment (authorized by Ohio statutes) whereby D's employer was required to deposit with the court each week 20% of D's take-home pay until the action is resolved. Under the terms of the garnishment order, if P prevails, P will be given the garnished amount (up to the amount of his judgment), but D will have no other liability, assuming that he does not make a general appearance. May the Ohio courts constitutionally proceed with P's action on this basis? _________________

15. A statute of the state of Ames provides that in any action for personal injuries arising out of an automobile accident, the plaintiff may obtain a pre-judgment attachment of the defendant's bank account simultaneously with the filing of the plaintiff's suit. However, the plaintiff may obtain the attachment only by filing an affidavit stating that, to the best of P's knowledge, D was involved in, and was the cause of, the accident; the judge must then find that P appears to be acting in good faith. The statute also provides that the court must grant D a hearing, within one month after issuance of the attachment, at which D may show that he will probably not be found liable in the suit; if D makes such a showing, the attachment must be rescinded. D now attacks the statute as a violation of his right to due process. Should D prevail? _________________

19. P, a resident of Las Vegas (in the District of Nevada) wishes to bring a federal-court suit against D1, a resident of Los Angeles (in the Central District of California) and D2 a resident of San Francisco (in the Northern District of California). The suit would be based on diversity, and concerns an auto accident which occurred in San Diego (in the Southern District of California). In which federal judicial district(s) may the suit be brought? _________________

20. Same facts as above question. Now, however, assume that D2 is a resident of Albuquerque, in the District of New Mexico. What district(s) have venue? _________________

CHAPTER 3

SUBJECT-MATTER JURISDICTION

22. D's sole residence is in Connecticut. Under a contract with P, D performed some construction work on P's weekend home in Connecticut. P also has a principal residence, located in New York (where P resides during the week). When D failed to do the work in the contracted-for manner, P sued D in federal court for the District of Connecticut for $100,000 (a reasonable assessment of the damages suffered by P). No federal questions are presented by P's suit. May the federal court for Connecticut hear the case? _________________

23. P1 is a citizen of New York. P2 is a citizen of New Jersey. D1 is a citizen of California. D2 is a citizen of New Jersey. P1 and P2 have brought a federal court action in the Southern

District of New York against D1 and D2, alleging that D1 and D2 have breached a contract. No federal question is present. The Southern District of New York is the district where the claim arose. The amount at stake is $100,000. May the Southern District of New York hear the case?

____

24. P1 is a citizen of Delaware; P2 is a citizen of New Jersey. They have brought a federal court action against D, a corporation with its principal place of business in New York and incorporated in Delaware. No federal question is present. $80,000 is at stake. Putting aside questions of venue, does the federal court have subject-matter jurisdiction over the dispute? ________________

27. P is an individual who is a citizen of Missouri. D, also an individual, is a citizen of Indiana. P asserts that he sold goods to D under a contract whereby D was to pay him $65,000, and that D has not paid for the goods. If suit is brought in federal court for the Southern District of Indiana (the district in which D resides), may that court hear the suit? ________________

28. P, an individual, is a citizen of Vermont. D, a corporation, is incorporated in and has its principal place of business in Washington. P signed a contract with D giving D marketing rights to an AI app developed by P. D then issued a press release (unrelated to the P-D contract), stating that P "is a good programmer, but he's not a very good or honest guy, as evidenced by his conviction last year for armed robbery." P has brought suit against D in federal district court for Vermont alleging: (1) in count 1, breach of the contractual royalty provisions, for which P claims damages of $55,000; and (2) in count 2, libel, for which P claims damages of $70,000. Assume the court has personal jurisdiction over D. May the court hear the case? ________________

29. P1 and P2 are individuals who are citizens of Kentucky. D is a corporation that is a citizen of North Carolina. The Ps both signed identically worded contracts with D, whereby the Ps were each to raise broiler chickens, which they would sell to D for a stated price per pound. D unilaterally cancelled both contracts at the same time. The Ps wish to bring a diversity action in North Carolina federal court for breach of contract, and plan to join together as plaintiffs against D under Federal Rule 20. (Assume that the claims are properly joinable under Rule 20(a) in that they arise out of the same "series of transactions" and involve at least one "question of law or fact [in] common.") The damages asserted by P1 are $80,000, and the damages asserted by P2 equal $40,000. May the claims by P1 and P2 be heard together in a single federal action? ________________

30. Same facts as prior question. Now, however, assume that P1 and P2 each have a claim for $45,000. May they join their claims against D together pursuant to Rule 20, so that they can be adjudicated in a single federal court suit? ________________

31. P and D are competing furniture stores. Each is operated in the form of a corporation headquartered in Georgia (and incorporated in Georgia); both stores serve the same small town. P has sued D in federal district court for the Middle District of Georgia. P makes two claims: (1) that certain advertising and marketing practices engaged in by D are a violation of the federal antitrust statutes; and (2) that those same practices are a violation of a Georgia statute prohibiting "unfair competition." Each claim involves more than

$100,000. D moves to dismiss claim (2) on the grounds that federal subject-matter jurisdiction is lacking over it.

(A) What doctrine determines the validity of D's motion? ________________

(B) Should D's motion be granted? ________________

33. P and D were both injured (P more seriously than D) when a car driven by P collided with a car driven by D. P is a citizen of Oklahoma; D is a citizen of Kansas. P has sued D in federal district court for the District of Kansas, asserting a claim whose amount in controversy is $100,000. D, who sustained only a few scratches and some damage to his car, has counterclaimed against P for $12,000. P moves to dismiss D's claim for lack of subject-matter jurisdiction.

(A) What doctrine determines whether D's claim should be dismissed?

____

(B) Should P's motion be granted? ________________

34. Same facts as prior question. Now, however, assume that there was a third car involved in the collision, driven by Xavier, a citizen of Kansas. P has not filed suit against Xavier, only against D. But D has concluded that both P and Xavier were at fault and were responsible for his injuries. Therefore, he has joined Xavier as an additional party (defendant) to the counterclaim which he is making against P; he seeks $12,000 against each of P and Xavier. If Xavier moves to dismiss the claim against him for lack of federal subject-matter jurisdiction, should the court grant his motion? ________________

35. P is a citizen of Washington. D is a citizen of Oregon. P has sued D for negligence, arising out of an auto accident in which a car driven by D collided with a car driven by P. The amount at stake for P is $100,000. This suit has been brought in federal court for the District of Oregon. D has taken advantage of the pending suit to file a counterclaim against P for breach of a contract which the two had signed several years ago (before the auto accident). D has added Wanda as a defendant to this counterclaim, on the grounds that Wanda induced P to breach the contract with D. Wanda is a citizen of Oregon. D's counterclaim plausibly seeks $200,000 in damages from each of P and Wanda. Wanda moves to dismiss D's claim against her on the grounds that the court lacks subject-matter jurisdiction over it. Should the court grant Wanda's motion? ________________

36. Pedro, a pedestrian, was hit and injured in New Jersey by a car owned by Denise, and driven by her employee, Ted. Pedro (a citizen of New York) has sued Denise (a citizen of New Jersey) in federal district court for the Southern District of New York; his claim is for $100,000. Ted is a Pennsylvania resident, but Pedro has not bothered joining him (because he believes Ted is judgment-proof.) Pedro began the action by serving Denise pursuant to the New York long-arm. Denise (knowing, as Pedro does not, that Ted has a small nest egg) has brought a third-party claim against Ted, in which she asserts that if she is forced to pay anything to Pedro, Ted owes that amount to her. Denise has served Ted, claiming authority of the New York long-arm. Ted has no connection with New York, but Denise has substantial connections with New York. Ted now moves to dismiss, on the grounds that the New York federal court has no personal jurisdiction over him. Should Ted's motion be granted? ________________

38. P is a citizen of Ohio. D is a citizen of Kentucky. P has brought suit in the Ohio state courts, asserting that D drove his car negligently, thereby injuring P. P has incurred $65,000 of medical bills, plus significant pain and suffering. If P prevails at all, the likely award will be at least $120,000. Nonetheless, in the state court action P seeks only $65,000. (P is aware that under Ohio law, the jury is not limited to the sum demanded in the complaint.) D has filed a timely notice of removal with the federal district court for Ohio. P has made a timely motion to have the case remanded to the Ohio state courts due to the federal court's lack of removal jurisdiction. Should P's motion for remand be granted? ________________

39. P is an individual who is a citizen of Pennsylvania. D is a corporation with its principal place of business in New Jersey, but incorporated in Delaware. P has sued D in the New Jersey state courts for breach of contract. P's claim seeks $100,000. D has filed a prompt notice of removal with the federal district court for New Jersey. P has moved to have the case remanded to the New Jersey state courts, on the grounds that removal was improper. Should P's motion be granted? ________________

40. P is a citizen of Arizona. D is a citizen of New Mexico. P has sued D in the New Mexico state courts for violation of a federally-registered trademark held by P. Suits alleging violation of the federal trademark laws may be brought in either state or federal court. D has filed a timely petition removing the case to federal court for the District of New Mexico. P moves to have the case dismissed for lack of subject-matter jurisdiction. Should P's motion be granted? ________________

41. P, a consumer, sues D, a drug manufacturer, in the court system of the state of Minnetonka. P and D are both citizens of Minnetonka. P asserts two claims: (1) that when P took a drug made by D, P relied on marketing materials produced by D that made false claims for the product, in violation of the federal "Truth in Pharmaceutical Marketing" ("TPM") statute; and (2) that the same marketing for that drug violated a Minnetonka state truth-in-advertising statute. D immediately removes the case to the federal district court for the state of Minnetonka. P claims that the removal was improper, because D is a citizen of the forum state.

Now, assume that the federal district court decides (rightly or wrongly) that the removal was proper. P would much prefer to have the case remain in state court. Therefore, P amends her complaint to drop the claim based on the federal TPM, leaving only claim (2) (the state-law claim) in the suit. P then moves to have the case returned to the state court on the grounds that the federal court no longer has subject-matter jurisdiction. D argues that because P brought the original suit with both claims, she should not be able to defeat removal by dropping the federal claim now

(a) Was the original removal proper? ________________

(b) Assuming that the original removal was proper, should the court remand the amended complaint to the Minnetonka state court? ________________

42. P, a citizen of North Carolina, has brought a state-law products liability suit against D1, D2, and D3, all citizens of South Carolina. P's suit has been brought in the North Carolina state courts. $1 million is at stake. D1 and D2 have signed and filed a notice of removal with the Eastern District of North Carolina (embracing the area where the state courthouse handling P's suit is located). D3 does not care whether the suit is removed or not, and has not signed the notice of removal. P moves to have the case remanded for lack of subject-matter jurisdiction. Should P's motion be granted? ________________

CHAPTER 4

PLEADING

43. One day, Paul called Larry, a lawyer whom Paul had never met. Paul said to Larry, "Larry, I've been in a terrible car accident. I was a passenger in a car driven by Dave. Dave ran a stop sign, plowed into another car, and I was badly injured. I've been in the hospital for two months, I've got severe lower back damage, and the doctors say I'll never be able to work again. I'd like to sue Dave." Larry accepted the truth of Paul's statements, asked only a few questions about how the accident occurred, and then prepared a complaint stating that Paul had been permanently injured, had lost the ability ever to work again, and was entitled to $1 million in damages. Who, if anyone, must sign this complaint before it is served on Dave in a federal court action based on diversity? ________________

44. Same facts as prior question. Assume that Larry honestly and in good faith believed everything that Paul told him. Larry did not ask for a copy of the police report. The actual police report showed that the driver was Dennis, not Dave. The case then went to trial. At trial, it turned out that Dennis, not Dave, was the driver, and that the suit was just Paul's attempt to find a "deeper pocket" to sue, since Dennis was judgment-proof. It also turned out at trial that Paul had only minor injuries, and had already been back at work at the time he made the telephone call to Larry. Dave has now finally won the case, but only after spending $10,000 in attorney's fees to defend the case. What, if any, action should Dave's lawyer take now that Dave has prevailed at trial? ________________

46. P and D entered into a contract. The contract turned out to be very unfavorable to P. P has uncovered evidence suggesting that D misrepresented certain major facts about the proposed contractual arrangement in order to induce P to enter into the contract. Therefore, P has brought a federal court action, based on diversity, against D. P's complaint recites the date and general subject matter of the contract, and then states, "D fraudulently induced P to enter into this contract." On account of this fraud, P asks the court to grant the equitable relief of rescinding the contract.

(A) Putting aside the correctness of the complaint's jurisdictional allegations and the adequacy of its demand for judgment, does the complaint satisfy the pleading requirements of the Federal Rules? ________________

(B) In light of your answer to (A), what procedural steps should D take? ________________

47. P, an individual, brought a federal diversity action for libel against D, a television station. Before filing an answer, D made a timely motion under Federal Rule 12(b)(6) for dismissal for failure to state a claim upon which relief can be granted. The motion was served on P on April 1. The essence of D's motion was that under applicable substantive law, a statement made over the airwaves by a television station cannot be libel, and is at most slander. The federal judge agreed with D, and on June 1 ordered P's claim dismissed. Now, on May 1, P wishes to amend his pleading to allege slander rather than libel. Assuming that D doesn't consent, must P get the court's permission to amend his pleading in this manner? ________________

48. P brought a federal diversity action against D, alleging that D breached an oral agreement to employ P for a five-year period. D, in his answer, denied each and every allegation of P, as permitted by Federal Rule 8(b). In what respect, if any, could D's answer have been improved? ________________

52. P, while standing on the sidewalk, was injured when a car driven by Driver and manufactured by Carco suddenly swerved in the street and struck her. P brought a federal court diversity action against Carco. Her complaint asserted that Carco had produced a dangerously defective product, and that Carco is strictly liable for P's injuries. At trial, P offered evidence that Carco was negligent in not ascertaining that the design of the car produced a significant likelihood of a sudden swerve to the right. Carco's lawyer did not object to this proof of negligence. The judge (the case was tried to a judge rather than to a jury) found that strict product liability does not apply to injuries caused to a bystander such as P, but also found that Carco is liable to P because of Carco's negligence in designing the car. Carco now moves to have the trial judge's verdict set aside, on the grounds that it is based upon a claim (negligence) that was not contained in P's complaint. How should the trial judge respond to this motion? ________________

CHAPTER 5

DISCOVERY AND PRETRIAL CONFERENCE

53. P was injured in an auto accident involving a car driven by D. P's lawyer deposed D. During this deposition, the fact emerged that D stood by the car after the accident, and watched while W, an eyewitness to the accident, gave a statement to the police. P's lawyer asked D during the deposition, "What was the substance of W's statement to the police about what occurred?" D's lawyer objected on the grounds that any answer would be hearsay, and instructs D not to answer. (Assume that it would indeed be hearsay for D to testify at trial regarding W's statement.) P now moves for an order compelling D to answer this question. Should the court grant the order sought by P? ________________

54. P brought a federal court diversity action against D. P's claim was that D willfully breached a contract with P. D raised the defense that the contract is unenforceable due to the Statute of Frauds. During a deposition of D conducted by P's lawyer, L, L ascertained that D had consulted with his own lawyer, X, before signing the contract. L then asked D, "Did you discuss with X the enforceability of the contract before you signed it?" D objected to the question on the grounds of attorney-client privilege. (This matter would indeed be privileged under the law of the state where the district court sits, if the question were asked of D at trial.) P now moves to compel D to answer the question. Should the court grant P's motion, and issue an order compelling an answer? ________________

55. P was injured in an automobile accident involving a car driven by D. P brought a federal diversity suit against D on a negligence theory. After commencement of the suit, D's lawyer, L, conducted an interview with an eyewitness to the accident, W. L wrote down those aspects of W's account of the accident that seemed most interesting to L. P's lawyer, after learning about this interview, submitted to D a Rule 34 Request for Production of Documents, requesting "any notes taken by L of any interviews with W." D and L refused to comply, so P made a motion to compel discovery. Should the court grant P's motion to compel production of the notes? ________________

56. P and D were involved in an automobile accident. P sued D in federal court based on diversity; the suit alleges that D behaved negligently. Shortly after the accident and before P filed his lawsuit, P furnished a statement to D's insurance company, at the insurer's request. At the time of the interview, P was not given a copy of the statement (which was in the form of a tape recording that was later transcribed). P's lawyer now submits, pursuant to Federal Rule 34, a request that D give P a copy of the transcript of P's statement. Is D obligated to give P a copy of this statement, assuming that P makes no showing of special need for this statement? ________________

57. P, driving one car, was injured by a collision with a car driven by D. (P believes that the accident occurred because D went through a stop sign.) P sued D for negligence in federal court based on diversity. P's lawyer hired an expert accident reconstructionist, Rufus T. Firefly, to: (1) examine the skid marks, the damage to the two automobiles, and any other physical evidence of how fast each car was going at the time of the accident; and (2) determine whether this speed proves that D definitely did not stop at the stop sign. As a result of his investigation, Firefly has formed an opinion that D definitely did not stop at the stop sign. P plans to call Firefly to testify at trial to this effect.

(A) How, if at all, can D learn that P will be calling Firefly at trial? ________________

(B) How, if at all, can D get details of what Firefly will say at trial? ________________

(C) Assume that D has learned of Firefly's identity and the fact that he will be called to testify at trial about the results of his investigation. If D wishes to take the deposition of Firefly to hear in detail Firefly's conclusions about what caused the accident, is D entitled to do so? If so, when? ________________

59. In a federal court action for antitrust, P, a corporation, claimed that D's predatory conduct had caused X to terminate a contract with P that was valuable to P. In a set of interrogatories, D asked P to state when and how the alleged interference by D with the P-X contract had occurred. P, in a set of answers signed by Prexy, P's president, responded that the interference had been in the form of a phone call by D's chairman, Charm, to X, on Sept. 15, 2007, in which Charm told X that P was preparing to breach the contract. Subsequent to the filing of this interrogatory answer, Prexy has learned that the conversation between Charm and X was a face-to-face one, and that it took place on Sept. 18, not Sept. 15. What obligation, if any, does P have to amend its interrogatory answer? ________________

60. D, a plastic surgeon, performed cosmetic surgery on P's face to reduce the size of her chin. P was mildly displeased with the results, and found a lawyer, L, willing to bring a malpractice action (in federal court based on diversity) against D. L has commenced the action, and now would like to know whether D is covered by malpractice insurance for any verdict that P might recover here. L would also like to know the limits of the policy, if one does exist. How may L get this information? ________________

61. P brought a federal court action against D in connection with an automobile accident. P learned that the accident was personally observed by W. P served upon W a set of interrogatories asking W to describe the accident as he saw it. Must W answer the interrogatories? ________________

62. P brought a diversity-based negligence action against D in federal district court for the Southern District of New York. One of the witnesses to the accident in question was W (who is not a party). W is an individual who was visiting in New York at the time of the accident, but who resides in the Southern District of Florida. P's lawyer wished to take W's deposition, but P's lawyer did not wish to travel to Florida to do so. Consequently, P served upon W at W's residence in Miami a notice of deposition, together with a notice stating that W's reasonable travel and lodging expenses for a trip to New York (where the deposition was to be held) would be paid by P. W has indicated that she will not submit to any deposition unless subpoenaed to do so. If P is ready to bear W's travel and lodging expenses to New York, may W be subpoenaed to appear in New York for her deposition? ________________

63. P and D were involved in an automobile accident. P sued D for negligence in federal court, based on diversity. P discovered the existence of a police report, issued by the police department of the City of Langdell (where the accident occurred). P served upon that police department a Rule 34 Request to Produce Documents, listing the police report as the document to be produced. Assuming that the City of Langdell is within the district where the action is pending, must the police department comply with the request?

____

64. P was hit by an automobile driven by D. P brought a federal diversity action against D alleging negligence. P claimed that he suffered serious whiplash in the accident, and that he has been physically disabled from working. D's lawyer had doubts about whether P was as severely disabled as he claims. Therefore, D's lawyer served upon P a notice to undergo physical examination, which stated, "Please present yourself at any time within the next two weeks at the office of Dr. John Smith, who will conduct a physical examination of you to determine the degree of your disability." Must P comply with this request?

____

65. P and D are each corporations engaged in the pharmaceutical business; they compete with each other. P has brought a federal patent infringement suit against D, and has added to it a pendent state claim alleging that D, by hiring a former employee of P, effectively stole certain trade secrets belonging to P. During the discovery phase, P has served upon D a Rule 34 document production request seeking documents containing details of certain secret manufacturing processes used by D, so that P can determine whether these are derived from P's own trade secrets. D is afraid that if it complies, two bad results may occur: (1) P may use the information, including the trade secrets, to compete with D; and (2) P may disclose those trade secrets to the world, thus stripping D's competitive advantage. What should D do to deal with these problems? ________________

66. P brought a product liability suit (based on diversity) against D. D is a corporation. P served D with a notice of deposition, which stated that D or its representative would be asked questions concerning how the product in question was designed. D designated Smith to be deposed on its behalf. Smith was D's Director of Product Safety at the time the product in question was designed, but had since left D's employ. Now, at trial, P seeks to introduce in evidence answers given by Smith in the deposition. The answers are offered for substantive purposes, and are offered even though Smith is available to testify at trial. Are the deposition answers admissible under these circumstances?

____

67. P and D were involved in an auto accident while each was driving a car. P brought a diversity action against D for negligence. D took the deposition of W, a bystander who observed the accident. W is available (indeed eager) to testify at trial, but neither party has called her. D now offers a portion of W's deposition testimony as evidence. Will this testimony be admitted if objected to by P? ________________

68. Same facts as prior question. Now, however, assume that W was called to the stand by P and gave live testimony. D now seeks to offer into evidence portions of W's deposition testimony which would cast doubt upon the accuracy of W's statements made at trial. Is this deposition material admissible? ________________

69. Cars driven by P and D were in an accident. P sued D in federal court for negligence. During the discovery process, P served upon D an interrogatory containing the following question: "State what, if anything, you told the police officer investigating the accident regarding whether you stopped at the stop sign located at the corner of Main and 21st Street just before the accident." D submitted the following response to this question: "I told the police officer that I did not stop at the stop sign."

(A) Suppose that at trial, D does not take the stand. May P introduce D's interrogatory statement for the purpose of proving that D did not in fact stop at the stop sign?

____

(B) Assume that at trial, (i) D testifies that he did stop at the stop sign; and (ii) P is permitted to introduce the interrogatory answer to impeach D's testimony. Will a properly-instructed jury be permitted to conclude that D stopped at the stop sign?

____

CHAPTER 6

ASCERTAINING APPLICABLE LAW

70. P has brought a negligence action against D (based on diversity) in federal district court for the District of Iowa. P's complaint alleges that P was a social guest in D's house, that P fell when a wooden step on a stairway inside the house broke, and that had D used ordinary reasonable care in keeping his house safe, he would have discovered the danger and avoided it. (The complaint does not claim that D knew of the defect, merely that a reasonable person in D's position would have learned of the defect and fixed it.) A five-year-old decision of the Iowa Supreme Court holds that a social guest is only a "licensee," not an "invitee," and that a property owner owes a licensee no duty of inspection. A number of courts in other states have in the last few years abolished the licensee/invitee distinction, and have held that a property owner owes a duty of reasonable inspection to a licensee as well as an invitee. The federal district judge in whose court P's action is pending believes that these newer decisions represent the much better view. However, there is no evidence that the Iowa Supreme Court would change its attitude on this issue, since the court has on more recent occasions rejected other chances to expand tort liability. Should the federal judge impose upon D the duty of making reasonable inspection of his premises?

____

72. P has sued D in federal district court for the Central District of California. The suit is based on diversity (since P is a citizen of California and D is a citizen of Arizona). P claims that D negligently drove an automobile, thus injuring P in an accident. The accident took place in Arizona. Under California state court decisions, any suit brought in the California state courts arising out of an auto accident is to be decided under California law if the plaintiff is a California resident, even if the accident took place in another state. This California approach is a minority and old-fashioned one; nearly every other state applies the rule of "lex locus delicti," whereby in auto accident cases the law of the state where the accident took place is the law that is used. The federal judge hearing the P-D suit believes that the majority "lex locus delicti" approach is the much sounder one. In the P-D suit the issue arises whether California state substantive law (under which contributory negligence is not a defense) or Arizona law (under which contributory negligence is still a defense) should be applied. The federal judge hearing the case believes that the California law (no contributory negligence defense) is the better approach. Which state's substantive law of negligence, California's or Arizona's, should be applied by the federal judge?

____

73. The state of Acme, in order to reduce health insurance costs, enacted a statute capping damages in any action for medical malpractice brought in the Acme state courts at $1 MM of compensatory damages, and zero punitive damages. P, a citizen of Beta, had a knee replacement done by D, a surgeon living in Acme; the operation was done in Acme. Due to D's gross negligence during the operation, the replacement failed and had to be replaced. P has now brought a diversity malpractice suit against D in Acme federal district court, seeking $1 MM of compensatory damages and $500,000 of punitive damages. Assume that federal courts, when they are free to make their own decision, typically award punitive damages in tort actions if the court believes that the defendant behaved with gross negligence and that the award of punitive damages will have a useful deterrent effect. If the federal court, after trial, believes that these conditions have been satisfied, may the court award P $100,000 in punitive damages? ________________

74. P has sued D in diversity in federal court for the Northern District of Georgia. P seeks to assert against D a tort claim relating to an accident, as well as a breach of contract claim arising from a prior business relationship between P and D, having nothing to do with the accident. Under a Georgia statute, a tort claim may not be joined with a contract claim against the same defendant in state court, if the two claims relate to different transactions. However, joinder of unrelated contract and tort claims against a single defendant is expressly allowed by FRCP 18(a). In the federal action, may P join his contract and tort claims against D in a single action? ________________

75. P and D signed a contract whereby P was to perform personal services for D. Almost immediately, it became clear to P that D was not living up to his part of the bargain, with respect to the duties that P was to be given. However, P tried to work things out with D for a long time (reasonable conduct by P in the circumstances), and therefore took no legal action for more than two years. He then brought a diversity action against D in federal district court for the District of Kansas, the state in which the contract was signed and was being performed. Under Kansas law, any action (whether legal or equitable) related to performance of a contract must be brought within two years of the performance or non-performance complained of. P does not seek damages in his federal suit; instead, he seeks to have the contract declared rescinded on account of D's nonperformance.

The federal courts have traditionally regarded actions to rescind a contract as being primarily equitable, and they apply the equitable doctrine of laches rather than any strict statute of limitations doctrine when the action is primarily equitable. Thus under general federal principles, P's suit will not be time-barred so long as P has acted within a "reasonable" period of time considering the circumstances. Should the federal court for the District of Kansas regard P's action as time-barred? ________________

76. P has brought a diversity suit against D in federal district court for Montana; the suit alleges negligence. In both the Montana state trial courts and the federal district court of Montana, the applicable rules provide for a six-person jury. By Montana statute, the verdict in a civil case needs to be by only a 5/6's majority. The state rule allowing a 5/6's majority was adopted to reduce the number of hung juries and re-trials, thus reducing court congestion. By a long-standing federal policy a federal civil jury must reach a unanimous verdict. (There is no federal statute or Rule of Civil Procedure which directly requires unanimity.) Should the federal district judge recognize a verdict on which five out of the six jurors agree? ________________

CHAPTER 7

TRIAL PROCEDURE

79. P has brought a medical malpractice suit against D in federal court based on diversity. P's complaint asserts that D performed an operation upon P to reduce the size of P's nose, and that the results were disastrous. The complaint asserts that the operation took place on October 13, 2025. D has moved for summary judgment pursuant to Rule 56, and has submitted in support of that motion an affidavit stating that he was not in the U.S. on October 13, 2025. D's moving papers give much additional information, all of which tends to indicate that D could not have performed the operation on the date P said D performed it (e.g., an affidavit from D's travel agent stating that D was in the south of France that day, as well as charges on D's phone bill showing calls made from the south of France to D's office on that date).P, in opposition to D's motion, has submitted an affidavit that furnishes a couple of details about the alleged operation (e.g., "On October 13, 2025, I went to D's offices at 456 Main Street. D was a brown haired man of about 50 years of age who wore glasses, and he performed the surgery on me."). P has not submitted any other information in opposition to D's motion. In reviewing these moving papers, the federal judge concludes that there is about a 90% chance that P is either honestly mistaken or is lying when she asserts that D performed the operation on her on that date. Should the federal judge grant D's motion for summary judgment? ____________

80. P sued D in federal district court for employment discrimination. The case was tried to a judge. Both sides put on their case. The judge announced from the bench that she would decide the case within several weeks. After four weeks, the judge issued a written opinion, which read in its entirety as follows: "The judge finds for D, on the grounds that while P has proven that D did not hire P, P has not proven that this refusal was on account of D's race, as required by the federal civil rights statute under which P brought suit." The judge has not issued any other statements or documents in connection with the case. Has the judge complied with applicable procedural requirements? ______________

81. P brought a federal suit against D for negligence relating to an automobile accident in which P was injured. The suit was based on diversity. The essence of P's claim was that D went through an intersection while the light was red, striking P's car. The case was tried without a jury. At trial, P presented a witness, W, who testified to having seen D go through the intersection when the light was red against D. P himself also testified that the light was green for him (and thus red for D) when D entered the intersection. The only witness or other evidence on behalf of D was D's own testimony, in which D asserted that the light was yellow when D passed through the intersection. The trial judge found in favor of D. The judge's findings of fact, after summarizing the testimony given by each of the witnesses, stated, "Although the only apparently objective witness supports P's account, I find that D's testimony was more credible, and I therefore conclude that the light was yellow at the time D entered the intersection. Accordingly, I find that D did not act negligently, and is therefore not liable."

P appealed the case to the Court of Appeals. The three-judge panel hearing the appeal has concluded, after reading the entire trial transcript, that there is a 70% or so chance that the light was red against D at the time D entered the intersection. The only issue on the appeal is whether the trial judge's finding of fact as to the color of light was a correct one. Should the appeals court affirm the lower court judgment? ______________

84. P sued D in federal court for the District of Colorado. The suit, which was based on diversity, alleged that D negligently injured P in an automobile accident. At the close of D's case, the judge instructed the jury that under Colorado law of comparative negligence (applicable here because of *Erie* doctrine) any contributory negligence by P would not bar P from recovery. However, the judge omitted to point out, as requested by D, that under Colorado law if P's fault was greater than D's, P may not recover at all. D's lawyer made no comment on the judge's jury instructions. The jury found in favor of P. On appeal, D now asserts that the trial judge's failure to give the requested "P more negligent than D" instruction constitutes reversible error. Assuming that the appellate court agrees that the judge's instruction was erroneous, should the appellate court affirm the verdict? ______________

85. P has brought a diversity-based contract action against D in federal court. The sole issue in the case is whether D in fact signed the document that P has proffered as "the contract." At trial, the only witnesses were P and D. P testified that D signed the contract. D testified that he did not sign the contract. No documentary evidence was produced (except for the alleged contract document itself). After both sides rested, the judge instructed the jury, and the jury found in favor of P. D has now moved for judgment as a matter of law (after having complied with any procedural prerequisites for this motion). In considering the j.m.l. motion, the trial judge has a fairly strong belief that D told the truth and that P lied; however, the judge also recognizes that if P's testimony is believed rather than D's, P should win the case. The judge has also concluded that a person would not be completely irrational in concluding that it was D, rather than P, who had lied. Should the judge grant the j.m.l. motion? ________________

86. P brought a negligence action against D in federal court, based on diversity. At the close of P's case, D immediately presented his first and only witness, and at no time made any motions. The jury found in favor of P. D then made a motion for j.m.l. Assuming that the trial judge agrees with D's contention that a reasonable jury could not possibly have found in favor of P, should the trial judge grant D's j.m.l. motion? ________________

87. P has brought a diversity-based product liability action against D in federal court. The jury has awarded damages (compensatory only) of $3 million, a sum which the trial judge believes to be at least twice what a reasonable damage award would be. However, the judge agrees with the jury's finding that D should be liable. The judge does not want to waste the litigants' and court's time by ordering a new trial. What should the judge do?

____

89. On July 1, P served on D a summons and complaint for a federal district court action alleging breach of contract. On July 15, D served an answer on P. There were no pleadings after the answer. At no time did P make a demand for a jury trial. On September 1, shortly before the case was to be tried, D served upon P a demand that the case be tried before a jury. Is D entitled to a jury trial? ________________

91. Insurer wrote a $100,000 policy on the life of X. X, who owned the policy, notified Insurer that the beneficiary should be W, X's wife. Two years later, just before X died, he wrote to Insurer, "I wish to change the beneficiary from W to S, my son." After X's death, both W and S made a claim to the policy proceeds (W's claim was on the basis that X was not mentally competent at the time he purported to change the beneficiary). Insurer instituted a Rule 22 interpleader action in federal court, with W and S as the defendants. Insurer and S were content to have the case heard by a judge, but W demanded a jury trial. Is W entitled to a jury trial on the issue of whether she is the proper beneficiary?

____

92. P, a 50-year-old married executive previously employed by D, a corporation, brings a federal diversity action against D. The suit claims that D breached their employment contract by firing P for posting on Facebook a photo of P at a party. In the photo, P is shown holding a bottle of whiskey, and has his arm around a woman, X, who appears to be a teenager; P has captioned the photo, "Isn't she a babe?" At the ensuing bench trial, both sides agree that the only relevant clause in the contract is one allowing termination for an "act of moral turpitude," a term that is not defined in the document. P testifies that (1) X was a family friend with whom P had no inappropriate relationship, criminal or otherwise; (2) the parties intended "moral turpitude" to cover only conduct that would be both criminal and reflective of serious immorality; and (3) nothing in the photo would suggest to a reasonable observer that P was behaving with moral turpitude. D's CEO testifies that the parties intended "moral turpitude" to include non-criminal acts reflecting a serious error of moral judgment, and that a reasonable observer who saw the photo and who knew that P was married to someone other than X would believe that P was showing poor moral judgment. The trial judge, in an opinion upholding the firing, concludes that as a factual matter D has proved a violation of the moral-turpitude clause. P has appealed to the U.S. Court of

Appeals, arguing that, as shown by the trial testimony, his conduct did not constitute a violation of the clause.

(A) What standard should the appeals court use in deciding whether the trial judge was correct in concluding that P violated the contract? ________________

(B) When the court applies the standard you listed in (A), should the court affirm or reverse the trial judge's verdict? ________________

93. P, an author, brings a federal court action against D, a publisher, claiming that a book published by D violates P's copyrights. The parties agree to have the case tried without a jury. The trial judge decides to hear the case in two stages, liability and then (if there is a finding of liability) damages. After discovery is complete, the judge grants partial summary judgment in favor of P under FRCP 56, on the grounds that there is no genuine dispute about whether D violated P's copyrights. The judge now proposes to hear testimony on the issue of damages. Before testimony begins, and with the consent of P, D files a notice of appeal contending that the judge improperly ordered summary judgment on the liability issue. What should the court of appeals do? ________________

CHAPTER 8

MULTI-PARTY AND MULTI-CLAIM LITIGATION

94. P and D were each seriously injured when a car driven by P collided with a car driven by D. P sued D in federal district court on a negligence theory; the case was based on diversity. D submitted a general denial as his answer. The jury found in favor of D. D has now brought a separate federal diversity-based action against P relating to the same accident; D's suit asserts that P's negligence caused the accident. Will D's suit be permitted to go to trial? ________________

95. Pedestrian was injured when she was struck by a delivery van driven by Worker. The van was owned by Boss, and was being driven by Worker as part of the job that Worker did for Boss. Pedestrian brought a federal court diversity-based action against Boss alleging that Worker drove negligently and that Boss was liable for that negligence under the doctrine of respondeat superior. Boss impleaded Worker as a third-party defendant under Federal Rule 14(a), on the theory that if Boss was liable to Pedestrian based on respondeat superior, Worker must indemnify Boss. The jury found against Pedestrian and thus in favor of Boss. Worker has now commenced a new federal action, alleging that Boss knowingly gave Worker a defective van to drive, thus preventing Worker from stopping, and contributing to injuries suffered by Worker in the same accident in which Pedestrian was injured. Should Worker's suit against Boss be allowed to go forward? ________________

96. In Connecticut, a car driven by Alan collided with a car owned by Bob but driven by Carol. Bob has sued Alan for negligence in Connecticut federal district court; the case is based on diversity. Bob's claim is for $100,000. Alan and Carol are citizens of Massachusetts; Bob is a citizen of Connecticut. The Connecticut long arm allows out-of-state mail service on anyone who is involved in an accident which takes place inside the state. Now,

Alan wishes to make a counterclaim (relating to the same accident) against Bob; Alan's claim is such that Carol must be made a co-defendant if it is feasible to do so (see FRCP 19(a)). Alan's claim is for $20,000 against Bob, and would be for another $20,000 against Carol if she is joined.

(A) May Alan bring a counterclaim against Bob and Carol together? ________________

(B) If Alan does not bring his counterclaim against Bob or Carol, may he bring a later state-court suit against them both? (Ignore jurisdictional problems with this second suit.) ________________

98. P brought, in federal court, an action against D for violation of P's federally-registered copyrights. (The suit alleged that D plagiarized language in a novel written by P.) Before D's time to answer ran, P amended his suit to add a second claim, that D libelled P by calling P a "dishonest writer." The alleged libel has nothing to do with the alleged copyright violation. Putting aside questions of personal and subject-matter jurisdiction, is P entitled, procedurally, to add this second claim to his action? ________________

99. Same basic fact pattern as prior question. Now, however, assume that P and D are citizens of the same state. Assume also that both the copyright claim and the libel claim are for more than $75,000. May the federal court hear the libel claim? ________________

100. P and D were both injured in a car accident, when the cars driven by each collided. P brought a federal court diversity action against D for negligence, seeking $100,000 of damages. D brought a counterclaim against P for negligence (relating to the same accident) in that same action; D joined to that counterclaim a second person, X (the owner of the car driven by P). D claimed that P and X each owed $30,000 on D's counterclaim. D then joined a second claim against X, for breach of contract, in an unrelated transaction; this claim was for $15,000. P is a citizen of Alabama, D is a citizen of Georgia, and X is a citizen of Florida.

(A) May the court hear D's claim against X for damages from the car accident? ________________

(B) May the court hear D's claim against X for breach of contract? ________________

102. P1 and P2 were both passengers in a twin-engine aircraft owned and operated by D1 (a commuter airline) and manufactured by D2. Both P1 and P2 were seriously injured when the plane caught fire while landing. P1 and P2 are both citizens of New York. D1 is incorporated in Delware and has its principal place of business in New York. D2 is both incorporated in, and has its principal place of business in, Kansas. P1 and P2 have brought a single federal court diversity action, in which D1 is charged with negligent inspection and operation, and D2 is charged with strict products liability. P1 and P2 each meet the amount in controversy requirement. Is the joinder of all parties proper? ________________

107. P1 and P2 are individuals whose applications to live in a particular federally-subsidized housing project were rejected by D, the state agency that administers the project. P1 and P2 brought a federal action alleging that D's refusal to furnish them with a statement of reasons for their rejection constituted a deprivation of their right to due process, in violation of a federal civil rights statute. P1 and P2 now seek to certify as a plaintiff class all individuals whose applications for this project were rejected where the rejection was not accompanied by a statement of reasons. They seek a declaratory judgment that D violated the civil rights of each class member, and an injunction against further violations. (They don't seek damages.) The identities of the would-be class members can be compiled quite readily from the records of D; there are approximately 700 such individuals. Assuming that the trial judge believes that the lawyers for P1 and P2, and P1 and P2 themselves, can adequately represent the interests of the 700 absent members, should the judge permit the action to go forward as a class action? If so, under what subdivision of Rule 23(b)? ________________

108. Same basic fact pattern as prior question. Assuming that the federal judge certifies the plaintiff class as requested by P1 and P2, must P1 and P2 pay for notice to all 700 absent class members? ________________

109. D operates a chemical plant in the Town of Pound. Late one night, an explosion occurred in the plant, and a cloud of toxic gas was released. The cloud drifted for several miles before dispersing, and hundreds of people appeared to be injured by it in various ways. One year after the explosion, P1, a resident of Pound who claimed to have been seriously injured by his exposure to the toxic cloud, filed suit against D for violation of federal environmental protection statutes. P, as sole named plaintiff, seeks certification of a class consisting of all individuals residing within five miles of the plant who were or may have been injured by the toxic substance released. The suit seeks compensatory damages on behalf of each class member. Should class certification be granted? If so, under what subdivision of Rule 23(b)? ________________

110. P1 instituted a federal class action against D. D is a large investment banking firm, and P1's suit alleged that D broke federal securities laws when it sold stock on behalf of Z Corporation. D and Z are both Delaware corporations with their principal place of business in New York. The suit took place in New York federal district court. The court certified as a class all persons who purchased Z Corp. stock during a certain time period. One of these individuals was X, a California resident with no significant contacts with either Delaware or New York. X ignored the notice telling him he had the right to opt out. The class action was decided in favor of D. X then instituted his own individual suit against D in California federal district court. D now argues that X should be bound by the prior class action results. X points out in rebuttal that he, X, had no minimum contacts with New York, and argues that he should not be bound by the results in the New York class action suit given this lack of minimum contacts. Is X's contention correct? ________________

111. P1 and P2 have instituted a federal suit against D, a large bank that issues many credit cards. The suit contends that credit cards issued by D were misleadingly advertised, in violation of the law of New York (the state where the federal action is pending). P1's claim is for $80,000 and P2's claim is for $90,000. P1 and P2 are both citizens of New Jersey. D is a citizen of New York. No federal question is present. P1 and P2 seek certification of a class consisting of all those who ordered credit cards from D in reliance on the misleading advertising, regardless of the amount of damage suffered by that person. (All these others have damages of at most $20,000 each.) Assuming that the requirements of Federal Rule 23(a) and 23(b)(3) are satisfied, should the court grant certification of the proposed class? ________________

112. Biff is the publisher of Biff's Notes, a series of study aids sold to college and high school students. Each year, Biff's acquires about one million new customers for its study aids, which cost an average of $14 each. P, a college student who is a customer of Biff's Notes, brought a federal antitrust suit against Biff, accusing him of price fixing, predatory tactics, and other Congressionally-forbidden tactics to maintain a dominant share of the study aid market. P has asked the court to certify a class consisting of all customers who have bought any study aids from Biff during the last four years. (Of the approximately four million Biff's customers during this period, the names and addresses of about 800,000 are identifiable by Biff's from its records, because they have sent in a card requesting free updates.) The court has certified this class under Rule 23(b)(3).

(A) Which, if any, of these customers must receive individualized notice of the pendency of the class action? ________________

(B) Assuming that at least some customers must receive such notice, who must pay for it?

____

(C) What if anything can the person who must pay for notice pursuant to (b) do to reduce the cost? ________________

113. Same facts as prior question. Assume that after the court has certified the action as a class action, P's lawyer and the lawyers for Biff work out a proposed settlement, by which a $1 discount coupon will be sent to each identifiable class member, and Biff's will reduce its prices by 10% for the next two years. What procedural steps, if any, must be taken?

____

114. P and X were passengers aboard an airplane owned and operated by D. The plane caught fire while landing, and P and X were both seriously injured. P filed a diversity suit against D in federal district court for the Southern District of Michigan, arguing that D flew the plane in a negligent manner. X now plans a separate suit against D. Before filing that suit, X has learned that P and he are both planning to use the same expert witness at trial, Edward, who will testify that D's pilot did not land the plane in accordance with the manufacturer's instructions. X's lawyer fears that if P tries his suit first, and does not properly prepare Edward for testimony, Edward will be seriously attacked in cross-examination, and will be a less useful witness in X's own later action against D. In this situation, what tactical step should X consider? ________________

115. Same facts as prior question. Assume that P is a citizen of Michigan, D is a citizen of Ohio, and X is a citizen of Ohio. Will the tactic you suggested in your answer to the prior question still work? ________________

116. Same facts as prior question. Now, however, assume that the federal district court rules that X is entitled to intervene as of right in the action. Does X's presence in the action satisfy the requirements of federal subject-matter jurisdiction? ________________

117. The United States government (represented by the Justice Department) has brought a federal court suit against the Ames Board of Education, charging that Ames is administering its public schools in a way that discriminates against Muslims. The essence of the complaint is that intra-district boundaries are being intentionally drawn on religious lines, and that predominantly-Muslim schools within Ames are receiving fewer resources than predominantly-non-Muslim schools. P is the parent of a Muslim Ames public school student, who wishes to intervene as of right in the action, as a co-plaintiff. Should such intervention be granted? _______________

118. A car driven by Xavier hit and injured two pedestrians, Al and Betty. The only insurance policy on Xavier's car was issued by Insurer, and has a $30,000 policy limit. Al is a citizen of the Southern District of New York; Betty is a citizen of the Western District of Oklahoma; Insurer is a citizen of the Western District of New York. Insurer is worried that it will have to defend Xavier in two distinct actions (one brought by Al and the other brought by Betty), and that defense costs plus judgments may total more than $30,000. Also, Insurer is worried that Al, Betty or both may sue in states allowing a direct action against the defendant's insurer. Insurer wants to be sure that it doesn't have to pay out more than $30,000 as the result of this accident. No suit has been commenced yet by either Al or Betty. Tactically, what should Insurer do? _______________

119. Same fact pattern as prior question. Can Insurer bring an action pursuant to federal Rule 22 on these facts? _______________

120. H and W, a married couple, jointly applied for a homeowner's insurance policy from Insurer. They then got entangled in a nasty divorce proceeding. While this proceeding was pending (and when the status of the marital home was still in doubt), a tornado destroyed the home. H now asserts that he is entitled to the entire proceeds by virtue of a prenuptial agreement signed between H and W; W asserts that she is entitled to the sole proceeds because she is the sole occupant of the house at the moment. W is a citizen of Indiana, where the home is located; H has now moved to Ohio, of which he is currently a citizen. Insurer is a citizen of Kentucky. Insurer's assets are heavily invested in junk bonds, which are relatively illiquid at the moment. Therefore, Insurer would like to delay as long as possible having to pay out the claim or even depositing the $500,000 policy proceeds in court during an interpleader proceeding. Assuming that none of the three states involved (Ohio, Kentucky and Indiana) has helpful interpleader laws, what tactical step should Insurer take? _______________

121. A commercial aircraft owned and operated by Airline, Inc. crashed into the tip of a peak in the Himalayas while en route from San Francisco to Nepal. Investigation of the "black box" and other instruments found in the wreckage indicated that the pilot believed that he was flying at 20,000 feet above sea level when he was in fact flying at only 9,000 above (less than the height of the mountain). The estate of P, one of the passengers killed in the accident, has sued Airline and Doeing (the plane's manufacturer) in a single federal court diversity action. The suit alleges that Airline was negligent in not discovering the altimeter problem, and that Doeing breached the implied warranty of merchantability by delivering a plane containing an altimeter that would fail.

Doeing's lawyer realizes that if the altimeter was defective, Doeing will be liable even if it behaved without negligence. The lawyer also realizes that if Doeing has breached the implied warranty of merchantability with respect to the altimeter, that warranty has also been breached by Altimeters R Us, the manufacturer of the altimeter (which is not a defendant thus far). What tactical step should Doeing take to ensure that Doeing does not get unfairly saddled with liability for an act (manufacture and delivery of a defective altimeter) that is really the fault of Altimeters R Us? _______________

122. Paula, a citizen of Ohio, wished to have a house constructed for her on land she owned in Ohio. She contracted with Dave, a general contractor, who is a citizen of Kentucky; the contract stated that Dave would build a house according to Paula's specifications on Paula's land, for a total construction price of $1MM. Dave decided to engage Ted as a large sub-contractor, and Ted agreed to indemnify Dave against any damages Dave might be required to pay on account of non-conforming work by Ted. Ted did not contract directly with Paula in any way. Dave is a citizen of Kentucky, and lives in the town of Covington. Ted is a citizen of Ohio, and lives in Cincinnati (about 50 miles from Covington).

Dave constructed the house; Paula paid for it, and moved in. Paula then discovered certain latent defects (caused by Ted's poor work), which rendered the house substantially less valuable. Paula has brought a suit against Dave in federal court for the Eastern District of Kentucky (where Covington is located); the suit is based in diversity, and seeks $200,000 damages for breach of contract. Paula has not joined Ted in the suit. Dave would now like to bring Ted into the suit, so that if Dave is required to pay up to $200,000 damages, Ted, in the same action, will be required to indemnify Dave for his amount. Although Ted has minimum contacts with Kentucky, the Kentucky long-arm statute is a very limited one which would not allow service on Ted in an action by Paula or Dave concerning either the Paula-Dave or the Dave-Ted contract.

(A) What can Dave do to bring Ted into this action? ________________

(B) What special FRCP provision will help you solve any problem relating to personal jurisdiction over anyone in the suit ? ________________

123. Same basic fact pattern as the prior question. Assume that Ted now wishes to file a claim against Paula, alleging that Paula libeled him by writing a letter to the local newspaper, which stated, "Ted secretly and crookedly induced Dave to save them both a few bucks by building my house in a sloppy and dangerous way." Ted's claim is for $100,000. Will the court hear Ted's claim against Paula? ________________

124. Same basic fact pattern as the prior two questions. Now, assume that after Paula has sued Dave, Dave has impleaded Ted, and Ted has made a claim against Paula for libel, Paula wishes to make a claim against Ted for deceit — she alleges that Ted conspired with Dave to induce her to pay for an improperly-constructed house. The claim does not involve a federal question, and is for $100,000. Will the court hear Paula's claim against Ted? ________________

125. Deborah and Dell, each driving a separate car, decided to drag-race one day. While doing so, one or both of them (this is not clear) collided with a car driven by Pete, injuring him. Pete has brought a federal diversity action against both Deborah and Dell, alleging that each, because of negligence, is jointly and severally responsible for his injuries. Pete is a citizen of Michigan; Deborah and Dell are both citizens of Wisconsin. Deborah would like to be able to make a claim against Dell for damage to her car, suffered in the same accident. However, Deborah does not want to make the claim in the current action, because she thinks that the federal judge assigned to this case is hostile to women drag-racers. If Deborah does not assert her claim against Dell in the present action, will she be able to bring a separate suit against Dell in Wisconsin state court after Pete's case is completed? ________________

126. Same facts as prior question. Suppose that Deborah does bring a claim against Dell as part of Pete's original action. Assume that Deborah's claim is for $100,000. Will the federal court take jurisdiction over Deborah's claim against Dell? ________________

CHAPTER 9

FORMER ADJUDICATION

128. P and D, each driving a car, collided. P suffered serious personal injuries, and her car was totally demolished. P brought an action in Ames state court for damages for her personal injuries, but not for any loss of property. P won the suit. P then commenced a second action against D, for the damage to her car, in Ames state court. Will the court hear this second action? ________________

131. Phillip was injured when a car he was driving collided with a car driven by Doreen. Phillip sued Doreen for negligence in Ames state court. The case was tried before a jury, and the jury found for Phillip, awarding him substantial damages. Judgment was entered. Then, Doreen brought a negligence suit against Phillip for property damage arising from the same transaction. This suit, too, was brought in Ames state court. In Doreen's suit, may she assert, and prove, that Phillip's negligence caused the accident? ________________

132. Same basic fact pattern as the prior question. Now, assume that after Phillip sued Doreen in Ames state court for negligence, Doreen declined to answer. A default judgment was entered against her for $100,000 in damages. Doreen then instituted an action, in Ames, against Phillip for negligence. Will the court allow Doreen to assert and prove that Phillip was negligent? ________________

134. Penny and Dan, each driving a car, were involved in what at first appeared to be a minor fender bender. Penny sued Dan for negligence in municipal court for the town of Langdell, a small claims court whose jurisdiction is limited to cases involving less than $5,000. This court has quite informal procedures; for instance, there is no right to jury trial, and there are no formal rules for the admissibility of evidence. The jurisdiction applies common-law contributory negligence. Penny sought $2,000 for property damage suffered by her. The judge found that Dan drove negligently and that Penny did not; he awarded the full $2,000 to Penny.

Dan shortly thereafter developed back trouble, which in the opinion of his doctor, stemmed from the collision with Penny. Dan sued in a court of general jurisdiction (in the state where Langdell is located) for $100,000 of compensatory damages for medical expense, and pain and suffering. Penny now asserts that Dan is collaterally estopped from either: (1) showing that Penny was negligent; or (2) denying that Dan himself was negligent. Which, if either, of these assertions is correct? ________________

135. Perry sued Denise for negligence, arising out of an auto accident. Since Perry was seeking only a modest sum for actual medical expenses, Denise agreed to settle the case for a $2,000 payment to Perry. The settlement document recited these facts, and made no statement about what effect the settlement would have on any other litigation. A judgment was entered in accordance with this settlement. Shortly thereafter, Xavier, who was injured in the same accident, sued Denise. Putting aside the issue of whether the mutuality doctrine or Xavier's status as a stranger to the first action prevents him from using collateral estoppel, is Denise entitled to deny her negligence as part of her defense of the action brought by Xavier? ________________

136. The Agriculture Department of the state of Ames bars any milk wholesaler from selling milk within Ames at a wholesale price of less than $1 per quart. Potter, an out-of-state wholesaler who wanted to sell milk at less than the $1 price, sued the Department of Agriculture in Ames state court. Potter's claim was that the price law discriminated against out-of-state commerce, in violation of the dormant Commerce Clause of the U.S. Constitution. The trial judge who heard the suit agreed with Potter's assertion. Potter, immediately after his victory, began selling milk at 90 cents per gallon. The Agriculture Department did not appeal. Instead, it actively defended a similar suit brought by Xavier, and lost that one at the trial level also. Subsequently, the Department appealed the loss to Xavier to the Ames Supreme Court (the highest court in the state), which found that the price floor was valid as a constitutional matter. Potter continued to sell 90 cent/gallon milk after the decision in Xavier's suit. The Agriculture Department then brought a suit to obtain an injunction against Potter's continuing to sell milk at less than $1 per gallon. Potter asserts that his victory in the earlier suit against him collaterally estops Ames from relitigating that issue with him now. Will Potter get the benefit of collateral estoppel on these facts? ________________

137. Peter and Paul were neighbors who agreed to share a cab ride to the airport one night. The cab was driven by David. On a poorly lit city street, the cab smashed into an abandoned car (whose owner was never traced) and Peter and Paul were both seriously injured. Peter brought a suit against David in Ames state court. Peter's lawyer aggressively and expertly litigated the case, but the jury found in favor of David. Special interrogatories given to the jury made it clear that the jury simply believed that David used all due care, and could not have prevented the accident by ordinary precautions. After this verdict, Paul brought a suit against David in Ames state court, also alleging negligence relating to the same accident. Assuming that Paul has no evidence of David's negligence to put forth except evidence used by Peter in the first suit, may Paul nonetheless assert and prove that David drove negligently and caused the accident? ________________

138. Parker was a lifelong smoker. The only two brands he ever smoked were Acme and Baker. On average, he smoked two packs of Acme per day, and one pack of Baker. He contracted lung cancer, and then brought a products liability suit against Acme in Ames state court, asserting that Acme was responsible for his lung cancer. Acme presented evidence that Parker's lung cancer was of a type not usually associated with cigarette smoking, that it was of a type usually associated with asbestos exposure, and that Parker had worked around asbestos for many years. The case was tried to a judge, who concluded that Parker had failed to prove by a preponderance of the evidence that cigarette smoking (regardless of brand) contributed substantially to his getting lung cancer. Parker then brought a suit against Baker, again in Ames state court, making the same type of allegations he had made against Acme. Baker now argues that Parker should be collaterally estopped from asserting that his lung cancer was caused by any brand of cigarette. Granting Baker's request will result in Parker's claim being dismissed before trial. Should Baker be permitted to use collateral estoppel to bar Parker from claiming that his lung cancer was caused by cigarettes? ________________

139. Fred and Greg went one day to a diner operated by Dave. Fred ordered a bowl of clam chowder. The meal went uneventfully, and Fred and Greg left. One week later, Fred sued Dave for strict product liability, alleging that the chowder was dangerously defective, and caused Fred to undergo food poisoning. The suit was tried in a court of general jurisdiction of the state of Ames, and Fred sought $2,000 in damages. Dave defended by trying to show that Fred's illness was in fact the flu, but the judge found in Fred's favor, and awarded $2,000 in damages. Nowhere during the trial was Greg mentioned.

Shortly after Fred's verdict against Dave, Greg instituted a suit against Dave in Ames state court. His suit alleges that he drank some of Fred's order of clam chowder, and that he too was food poisoned. Greg's suit seeks $100,000 in damages, stating that while the hospital was treating him for food poisoning, it gave him a drug which caused him to go into convulsions, and that Dave must be liable for all of the resulting injury to Greg. At the trial, Greg seeks to collaterally estop Dave from denying that the clam chowder was dangerously defective (though he is willing to let Dave attempt to prove that the defectiveness was not the proximate cause of Greg's own injuries). Should Greg be allowed to use collateral estoppel in this manner? ________________

140. A group of plaintiff lawyers decided that the time was ripe for bringing a serious strict product liability action against one or more of the leading talcum powder companies whose products allegedly cause cancer. They singled out the A+ Talcum Co. as their primary defendant. They then advertised in consumer magazines for possible plaintiffs who had suffered talcum-related cancer. After interviewing dozens of potential plaintiffs, they finally settled upon Angie as their first plaintiff. They picked Angie because her case was especially appealing for several reasons, including the strong link between her talcum use and her cancer; also, they think she'll be a very compelling witness. Angie's case was tried to a jury in Ames state court. After a long trial, the jury found that talcum powder produced by A+ was dangerously defective, that A+ did not issue adequate warnings, and that A+ should therefore be liable to Angie for $200,000.

After this victory, the same group of lawyers selected Betty as the next plaintiff. Her case also seems to be strong, though not as strong as Angie's for several reasons (e.g., she would not make as appealing a witness as Angie). Betty's lawyers now propose that A+ be collaterally estopped from denying that its talcum power is a dangerously defective product, and from denying that its warning labels (at least during the years that were at issue in Angie's suit) were inadequate. Should this use of collateral estoppel be allowed? ________________

141. In the courts of the state of Ames, Abel sued Baker for negligence arising out of an automobile accident. The judge concluded that Baker was negligent, and entered judgment in favor of Abel. Shortly thereafter, Conroy sued Baker for negligence arising out of the same auto accident; this suit is taking place in the courts of the state of Bates. The Ames Supreme Court allows broad offensive use of collateral estoppel, and would allow Conroy to make use of collateral estoppel against Baker on the issue of Baker's negligence in the accident, if Conroy's suit had been filed in Ames. The Supreme Court of Bates, by contrast, is a more old-fashioned jurisdiction which almost never allows offensive use of collateral estoppel by a stranger to the first action. Conroy seeks to collaterally estop Baker from denying Baker's negligence in the accident.

(A) Should Conroy be given the benefits of collateral estoppel here? ________________

(B) Will the answer to (A) be left to the court's discretion, or will it be it imposed by some non-discretionary requirement? ________________

142. Same basic fact pattern as prior question. Now, however, assume that the second action (by Conroy) was filed not in the state courts of Bates, but rather, in federal district court for the District of Bates. Should/must the federal judge give Conroy the benefit of collateral estoppel against Baker? ________________

143. Same basic fact pattern as prior two questions. Now, however, assume that the first suit is in federal court for the District of Ames (sitting in diversity), and the second suit is in the state court of Bates. Again, assume that the Ames courts allow broad use of collateral estoppel, and would therefore allow Conroy to use collateral estoppel against Baker on the issue of Baker's negligence if Conroy's suit was filed in Ames. Must the state court of Bates allow Conroy to use collateral estoppel? ________________

ANSWERS TO SHORT-ANSWER QUESTIONS

1. Yes. It is quite clear that a court may constitutionally exercise jurisdiction over anyone who is ***domiciled*** in that state. Even though D has temporarily changed his residence to California, his domicile remains Connecticut. This is because one's domicile is the last place of which it was true both that one resided there and that one had the indefinite intent to remain there. Since D does not intend to remain in California, California cannot be his domicile, so we look at the next prior place he resided, Connecticut. (In fact, Connecticut would still be D's domicile even if he intended to move to New York after he finished his California job.)

2. No, probably. According to *Worldwide Volkswagen v. Woodson*, 444 U.S. 286 (1980), the mere fact that a product finds its way into a state and causes injury there is not enough to subject the out-of-state manufacturer or vendor to personal jurisdiction there. Instead, the defendant must have made some effort to ***market*** in the forum state. Here, D was not attempting to market in South Carolina, even though he knew that the doughnuts in question would find their way to South Carolina. Therefore, even though P resides in and is presently located in South Carolina, and all the witnesses are there, it would probably be a violation of due process for the South Carolina courts to subject D to personal jurisdiction there.

4. No. First, notice that P's suit requires only *specific* jurisdiction, not *general* jurisdiction, over D. That is, P's claim arises out of the contacts between D and the forum state (the sale, through D's authorized distributor, of a machine made by D to a New Jersey-based customer, and the consequent in-state injury to P caused by that machine). Next, we need to know what kinds of connections between an out-of-state or foreign manufacturer and the forum state will suffice for specific jurisdiction. The Supreme Court has held that for a state to constitutionally exercise specific jurisdiction over an out-of-state or foreign manufacturer of an item that causes in-state injuries, it is *not* enough that it was merely *foreseeable* to the manufacturer that the item would find its way into the forum state and cause injury there (*World-Wide Volkswagen*). Instead, something more of a connection between the manufacturer and the forum state is required. But specific jurisdiction *can* be constitutionally exercised if the defendant manufacturer ***"purposefully availed itself"*** of the opportunity to serve the forum state's market. Here, this "purposeful availment" (or "targeting") test is satisfied, because D not only urged Distrib to make as many American sales as possible, but approved Distrib's plan to open a New Jersey office from which, as D knew, Distrib intended to serve the lucrative New Jersey market. That's enough to constitute a targeting by D of the New Jersey market.

5. The court should grant both motions. First, notice that P's suit requires *general* (not specific) jurisdiction over both D and D-Sub in order to proceed. That's because the suit arises out of a valve made and installed abroad, so that the suit does not arise out of whatever contacts D and/or D-Sub might have with the forum state. (Remember that when the plaintiff's claim does not arise out of any connection between the defendant and the forum state, the resulting exercise of jurisdiction is "general" rather than "specific.") For a court to exercise general jurisdiction, the due process clause of the U.S. Constitution's 14th Amendment requires much greater voluntary connections between the defendant and the forum state than where "specific" jurisdiction is involved. In fact, where the defendant is a corporation, the forum state may normally exercise general jurisdiction over it only if the corporation is ***"at home"*** in the forum state. And a corporation is deemed to be "at home" in a state only if the corporation is either ***incorporated in*** that state or has its ***principal place of business there***. *Daimler AG v. Bauman.*

Since neither D nor D-Sub is either incorporated in Texas or has a principal place of business in Texas, neither defendant is "at home" in Texas. Therefore, Texas cannot exercise general jurisdiction against either defendant. So although P would be able to sue both D and D-Sub for an accident occurring *in Texas* arising out of a defective valve sold by D-Sub to a *Texas-based* boiler customer (that would be an exercise of *specific* jurisdiction, making the defendant's purposeful availment of the Texas market sufficient for jurisdiction), P may not sue either D or D-Sub for this *non-Texas-based* accident. And notice that this result does not depend solely on the fact that the accident occurred outside the U.S. — the same result (no general jurisdiction by Texas) would occur if the accident had happened somewhere in the U.S. but outside of Texas.

6. **(A) Motion denied; specific jurisdiction.** First, notice that Montana's only significance in the litigation is that it is the state in which the Sedan was purchased (by Owner), from Deal's showroom there. At the outset, we know that if the Montana court is to have jurisdiction over Driver's claim, that jurisdiction will have to be *specific*, not general. (That's because, under *Daimler v. Bauman*, for general jurisdiction to lie against a corporate defendant, the defendant must be "at home" in the forum state, a status that exists only if the corporation is either incorporated in the forum state or has its principal place of business there. Montana does not qualify on either score.)

For the Montana court to have specific jurisdiction over Drive's claim, two requirements will have to be met: (1) Big must have "minimum contacts" with Montana; and (2) it must be the case that Drive's claim in some sense "arose out of or relates to" Big's contacts with Montana. As to requirement (1): in determining whether a corporate defendant has minimum contacts with the forum state, the general inquiry is whether the defendant somehow "targeted" the forum state as a place to sell its goods. *World-Wide Volkswagen* expresses the test this way: the defendant's "conduct and connection with the forum state" must be sufficient that we can say the defendant "should reasonably anticipate being haled into court there." Normally, *World-Wide* says, for that to be true the defendant must have made efforts "to ***serve, directly or indirectly, the market for its products" in the forum state***; it's not enough that, say, the presence of the defendant's product in the forum state was an "isolated occurrence," or was due entirely to the unilateral activities of the plaintiff.

When this standard is applied to Montana, it's clear that Big's contacts with the state *are* enough to constitute minimum contacts. Big has not only selected Deal to be an authorized dealer located in the state, but has by contract commanded Deal to extensively market Big's vehicles in a defined territory within the state; that's more than sufficient to show that Big made efforts "to serve, directly or indirectly, the market for its products" in Montana.

As to requirement (2) (claim "arose out of" D's forum-state contacts), it is highly likely that Montana satisfies this requirement too. There is no Supreme Court case in which the Court had to decide whether the fact that a defective product was purchased in the forum state (but later caused an accident elsewhere) is by itself enough to meet the requirement for specific jurisdiction that the claim "arose out of" the defendant's forum-state connections. But language in some of the Court's opinions suggests that this will be enough. Plus, we can say that that if Owner had not bought the Sedan in Montana, the accident would not have occurred at all; the fact that the in-forum-state purchase was thus a "but for" cause of the accident sounds intuitively like enough of a connection to compel the conclusion that the claim "arose out of" Big's decision to cause the car in question to be sold in the state. Therefore, the Montana court has specific jurisdiction over Drive's suit.

(B) Motion granted; no jurisdiction. The only connection between Pass' claim and North Dakota is that Pass was a resident of the state at the time of the accident and recovered there from his injuries. The first requirement to check for is whether Big has minimum contacts with North Dakota. We are told that Big has no operations, or authorized dealers, in North Dakota; we are also indirectly told that neither Big nor any of the five authorized dealers is making any sales or marketing efforts directed at North Dakota consumers. Therefore, it cannot be said that Big has made efforts "to serve, directly or indirectly, the market for its products" in North Dakota (*World-Wide Volkswagen*). The fact that a few (fewer than 10) Big vehicles are located in the state (all of which have been brought there by the unilateral action of their owners who moved into the state) doesn't change this. Therefore, Big has not "purposely availed itself of the privilege of conducting activities within the forum state" (*Hanson v. Denckla*), so it doesn't have minimum contacts with the state. That's enough to foreclose the possibility that North Dakota has specific jurisdiction over Big, and we don't even need to get to the question of whether the claim in some sense "arose out of" Big's voluntary contacts with North Dakota. (If we *did* have to resolve that question, the answer would be "no" – the claim did not arise out of Big's North Dakota contacts.)

(C) Motion granted; no jurisdiction. Kentucky is of course both Ped's state of residence and the state in which the accident occurred. The latter fact is enough by itself to allow us to conclude that Ped's claim "arose out of" Kentucky contacts. But in any event, Kentucky can only have jurisdiction over Big if Big has minimum contacts with the state.

On the minimum-contacts issue, the analysis is exactly the same as for North Dakota in part (B): we know that Big has no operations or authorized dealers in Kentucky, and that neither Big nor any of its authorized dealers is trying to market Big's products in Kentucky. That's enough for us to say that Big has not made efforts to serve the market for its products in Kentucky. And that, in turn, is enough to let us say that Big does not have minimum contacts with the state.

(D) Motion denied; general jurisdiction. Tennessee is, of course, the state in which Big has its principal place of business. That means that, according to *Daimler v. Bauman*, Big is "at home" there. That fact alone means that the Tennessee courts have general jurisdiction over Big. By "general jurisdiction," we mean "the power to hear any claim against the defendant, whether or not the claim arose out of any voluntary connections between the defendant in the forum state." Therefore, we don't even need to figure out whether Owner's claim "arose out of" Big's voluntary connections with Tennessee. This is probably the easiest of the five subparts of this question to answer, because it requires no judgment: as soon as we know that the suit has been filed in the defendant's state of principal place of business, the entire personal jurisdiction issue is *automatically* resolved. (The same would be true if Owner sued Big in

Delaware, Big's state of incorporation; a corporation is automatically at home in its state of incorporation, and can therefore always be sued there, even on a claim that has no connection with the state.)

(E) Motion granted; no jurisdiction. It's obvious that Big has minimum contacts with Ohio: where a corporation manufactures items that produce annual revenues of $20 million, that fact alone is enough to constitute minimum contacts, since a defendant's establishment in the forum state of such a consequential operation is a voluntary choice to make use of the state's resources and laws, and the defendant should "reasonably anticipate being haled into court there" (*World-Wide Volkswagen*) as a result.

But since Big is not "at home" in Ohio (it's only at home in its state of principal place of business and state of incorporation), any jurisdiction there would have to be of the "specific" variety, which would require that Truck's claim "arose out of" the defendant's connections with the forum state. This requirement isn't met: the Sedan wasn't produced in Ohio, the accident didn't happen there, and none of Big's in-Ohio activities had anything to do with the accident that has given rise to Truck's claim. Therefore, this is a classic situation in which a corporate defendant will be effectively immune from suit in a state even though it conducts major operations in that state.

7. **(A) No, motion denied.** First, since StentCo is neither incorporated in Minnesota nor with its principal place of business there, the company is not "at home" in the forum state. Therefore, personal jurisdiction over it, if such exists at all, would have to be specific rather than general. Consequently, for jurisdiction to exist as to the claim of any plaintiff in the P1-P6 group, it will have to be the case both that: (1) StentCo has minimum contacts with Minnesota; and (2) the claim "arises out of" StentCo's voluntary contacts with Minnesota. As to (1) (minimum contacts), this requirement is clearly satisfied here: by shipping multiple millions of dollars of devices into the forum state each year, the company has clearly made efforts to "serve directly or indirectly, the market for its products" in the state (*World-Wide Volkswagen*), and such "purposeful availment" of the opportunity to do business in the forum state suffices to establish minimum contacts. And to (2) (claim "arose out of"), this requirement is also easily satisfied as to the claims of P1-P6: each patient received implantation of the device in the forum state, and then had the device removed in the forum state following StentCo's notice-of-mandatory-recall; certainly the first of these events (and probably the second, as well) would have sufficed to satisfy the requirement that the claim arose out of the defendant's voluntary contacts with the forum state.

(B) Yes, motion granted. As with part (A), personal jurisdiction will have to be specific rather than general, if jurisdiction exists at all. The minimum-contacts part of the test is of course satisfied, as described in the answer to part (A). But the "arose out of" part of the test is *not* satisfied with respect to P7's claim, because there is no aspect of P7's claim that has anything to do with events in Minnesota. It's true that P7 is alleging exactly the same conduct by StentCo, and the same resulting injury, as are asserted by P1 through P6; therefore, P7 can accurately argue that there would be virtually no extra burden on StentCo (or the court) from allowing P7's claim to be joined to the six virtually-identical claims that are already properly before the court. But the U.S. Supreme Court, in *Bristol-Myers Squibb v. Superior Court* (2017), on essentially the same facts, expressly rejected this argument raised by "nonresident plaintiffs." The Court there held that each plaintiff's claim must *independently* arise out of voluntary contacts between the defendant and the forum state, and the fact that some plaintiffs' claims (e.g., the claims of P1-P6) have the necessary forum-state connection, does not mean that a lesser connection between the defendant and the forum state will suffice for some other plaintiff's claim (e.g., P7's claim) than if the latter were the only claim in the suit.

8. No, because the Caledonia statute does not violate D's due process rights. The facts are essentially identical to those in *Mallory v. Norfolk Southern Ry*, where Pennsylvania enacted a statute almost word-for-word like the Jurisdiction Act here. The Supreme Court held that because of a very old prior decision (from 1917), a state may pass such a statute and constitutionally use it to confer general jurisdiction (i.e., jurisdiction over any suit, even if the matter being litigated has nothing to do with the state) over all claims made against the registrant. The court said in *Malory* that (1) the Pennsylvania registration statute fell within the general rule that a party can effectively ***consent*** to general jurisdiction, regardless of whether the party has minimum contacts with the state; and (2) registering to do business under that statute was a valid form of "consent," even though even though the registrant had no choice but to register if it wanted to do any business in the state.

Because the jurisdiction here is "general," the fact that D does not have minimum contacts with Caledonia is irrelevant (though without the statute, Caledonia wouldn't even have *specific* jurisdiction because of this lack of minimum contacts).

11. Yes. Software Co.'s suit is a "federal question" suit. That is, Software Co.'s claim "arises under the constitution, laws, or treaties of the United States," since the source of the claim is the federal copyright statute. In federal question suits, the federal court will hear the case if the defendant has minimum contacts with the forum state, even though the courts of the state might not (for reasons of fairness or judicial economy) have heard a suit against that defendant. So the fact that the Washington courts would not hear any suit against Clone Co. is irrelevant — since Clone Co. has the constitutionally-required minimum contacts with Washington, the federal court will hear the suit. (But this is not the rule for suits based on diversity.)

12. No. In diversity cases, the federal courts only exercise the personal jurisdiction that is allowed by the law of the state in which they sit, even if the state law does not go to the limits of what the state could do commensurate with due process. So the rule for diversity actions is quite different from that for federal question actions — this fact pattern is virtually identical to the fact pattern of the prior question except that we are dealing with diversity rather than federal question; yet the result is that here there is no federal-court jurisdiction and in the prior question there is.

13. No, because the Ds' due process rights would not be violated by the action. First, the relevant due process clause is *not* the Fourteenth Amendment (which applies only to actions taken by a *state*, such as the exercise of personal jurisdiction by the state's courts). Rather, whatever due process rights the Ds may have in federal courts are determined by the *Fifth* Amendment's due process clause (which is what applies to actions by the *federal* government, including the federal courts' exercise of personal jurisdiction).

Next, the definition of Fifth Amendment "due process" for the Ds' claims is ***not as broad*** as the definition of that term in the Fourteenth Amendment. It's true that a key purpose of the Fourteenth Amendment's due process clause (which requires "minimum contacts") is to give the defendant freedom from unfairly being required to defend a faraway state-court action. But there's a second purpose for requiring minimum contacts under that clause: to ***protect the sovereignty*** of each state against incursion by other states. However, the *Fifth* Amendment requirement of due process, since it's an obligation of the federal government, is ***not required to protect the sovereignty of any state.*** So the *only* purpose of Fifth Amendment due process is fairness to the defendant in being forced to defend in the U.S. Thus that fairness is what the federal court here must evaluate.

The federal government has a strong interest in giving civil redress to any American injured abroad by a terrorist act. Therefore, it is not unfair to require the foreign terrorist who causes such an injury to defend in any federal court throughout the U.S., even if the terrorist has not committed any act in the U.S., and cannot be said to have minimum contacts with the U.S. as a whole. Thus the RTA, in asserting federal-court jurisdiction over the foreign terrorist Ds in any U.S. federal court, regardless of the absence of minimum contacts, does not violate the Ds' Fifth Amendment due process rights. (The facts and holding are similar to those of *Fuld v. Palestine Liberation Org.*, where the federal equivalent of the RTA applied only to members of the PLO who killed or injured an American abroad; the Court found no Fifth Amendment violation.)

14. No. The landmark case of *Shaffer v. Heitner* states that *quasi in rem* jurisdiction over a defendant may not be exercised unless the defendant has such minimum contacts with the forum state that *in personam* jurisdiction could be exercised over him. Since D has no contacts at all with Ohio (except for the very fortuitous fact that D's Pennsylvania-based job is with an Ohio-headquartered company), the Ohio courts could not exercise personal jurisdiction over D. Consequently, under *Shaffer v. Heitner*, Ohio may not achieve the same result by seizing part of D's wages to serve as the means for satisfying a possible judgment. The fact that P happens to be an Ohio resident is irrelevant — what counts is D's contacts with the forum state.

15. Yes. Under *Connecticut v. Doehr*, 501 U.S. 1 (1991), the court is to apply a three-part balancing test in determining whether a statute allowing for prejudgment attachment satisfies the due process rights of the person whose property is being attached (here, D): the court weighs the harm to D's property right, the risk of an erroneous deprivation, and the strength of the other party's (here, P) interest in obtaining the prejudgment attachment. Here, the impact on D is significant, since D can't spend the money in the account (and even a temporary, up-to-one-month deprivation would probably be found to be material). The risk of erroneous deprivation is substantial, because P's one-sided conclusory allegations (with no rebuttal by D or opportunity to cross-examine P or to present witnesses) leave the judge no real ability to assess the likelihood that P will prevail on the merits. The strength of P's interest in the attachment is weak, because the statute does not require P to show that D is about to transfer funds or do anything else that would make it hard for P to collect any judgment he might obtain. All in all, the statute here is marginally better than the one struck down in Doehr, but similar enough to it that it, too, would almost certainly be found to violate due process.

19. Central, Northern and Southern Districts of California. In both diversity and federal question cases, venue lies in any district where any defendant resides, so long as, if there is more than one defendant, all the defendants reside in the state containing that district. 28 U.S.C. §1391(a)(1). This yields the Central and Northern Districts of California. Additionally, for both diversity and federal question cases, venue lies in any judicial district "in which a substantial part of the events or omissions giving rise to the claim occurred, or a substantial part of property that is the subject of the action is situated. ..." 28 U.S.C. §1391(a)(2). This yields the Southern District of California, where the accident took place. There is no provision allowing venue based on the residence of the plaintiff.

20. Southern District of California. As noted in the prior answer, venue based on defendants' residence exists only if all defendants are at least residents of the same state. Since this is not true here, the fact that the Central District of California and the District of New Mexico are each home to one defendant is irrelevant. Only the "place of events" section, §1391(a)(2), gives venue, which as in the prior question is the Southern District of California.

22. Yes. For there to be subject-matter jurisdiction, there must of course be diversity of citizenship. That is, P and D must be "citizens" of different states. "Citizenship" for this purpose is not synonymous with "residence." Instead, a person is a "citizen" only of the state where he is *domiciled*, i.e., has his principal residence. On these facts, P's principal residence is clearly New York, and Connecticut is merely his secondary residence. Therefore, P is a "citizen" of New York, and he has diversity of citizenship with D. Consequently, the court may hear the case.

23. No. Since there is no federal question present, the federal subject-matter jurisdiction must be supplied by diversity if at all. But by a judge-made construction of the federal diversity statute, there must be ***"complete"*** diversity. That is, it must be the case that no plaintiff is a citizen of the same state as any defendant. Since P2 and D2 are both citizens of New Jersey, diversity is deemed not to exist even though there is also a pair of opponents (P1 and D1) who are citizens of different states from each other. See *Strawbridge v. Curtiss*, 3 Cranch 267 (1806).

24. No. A corporation (whether plaintiff or defendant) is deemed to be a citizen ***both*** of the state where it has its principal place of business ***and*** the state where it is incorporated. 28 U.S.C. §1332(c)(1). Putting this rule together with the rule requiring complete diversity, it becomes the case that D can be sued only if none of the Ps is a citizen of ***either*** Delaware or New York. Since P1 is a citizen of Delaware, complete diversity is lacking and there is no diversity jurisdiction.

27. No. For diversity actions, the ***amount in controversy*** must exceed $75,000. See 28 U.S.C. §1332(a). Since P is claiming only the amount of money due under the contract, and that amount comes to less than $75,000, this requirement is not satisfied. (Nor can costs, interest or attorney's fees generally be included to meet the amount.)

28. Yes. A plaintiff may ***"aggregate,"*** i.e., add together, all of his claims against a single defendant, for purposes of meeting the $75,000 diversity amount in controversy requirement. This is true even if no single claim meets the jurisdictional amount by itself.

29. Yes. In *Exxon Mobil Corp. v. Allapattah Services, Inc.*, 125 S.Ct. 2611 (2005), the Supreme Court held that when multiple plaintiffs join under Rule 20, as long as one satisfies the amount in controversy requirement, the doctrine of supplemental jurisdiction permits the other(s) to join in with claims that don't meet the requirement. So here, because P1's claim is for more than $75,000, P2 can join the action under Rule 20(b) even though P2's claim is for less than $75,000.

31. (A) Supplemental Jurisdiction.

(B) No, probably. This fact pattern is a classic illustration of the doctrine of ***supplemental*** jurisdiction. Supplemental jurisdiction, codified in 28 U.S.C. §1367, provides that in cases where "the district courts have original jurisdiction [over a federal question], the district court shall have supplemental jurisdiction over all other claims that are so related to claims in the action within such original jurisdiction that they form part of the same case or controversy under Article III. …" Supplemental jurisdiction applies to additional claims between the same two parties, as well as to "pendent parties" (third parties brought into the suit who are under the federal court's jurisdiction), provided that both claims derive from a ***common nucleus of operative fact*** (a requirement implied by the statute's reference to "Article III case or controversy").

Here, the federal court would not ordinarily have jurisdiction over the state unfair competition claim, because that claim apparently does not present a federal question, and there is no diversity between the parties (since both are citizens of Georgia). But since the antitrust claim presents a federal question, and since the practices that are being relied on by D to support that federal claim are the same as the practices that are alleged to violate the state statute, both claims derive from a "common nucleus of operative fact," and P would ordinarily be expected to try them all in one suit. The federal court would still be free to use its ***discretion*** under §1367(c) to decline to hear the state-law claim, but on these facts it probably would hear the claim (since considerations of judicial economy and convenience militate in favor of hearing both claims).

31. (A) Supplemental jurisdiction. Where the plaintiff has a valid diversity claim against the defendant, the doctrine of ***supplemental jurisdiction*** often allows additional claims or parties to be brought into the litigation, even though the additional claim or party does not satisfy the requirement of diversity or the amount in controversy requirement ($75,000) applied in diversity actions.

(B) No. Supplemental jurisdiction will always encompass a defendant's compulsory counterclaim. According to Federal Rule 13(a), a counterclaim is compulsory "if the claim (A) arises out of the transaction or occurrence that is the subject matter of the opposing party's claim; and (B) does not require adding another party over whom the court cannot acquire jurisdiction." By this test, D's counterclaim against P was a compulsory one, since both claims arose out of the same auto accident. Accordingly, the court will hear the counterclaim as part of its supplemental jurisdiction, even though that counterclaim does not independently meet the amount in controversy requirement for diversity suits.

34. No. Just as the federal courts virtually always allow supplemental jurisdiction over a compulsory counterclaim, so they also allow supplemental jurisdiction over an additional party to a compulsory counterclaim. Consequently, the fact that Xavier is a citizen of the same state as D (thus technically preventing complete diversity from existing) will be disregarded by the court. Although 28 U.S.C. §1367(b) does restrict certain types of joinder when the original claim is based on diversity, these restrictions do not apply to claims by defendants, nor do they apply to Rule 13 counterclaims.

34. Yes. D's claim against P is a ***permissive*** counterclaim (Rule 13(b)), since it does not arise out of the transaction or occurrence that is the subject matter of the plaintiff's claim. Because this permissive counterclaim and the original claim do not derive from a common nucleus of operative fact, the counterclaim does not satisfy the standard of 28 U.S.C. §1367, and it will

not fall under a court's supplemental jurisdiction. For the same reason, D's claim against Wanda does not fall under supplemental jurisdiction. Therefore, D's claim must independently meet the federal subject-matter jurisdictional requirements — that is, there must be either diversity or a federal question, and any applicable amount in controversy requirement must be satisfied. Since there is no federal question, and since D and Wanda are citizens of the same state (Oregon), the federal subject-matter jurisdictional requirements are not satisfied, and Wanda is entitled to dismissal.

36. Yes. A Rule 14 third-party claim brought by a third-party plaintiff (the defendant in the main action) against a third-party defendant is always considered to be within the supplemental jurisdiction of the court. 28 U.S.C. §1367. However, the fact that supplemental jurisdiction will encompass the third-party claim against Ted under §1367 does not mean that the requirements of ***personal*** jurisdiction don't have to be satisfied as to Ted. For the third-party claim against Ted to be heard by the New York federal court, it must still be the case that Ted has minimum contacts with New York, which the facts say he does not.

38. Yes. The federal courts only have removal jurisdiction of a case which could have been brought as an original action in the federal courts. For this purpose, "could have been brought" includes all requirements of federal subject-matter jurisdiction, including any applicable amount in controversy requirement. Since P's claim could only have been brought as a diversity action (no federal question is present), that claim must be for more than $75,000 to satisfy the amount in controversy requirement. P is deemed to be ***master of her complaint***, and if she seeks less than $75,000, that is dispositive even though her claim could quite properly have been for more than the jurisdictional amount. So the federal judge, as in any situation where removal is not proper, should remand the case to state court.

39. Yes. The most important single fact to remember about federal removal jurisdiction is that where a case is based solely on diversity, the defendant ***may not remove if he is a citizen of the state where the action is pending***. (This restricts removal and diversity cases to situations in which the defendant would suffer from having to litigate "away" rather than "at home" if removal were not allowed.) Since a corporation is deemed to be a citizen of the state where it has its principal place of business as well as the state where it is incorporated, D is deemed a citizen of both New Jersey and Delaware, and may therefore not remove an action pending in the New Jersey courts.

40. No. Where the plaintiff's claim raises a federal question, the defendant may remove even though the state court suit is pending in the state of which the defendant is a citizen. This is the principal difference between removal jurisdiction in federal question actions and removal in diversity suits (where a defendant may not remove if the suit is pending in his home state, as shown by the prior question).

41. (A) Yes, the removal was proper. P is incorrect to argue that the fact that D is a citizen of the forum state prevents D from removing. If this were a case *founded only on state law* (so that what would be removed would result in a federal diversity case), P's argument would be correct, because in diversity cases, the suit may be removed only if ***no proper defendant is a citizen*** of the state where the action is pending (Minnetonka). But here, the original state case includes a claim based on federal law, so the suit as moved to federal court would raise a federal question, rather than being a diversity-only case. Since the pre-requisite for removal that no defendant be a citizen of the forum state does not apply to federal-question suits (only to diversity suits), the removal was proper. See 28 U.S.C. §1441(b).

(B) Yes. According to the Supreme Court's holding in *Royal Canin U.S.A. v. Wullschleger*, P was entitled to amend her current federal complaint to drop her claim that D violated the federal statute. That's because P is "master or mistress" of her complaint, so she's free to drop the federal claim, even if she is doing this solely for the purpose of defeating removal. And after she dropped the federal-law claim, all that was left was a state-law claim, over which the court has no jurisdiction (because the "complete diversity" requirement is not met, since P and D are citizens of the same state). (*Royal Canin, supra.*) Therefore, a remand by the federal court to the Minnetonka state could was proper.

42. Yes. Where there are multiple defendants, ***all*** defendants, not just a majority, must sign the notice of removal.

43. Larry. Federal Rule 11, first sentence, provides that "every pleading … must be signed by at least one attorney of record in the attorney's name. … "

44. Move for Rule 11 sanctions against Paul and/or Larry. Rule 11 states that "by presenting [a pleading] to the court … an attorney or unrepresented party certifies that to the best of the person's knowledge, information, and belief, formed after an ***inquiry reasonable under the circumstances*** … (3) the factual contentions have ***evidentiary support***." The rule goes on to say that if there is a violation, "the court may impose an appropriate sanction." Possible sanctions include "an order to pay a penalty into court."

Although Larry acted in good faith in signing the pleading, he almost certainly did not have a belief, made after a "reasonable inquiry," that there was evidentiary support for the proposition that Dave was the driver. For instance, reasonable inquiry would probably have included getting a copy of the police report, which would have led Larry to realize that Dennis, not Dave, should be the defendant. Assuming that the court agrees that Larry acted without making reasonable inquiries, the court could award sanctions against either Larry or Paul. Since Paul is the more guilty of the two (his wrongdoing was deliberate), the court will almost certainly award sanctions against Paul, and possibly against Larry as well. The court should probably order Paul and/or Larry to pay Dave the $10,000 that Dave has spent in attorney's fees defending the suit.

46. (A) No. Federal Rule 9 sets out certain matters that must be pleaded in extra detail, called "special matters." One of these is fraud, as detailed in Rule 9(b): "In alleging fraud or mistake, a party must state with particularity the circumstances constituting fraud or mistake." P's conclusory statement that D fraudulently induced him to enter into the contract (without a statement of what the fraudulent misrepresentations were, or how D knew that these representations were false) seems not to satisfy this requirement of particularity.

(B) Make a Rule 12(e) motion for more definite statement. If this motions fails, then at the least, D would be entitled in discovery to probe the details of how P thinks D behaved fraudulently.

47. Yes. Rule 15(a)(1) says that a party may amend a pleading a single time by right, but only only where (1) the amendment is made no more than ***21 days*** after the party originally served the pleading; or (2) in a case where a responsive pleading is required, the amendment comes no more than 21 days after ***service of that responsive pleading***, or within 21 days after the responder served a ***motion*** under Rule 12(b), (3) or (f), whichever of these 21-day periods occurs ***earlier***. So once D made his April 1 motion, that event started P's 21-day amendment-of-right clock ticking. After April 21, P could amend only with either D's written permission, or leave from the court. Rule 15(a)(2). (But 15(a)(2) says that "the court should freely give leave when justice so requires." In all probability, the court will conclude that justice requires that P be given a chance to amend here, since P could not necessarily have foreseen, when drafting the complaint, that a broadcast statement would be held to constitute "slander" rather than "libel" under state law.)

48. By asserting the affirmative defense of Statute of Frauds. Rule 8(c) states that a party must "affirmatively state" a number of defenses, including Statute of Frauds. A defendant who does not specifically plead an affirmative defense may be held at trial to have waived the right to present evidence on that defense.

52. Deny it. The first sentence of Rule 15(b) provides that "when an isssue not raised by the pleadings is tried by the parties' express or implied consent, it must be treated in all respects as if raised in the pleadings." When Carco remained silent in the face of P's presentation of evidence on negligence, Carco was implicitly consenting to the trial of this issue, so the court will treat the case as if the complaint alleged negligence by Carco.

53. Yes. Even though it is true that the answer would consist solely of hearsay material, which would be inadmissible at trial, Rule 26(b)(1) states that the information sought in discovery "need not be admissible at the trial if the discovery appears reasonably calculated to lead to the discovery of admissible evidence." Here, D's answer to the question will at least tell P whether it is worthwhile to conduct discovery of W (which may in turn produce admissible evidence), and may lead to admissible evidence in other not easily foreseen ways. Therefore, the court will almost certainly hold that the defendant must answer the question.

54. No. According to Federal Rule 26(b)(1), first sentence, parties may obtain discovery "regarding any ***nonprivileged*** matter that is relevant to any party's claim or defense[.]" In diversity actions the rules of privilege are those of the state whose substantive law controls the action. The facts tell us that according to state law here, the question asked by L would require D to divulge information protected by the attorney-client privilege. Therefore, the court will not order D to answer the question.

55. No. The notes clearly fall within the ***work-product immunity*** of Federal Rule 26(b)(3). In fact, the notes probably come within the "***absolute***" protection given by 26(b)(3)(B), under which, if the court orders discovery of materials prepared in anticipation of litigation or for trial, the court "must protect against disclosure of the mental impressions, conclusions, opinions, or legal theories of a party's attorney or other representative concerning the litigation[.]" Since L has written down only what he thinks is important, his notes of necessity contain his "mental impressions" and probably his "opinions." Therefore, the court is almost certain to reject discovery of those notes even if P needs them very badly (e.g., because W has died).

56. Yes. Rule 26(b)(3)(C) provides that even though a party's statement made to the other party is technically work product, it is still discoverable: "Any party or other person may, on request and without the required showing [of special need], obtain the person's own previous statement about the action or its subject matter." So P is entitled to the transcript even without any showing of special need.

57. (A) D need not do anything; P has an obligation to automatically disclose this information. Under Rule 26(a)(2)(A), "A party shall disclose to other parties the identity of any person who may be used at trial to present [expert] evidence. ..." This disclosure is "automatic," in the sense that the adversary does not have to ask for it. The disclosure must be made at least 90 days before trial; Rule 26(a)(2)(D).

(B) Again, D need not do anything; P has an obligation to provide a report prepared by Firefly. Under 26(a)(2)(B), the party preparing to call a retained expert must automatically provide to the other party "a written report — prepared and signed by the [expert] witness." The report must contain "a complete statement of all opinions the witness will express and the basis and reasons for them," as well as the data relied on, any exhibits to be used, the witness' qualifications and publications, the compensation to be paid the witness for testifying, and even a list of all cases in which the witness has testified as an expert in the previous four years. *Id.*

(C) Yes, after the report is provided. FRCP 26(b)(4)(A) says that a party may "depose any person who has been identified as an expert whose opinions may be presented at trial." The rule goes on to specify that where a report is to be provided by the expert, as Firefly would have to do here (see (b) above), the deposition may not be conducted until after the report has been provided.

59. P must amend its response unless the error has already been called to D's attention. Under Rule 26(e)(1), "A party who has made a disclosure under Rule 26(a) — or who has responded to an interrogatory, request for production, or request for admission — must ***supplement or correct*** its disclosure or response: (A) in a timely manner if the party learns that in some material respect the disclosure or response is incomplete or incorrect, and if the additional or corrective information has not otherwise been made known to the other parties during the discovery process or in writing[.]" Since P has now learned that its answer was materially incorrect (the place and date of this key conversation would surely be material), P must file an amended response, so long as D has not learned of the error in some other way.

60. L does not need to do anything; D's lawyer must disclose this information automatically. Automatic disclosure regarding liability insurance is mandatory. Under Rule 26(a)(1)(A), "[A] party must, without awaiting a discovery request, provide to the other parties: ... (iv) for inspection and copying as under Rule 34, any insurance agreement under which an insurance business may be liable to satisfy all or part of a possible judgment in the action or to indemnify or reimburse for payments made to satisfy the judgment." This mandatory disclosure must occur early on in the case.

61. No. Only ***parties*** may be served with, and required to respond to, interrogatories. See Federal Rule 33(a). If a party wishes to get discovery from a non-party witness, this must usually be done by taking the witness' deposition.

62. No. Federal Rule 45(c)(3)(A)(ii), which protects persons subject to subpoenas, states that a court shall quash a subpoena if it "requires a person who is [not] a party ... to travel more than 100 miles from where the person resides, is employed, or regularly transacts business in person[.]" Since a 1,300-mile trip from Miami to New York goes far beyond the 100 miles ordinarily contemplated for a subpoena, it is highly unlikely that a court would uphold the necessary subpoena. (But if P's lawyer is willing to travel to Miami to conduct the deposition, the lawyer can serve the subpoena for deposition on W at W's residence. And, by the way, that's true even if P's lawyer is not admitted to practice in Florida — see Rule 45(a)(3)(B), authorizing an attorney as an officer of the court to issue a subpoena for a deposition in another district, "if the attorney is authorized to practice in the court where the action is pending.")

63. **No.** A Rule 34 request to produce documents may be served ***only on a party***. To compel the police department to deliver the report, P must cause the clerk of the court to issue a subpoena duces tecum on the department, pursuant to Rule 45(b).

64. **No.** Unlike nearly all the other discovery tools, the right to require another party to undergo a physical examination may be accomplished only by ***obtaining a court order***. According to Rule 35(a), if the mental or physical condition of a party is "in controversy," the court where the action is pending may order that party to submit to a physical or mental examination. The order may only be made upon a showing of "good cause." Here, if D makes a motion to have P subjected to a physical examination, the court will almost certainly grant D's motion, since P's physical condition is clearly in controversy, and there is no other good way to ascertain the truth of P's claim of disability.

65. **Seek a protective order limiting how the information can be used.** Federal Rule 26(c) allows the federal court to issue, on motion by a party from whom discovery is sought, a protective order protecting the requesting party from annoyance, embarrassment, oppression, etc. One of the steps the court can order is "that a trade secret or other confidential research, development, or commercial information not be revealed or be revealed only in a specified way." Rule 26(c)(1)(G). D should seek an order that the information sought be used by P only for purposes of the litigation, that it not be used in P's business operations, and that it not be disclosed to any third parties. The Supreme Court has held that such an anti-disclosure protective order will generally not violate the First Amendment free speech rights of the other party (here, P). See *Seattle Times Co. v. Rhinehart* 467 U.S. 20 (1984).

66. **Yes.** Federal Rule 32(a)(3) states, "An adverse party may use for any purpose the deposition of a party or anyone who, when deposed, was the party's officer, director, managing agent, or designee under Rule 30(b)(6) or 31(a)(4)." Here, at the time of deposition, Smith was a person designated under Rule 30(b)(6) (by which the deposing party serves a notice of deposition on the corporation without naming an individual, and the corporation designates the person to answer the questions). Therefore, Smith's answers can be used against D even though Smith was no longer in D's employ at the time of the deposition. This is true even if Smith is available to testify at trial.

67. **No.** A non-party deponent's deposition testimony may be admitted for substantive purposes only under narrowly-defined circumstances, relating to the witness' unavailability to give live testimony. See Federal Rule 32(a)(4).

68. **Yes.** "Any party may use a deposition to ***contradict or impeach*** the testimony given by the deponent as a witness, or for any other purpose allowed by the Federal Rules of Evidence." Federal Rule 32(a)(2). The use here is for impeachment, so it's covered by 32(a)(2).

69. **(A) Yes.** Federal Rule 33(c) states that "an answer to an interrogatory may be used to the extent allowed by the Federal Rules of Evidence." Since an interrogatory may only be addressed to a party, and since by Federal Rule of Evidence 801(d)(2)(A), a party's statement is not classified as hearsay and is admissible against him for any purpose, an interrogatory answer will always be admissible against the party who made it. Therefore, D's interrogatory answer may be used substantively against him.

(B) Yes. Although a party's interrogatory answer is always admissible against him (whether for substantive or impeachment purposes), that answer is not "binding" on him. That is, the party who has given the interrogatory answer is always free at trial to state that his answer was wrong, and it is up to the jury to decide whether to believe what the defendant says at trial or what he said in the interrogatory. (Contrast this with the response to a Rule 36 request to admit, which *is* binding on the party making the admission.)

70. No. This is a classic *Erie* situation. There is neither a state nor a federal statute (or Federal Rule) on the matter. State common law creates the right being sued upon. Therefore, the federal court in diversity ***must apply the common law (judge-made law) of the state where the federal court sits***, and may not apply the federal judge's own opinion of what a desirable rule would be. Since all the evidence is that the Iowa Supreme Court would not impose any duty of inspection on D here, the federal court may not impose any such duty either.

72. California's. In deciding an *Erie* case, the federal judge must apply the law of the state where the federal court sits. This principle includes the forum state's ***conflict-of-laws principles*** as well as its substantive principles. Therefore, the federal judge must apply California's conflicts rules. Since California's conflicts rules would make California rather than Arizona law applicable, the court must follow California's substantive rules as well. One way to remember this is to apply the general principle that the federal court must ***reach the same underlying decision*** as the court of the state where the federal judge sits. (Observe that if California would apply Arizona law, then the task for the federal judge is not to apply what it thinks Arizona's state courts would decide, but rather, to apply what it thinks California's courts would think that Arizona's laws are.)

73. No. There is no Federal Rule or federal statute on point, and the case is a diversity suit based solely on state law. Therefore, conventional *Erie* analysis applies: if the state interest is essentially substantive, then the federal court must apply state law, unless there are very strong federal procedural interests in not doing so. Here, although the state statute has a small procedural aspect (it refers to what should happen in litigation in the Acme courts), the state is pursuing a heavily-substantive interest: Acme is mainly trying to affect how much money malpractice plaintiffs can recover. Furthermore, the choice of federal or state law is highly outcome-determinative; P has a shot at large punitive damages (and uncapped compensatory damages) if federal common law principles apply, but no shot at punitive damages (and a $1 MM compensatory cap) if state law applies. Because of this highly outcome-determinative aspect of the choice, out-of-state patients in P's situation will have a strong incentive to forum-shop (by suing in diversity) if federal common law is to be applied. On the other side of the balance, there is no strong federal procedural interest (such as an interest in national uniformity of procedures) that will be negatively affected by following state law. So this is an easy case: the heavily substantive, and heavily outcome-determinative, state law imposing damage caps must be applied. See, e.g., *Gasperini v. Center for Humanities*, 518 U.S. 415 (1996): "A statutory cap on damages would supply substantive law for *Erie* purposes."

74. Yes. This is an instance in which the federal policy is embodied in a Federal Rule of Civil Procedure that is exactly on point, and that is in direct conflict with the relevant state rule. In situations involving such a direct conflict, *Erie* doctrine (and the avoidance of forum shopping) does not apply at all. Instead, the sole question is ***whether the federal rule is a valid one***. See *Hanna v. Plumer*, 380 U.S. 460 (1965) and *Shady Grove Orthopedic Assoc. v. Allstate Ins. Co.*, 130 S.Ct. 1431 (2010). Since no Federal Rule of Civil Procedure has ever been found invalid under the Rules Enabling Act (i.e., no rule has ever been found to violate the Enabling Act's ban on the abridgement or enlargement of a litigant's substantive rights), Rule 18(a)'s rule of permissive joinder is certainly valid. Therefore, the federal court must follow Rule 18(a), and must disregard the policy behind the conflicting state rule.

75. Yes. In diversity suits, the federal court must ***apply the state-law statute of limitations***. Even though a statute of limitations has a "procedural" aspect, the choice of statute of limitations is heavily outcome-determinative. For example, here P will be allowed to maintain his suit if the federal laches approach is used, but will not be allowed to maintain suit at all if the state statute of limitations is used — the choice of law, therefore, is ***completely*** outcome determinative. The doctrine that state statutes of limitations control in diversity actions is the central holding of one of the most important *Erie* cases of all, *Guaranty Trust Co. v. York*, 326 U.S. 99 (1945).

76. No. Here, as in the previous question, we have a conflict between a federal policy not embodied specifically in a Federal Rule, and a state policy or statute. Therefore, we must balance the two. The state interest here is relatively weak, and is in any event not thwarted by following the federal policy (since the number of hung juries and thus re-trials in state court will probably not be increased if the federal court has a hung jury). Conversely, the federal policy is a long-standing and apparently strong one — it is related to the Seventh Amendment's policy of giving maximum weight to the jury system, for instance. Similarly, there is a strong federal interest in having a treatment of the unanimity issue that is the same from one federal courtroom to another. Also, the choice of law is quite unlikely to be outcome determinative — it is hard to say, for instance, whether having a less-than-unanimous jury verdict would help P or D, since it is unclear who would get five but not six votes. And the choice of law is unlikely to promote forum shopping — it is hard to imagine that P will sue in state rather than federal court because juries in the former don't have to be unanimous.

All in all, the federal interests seem so much stronger than the state interests, and the risk of forum shopping so small, that the court will probably decide to follow the federal policy requiring unanimity.

76. No. Federal Rule 56(c) states that the motion for summary judgment may be rendered only if all the materials submitted by both parties "show that there is no genuine dispute as to any material fact. …" It is not enough that the judge concludes that the moving party is very likely to win at trial — the judge must conclude that ***as a matter of law*** all issues must be decided in favor of the movant, before the judge may grant summary judgment. Here, there is some chance (although admittedly not a very good chance) that P will be able to come up with more evidence that D really did perform the operation on the day stated, or will be able to show that D's evidence was fraudulent. Alternatively, P may be able to show that D performed the operation on a different day. Since the issue of whether D performed the operation is very fact-bound, and there seems to be an honest dispute, the court should deny D's motion even though it appears very probable that D will prevail at trial.

80. No. Federal Rule 52(a) provides that "In an action tried on the facts without a jury ... the court must find the facts specially and state its conclusions of law separately." The judge has almost certainly failed to find the facts "specially" — this word indicates that the judge must state the facts with some particularity, so that a reviewing court will know whether the judge has conducted the trial in an adequate way and has reached a verdict in accord with the weight of the evidence. At a minimum, the judge should have summarized the evidence of intentional discrimination produced by P (if any), and should have described why she did not find this evidence sufficient. If P were to appeal this case, the appellate court would probably remand it to the district court for an opinion that recites the facts and conclusions of law much more specifically.

81. Yes. One of the most important sentences in the entire Federal Rules of Civil Procedure is in Rule 52(a): "Findings of fact, whether based on oral or other evidence, must not be set aside unless ***clearly erroneous***, and the reviewing court must give due regard to the trial court's opportunity to ***judge the witnesses' credibility.***" Here, each witness' testimony is internally consistent, and there are no documents that contradict any witness' story. Therefore, the case boils down completely to whether one believes P and W on the one hand, or D on the other. This is the very sort of credibility determination that the Federal Rules leave to the trial court. Thus even though the appellate court believes that there is a 70% chance that the trial judge made an error, the appellate court should not reverse or even order a new trial. (The main rationale for this deference to the trial judge's findings, especially on matters of credibility, is that the trial judge can ***see*** things in court that are not apparent from the trial transcript. For instance, both P and W may have appeared to be evasive, pausing a long time before answering questions, failing to look the questioner in the eye, etc.; by contrast, D might have appeared to be a quite straight shooter whose demeanor strongly suggested honesty.)

84. Yes, probably. Federal Rule 51(d)(1) provides that "A party may assign as error: (A) an error in an instruction actually given, if that party properly objected; or (B) a failure to give an instruction, if that party properly requested it and — unless the court rejected the request in a definitive ruling on the record — *also properly objected.*" As you can see from the italicized phrase, a request for a particular instruction, made before the judge gives his instructions, is not a substitute for an after-the-instruction objection. Therefore, by the strict language of Rule 51, D waived his right to an instruction on this point by failing to object before the jury retired. There is some chance that the appellate court might conclude that this error was "plain error" which should be reversed despite the lack of an objection; however, most appellate courts in the federal system are reluctant to reverse even for plain error in instructions, on the theory that this wastes judicial resources (since a new trial is necessary, whereas with a timely objection the judge might have corrected his mistake and obtained a properly-instructed jury verdict the first time around).

85. No. When a judge decides a j.m.l. motion (as when she decides a motion for directed verdict), the judge's job is not to substitute herself for the jury. Instead, her task is to decide whether a reasonable juror could possibly find in favor of the non-movant; if the answer to this is "yes," the j.m.l. or directed verdict must be denied. Where the non-movant (here, P) presents testimony which if believed is adequate to make out a claim, the judge will rarely grant the motion even though the judge believes the contradicting testimony supporting the movant. On the other hand, if the trial judge believed that P's testimony was so implausible, so internally self-contradictory, or so completely contradicted by other evidence that no rational juror could believe it, then it would be proper for the judge to grant the motion.

86. No. Rule 50(a)(2) says that a j.m.l. motion may be made "at any time before the case is submitted to the jury." 50(b) then says that any j.m.l. motion made after trial must be a "renewed motion," i.e., a *repeat of a motion made before* the case was submitted to the jury. Since on our facts D never moved for j.m.l. before the case went to the jury, he has waived his right to seek a j.m.l. now (post-trial). This means that the most D can get, either from the trial judge or on appeal, is a new trial, not an entry of judgment in his favor.

87. Grant a remittitur. That is, the judge should conditionally order a new trial — the new trial will occur unless P agrees to a reduction of the damages to an amount set by the court, probably $1.5 million. It will then be up to P whether to accept this "deal" or not. If P accepts, he may not appeal the remittitur thereafter, and must be content with the $1.5 million. If P declines the remittitur, he must go through a new trial, which he may lose entirely.

88. No. According to Federal Rule 38(b), "On any issue triable of right by a jury, a party may demand a jury trial by: (1) serving the other parties with a written demand — which may be included in a pleading — no later than *14 days after the last pleading directed to the issue* is served; and (2) filing the demand [with the court.]" This means that the last time D could demand a jury trial was 14 days after he served his answer, or July 29. After that, he waived his right, and only in very exceptional cases will the court relieve him from this waiver.

89. Yes. The issue is whether the action is legal or equitable. It may well be that prior to the enactment of the Federal Rules of Civil Procedure in 1938, interpleader was regarded as an equitable action. But today, the court determines whether a claim is equitable or legal not by reference to the procedural device by which the parties come before the court (here, interpleader) but rather, by reference to the ***underlying claim***. Here, the underlying issue is basically an issue of contract law (was X competent to change the policy beneficiary?), and such a contract-law issue will almost always be legal rather than equitable. Since the underlying issue is legal, each party has the right to demand a jury trial as to that issue (and if one party so demands, there will be a jury trial even though the other parties do not want one). See *Ross v. Bernhard*, 396 U.S. 531 (1970) (for determining whether the claim is legal or equitable, "nothing now turns upon … the procedural devices by which the parties happen to come before the court").

92. (A) Whether the judge's finding of a violation was "clearly erroneous." FRCP 52(a)(6) says that in bench trials (i.e., trials without a jury), "Findings of fact, whether based on oral or other evidence, must not be set aside unless ***clearly erroneous***, and the reviewing court must give ***due regard*** to the ***trial court's opportunity to judge the witnesses' credibility***." The trial court's findings here are essentially about factual matters, including what the parties meant by the ambiguous term "moral turpitude" and how a reasonable observer would have interpreted the photo. So the "clearly erroneous" standard is the standard the appeals court must apply.

(B) Affirm. Since the appeal essentially turns on issues of fact, P can win only by showing that the trial court's determination on these issues was clearly erroneous. P and D's CEO gave conflicting on-point testimony on the issues. Therefore, their relative credibility as witnesses was an important part of the trial judge's findings of fact. Because of the importance of witness credibility here, the challenged findings do not meet the hard-to-satisfy requirement that they be "clearly erroneous," and the appeals court must affirm. And that's true even if the appeals judges think that they would probably have reached a different conclusion had they been trying the case.

93. Dismiss the appeal for lack of jurisdiction. The federal courts, like those of most states, impose the ***"final judgment rule."*** Under 28 U.S.C. §1291, the U.S. Courts of Appeals only have jurisdiction over "final decisions of the district courts." Normally, the federal district judge is not deemed to have made a "final decision" for purposes of §1291 until the judge has entered a "final judgment" in the entire case. The issuance of an order of partial summary judgment here was not a final judgment, since the entire case has not been disposed of. There are some exceptions to the final judgment rule in federal litigation (e.g., the "collateral order" exception), but these exceptions are narrow, and none of them comes close to applying here. Therefore, the Court of Appeals cannot hear the appeal even if it wants to, because it lacks jurisdiction. And the lack of jurisdiction is not waivable by the agreement of the parties, so P's consent to the interlocutory appeal doesn't make any difference. See *Liberty Mutual Insur. Co. v. Wetzel*, 424 U.S. 737 (1976).

94. No. Since D's present claim arises out of the "same transaction or occurrence" that was the subject of P's claim in the first suit, D's claim was a ***compulsory*** counterclaim in the first action. That is, D was required to assert that claim as a Rule 13(a) compulsory counterclaim in the first action, or face losing it. Since D did not do so, he will be barred from bringing the claim as a separate suit now (even though the result in the first trial indicates that D is probably correct in asserting that the accident was caused by P's negligence).

95. No. The rule that compulsory counterclaims must be asserted in the initial action or waived applies not only to defendants, but to any other parties. Thus Federal Rule 13(a) does not refer to defendants specifically, but instead to any "pleading" by any "pleader" — the pleader is required to raise any claim against "any opposing party" if that claim arises out of the same transaction or occurrence that is the subject matter of the opposing party's claim. Since Worker's claim against Boss for injuries results from the same transaction or occurrence (the accident with Pedestrian) as Boss's third-party claim against Worker, Worker must assert his claim as a counterclaim against Boss, or lose it. Since he did not so assert it, he will be found to have waived it.

96. (A) Yes. Compulsory counterclaims fall within the ***supplemental jurisdiction*** of the court under 28 U.S.C. §1367. Since Alan's counterclaim arises out of the same transaction or occurrence as Bob's claim, Alan's counterclaim is compulsory and will satisfy the "same case or controversy" requirement of §1367. Since §1367(b), which excludes certain types of claims in diversity actions, does not mention counterclaims, Alan's claim will fall within supplemental jurisdiction, and it will not matter that Carol and Alan, opposing parties, are citizens of the same state. Nor does it matter that Alan's claim totals less than $75,000. (The supplemental jurisdiction statute, where it applies, obviates the need to meet the usual requirements of subject-matter jurisdiction, such as complete diversity and amount in controversy.)

(B) No. Alan's federal-court counterclaim was compulsory, so by not asserting it he lost it. If Alan had not been able to get ***personal*** jurisdiction over Carol, his counterclaim against Bob would not have been compulsory, because Rule 13(a)(1)(B) says that a counterclaim is compulsory only if it "does not require adding another party over whom the court cannot acquire jurisdiction." But since Carol had minimum contacts with Connecticut, and Connecticut had a long arm authorizing service out-of-state on Carol, jurisdiction was not a problem. The supplemental jurisdiction statute would have taken care of any subject-matter jurisdictional problem.

Therefore, Alan's claim was an ordinary compulsory counterclaim, even though it needs for just adjudication the presence of a third person not previously a party to the action. Since a state court will normally bar a claim that would have been a compulsory counterclaim in an earlier federal action, Alan will be barred.

98. Yes. Federal Rule 18(a) provides, "A party asserting a claim ... may join, as independent or alternative claims, as many claims as it has against an opposing party." Since P and D are opposing parties based on P's initial copyright claim, P has the right to add whatever claims against D he wishes, even if these other claims have nothing to do with the original copyright claim.

99. Probably not. Since P and D are citizens of the same state, there is no diversity jurisdiction. This is not a problem for the copyright claim, since that is founded upon federal law. But the libel claim is based upon state law. If the libel claim were closely related to the copyright claim (e.g., both related to the same transaction or occurrence), the libel claim could be heard together with the copyright claim under the doctrine of supplemental (formerly pendent) jurisdiction. The supplemental jurisdiction statute, 28 U.S.C. §1367, allows parties to join claims that are so related as to form part of the "same case or controversy" in the same suit. But since the two claims have nothing to do with each other, supplemental jurisdiction does not apply here. Therefore, there is no federal subject-matter jurisdiction over the libel claim, and it cannot be heard by the federal court.

100. (A) Yes. D's claim against X for the car accident is a compulsory counterclaim. (That is, D's claim against P is a garden-variety compulsory counterclaim, and X is an additional party to that counterclaim joined pursuant to Rule 13(h).) Compulsory counterclaims, and the joinder of additional parties to compulsory counterclaims, fall within the court's supplemental jurisdiction under 28 U.S.C. §1367 because they concern a "common nucleus of operative fact." Consequently, it does not matter that D's claim against X fails by itself to meet the amount in controversy requirement; supplemental jurisdiction obviates the need for the usual diversity jurisdiction in this case. (In fact, it wouldn't even matter that D and X were citizens of the same state.)

(B) No. This second claim by D against X is allowed procedurally only because of Rule 18(a)'s joinder of claims provision (which allows any party, not just the plaintiff, to join additional claims against an opposing party who is already in the action). But Rule 18(a) joinder of claims does not fall within the court's supplemental jurisdiction unless the claims are so related as to form part of the same case or controversy (the "common nucleus of operative fact" standard). We are told that the breach of contract claim is based on an unrelated transaction. Since it does not fall under supplemental jurisdiction, the unrelated claim must independently meet federal subject-matter jurisdictional requirements. Because D's second claim against X is not for more than $75,000, that second claim cannot be heard.

102. No. In general, multiple plaintiffs may join together, and may join multiple defendants, provided that (1) the claims arise out of the "same transaction, occurrence, or series of transactions or occurrences" and (2) there is at least one question of law or fact in common. FRCP 20. Since all claims involve a single occurrence (the accident) and a single question of law or fact (who caused that accident?), this two-part test is easily satisfied.

However, the ***usual requirements of subject matter matter jurisdiction*** (as well as personal jurisdiction) ***apply to joinder of parties.*** Since D1 has its principal place of business in New York, it is deemed to be a citizen of New York (as well as of Delaware, its state of incorporation.) This means that there is not the required complete diversity of citizenship (i.e., it is not the case that no plaintiff is a citizen of the same state as any defendant.) Since the action involves no federal question, and there is no diversity, the action could go forward as pleaded only if supplemental jurisdiction somehow eliminated the requirement of complete diversity. But the supplemental jurisdiction statute, 28 U.S.C. §1367, states in subsection (b) that in diversity actions the district courts shall ***not*** have supplemental jurisdiction over claims by plaintiffs (like P1 and P2) against persons made parties under Rule 20 (such as D1) if the result would be inconsistent with the requirements of diversity. Because §1367 does not apply in this case, each claim and each party must independently meet federal subject-matter jurisdictional requirements. Consequently, D1 will have to be dropped from the action (though the action may proceed as a suit by P1 and P2 against D2).

107. Yes, under Rule 23(b)(2). First, a proposed class action must meet the four requirements of Rule 23(a): numerosity, common questions of law or fact, typicality of claims or defenses, and adequate representation. Seven hundred members seems sufficiently numerous. There are certainly questions of law or fact common to the class — for instance, each class member's claim presents the issue of whether due process is owed to a rejected housing applicant. The claims of P1 and P2 seem quite typical of the claims of other class members, since all are rejected applicants claiming a due process right. Finally, the facts tell us to assume that there is adequate representation.

Now that Rule 23(a) is satisfied, we must still find some subdivision of Rule 23(b) that is satisfied. The most likely candidate is (b)(2): "The party opposing the class has acted or refused to act on grounds that apply generally to the class, so that final injunctive relief or corresponding declaratory relief is appropriate respecting the class as a whole. ..." Here, the plaintiffs are seeking a declaratory judgment that due process is owed to a housing applicant, and an injunction against denying due process to future applicants. Since D is apparently treating all rejected applicants the same way (by not giving them a statement of reasons for the rejection, or other trappings of due process), the "generally applicable to the class" requirement seems satisfied.

108. No. In a (b)(1) or (b)(2) class action, notice is not required by Rule 23 (in contrast to (b)(3) actions). Instead, Rule 23(c)(2)(A) leaves it up to the discretion of the judge whether to order notice to some or all members of a (b)(2) class action. The reason for this is that if the suit is successful, it will result in an injunction or declaratory judgment applicable to ***all*** members of the class, whether notified or not, and class members will not be able to opt out, so that no good would probably come of class-wide notice. On these facts, it is unlikely that the judge will order notice given to each individual (though the judge might order publication notice, or notice sent to a small sample).

109. Unclear, but probably not. Even assuming that the four requirements of 23(a) can be satisfied, P's only chance of certification would be as a (b)(3) action. (A Rule 23(b)(1) action is out, because there is no risk of inconsistent or varying adjudications, or prejudice to the absentees — even if D was ordered to pay damages to P and not to some absentee, or vice versa, there would be no inconsistency or prejudice. Similarly, (b)(2) is out, because the suit does not seek declaratory or injunctive relief.)

For a (b)(3) action to be certified, the court must find that "questions of law or fact ***common*** to the class members ***predominate*** over any questions affecting only individual members." This requirement seems not to be met here: while there is a common question of liability, the more interesting and time-consuming questions will probably relate to causation (given that a particular class member was sick or injured, was this because of the toxic cloud?) and damages, issues which are not common. In general, mass-toxic-exposure cases do not meet the "common questions predominate" requirement. See, e.g., *Amchem Products, Inc. v. Windsor*, 521 U.S. 591 (1997), finding that a mass-asbestos-exposure case did not meet this requirement. Similarly, it is unclear that the court should conclude that "a class action is superior to other available methods for fairly and efficiently adjudicating the controversy," as required by Rule 23(b)(3).

Lastly, in all class actions (not just (b)(3) actions), the court must find that the named parties "will fairly and adequately protect the interests of the class." Rule 23(a)(4). Again, it's questionable whether P1 —who claims to have been actually injured physically — can adequately represent all absent members (e.g., those that have suffered exposure but have not yet have suffered visible injury). Cf. *Amchem Products*, *supra* (lack of adequate representation found in mass-asbestos-exposure case).

110. No. In *Phillips Petroleum Co. v. Shutts*, 472 U.S. 797 (1985), the Supreme Court held that an "absent" member of the plaintiff class (i.e., one who does not participate in the suit, but who also does not opt out) will nonetheless be bound by the results of the case, even if the absent member does not have minimum contacts with the state where the class action is pending. Thus even though X had absolutely no contacts with New York, where the class action took place, he is bound by the results since he did not opt out.

111. Yes. According to *Exxon Mobil Corp. v. Allapattah Services, Inc.*, 125 S.Ct. 2611 (2005), as long as the ***named members*** of the class each have claims that satisfy the amount in controversy requirement, the supplemental jurisdiction statute is to be read so as to permit ***non-named*** persons with claims for ***less than that amount*** to be part of the plaintiff class. So the action will be certified even though the unnamed members don't independently have claims exceeding $75,000.

112. (A) All 800,000 identifiable members. Individual notice must be given (usually by mail) to any class member who can be "identified through reasonable effort." *Eisen v. Carlisle & Jacquelin*, 417 U.S. 156 (1974). Thus the 800,000 customers whose names and addresses are on file at Biff's offices must each be sent notice by mail. This is true even though the average Biff's Notes cost just $14, and thus even though the cost of notice is large, if not prohibitive, compared with the possible recovery. Additionally, the court may order publication notice to reach the approximately 3,200,000 customers whose names are not on file.

(B) P must pay the entire cost. This is true even if the court concludes that P would probably prevail at trial, and even if the court concludes that the cost of notice is so great relative to P's possible recovery that imposing the cost of notice on P will effectively kill the action.

(C) P could define a sub-class, and give notice only to that class. For instance, P could restrict his suit only to those who bought during the most recent year, or only to those who bought more than a certain quantity of books, or to those who bought only certain titles. The advantage would be that P's costs of notice diminish. The disadvantage, of course, would be that any recovery would be reduced, and the fees awarded by the court to P's lawyer in the event of victory would be correspondingly reduced.

113. Notice of the proposed settlement to absent class members, and judicial approval of the settlement. Rule 23(e) provides that "The claims, issues, or defenses of a certified class may be ***settled*** ... only with the ***court's approval***. The following procedures apply to a proposed settlement ... : (1) The court must direct ***notice in a reasonable manner*** to all class members who would be bound by the proposal." In the case of a large class, each member of which has very small claims, the court will probably not order notice by mail to anyone, but will instead probably permit publication notice. In deciding whether to approve the settlement, the court will consider principally whether it is fair to the absent class members (since there is a danger that P's lawyer and Biff will collude, by agreeing to pay P's lawyer a large amount and paying smaller damages to class members than would be appropriate based on the strength of P's case).

114. Seek the court's permission to intervene under Federal Rule 24(b). Since X's proposed claim and P's existing action have a "common question of law or fact," X can move the Michigan federal court for leave to intervene as a co-plaintiff in P's suit. Clearly there is one major question of law/fact that the two claims have in common: whether D flew the plane in a negligent manner. The fact that there is also at least one non-common question of fact (each plaintiff's damages) should be irrelevant. It will be up to the district court's discretion whether to allow the intervention. (The requirements for intervention of right under Rule 24(a) do not seem to be satisfied — X is not really "so situated that disposing of the [main] action may as a practical matter impair or impede [X's] ability to protect its interest ...," since X ought to be able to find a different expert witness, or to improve Edward's testimony even if he gives poor testimony in P's action.)

115. No. The action is in diversity, which means that there must be complete diversity (no plaintiff from the same state as any defendant). If X's motion for permissive intervention is allowed, X will be treated as a plaintiff. Since he will then be a citizen of the same state (Ohio) as D, diversity will be ruined. Supplemental jurisdiction does not apply to permissive intervention — 28 U.S.C §1367(b) provides that intervenors under Rule 24 must meet jurisdictional requirements for diversity actions and cannot rely on the court's supplemental jurisdiction.

116. No. The supplemental jurisdiction statute makes no distinction between intervention as of right and permissive intervention. 28 U.S.C. §1367(b) clearly states that persons seeking to intervene under Rule 24 will not be allowed if their presence would destroy diversity (as it would here).

117. Yes, probably. For a person to be entitled to intervention as of right, Rule 24(a) requires that the applicant claim "an interest relating to the property or transaction that is the subject of the action, and [be] so situated that the disposing of the action may as a practical matter impair or impede the [applicant's] ability to protect its interest, unless existing parties adequately represent that interest." P certainly has an interest relating to the same transaction as the main action: the procedure by which Ames draws district boundaries and administers its schools. There is also a danger to P that his ability to bring a successful action in the future might be compromised by a poor result in the U.S.'s action — if the Justice Department does a lackluster job and loses the case (e.g., the court finds that there was no religion-based discriminatory intent on Ames' part), a subsequent court is unlikely to permit the issue of intentional discrimination to be completely relitigated (even though the rules of collateral estoppel do not formally bind P, since P was an absentee to the U.S.-Ames original action).

The toughest question is whether "existing parties adequately represent [the applicant's] interest" — either the U.S. or Ames can make a plausible argument that the Justice Department is adequate to represent P's interests. But P can argue in turn that the U.S. government may be pursuing other interests (e.g., a desire to settle such suits in return for partial relief, rather than litigating them to the fullest extent to get complete compliance with the law), and that P's interests are therefore not completely congruent with the U.S.'s.

On balance, the court will probably rule that P is entitled to intervene as of right (and will almost certainly at least allow P to intervene permissively).

118. Bring a federal statutory interpleader proceeding, under 28 U.S.C. §1335. That section allows a person holding property claimed by two or more adverse claimants to interplead those claimants. Thus Insurer can commence a federal proceeding "against" both Al and Betty, and say in effect to the court, "Here's the $30,000; you decide how this should be split among Al and Betty. Return any excess to us." Even though this is a suit brought, in essence, in diversity, the amount in controversy requirement is only $500 (not $75,000). Also, the requirement of complete diversity is canceled, and all that is required is that some two claimants be citizens of different states (satisfied here since Al is a citizen of New York and Betty is a citizen of Oklahoma).

119. No. Federal Rule 22 does allow an interpleader action to be brought by a stakeholder (whether the stakeholder acts as plaintiff, or is already a defendant in an existing proceeding brought by one or more claimants). But Rule 22 interpleader, unlike statutory interpleader, does not give any relief from the normal requirements of personal jurisdiction, subject-matter jurisdiction, and venue. In a Rule 22 interpleader action, there must be complete diversity between the stakeholder on the one hand and all of the claimants on the other hand. Since Insurer and Al are both citizens of New York, the required complete diversity is not present. Also, a Rule 22 interpleader action must satisfy the ordinary $75,000 amount in controversy requirement for diversity actions, which the controversy here does not. (What counts for a Rule 22 action is the size of the stake, not the aggregated sizes of the various claims against the fund.)

120. Use Federal Rule 22 interpleader. The most promising place for Insurer to start such a proceeding is in federal court for the district of Indiana where the home is located; H, as a former resident of Indiana and one who still asserts a property interest in Indiana real estate, certainly has minimum contacts with Indiana and is therefore subject to personal jurisdiction (assuming that the Indiana long arm allows him to be served, which is quite likely). Although Rule 22 suits require complete diversity (in the sense that the stakeholder not be a citizen of the same state as any of the claimants), this requirement is satisfied here, since neither H nor W is a citizen of Insurer's home state of Kentucky. The amount-in-controversy requirement is satisfied, since more than $75,000 is at stake. The district where the home is located suffices for venue also, since that is the district where a "substantial part of property that is the subject of the action is situated." 28 U.S.C. §1391(a)(2).

The big advantage for Insurer of Rule 22 interpleader versus statutory interpleader is that under Rule 22 interpleader, Insurer does not have to deposit the "stake" (the $500,000 policy proceeds) with the court at the outset of the proceeding, or post a bond in that amount, as it would for statutory interpleader. Therefore, Insurer gets the use of the money while the suit is pending.

121. Doeing should implead Altimeters pursuant to Federal Rule 14(a). A defendant may, as a third-party plaintiff, cause a summons and complaint to be served "on a nonparty who is or may be liable to it for all or part of the claim against it." Rule 14(a)(1). By impleading Altimeters, Doeing is stating that if it is liable for breach of warranty, Altimeters must be derivatively liable to it. (This is a correct statement of warranty law.)

122. (A) Dave can implead Ted pursuant to Federal Rule 14(a). Since Ted will be liable over to Dave for anything that Dave is required to pay Paula, Ted's liability is derivative. Therefore, it is appropriate for Dave to bring a third-party action against Ted, even though Paula has not made any claims against Ted directly.

(B) Dave has to solve two problems: (1) diversity and (2) personal jurisdiction. As to (1), a claim by a third-party plaintiff against a third-party defendant will come within the court's ***supplemental*** jurisdiction, provided that it and the main claim concern a "common nucleus of operative fact." The supplemental jurisdiction statute, 28 U.S.C. §1367, does not specifically exclude claims by third-party plaintiffs under Rule 14, as it excludes some claims made by plaintiffs. Thus the fact that Paula and Ted are both citizens of Ohio, and are in a very general sense opposing parties (theoretically nullifying the complete diversity usually required) doesn't matter — so long as Paula and Dave, the original parties, are diverse, the citizenship of the third-party defendant is ignored. As to (2), see the answer to Part (C), immediately below.

(C) FRCP 4(k)(1)(B)'s "100-mile-bulge" provision. Under ordinary principles, Dave would not be able to get personal jurisdiction over Ted, because he would not be able to make service on him — the federal court sitting in diversity only allows service on out-of-staters to the extent that the long arm of the state in which the federal court sits would so allow. Here, since Kentucky would not allow service over Ted, the federal court would not normally be permitted to allow such service either (even though Ted has minimum contacts with Kentucky). But the special "100-mile bulge" provision of Federal Rule 4(k)(1)(B) comes to Dave's rescue: according to that Rule, anyone who is brought in as a third-party defendant pursuant to Rule 14 may be served in a place that is "not more than 100 miles from where the summons was issued[.]" Since Cincinnati is within 100 miles of Covington (where the action is pending), Ted may be served at his residence.

123. Yes. Rule 14(a)(2)(D) provides that the third-party defendant "may also ***assert against the plaintiff*** any claim arising out of the transaction or occurrence that is the subject matter of the ***plaintiff's claim against the third-party plaintiff.***" Since Paula's claim against Dave and Ted's claim against Paula both relate to construction of Paula's house, Ted's claim against Paula will presumably be found to meet this "same transaction or occurrence" test. The bigger potential problem is that Ted and Paula are both citizens of Ohio, and all claims are based solely on diversity. There would thus not seem to be the complete diversity required. However, a claim by a third-party defendant against the original plaintiff falls within the court's supplemental jurisdiction under 28 U.S.C. §1367, since the claim is closely related to the original Paula v. Dave claim. Since §1367(b) does not exclude claims by third-party defendants against original plaintiffs, the lack of diversity doesn't matter.

124. No. A claim by the original plaintiff against the third-party defendant does ***not*** fall within the court's supplemental jurisdiction. The supplemental jurisdiction statute, in 28 U.S.C. §1367(b), specifically bars claims made by the original plaintiff against "persons made parties under Rule 14, 19, 20, or 24" (here, Paula). Paula's claim against Ted would have to be brought under Rule 14(b), which allows a plaintiff to "bring in a third party" if Rule 14 would allow that defendant to bring in the third party (here, Ted), which Rule 14(a)(2)(D) would allow.

125. Yes. If Deborah were to make a claim against Dell as part of Pete's existing action, Deborah's claim would be a ***cross-claim*** under Rule 13(g). However, Deborah is ***not required*** to make this cross-claim against Dell — cross-claims under the Federal Rules are always optional, never compulsory (in contrast to counterclaims, which are compulsory if they arise out of the same transaction or occurrence as the original claim). Thus Deborah will not be barred from bringing a separate state-court action against Dell later on (though the doctrine of collateral estoppel will probably prevent her from relitigating issues that were actually litigated by her in the original action).

126. Yes. As discussed in the prior answer, Deborah's claim against Dell would be a cross-claim, asserted pursuant to Rule 13(g). Cross-claims fall within the court's supplemental jurisdiction, under 28 U.S.C. §1367, since they are by definition closely related to the original action and since they are not excluded by subsection (b). Therefore, the ordinary requirements of federal subject-matter jurisdiction are ignored, so it doesn't matter that Deborah and Dell are both citizens of the same state, or that Deborah's claim is for less than the $75,000 amount in controversy ordinarily required for diversity suits.

128. No, probably. The twin doctrines of ***merger*** and ***bar*** (collectively known as ***"claim preclusion"***) prevent a plaintiff from "splitting her cause of action" between two suits. If a plaintiff splits a cause of action and wins the first suit, her second claim is said to be "merged" into the favorable first judgment; if she loses the first suit, her second claim is held to be "barred" by the unfavorable first result.

Most courts today follow the "transaction" test for determining what constitutes a cause of action. By this test, both P's personal injury claim and her property damage claim formed a single cause of action, since they stemmed from a single transaction (the auto accident). Therefore, most courts would treat P as losing her property damage claim because it was merged into her previously-asserted personal injury claim.

131. No. Doreen is ***collaterally estopped*** from relitigating the issue of Phillip's negligence in the accident. This is because: (1) the issue of Phillip's negligence was ***fully and fairly litigated*** in the first action; (2) that issue was ***actually decided*** (since the finding in favor of Phillip, under the substantive law of Ames, was inconsistent with any negligence on Phillip's part); and (3) the finding was ***necessary*** to the verdict (since if Phillip had been negligent, he could not have recovered under Ames' law on contributory negligence).

132. Yes. Collateral estoppel does not apply here. For collateral estoppel to apply to an issue, that issue must have been actually litigated at the first trial. When a default judgment is entered, no issue is deemed to have been litigated.

134. Neither. Where the first trial takes place in a court that not only has very limited jurisdiction but also very informal procedures, the findings of that court will generally ***not*** be given collateral estoppel effect. The reason is that the findings of such a court are viewed as insufficiently trustworthy to determine the outcome of a much larger later controversy. (The mere fact that a jury trial was not available would not by itself be enough to deprive the first court's findings of collateral estoppel effect, but the absence of rules of evidence probably *would* be enough.)

135. Yes. A ***settlement*** normally has ***no collateral estoppel effect*** on other suits. Therefore, Xavier will not be able to treat the settlement as establishing Denise's negligence, even though a judgment against Denise was entered pursuant to that settlement. (Also, the rule against giving collateral estoppel effect to settlements can be viewed as a specific application of the general rule that collateral estoppel effect will only be given to issues that were litigated in the first action.)

136. No, probably. Collateral estoppel does not usually apply to "pure" issues of law, but does usually apply to "mixed" issues of law and fact, i.e., the application of a given legal principle to a particular fact situation. However, even if the first decision involves (as it does here) a mixed question of law and fact rather than a pure question of law, most courts believe that they have ***discretion*** to decline to apply collateral estoppel where there has been a ***significant change in legal principles*** between the first and second suits. Courts are especially likely to exercise that discretion where use of collateral estoppel would "impose on one of the parties a significant disadvantage, or confer on him a significant benefit, with respect to his competitors." Rest. 2d Judgments, §28, Comment c. Here, use of collateral estoppel would give Potter a perpetual advantage over his competitors (he can undercut their price slightly, and they cannot ever match him). The court is very unlikely to grant Potter, just because of the fortuity of his earlier victory, such a permanent advantage. This is especially true where, as here, the intervening decision was by a higher court than decided the original case in favor of the party now seeking collateral estoppel.

137. Yes. ***A stranger to the first action will never be bound***, either for claim preclusion or collateral estoppel purposes, by the results of that first suit. Peter and Paul were not privies, since their cab-sharing relationship does not fall within any of the traditional relationships recognized as constituting privity by the common law (e.g., master/servant, insurer/insured, etc.). Thus Paul is entitled to get his "day in court," even if that amounts to merely trotting out the same evidence as already used by Peter against David.

138. Yes. Until the 1960s, many courts might have automatically denied Baker's attempt to use collateral estoppel, on the now-discredited doctrine of mutuality (by which since Baker was a stranger to the first action, it could not claim the benefits of collateral estoppel in the second action). But today, virtually all jurisdictions ***reject*** the automatic principle of mutuality. Instead, most courts decide on a case-by-case basis whether to allow collateral estoppel use by a stranger. When it is the defendant in the second action who seeks to use collateral estoppel, and seeks to use it against a party who was a plaintiff in the first action, the case for allowing collateral estoppel is at its strongest. Thus here, Parker had the opportunity to fully and fairly litigate the causation issue during his first trial, and Baker is merely trying to use collateral estoppel as a shield rather than a sword in the second action. Nearly all courts would allow Baker to use collateral estoppel here.

139. No. Greg is not only a stranger to the first action but is attempting an ***offensive*** use of collateral estoppel. (That is, he is a plaintiff in the second action.) Therefore, the court will do a case-by-case balancing (similar to that performed by the Supreme Court in *Parklane Hosiery v. Shore*) to decide whether to allow estoppel here. Two factors strongly militate against allowing estoppel here: (1) the first suit was for relatively little money ($2,000), so Dave did not have an incentive to litigate it to the hilt; and (2) the possibility of a later action by Greg (or anyone else relating to that particular serving of chowder) was quite unlikely from Dave's perspective, so Dave was not at all on notice that issues might be decided as to which collateral estoppel would later be possibly applicable. Together, these factors make it most unlikely that the court would estop Dave from attempting to disprove Greg's allegation of dangerously defective chowder.

140. No. Again, we have a situation where a stranger to the first action is proposing to make offensive use of collateral estoppel. Here, we have a stark case of the ***"multiple plaintiff anomaly"*** — if Deadly wins any given suit, it still has to completely relitigate the merits with the next plaintiff in line, yet under collateral estoppel one defeat by Deadly would cause it to lose against everyone later in line. The unfairness to Deadly from allowing collateral estoppel here is further exaggerated by: (1) the fact that the plaintiffs' lawyers have intentionally chosen the most appealing plaintiff to go first; and (2) the fact that the lawyers intentionally declined to join the additional victims as plaintiffs in the first suit, preferring to have them "wait in the wings." Therefore, it is unlikely that Deadly will be deprived of its chance to relitigate the issue of whether its talcum powder is dangerously defective or its warnings inadequate.

141. (A) Yes.

(B) The answer is required by the Full Faith and Credit Clause of the U.S. Constitution. The Full Faith and Credit Clause of the U.S. Constitution (Article IV, Section 1) requires each state to give to the judgment of any other state the same effect that that judgment would have in the state which rendered it. This requirement extends to the ***res judicata effect*** of the first state court's judgment. Here, therefore, Bates must give to the judgment of the Ames court the same effect that the Ames court system would give to that prior judgment. Since Ames would grant preclusive effect to the judgment against Baker (i.e., Ames would let Conroy collaterally estop Baker), Bates must do the same. This is true even though the Bates courts, if left to their own devices, would prefer not to give collateral estoppel effect to the judgment against Baker.

142. Yes, the federal judge must do so. A federal statute, 28 U.S.C. §1738, requires federal courts to give state court judgments the same effect (including res judicata effect) as the state itself would give them. Therefore, the federal court is bound by §1738 to give the state court judgment the same effect the state itself would give it. Thus the federal judge must grant collateral estoppel against Baker solely on the grounds that the Ames court would do so.

143. Yes. No congressional statute, and no specific constitutional provision, requires the state court to follow the prior federal judgment's preclusive effect. However, *Semtek v. Lockheed Martin* requires the Bates state court to apply the same rule of preclusion as would be applied by the Ames courts (which are the courts of the state where the federal diversity court that rendered the first judgment sits). Since the Ames courts would allow Conroy to make offensive use of collateral estoppel against Baker on this issue if the first judgment had been rendered by an Ames state court, the courts of Bates must allow that same use.

MULTIPLE-CHOICE QUESTIONS

Here are 27 multiple-choice questions. The fact patterns in these questions are principally derived from *Steve Emanuel's First-Year Q&As* (2d Ed.), an 1,124-question book revised by Prof. Alex Ruskell of the University of South Carolina School of Law and published by Wolters Kluwer. The questions in that book are short-answer (yes/no); I have adapted these questions to a multiple-choice format, and have extensively rewritten the answers, especially for this *CrunchTime* volume.

— SE

1. Paula and Pete were hit by a truck driven on the job by an employee of Trucking Corp., a corporation incorporated in Delaware engaged in the trucking business. The accident occurred in California, where Paula and Pete were living at that time. Trucking's headquarters (from which the top executives direct the company's operations) are in Michigan, but most of its lower-level employees and customers are based in or near Miami, Florida, and most of its trucking routes are entirely within Florida. After the accident, Paula and Pete moved to Miami, where they planned to retire.

   After moving, Paula and Pete contacted a lawyer, who filed suit for them against Trucking in federal district court for the Southern District of Florida (which includes Miami). The suit, which said that it was based on diversity jurisdiction, alleged that Paula and Pete had each suffered personal injuries in excess of $75,000. Trucking moved to dismiss the case for lack of subject matter jurisdiction.

   Trucking's motion should be:

   (A) Granted, because the plaintiffs were citizens of California when they were injured.
   (B) Granted, because Trucking and the plaintiffs are all citizens of Florida.
   (C) Denied, because diversity subject matter jurisdiction exists.
   (D) Denied, because Trucking is a citizen of Delaware and the plaintiffs are not.

2. P has filed suit against D in the U.S. district court for Nevada. The suit asserts a federal claim, that D committed racial discrimination against P in Dallas (which is located in the Northern District of Texas). D is a citizen of California (he lives in San Francisco, in the Northern District of California). P lives in Nevada. D has now moved for a change of venue to the Northern

District of California, or alternatively, to the Northern District of Texas. Which of the following is correct?

(A) The court may properly transfer the action to the Northern District of California but not to the Northern District of Texas.

(B) The court may properly transfer the action to either the Northern District of California or to the Northern District of Texas.

(C) The court must dismiss the action, since it was commenced in an improper forum.

(D) The court may, in its discretion, either retain the action for trial in Nevada, transfer it to the Northern District of California, or transfer it to the Northern District of Texas.

3. Pedro, a citizen of Illinois, has filed suit against David in an Illinois state court located in Chicago. The suit alleges that David committed acts in Missouri which violated Pedro's rights under federal employment-discrimination statutes. David is a citizen of Illinois, living in Springfield, Ill. (located, for federal-district-court purposes, in the Central District of Illinois). David has filed a petition for removal to the federal district court for the Northern District of Illinois (encompassing Chicago). Pedro has opposed the removal petition. Should the action be removed?

(A) No, because the action could not have originally been brought in the U.S. district court for the Northern District of Illinois, the court to which removal has been requested.

(B) Yes, because Pedro's action arises under a federal statute, and the action would be removed to the federal district encompassing the place where the state action is pending.

(C) Yes, because state courts, even those of general jurisdiction, do not have subject matter jurisdiction over federal claims.

(D) No, because David is a citizen of Illinois, the state containing the district to which the action would be removed.

4. Dressco, a corporation, manufactures ladies' dresses. In the state of Arkansas, Dressco does not maintain any official office. Dressco conducts no advertising directed at Arkansas residents, and derives only a small portion of its total revenues from that state. Dressco's sole activities in the state consist of the activities of Jones, a commission salesman for Dressco, who works out of his house soliciting orders from Arkansas-based department stores. When an Arkansas department store places an order, the order is not accepted by Jones, but is instead sent to Dressco's home office in New York for approval. All orders are shipped from New York directly to the department store which placed the order. Dilbert's, an Arkansas department store that placed one order with Dressco via Jones, received what it believed to be defective merchandise, and sued Dressco in the Arkansas courts. May the Arkansas courts constitutionally take jurisdiction over Dressco in the action brought by Dilbert's?

(A) Yes, because by hiring Jones to solicit orders from Arkansas-based stores, Dressco has purposely availed itself of the opportunity to do business in Arkansas.
(B) No, because Dressco's connections with Arkansas were too small to constitute the minimum contacts required for personal jurisdiction by the due process clause.
(C) Yes, because Dressco shipped goods to the plaintiff in Arkansas.
(D) No, because Dressco is not incorporated in Arkansas and does not have its principal place of business there.

5. Dennis owns a corporation, D-Goods Inc., whose sole function is the operation of a women's leather-goods store in Tulsa, Oklahoma. Until 2010, Dennis bought all of his goods for D-Goods from an Oklahoma-based jobber. But in 2010, Dennis decided to travel to New York City's leather district to see what goods he could buy there. On behalf of the business, he purchased $10,000 of merchandise in New York, then flew back to Tulsa. Two months later, while on company business in Pennsylvania, Dennis collided with a car driven by Paul, a New York resident. Paul sued Dennis in New York state court. Except for the buying trip, neither Dennis nor D-Goods has ever conducted any activities connected with New York. May the New York courts properly take jurisdiction over D-Goods for purposes of this negligence suit?

(A) Yes, because by Dennis' travelling to New York and purchasing business merchandise there, D-Goods purposely availed itself of the opportunity to do business in New York.
(B) No, because D-Goods is not incorporated in New York, and does not have its principal place of business there.
(C) Yes, because the New York courts have a constitutionally-sufficient interest in furnishing a local forum for redress of personal injuries suffered by New York residents.
(D) No, because the gap in time between D-Goods' New York activities and the accident was too long.

6. Toyco is a toy manufacturer whose sole office is located in New York. Penny is a young Florida citizen who claims to have been seriously injured in Florida by a toy made by Toyco in New York and shipped to a store in Florida, from which Penny's mother bought it. Penny has brought a diversity action against Toyco, based on strict product liability, in the U.S. District Court, Southern District of Florida. Assume that if the action had been brought in the Florida state courts, no Florida statute would have authorized the Florida courts to take jurisdiction over a tort action by Penny against Toyco. In the federal action, Penny caused a licensed process server to travel to New York, where the process server visited Toyco's headquarters, and personally handed the summons and complaint to Toyco's president. Does the federal court for the Southern District of Florida now have personal jurisdiction over Toyco?

(A) No, because Toyco does not have minimum contacts with the state of Florida.
(B) Yes, because the Florida courts could constitutionally have taken jurisdiction over Toyco in a tort suit by Penny.

(C) No, because no Florida statute would have permitted the exercise of jurisdiction over Toyco.
(D) Yes, because Toyco's president was personally served.

7. Ted worked for a messenger service owned by Dan. While Ted was driving a Dan-owned car on business in the District of Columbia, he hit and injured Peter, a pedestrian who resides in Delaware. Peter brought a diversity action against Dan in federal court for the District of Columbia, on a theory of respondeat superior. Personal service was properly made, pursuant to FRCP 4(e)(2), on Dan, a D.C. resident. Dan now wishes to implead Ted as a third-party defendant (since if Dan is held liable to Peter, Dan will be entitled under common-law principles to an indemnity from Ted, the actual cause of the accident). Ted is a resident of Virginia, and lives in Arlington, just a few miles from D.C. Dan caused a licensed process server to serve Ted personally at Ted's home in Arlington. Assume that the District of Columbia has no long-arm statute allowing state-court jurisdiction over any defendant who cannot be physically found within District itself. Does the federal court for D.C. have personal jurisdiction over Dan's third-party claim against Ted?

(A) Yes, because Ted was a third-party-defendant who was served within 100 miles of the federal courthouse.
(B) No, because there is no D.C. long-arm statute that would authorize state-court jurisdiction over Ted.
(C) Yes, because service was properly made on Dan within D.C., the state or district where the federal suit is pending.
(D) Yes, because Peter, Dan and Ted are all citizens of different states or districts.

8. Paolo is a resident of New Mexico. Dwight is a resident of either Arizona or Mexico (the parties disagree about which is the correct state of residence for Dwight). Paolo has sued Dwight in diversity in federal court for New Mexico, and made service on Dwight in Arizona in a manner that he believed to be authorized by the New Mexico long-arm statute. Dwight then filed a motion under Federal Rule 12(b)(6) for failure to state a claim upon which relief can be granted; this motion asserted that Paolo's claim was barred by the applicable statute of limitations. The court considered and rejected Dwight's motion. Dwight then made another motion to dismiss pursuant to Rule 12(b), claiming that: (1) venue was improper; and (2) the court lacked subject-matter jurisdiction, because Dwight and Paolo are both citizens of New Mexico. Paolo has asserted that Dwight has waived the right to assert either ground for dismissal. How should the court rule on Paolo's claim of waiver?

(A) It should find that Dwight has waived his right to assert either the venue ground or the subject-matter jurisdiction grounds.
(B) It should find that Dwight has waived the venue ground but not the subject-matter-jurisdiction ground.
(C) It should find that Dwight has waived the subject-matter-jurisdiction ground but not the venue ground.

(D) It should find that Dwight has not waived either the venue ground or the subject-matter jurisdiction ground.

9. Pound is a resident of New York. Donald's Corp. is a New Jersey corporation that operates a single hamburger restaurant in that state. While Pound was driving through New Jersey, Donald's served Pound a hamburger. Pound ate the hamburger in New Jersey, but became violently ill upon his return to New York. Pound sued Donald's in New York state court for negligence and product liability. Service on Donald's was carried out by means authorized by the New York long-arm statute. Donald's made a special appearance in the New York court (as is permitted by New York procedural law) for the sole purpose of contesting personal jurisdiction over it. The New York court found that it had personal jurisdiction over Donald's.

   Donald's then failed to answer the complaint, and the New York court issued a default judgment against it. Since all of Donald's assets were in New Jersey, Pound brought a suit in New Jersey to enforce the New York judgment. In the New Jersey suit on the judgment, Donald's has now convinced the New Jersey court that under applicable U.S. Supreme Court decisions, the New York court erred in deciding that it could constitutionally exercise personal jurisdiction over Donald's, because Donald's did not knowingly and voluntarily take action that would bring its products into New York. Must the New Jersey court enforce the New York judgment against Donald's, thus allowing Pound to seize Donald's property to satisfy that judgment?

   (A) Yes, because the Full Faith & Credit Clause virtually always requires a court to enforce the judgment issued by another state even if the second court believes the first court had no jurisdiction.
   (B) No, because an exception to the Full Faith & Credit Clause applies where the second state believes that the first state lacked jurisdiction to enter the original judgment.
   (C) Yes, because Donald's litigated the jurisdiction issue in the New York proceeding.
   (D) No, because Donald's made only a special, not a general, appearance in the New York proceeding.

10. PigOut Inc. is a franchiser of fast food restaurants. Devon Corp. holds a franchise issued by PigOut for a particular restaurant location. PigOut is incorporated in Delaware, and has its principal place of business in New York. Devon is incorporated in Florida, and has its principal place of business in Delaware. PigOut wishes to terminate Devon's franchise. Therefore, PigOut has brought an action in Florida federal district court for a declaratory judgment that by the terms of the franchise contract, PigOut is entitled to terminate Devon's franchise. PigOut's complaint raises no substantive issues other than issues of state contract law.

    Devon has submitted an answer asserting that PigOut wishes to terminate Devon's franchise so that Pigout can operate Devon's store itself; Devon asserts that this cancellation would be a violation of federal antitrust laws. Both PigOut and Devon wish the action to proceed in federal court, to avoid the congestion of the Florida state courts. The federal judge is convinced that Devon's antitrust defense is not frivolous. The amount at stake is in excess of $100,000. Does the federal court for Florida have subject matter jurisdiction over the case?

(A) Yes, because there is diversity of citizenship between PigOut and Devon.
(B) Yes, because Devon's answer raises a federal question.
(C) Yes, because the parties may agree to waive lack of subject matter jurisdiction.
(D) No, because no federal question is raised by PigOut's complaint.

11. Paula, a pedestrian, was injured when a mail truck owned by the U.S. and driven by Dexter (a post office employee), hit her while she was crossing the street. Paula reasonably believed that both the U.S. and Dexter were liable to her. Applicable statutes, and court decisions interpreting those statutes, indicate that a suit against the U.S. under the Federal Tort Claims Act may only be brought in federal court. Therefore, Paula sued both the U.S. and Dexter in federal district court for Nevada. Both Paula and Dexter are citizens of Nevada. Paula's claim is for $200,000 against the U.S., and for $50,000 against Dexter. Paula's claim against the U.S. is based on the Federal Tort Claims Act; her claim against Dexter is based on a state-law negligence theory. Dexter has moved to have the claim against him dismissed for lack of subject-matter jurisdiction. Should Dexter's motion be granted?

(A) No, because Paula's claim against Dexter did not raise a federal question, and there is no diversity of citizenship as between Paula and Dexter.
(B) Yes, because the doctrine of supplemental jurisdiction permits Paula to assert her state-law claim against Dexter, given the presence of a federal-question claim between Paula and the U.S. arising out of the same transaction as the Paula-Dexter claim.
(C) Yes, because the value of the claim against the U.S. and the value of the claim against Dexter may be aggregated in determining whether the amount in controversy requirement is satisfied.
(D) No, because the doctrine of supplemental jurisdiction does not allow the addition of the state-law claim against Dexter since the U.S. is not a co-defendant with Dexter on that state-law claim.

12. Patricia, a citizen of New York, ate dinner one night at a restaurant operated in New York by David, a citizen of Connecticut. For dessert, Patricia had an apple pie at the restaurant. Patricia became violently ill shortly thereafter, and tests indicated that the pie contained botulism. David had bought the pie from Terry, a New York citizen who is in the business of baking and selling pies to restaurants. Terry had bought the apples for the pie from Thad, a farmer who is also a citizen of New York.

After months of hospitalization, Patricia commenced a product liability action in New York federal district court against David. Her claim was for $200,000. David then impleaded Terry and Thad as third-party defendants pursuant to Federal Rule 14, asserting that if he was liable to Patricia, Terry and Thad would both be liable to him. (This represents a correct statement by David of the applicable substantive rule in a product liability action brought against a restauranteur who makes a claim over against his suppliers.) Patricia then made a product liability claim against Terry for $200,000, as allowed by Federal Rule 14. Terry has now moved to dismiss Patricia's claim against Terry for lack of subject matter jurisdiction. Also, Thad has now moved to dismiss David's third-party claim against him on similar grounds of lack of subject-matter jurisdiction. How should the court decide the two motions?

(A) It should grant Terry's motion but not grant Thad's, because the Patricia-v-Terry claim does not fall within the court's supplemental jurisdiction but the David-v-Thad claim does.
(B) It should grant Thad's motion but not grant Terry's, because the David-v-Thad claim does not fall within the court's supplemental jurisdiction but the Patricia-v-Terry claim does.
(C) It should not grant either motion, because both the Patricia-v-Terry claim and the David-v-Thad claim fall within the court's supplemental jurisdiction.
(D) It should grant both motions, because neither the Patricia-v-Terry claim nor the David-v-Thad claim falls within the court's supplementation jurisdiction.

13. The statute of limitations for federal patent-infringement suits is three years from the date of the violation. On July 1, 2009, P Co. filed with the federal court a complaint alleging that D violated a particular patent belonging to P. The complaint alleged that D imported a certain machine into the United States on July 14, 2006, thereby committing the patent violation. On July 10, 2009, P made personal service of the complaint upon D. On July 25, P, after realizing that it had cited the wrong patent number in its complaint, served upon D an amended complaint listing the correct patent number. (All other aspects of the complaint were the same as in the original complaint.) On July 27, P filed the amended complaint with the court. If D now seeks to dismiss the amended complaint on statute-of-limitations grounds, should the court grant D's motion?

(A) Yes, because the action will be treated as having been commenced on July 27, 2009, after the expiration of the limitations period.
(B) Yes, because the action will be treated as having been commenced on July 25, 2009, after the expiration of the limitations period.
(C) No, because the action will be treated as having been commenced on July 10, 2009, within the limitations period.
(D) No, because the action will be treated as having been commenced on July 1, 2009, within the limitations period.

Questions 14-15 are based upon the following facts:

Paul was injured while operating a drill press manufactured by Manco. Paul properly commenced a diversity action against Manco in the appropriate U.S. district court. Prior to trial, Paul moved to compel discovery of a report which had been made to Manco by Brown, a claims investigator for Manco. At the request of Manco — which feared that Paul might sue it — Brown had, immediately after the accident, inspected the machine and investigated the circumstances of the accident. (Manco's lawyer played no part in Manco's decision to commission Brown to prepare the report.) The machine was subsequently destroyed in a fire and Brown has retired, leaving no forwarding address. The trial judge granted Paul's motion, ordering Manco to furnish the report. [Ruling 1]

The case was tried to a jury. A verdict was returned in favor of Paul for $100,000. Manco moved for a new trial. The trial judge issued an order granting a new trial unless Paul accepted a reduction in the verdict from $100,000 to $25,000. [Ruling 2] Paul asserted that the judge did not have authority to issue such an order, but reluctantly agreed to the reduction under protest. A judgment for $25,000 was entered. Paul then changed his mind about the wisdom of having agreed to the reduction, and appealed Ruling 2.

14. Ruling 1 was:

    (A) incorrect, because work product prepared in anticipation of litigation or trial is not discoverable.
    (B) correct, if Paul showed that there was a substantial need for the information and that he was otherwise unable to obtain it without undue hardship.
    (C) incorrect, because the report was prepared at Manco's request, rather than at the instigation of Manco's attorney.
    (D) correct, regardless of whether the report was prepared in anticipation of litigation.

15. Paul's appeal from Ruling 2 will be:

    (A) Successful, since the court's order violated Paul's Seventh Amendment right to a trial by jury upon the issue of damages.
    (B) Successful, unless the trial court abused its discretion in making Ruling 2.
    (C) Unsuccessful, because Paul elected to accept the remittitur.
    (D) Successful, because the judge-ordered reduction to less than $75,000 was unlawful in that it took the case below the amount-in-controversy threshhold for diversity actions.

16. Printz, driving one car, was injured by a collision with another car driven by Della. Printz believed that the accident occurred because Della went through a stop sign. Printz sued Della for negligence in federal court based on diversity. In preparing for trial, Printz's lawyer discovered a witness, Wanda, who saw the accident and agreed that Della had gone through a stop sign. Della decided to take no discovery in the case. Printz made no disclosure to Della of Wanda's existence, because Della never asked

for this or any other information and Printz consequently believed that no disclosure was required.

At trial, after Printz's case in chief (during which Wanda was not called as a witness), Della presented testimony by Wilbur, who said that he had seen the accident and that Della did not go through the stop sign. In rebuttal, Printz offered the testimony of Wanda that Della *did* go through the stop sign. Della made a procedurally-proper motion objecting to Wanda's testimony on the grounds that Printz had failed to give Della proper notification of Wanda's existence. How should the court rule on the admissibility of that testimony?

(A) Allow the testimony, because Della failed to make a timely discovery request for the information.
(B) Exclude the testimony if and only if it is being offered as part of Printz's substantive case, because Printz was required to disclose Wanda's name and address to Della early in the case without awaiting a discovery request.
(C) Exclude the testimony whether it is being offered as part of Printz's substantive case or merely offered to impeach Wilbur's testimony, because Printz was required to disclose Wanda's name and address to Della early in the case without awaiting a discovery request.
(D) Allow the testimony, because the proper judicial response to any discovery infraction that Printz may have committed is the award of attorney fees or other financial sanctions to Della.

17. P has brought a negligence action against D (based on diversity) in federal district court for the District of Iowa. P's complaint alleges that P was a social guest in D's house, that P fell when a wooden step on a stairway inside the house broke, and that had D used ordinary reasonable care in keeping his house safe, he would have discovered the danger and avoided it. (The complaint does not claim that D knew of the defect, merely that a reasonable person in D's position would have learned of the defect and fixed it.)

The Iowa Supreme Court's only ruling on the issue of whether a property owner owes a duty of inspection to a licensee is a 1924 decision, *Smith v. Bowen*, in which the court held that no such duty is owed to a licensee. The only other Iowa court to ever rule on the matter is the Iowa Appeals Court (the sole intermediate-level court in the state), which has recently held in *Lopez v. Cohen* that the Iowa Supreme Court would not follow *Smith v. Bowen* today, and that a duty of inspection *is* owed to a licensee. In states other than Iowa, the vast majority of courts to have considered the issue recently have concluded that a duty of inspection should be owed to a licensee.

In *P v. D*, should the federal judge instruct the jury that landlords owe invitees a duty of inspection?

(A) Yes, if the federal court believes that the Iowa Supreme Court would probably impose such a duty if the issue were before it today.

(B) Yes, because the federal court is required to follow the ruling of the highest Iowa court to have considered the issue in recent years, the Appeals Court opinion in *Lopez v. Cohen.*

(C) No, because the federal court is required to follow the ruling in *Smith v. Bowen* unless and until that opinion is officially overturned by the Iowa Supreme Court.

(D) Yes, because the federal interest in having a uniform national approach to the matter outweighs any Iowa interest in pursuing a contrary approach.

18. P has sued D in diversity in federal court for the District of Kansas. P's suit was filed with the court on July 1, and served on D on July 2. The complaint alleges that a product sold by D to P was negligently manufactured and injured P; this is a cause of action sounding primarily in tort. On August 1, P amended his complaint to add a claim that the product sold by D breached the implied warranty of merchantability, and that D is therefore liable regardless of fault. Under Kansas law, a breach of warranty claim is deemed to be a contract claim. Also under state law, P's time to sue expired on July 15.

    Under Kansas law, a claim added by an amendment to a previously-filed action dates from the date of the amendment, for statute of limitations purposes. This rule was adopted by the state supreme court out of a belief that too many plaintiffs were filing sloppily-drafted complaints just before expiration of the statute of limitations and then amending the complaints to plead more accurately. But according to FRCP 15(c), a claim added by amendment against the original defendant and arising out of the same transaction as the original claim "relates back," so that it is deemed to date from the filing of the original action. (FRCP 15(c) was enacted to avoid throwing plaintiffs out of court if they needed to make slight amendments to pleadings after the statute of limitations had run.) Should the federal court treat P as being time-barred?

    (A) Yes, because *Erie* doctrine requires the court to apply state rather than federal law whenever the claim is created by state law.

    (B) Yes, because the choice of rule in this situation is heavily outcome-determinative.

    (C) No, because the federal court must apply FRCP 15(c), since that rule is a validly-enacted rule that is directly on point.

    (D) No, if the court concludes that the federal interest in allowing plaintiffs reasonable flexibility in pleading outweighs the countervailing state interest in discouraging sloppy pleading.

Questions 19-20 are based on the following fact pattern:

Denise, driving her car, struck and injured Pete, a pedestrian. Pete sued Denise in the courts of the state of Ames, which follows the Federal Rules of Civil Procedure and the Federal Rules of Evidence. Pete's suit charged that Denise drove negligently. The substantive law of the state of Ames imposes on Pete both the burden of production as to negligence and the burden of persuasion (by a preponderance of the evidence) on this issue. The case was tried to a jury. As part of Pete's case, Pete produced credible evidence that shortly after the accident, Denise was stopped by the police, asked to take a breathalyzer exam, and refused to do so. According to the statutory law of Ames, refusal to take a breathalyzer upon request by the police gives rise to a rebuttable presumption of intoxication (which under state law is a form of negligence when the person is the driver).

19. During his case, Pete came up with no evidence of Denise's negligence other than the evidence tending to show that Denise had refused to take the breathalyzer exam. Denise cross-examined Pete's witnesses on the breathalyzer issue, in such a way that a reasonable jury watching the testimony could have gone either way on the issue of whether Denise refused to take a breathalyzer test requested by the police. Denise's cross-examination of Pete's witnesses also would have allowed (but not required) a reasonable jury to conclude that even if Denise failed to take a breathalyzer, she was not in fact intoxicated at the time of the accident.

    At the close of Pete's case, Denise made a motion for a directed verdict, based on Pete's failure to prove negligence. Should the trial judge grant Denise's motion?

    (A) Yes, because a reasonable jury might disbelieve Pete's evidence that Denise failed to take the breathalyzer test.
    (B) Yes, because a reasonable jury might not believe that Denise's failure to take the breathalyzer constituted negligence.
    (C) No, because Pete's proof suggesting that Denise failed to take the breathalyzer test, coupled with the statutory presumption, satisfied Pete's burden of production on the issue of negligence.
    (D) No, because Pete's proof suggesting that Denise failed to take the breathalyzer test, coupled with the statutory presumption, satisfied Pete's burden of persuasion on the issue of negligence.

20. For this question only, assume that the trial judge denied Denise's directed-verdict motion, and ordered Denise to put on her case. Denise came up with some evidence indicating that she was not in fact intoxicated despite her refusal to take the breathalyzer exam; this evidence was enough that a reasonable jury could be persuaded that Denise was not in fact intoxicated. At the close of Denise's case, the judge instructed the jury as follows: "Under our law, the defendant's refusal to take a breathalyzer exam when asked to do so by the police gives rise to a presumption of intoxication. If you find that Denise refused to take the breathalyzer, then you must find that Denise was intoxicated unless Denise persuades you by a preponderance of the evidence that she was not intoxicated." Are the judge's instructions correct?

    (A) No, because the existence of the presumption, coupled with Pete's evidence that Denise refused to take the breathalyzer, did not shift to Denise the burden of persuasion on the issue of Denise's negligence.

(B) Yes, because the existence of the presumption, coupled with Pete's evidence that Denise refused to take the breathalyzer, shifted to Denise the burden of production on the issue of Denise's negligence.
(C) Yes, because the existence of the presumption, coupled with Pete's evidence that Denise refused to take the breathalyzer, shifted to Denise the burden of persuasion on the issue of her negligence.
(D) No, because if the jury believed that Denise refused to take the breathalyzer test, the jury was required to find that Denise was intoxicated regardless of any other evidence of non-intoxication produced by Denise.

21. P has sued D in a diversity action brought in the federal court for the District of Iowa. According to properly-adopted local court rules for the Iowa District Court, a civil jury shall consist of eight members. P's claim against D was tried before an eight-person jury, and the jury split 7-1 in favor of P. May a verdict be entered in favor of P?

(A) No, because the Seventh Amendment requires that all jury verdicts in any federal civil case be unanimous.
(B) No, because the verdict of a jury of fewer than 12 members must be unanimous.
(C) Yes, if the local district has enacted a court rule allowing for non-unanimous verdicts.
(D) Yes, but only if the parties have stipulated that a non-unanimous verdict shall be valid.

22. P brought a negligence action for damages against D in federal court, based on diversity. The case was tried to a jury. At the close of P's case, D immediately presented his first and only witness, then rested. Neither party made any motions. The court submitted the case to the jury. The jury found in favor of P. D then made a motion for Judgment as a Matter of Law (JML). Should the trial judge grant D's JML motion?

(A) No, because D has waived his right to seek this form of relief.
(B) No, because entry of judgment for D would violate P's Seventh Amendment rights.
(C) Yes, if the judge agrees with D's contention that a reasonable jury could not possibly have found in favor of P.
(D) Yes, if the judge believes that the verdict in P's favor was substantially against the weight of the evidence.

23. P has brought a federal trademark infringement action against D. P seeks two types of relief: (1) an injunction prohibiting D from further violating P's trademark; and (2) money damages for the past violations. D seeks a jury trial on any issues for which he has a jury trial right.

Which of the following statements is correct:

I. D has a right to a jury trial on the injunction claim but not the money-damages claim.
II. D has a right to a jury trial on the money-damages claim but not the injunction claim.
III. The trial judge should first try the damages claim with a jury, then try the injunction claim without a jury.

(A) I only
(B) II only
(C) II and III
(D) Neither I, II or III.

24. P has brought a tort action against D, arising out of an automobile accident that occurred in November, 2000. The case is pending in federal district court for the District of Connecticut. The case is based on diversity, and P's claim is for $100,000. D now seeks to assert a counterclaim against P; the counterclaim is for $30,000, and alleges that P breached a 1999 contract with D made in Connecticut, under which P agreed to buy some merchandise from D. Which of the following are true statements about D's counterclaim:

I. D's counterclaim is permissive.
II. D's counterclaim may be asserted even though it doesn't independently meet the $75,000 amount-in-controversy requirement.
III. If D fails to assert the counterclaim in this action, he will not be able to bring it in a later, separate Connecticut state-court action.

(A) I only
(B) II only
(C) III only
(D) II and III

25. Studio Corp., a motion picture company, is the owner of the "Richie Rat" and "Porky Pig" cartoon characters. Because of these characters' enormous popularity, a number of small entrepreneurs produce T-shirts, sweatshirts, dolls, and other objects with the likenesses of one or the other character on them, without authorization from Studio. Studio has brought a federal district court action against Dave and Dennis, alleging federal copyright violation. Studio is incorporated in Delaware and has its principal place of business in California. Dave is an individual who is a citizen of California. Dennis is an individual who is a citizen of Florida. Dave and Dennis have no connection with each other or with Studio. Studio claims that Dave has unauthorizedly put a picture of Richie Rat on a series of T-shirts, and that Dennis has unauthorizedly created a series of dolls that look like Porky Pig. Studio is seeking an injunction plus $10,000 in damages from Dave, and an injunction plus $20,000 in damages from Dennis.

Which of the following is the most correct statement about the action:

(A) The case may not go forward against either Dave or Dennis because neither claim meets the amount in controversy requirement.

(B) The case may go forward against Dennis but not Dave, because Dave is not diverse with Studio.

(C) The case may go forward against both Dave and Dennis, because all jurisdictional requirements are satisfied and the joinder of defendants is proper.

(D) Dave and Dennis may not be joined in a single action, because the complained-of acts are not part of a single transaction or single series of transactions.

26. A cooperative located in the City of Langdell has 12 apartments and, thus, 12 shareholders. The members of the co-op wish to bring a federal court securities action against Desmond, the prior owner of the building. The suit would allege that Desmond created a false prospectus (concealing defects in the building's structure known to him), and then sold shares in the corporation holding title to the building, in violation of a federal securities law provision. Each of the 12 members has a claim worth in excess of $100,000. The co-op members would like to bring their suit as a class action, with three co-op members (selected by vote of all 12) named as representative plaintiffs. Are they likely to be able to do so?

(A) Yes, because common questions of law or fact predominate, and the class action method is superior to other available methods.

(B) No, because there is no evidence that the representatives will fairly and adequately protect the interests of the class.

(C) No, because there are not enough class members to make joinder of them all as ordinary co-plaintiffs impracticable.

(D) Yes, because the suit alleges that Desmond acted on grounds that apply generally to the class.

27. The Attorney General for the state of Ames had evidence that Natural Foods, a cereal company, was making inflated health claims about its new Oat Bits cereal. Natural Foods claimed that Oat Bits "cuts by 90% your chances of getting colon cancer." The Attorney General brought a civil suit in Ames state court against Natural Foods, seeking a declaratory judgment that this claim was false, and also seeking a civil fine. Natural Foods defended the case vigorously, but lost, with the court finding that the health claim was false and awarding a $10,000 civil fine against Natural Foods.

Subsequently, Paul, a consumer, filed a $1 million strict product liability and negligence action against Natural Foods. The suit was brought in federal court for the district of Langdell, and was based on diversity. The suit alleged that Paul ate Oat Bits constantly, relied on the message, ignored pains in his stomach and thus did not consult a doctor for the pains. When he finally consulted a doctor, Paul alleged, he found out that he had advanced colon cancer, which might have been caught and treated earlier while it was still curable had he not been lulled into a false feeling of security by Natural Foods' health claims about Oat Bits.

Paul now seeks to prevent Natural Foods from relitigating the issue of whether Oat Bits really cuts a person's risk of colon cancer by 90%. Should Natural Foods be so prevented?

(A) Yes, because even though this would constitute an offensive use of collateral estoppel by a stranger to the first action, it is not unfair to prevent Natural Foods from relitigating the colon-risk issue.

(B) No, because courts rarely permit offensive use of collateral estoppel by a stranger to the first action, and this case does not present good reason for departing from the general rule.

(C) No, because under the requirement of mutuality of estoppel, a stranger to the first action would not be bound by the results of the first action and therefore may not benefit from those results.

(D) Yes, because the principle of Full Faith & Credit compels the federal court for Langdell to enforce the judgment of the Ames state court.

ANSWERS TO MULTIPLE-CHOICE QUESTIONS

1. **C** Trucking's motion amounts to an assertion that there is no diversity jurisdiction. (There's no federal-question claim, so the suit must be based on diversity if there is to be subject-matter jurisdiction at all.) For diversity to exist, (1) no plaintiff may be the citizen of the *same state* as any defendant, and (2) the amount in controversy must exceed $75,000.

   A plaintiff is deemed to be a citizen of the state where she resides *at the time the suit is filed* (not where she resides at the earlier time when the cause of action accrued). Therefore, Paula and Pete are citizens of Florida, not California. A corporation is deemed to be a citizen of both the state in which it is incorporated and the state in which it has its principal place of business. Under the ***"nerve center"*** test adopted by the Supreme Court in 2010 (*Hertz Corp. v. Friend*), a corporation's principal place of business is deemed to be the state in which its ***headquarters are located***, not the state in which it does the most business or has the most employees. Therefore, Trucking is a citizen of both Michigan and Delaware, but not of Florida. Thus we have Florida vs. Michigan/Delaware, which satisfies the requirement of complete diversity. Consequently, **C** is correct.

   Choice **A** is incorrect because diversity subject matter jurisdiction is not dependent on the plaintiff's state of citizenship at the time the cause of action accrued, just the state at the time the action was filed. Choice **B** is incorrect because a corporation is a citizen (only) of the states in which it is incorporated and in which it has its principal place of business, and as noted above neither of these is Florida despite the fact that Trucking does more daily activities there than elsewhere.

   Choice **D** is incorrect because, although it reaches the correct result, it does so based on incorrect logic; as explained above in the discussion of Choice (C), no plaintiff can be a citizen of *either* the corporate defendant's state of incorporation or the latter's state of principal-place-of-business.

2. **B** Suits brought in federal court (whether under diversity or federal-question) may be commenced in the judicial district in which either (1) any defendant resides, if all defendants reside in the same State, (2) a substantial part of the events or omissions on which the claim is based occurred or a substantial part of the property in question is located, or (3) any defendant may be found, if there is no district in which the action may otherwise be brought. 28 U.S.C. § 1391(b). When venue is improper, a U.S. district court may, on its own motion or on the motion of any defendant, either transfer the action to another U.S. district court in which the matter could have originally been commenced, or dismiss the lawsuit; 28

U.S.C. § 1406(a). Since the action could have been commenced in either the Northern District of California (where D resides) or the Northern District of Texas (where the discrimination took place), the Nevada federal court may transfer it to either of those districts, making Choice **B** correct.

Choice **A** is incorrect because transfer to N.D. Tex. would be proper (as would transfer to N.D. Cal.) Choice **C** is incorrect because, although the court *may* dismiss the action (since it was brought in an improper district), the court doesn't *have to* do so, and may instead exercise its discretion to transfer the case to a proper district. Choice **D** is wrong because the court may not keep the case — venue in the district of Nevada is not proper, since that district does not satisfy any of the three alternative venue tests (there is no venue based on plaintiff's residence).

3. **B** Where a suit is properly commenced in a state court and jurisdiction is based on a federal question, the defendant may remove the action to the U.S. district court for the judicial district that encompasses the state court. 28 U.S.C. §1441(b). Since the action here involves a federal question, David is entitled to have the litigation removed to the Northern District of Illinois, since that's the federal district court that encompasses Chicago (the place where the state action was pending.) Therefore, Choice **B** is correct.

Choice **A** is incorrect because where removal is otherwise proper, the fact that the action could not have originally been commenced in the U.S. district court to which it is removed is irrelevant. (Pedro could not have initially brought suit in the Northern District because venue based on plaintiff's residence doesn't exist.)

Choice **C** is incorrect because state courts of general jurisdiction are ordinarily competent to hear federal claims, and that is certainly true of employment-discrimination claims. Finally, Choice **D** is incorrect because the defendant's state of citizenship is not pertinent where removal is based upon a federal claim. (It's true that in a *diversity* case, a defendant can't remove if she's a citizen of the state where the action is pending — but this rule doesn't apply to federal-question suits.)

4. **A** These facts are quite similar to those of *International Shoe v. Washington*, 326 U.S. 310 (1945), in which the Supreme Court held that the out-of-state company had the requisite "minimum contacts" with the forum state. Dressco's decision to hire a salesman to solicit orders from inside the state is enough to justify the conclusion that Dressco: (a) ***purposely availed itself of the chance to do business*** in the state, and therefore (b) should have anticipated being required to litigate in the state, at least where the claim related to an in-state transaction. Choice **A** is therefore correct.

Choice **B** is incorrect for the same reasons that Choice **A** is correct. Choice **C** is incorrect because the mere shipment of goods into the forum state is not sufficient for minimum contacts; for instance, if Dressco had maintained a website that it intended for New York-area customers only, and Dilbert's had happened to place the only order from Arkansas filled by Dressco that year, the shipment of goods into Arkansas would not have sufficed.

Choice **D** is incorrect because it states the requirements for "general" jurisdiction (i.e., suits not relating to the defendant's forum-state contacts), not those for "specific" jurisdiction (suits relating to the in-state contacts). See *Daimler AG v. Bauman.* The claim here relates to a shipment made by Dressco into the forum state (Arkansas), so only the easier-to-satisfy requirements for specific jurisdiction have to be satisfied.

5. **B** If Dennis were being sued on a claim ***arising out of D-Goods' New York-based activities*** (e.g., an auto accident that occurred while he was in New York on the leather-buying trip), what would be involved is "specific" jurisdiction, and Dennis' trip to New York would probably represent the constitutionally-required minimum contacts with that state. (Dennis and D-Goods would have purposefully availed themselves of the opportunity to do business in New York.) But here, the claim does not relate to Dennis' in-forum-state activities. According to *Daimler AG v. Bauman,* claims that do not arise from in-forum-state activities of a defendant corporation (i.e., claims based on "general jurisdiction") may only be litigated in the forum state if the corporation was "at home" in the forum state. And a corporation will be deemed at home in the forum state only if it either is incorporated in that state, or has its principal place of business there. *Id.* Since D-Goods is not incorporated in New York and has no principal place of business there, the New York court cannot exercise general jurisdiction over it. Therefore, Choice **B** is correct.

Choice **A** is incorrect because the logic there would apply only if the claim were one related to D-Goods' purposeful in-state activities. Choice **C** is incorrect because, although a state has an interest in affording a local forum for redress of residents' injuries, that interest is relatively weak when the injuries occurred out-of-state and involve a tortfeasor with no or few connections with the forum state. Choice **D** is incorrect because the gap in time between the defendant's in-state activities and the out-of-state activities giving rise to the claim is irrelevant — if the claim does not relate to the in-state activities of a corporate defendant, the corporation won't be subject to general jurisdiction unless it's incorporated in the forum state or has its principal place of business there, and even a complete temporal overlap between the in-state activities and the out-of-state ones that triggered the claim will not change this.

6. **C** FRCP 4(k)(1)(A) says that, with a couple of exceptions not relevant here, a federal court — whether in a diversity or federal-question case — may not exercise jurisdiction unless the defendant is ***"subject to the jurisdiction of a court of general jurisdiction*** in the ***state where the district court is located."*** Since the

facts tell us that there is no Florida long-arm that would allow jurisdiction over an out-of-state corporation in Toyco's position, the federal court sitting in Florida may not take jurisdiction either. Therefore, **C** is the correct choice.

Choice **A** is incorrect because Toyco probably *does* have minimum contacts with Florida (having shipped a defective toy to Florida that caused an injury there), and in any event the presence of minimum contacts will not override the effect of Florida's unwillingness to subject Toyco to jurisdiction for a state-court action. Choice **B** is incorrect because the Florida courts' ability to constitutionally exercise jurisdiction over Toyco is necessary but not sufficient to the Florida federal court's exercise of jurisdiction — it must be the case *both* that the Florida courts could have constitutionally exercised jurisdiction over the out-of-state defendant (i.e., that the defendant have minimum contacts with Florida) *and* that Florida statutes in fact authorize the exercise of such jurisdiction. Choice **D** is incorrect because the fact that a defendant is served by a proper method (in this case, personal service on a corporate officer is expressly deemed valid by FRCP 4(h)(1)) does not mean that the defendant was "amenable" to service, a separate requirement described above in the discussion of why Choice **C** is correct.

7. **A** This question illustrates the utility of the ***"100-mile bulge"*** provision of Federal Rule 4(k)(1)(B). Rule 4(k)(1)(B) says that when a person is brought in as a third-party defendant pursuant to Federal Rule 14, service may be made outside the state where the district court sits, provided that the place of service is "not more than 100 miles from where the summons was issued[.]" Since Arlington is less than 100 miles from the federal courthouse in the District of Columbia (which is the place from which the summons is deemed to have been "issued"), service was valid under the 100-mile bulge provision even though the non-federal courts of the District (analogous to state courts) would not have been able to exercise jurisdiction due to the lack of a local long-arm statute. Therefore, Choice **A** is correct.

Choice **B** is incorrect because the availability of the 100-mile-bulge provision makes the fact that no D.C. long-arm would reach Ted irrelevant. (If not for the existence of the bulge provision, this choice would be correct, since as a general rule a federal court can't exercise jurisdiction over an out-of-state defendant who couldn't be reached by the long-arm of the state where the federal court sits.) Choice **C** is correct because the fact that service was made by a proper *method* doesn't answer the separate question of whether the defendant was within the proper territory for service, a question answered above in the discussion of Choice A. Choice **D** is incorrect because the citizenship of the parties is relevant to the issue of federal subject-matter jurisdiction (here, based on diversity), not to the issue of jurisdiction over the parties, which is the issue raised by the question.

8. **B** Under FRCP 12(h)(1)(A), a defense of improper venue is waived if a person makes any Rule 12 motion and omits the venue defense from that motion. That's what happened here — Dwight's first motion was under 12(b)(6), and it failed to include the 12(b) venue motion. On the other hand, according to FRCP 12(h)(3) the defense of lack of subject matter jurisdiction may be raised (either by a party or by the court) at any time, and can never be waived. Therefore, Choice **B** is correct.

   For these same reasons, Choices **A**, **C** and **D** are incorrect.

9. **C** The Full Faith and Credit Clause of the Constitution (Article IV, §1) provides that where a judgment from State 1 is sued upon in State 2, the courts of State 2 must give that judgment the same effect as it would have in State 1. There is an exception if the State 1 judgment was by default, but there is an exception to this exception if the defendant ***actually litigated the jurisdictional question*** in State 1 and lost. Since here, D litigated the jurisdictional issue in the New York courts and lost, he may not "collaterally attack" the New York judgment when it is sued upon for enforcement in New Jersey, even if the New Jersey court is absolutely convinced that the New York courts misunderstood federal due process principles. (D should have appealed the New York decision to the Supreme Court, rather than trying to make a collateral attack in New Jersey.) *Baldwin v. Iowa State Travelling Men's Association*, 283 U.S. 522 (1931). Therefore, choice **C** is correct.

   Choice **A** states a general rule that is correct in most cases. But the rule as stated says that the State 2 court is nearly always required to ignore the State 1 jurisdiction issue and enforce the judgment, and that's not so where the defendant defaulted in the State 1 proceeding without litigating the jurisdiction issue there. So Choice **A** is not as precise, and therefore as good, an answer as Choice **C**.

   Choice **B** is wrong because the State 2 court is free to decline to enforce the State 1 judgment on the grounds that the State 1 court lacked jurisdiction *only* if the defendant did not litigate the jurisdiction issue (or otherwise appear) in the State 1 proceeding; here, Donald's *did* litigate that issue in New York.

   Choice **D** is wrong because the fact that Donald's made only a special appearance in the New York proceeding is irrelevant to the New Jersey court's duty to enforce the New York judgment. The fact that the appearance was "special" meant merely that Donald's could, after losing on jurisdiction in New York, have then defended on the merits without thereby being deemed to have consented to jurisdiction; this would have protected Donald's right to raise the jurisdiction issue in any *New York* appeal, but did not protect Donald's right to make a collateral attack in New Jersey.

10. **D** First, there is no diversity of citizenship, since a corporation is deemed to be a citizen of both the state of incorporation and the state of principal place of business, making both PigOut and Devon citizens of Delaware. Therefore, the sub-

ject matter jurisdiction must be of the federal-question sort. But to support federal-question jurisdiction, the federal question must normally be part of a "well-pleaded complaint." In other words, the federal question must normally be an integral part of the plaintiff's cause of action (as revealed by the plaintiff's complaint); it is not enough that the plaintiff anticipates a defense based on federal law, or even that the defendant's answer explicitly states a federal defense. There is a rarely-applied exception for cases where resolution of the plaintiff's state-law claim requires resolving an important "embedded" issue of federal law as to which the federal government has a strong interest in a uniform answer (e.g., a state-law claim whose validity turns on the interpretation of the federal tax-collection statute; see *Grable & Sons Metal Products, Inc. v. Darue Engineering & Manufacturing* (U.S. 2005)). But the exception doesn't apply here, given that there are no strong federal interests involved and federal law doesn't have to be consulted to decide plaintiff's own claim (just the defendant's claim). Therefore, the general rule applies: since PigOut's claim is founded solely upon state law (contract law), it is irrelevant that D has asserted a defense that derives entirely from a federal statute. See *Louisville & Nashville R.R. v. Mottley* (U.S. 1908). Therefore, choice **D** is correct.

Choice **A** is incorrect because, as discussed in the first sentence above, there is not diversity of citizenship between PigOut and Devon. Choice **B** is incorrect because, as described above, the fact that the defendant's answer raises a federal question does not suffice to generate federal-question jurisdiction; the federal question must, except in rare cases, appear as part of the plaintiff's complaint. Choice **C** is incorrect because lack of federal subject-matter jurisdiction is one of the few defenses that cannot be waived by the parties.

11. **B** The supplemental jurisdiction doctrine (codified in 28 U.S.C. § 1367) says that when there is a "core" claim that qualifies for diversity or federal-question jurisdiction, certain other related claims may be added even though those other claims do not independently satisfy the requirements of subject-matter jurisdiction. One aspect of supplemental jurisdiction is that if there is a federal-question claim against D1, a state-law claim against D2 (who is not a party to the federal-question claim) may be added as long as the claim against D2 and the federal-question claim against D1 arises out of a ***common nucleus of operative fact.*** Since the two claims by Paula arise out of a single accident and conduct (Dexter's driving of the mail truck), this requirement is met here. Therefore, choice **B** is correct.

Choice **A** is incorrect because the absence of a federal question in the Paula-Dexter claim and the absence of diversity between the two don't matter, since supplemental jurisdiction applies as described above. Choice **C** is incorrect for two reasons: (1) Paula is probably not permitted to meet the amount in controversy requirement by aggregating the amount of her claim against one defendant to the amount of her claim against another defendant; and (2) such aggregation wouldn't help anyway, since there would still be a lack of diversity between Paula and Dexter (only supplemental jurisdiction can take care of that problem).

Choice **D** is incorrect because supplemental jurisdiction allows the tacking on of a state-law claim against D2 to a federal-question claim against D1, even if D1 is not a party to the state-law claim against D2 (as long as the federal-question and state-law claims arise out of the same nucleus of fact.)

12. **A** Terry is a third-party defendant. A claim by the original plaintiff against the third-party defendant does not fall within the court's supplemental jurisdiction, so it must have independent jurisdictional grounds. In the absence of a federal question and in the absence of supplemental jurisdiction, Patricia and Terry must be citizens of different states, which they are not. Consequently, the court has no subject-matter jurisdiction over the Patricia-v-Terry claim, and it must be dismissed.

On the other hand, a claim by the original defendant (acting as a third-party plaintiff) against a third-party defendant *does* fall within the court's supplemental jurisdiction. Therefore, the David-v-Thad third-party claim may be heard under the supplemental-jurisdiction doctrine, even though that claim does not raise a federal question and even though David and Thad are citizens of the same state.

Since choice **A** states that only the Patricia-v-Terry claim should be dismissed, it is correct. The other choices are incorrect on the same reasoning.

(Observe, by the way, that there is a good rationale for denying supplemental treatment to Patricia's claim against Terry: Patricia would not have been able to institute an initial suit against both David and Terry, because of the lack of diversity between Patricia and Terry; it seems improper to allow Patricia to do indirectly [by dropping Terry from the initial suit, waiting for David to implead Terry as he would surely do, then making a third-party claim against Terry] what she may not do directly. There's not a similarly good rationale for being as sceptical of the David-v-Thad impleader claim, since David was dragged into the case against his will, and we therefore don't have to worry about giving him an incentive to use clever means of getting into the federal courts.)

13. **D** To solve this problem, you need to know two things about how the federal courts compute the commencement date of a civil action. First, in cases in which the plaintiff's claim arises under the federal Constitution or a federal statute (i.e., federal-question cases), the action is deemed commenced, for statute of limitations purposes, by the filing of a complaint ***with the court***. (FRCP 3.) (In a diversity suit, state law determines what constitutes the commencement of the action for statute of limitations purposes.) Therefore, at least as to P's original complaint, P will be deemed to have commenced the suit on July 1, prior to the running of the 3-year statute on July 14.

The second thing to understand is the effect of FRCP 15(c)(1), which deals with the filing date of amended pleadings. That section provides for ***"relation back,"*** i.e., for treating the amended pleading as having been served as of the date of the original pleading, in certain circumstances. Relation back applies when "the amendment asserts a claim or defense that arose out of the conduct, transaction, or occurrence set out — or attempted to be set out — in the original pleading." 15(c)(1)(B). Here, the same transaction (importation of a particular machine violating P's patents) is charged in both complaints, despite the fact that the patent number changed. Therefore, the amended complaint relates back to the original July 1 complaint filing, making the amended complaint timely.

Therefore, choice **D** is correct. For exactly the same reasons, choices **A**, **B** and **C** are incorrect.

14. **B** A party may ordinarily obtain discovery of documents and other tangible items prepared in anticipation of litigation or for trial (1) by or for another party, or (2) by or for that other party's representative (including her attorney), only upon a showing that (1) the party seeking such discovery has a *substantial need* for the items, and (2) that party is *unable, without undue hardship*, to obtain the equivalent thereof by other means; FRCP 26(b)(3)(A). In effect, **B** restates this rule, so it's correct.

Choice **A** is incorrect because, even though the report was prepared by Brown in anticipation of litigation or trial, it would still be discoverable if Paul could show a substantial need for the document and that he was unable to otherwise obtain it (or its equivalent) without undue hardship. Choice **C** is incorrect because the "work product" privilege extends to litigation-related documents created by another party (not just to items prepared by or for that party's lawyer). Finally, Choice **D** is incorrect because whether the report was prepared in anticipation of ligitation would make a difference to the correctness of the judge's ruling allowing discovery — if the report was not prepared in anticipation, it would be automatically discoverable as long as it was "relevant to any party's claim or defense" (FRCP 26(b)(1)); if instead the report was prepared in anticipation of litigation, it would be discoverable only if Paul could show substantial need and inability to obtain the equivalent without undue hardship.

15. **C** A plaintiff who accepts a remittitur in federal court may not challenge the trial court's ruling on appeal. By accepting the remittitur, and thereby avoiding the delay and cost of a new trial, the plaintiff will be deemed to have relinquished her right to appeal the court's order. If Paul was dissatisfied with the remittitur, he should have appealed Ruling 2 immediately, on the basis that the judge had abused his discretion (i.e., there was no good faith basis for reducing the verdict of $100,000 to $25,000). The fact that Paul agreed to the reduction "under protest" is irrelevant. So Choice **C** is correct.

Choice **A** is incorrect because remittiturs are not violations of the Seventh Amendment, even though in a sense they take away the jury's verdict. (The rationale for this is that the plaintiff is considered to have voluntarily agreed to the remittitur; i.e., the plaintiff is always free to reject the remittitur and to have the case re-tried by a jury). Choice **B** is incorrect because, whether the trial court abused its discretion or not in ordering a new trial, Paul waived his right to appeal the court's order by accepting the decreased sum. Finally, Choice **D** is incorrect because the amount-in-controversy is a test applied only at the beginning of the case — so long as at that point it cannot be said to a legal certainty that plaintiff's claim cannot exceed $75,000, the fact that later proof (or judicial finding) indicates that the claim was worth less than $75,000 is irrelevant.

16. **B** Under FRCP 26(a)(1)(A), a party must, without awaiting a discovery request from the other party, provide to the other party "the name and, if known, the address and telephone number of each individual likely to have discoverable information ... that the disclosing party may use to support its claims or defenses, unless the use would be solely for impeachment...." FRCP 37(c)(1) says that where a party "fails to provide information ... as required by Rule 26(a) or (e), the party is not allowed to use that information or witness to supply evidence ... unless the failure was substantially justified or is harmless." Since Printz did not have substantial justification for the failure to disclose (an incorrect belief that the disclosure is not required unless it's specifically requested by the other side is clearly not "substantial justification"), and since the failure to disclose was not harmless, the trial judge has no choice but to exclude the evidence from being introduced substantively. Since choice **B** essentially re-states this rule, it is the correct answer.

Choice **A** is incorrect because the obligation in 26(a)(1)(A) applies even if the other party never makes a discovery request. Choice **C** is incorrect because the above-quoted portion of 26(a)(1)(A) makes the duty of automatic disclosure inapplicable if the disclosing party plans to use the witness' discoverable information "solely for impeachment," and choice **C** incorrectly asserts that the duty of disclosure would apply even in this solely-for-impeachment situation. Choice **D** is incorrect because, although the court is permitted to award Rule 37 sanctions for such a failure to make automatic disclosure, Rule 37(c)(1) makes it clear that such sanctions are in addition to, not in lieu of, exclusion of the evidence that should have been disclosed.

17. **A** This is a classic *Erie* situation — there is no state or federal statute or rule on the matter, and state common law creates the right being sued upon. In this situation, *Erie* means that the federal judge's duty to is to figure out what the state's highest court would most likely do if the issue were presented today; then, the federal court is required to do the same. Since Choice **A** states this obligation, it is the correct answer.

Choice **B** is incorrect because a recent ruling by an intermediate court is significant only to the extent it helps predict what the state's highest court would do; Choice B suggests that the intermediate court's approach is dispositive, and that is not a correct statement of how the federal court should approach the problem. (That is, if the federal court thinks that the Iowa Supreme Court would not impose an inspection obligation, the federal court must follow suit even if the recent intermediate-court opinion says otherwise.) Similarly, Choice **C** is wrong because the fact that an old highest-state-court opinion went one way doesn't resolve the relevant issue, which is what the highest-state-court would do *today*. And Choice **D** is wrong because where (as here), the issue is a pure substantive issue of state common-law, there is no weighing of state and federal interests to be done.

18. **C** This fact pattern presents a flat-out conflict between an applicable Federal Rule (15(c)(1)) and a state rule or policy. So as long as the Federal Rule is valid under the Rules Enabling Act (i.e., it does not enlarge or reduce a party's "substantive right"), it will prevail over the competing state policy. The highly technical nature of Rule 15(c)(1)'s relation-back approach means that it is almost certainly valid. Therefore, a federal court will apply the Rule, and allow P to add his breach of warranty claim, even though he could not do so in state court. This is true even though there is something of an outcome-determinative effect here: P gets to pursue his warranty claim even though he would not get to pursue it if the case were in state court. The important thing to remember is that we do not use the *Byrd v. Blue Ridge* "balancing" approach when a Federal Rule is directly on point; instead we apply the Federal Rule so long as it is valid (which every Federal Rule has been found to be so far). See *Hanna v. Plumer*, 380 U.S. 460 (1965), and *Shady Grove Orthopedic Assoc. v. Allstate Ins. Co.*, 130 S.Ct. 1431 (2010), each of which describes the method of analyzing a conflict between an on-point Federal Rule and a state rule or policy.

Choice **A** is incorrect because, among other things, it falsely implies that even purely-procedural issues must be resolved by application of state law if the underlying claim is state-created; *Hanna v. Plumer* says that a valid federal procedural rule takes priority over a valid state rule or policy in this situation. Choice **B** is incorrect because where a valid federal procedural rule is on point, the fact that the choice of federal versus state rule is heavily outcome-determinative is irrelevant; the federal rule must be applied anyway. Choice **D** is wrong because, again, in this valid-and-onpoint-federal-rule scenario, the court does not engage in a weighing of the competing state and federal interests; it simply applies the federal rule.

19. **C** The trial judge may grant Denise's motion for judgment as a matter of law only if the judge believes that Pete has not carried his burden of production, that is, his burden of producing some credible evidence (evidence that might be believed by a reasonable jury) that Denise behaved negligently. The presump-

tion (failure to take a breathalyzer equals intoxication and thus negligence) is enough to get Pete past this burden of production — by offering credible proof that Denise did not take the breathalyzer (the "basic" fact), Pete will be deemed to have met the burden of producing evidence that Denise was negligent (the "presumed" fact). (In fact, since Pete has now carried his burden of production, this burden is now shifted to Denise: unless Denise comes up with credible evidence of her non-negligence, the court will have to instruct the jury at the end of Denise's case that it should find for Pete on this issue.) Therefore, **C** is correct.

Choice **A** is incorrect because, although it is possible that a reasonable jury on these facts might disbelieve Pete's evidence that Denise failed to take the breathalyzer test, this possibility is certainly not a justification for the judge to take the case from the jury — a reasonable jury might, alternatively, *believe* Pete's evidence on the breathalyzer, so the judge must let the jury decide whether to believe that evidence.

Choice **B** is incorrect for basically the same reason as Choice **A** is incorrect. It's true that a reasonable jury might believe that Denise was not intoxicated even though she failed to take a breathalyzer (i.e., that Denise, through her cross-examination, successfully rebutted the presumption of intoxication from failure to take a breathalyer). But the fact that a reasonable jury *might* reach such a conclusion doesn't justify the court in taking the issue away from the jury — only if a reasonable jury would *necessarily* believe that Denise had rebutted the presumption could the court direct a verdict on the ground in choice **B**, and that is not the case here (since the facts say that the jury could go either way on this issue).

Choice **D** is incorrect because, in a motion for directed verdict, the non-movant's satisfaction of the burden of *persuasion* is irrelevant. The only issue raised by a motion for directed verdict is whether the *non*-movant has satisfied his burden of *production* on the issue (i.e., his burden of producing enough evidence on the issue that a reasonable jury might find for him). So the fact that a reasonable jury might possibly find by a preponderance of the evidence that Denise did not decline to take a breathalyzer (i.e., the fact that the jury might conclude that Denise carried a burden of persuasion on the breathalyzer issue) is irrelevant on the present issue of whether to direct a verdict against Pete.

20. **A** Under the ***"bursting bubble"*** approach to presumptions imposed by Federal Rule of Evidence 301, "a presumption imposes on the party against whom it is directed the burden of going forward with evidence to rebut or meet the presumption, but ***does not shift to such party*** the burden of proof in the sense of the ***risk of non-persuasion***, which ***remains*** throughout the trial upon the party on whom it was originally cast." Thus although the presumption "refusal to take breathalyzer equals intoxication" meant that once Pete showed such refusal, the burden of *production* as to intoxication shifted to Denise (see answer to prior question), this presumption did not help Pete get rid of the burden of *persuasion*.

At the end of the trial, just as at the beginning, the burden remained on Pete to show by a preponderance of the evidence that Denise was in fact intoxicated. Thus if the jury believed that there was exactly a 50% chance that Denise was intoxicated, Pete loses, just as if there had been no presumption at all. To the extent that the judge's instructions indicated that Denise would lose if the jury was completely undecided, those instructions are wrong. Therefore, Choice **A** is correct.

Choice **B** is incorrect because, although the existence of the presumption shifted to Denise the burden of *production* on the issue of Denise's negligence (see the answer to the prior question), this shift does not bear on the accuracy of the judge's instructions, which relate solely to the burden of *persuasion.*

Choice **C** is incorrect because the existence of the presumption does not shift the burden of persuasion, as explained in the first paragraph of this answer. Choice **D** is incorrect because the facts tell you that the presumption is rebuttable; Choice D, if correct, would render the presumption irrebuttable.

21. **D** The six-person jury is allowable under FRCP 48, which states that "a jury must initially have at least 6 and no more than 12 members[.]" But Rule 48 further requires the jury verdict in federal civil trials both to be unanimous and to be returned by at least 6 members, unless the parties stipulate otherwise. Unless P and D stipulated that a less-than-unanimous verdict would suffice, the trial must be treated as a "hung jury" and the case retried. Therefore, Choice **D** is correct.

Choice **A** is incorrect because the Seventh Amendment has generally not been interpreted to require unanimity in federal civil jury trials. (Also, even if the Seventh Amendment requires unanimity in cases covered by the Seventh Amendment, the Amendment does not apply to all civil cases, only to ones "at common law.") Choice **B** is incorrect because, as explained above, the parties may stipulate to waive the requirement of unanimity (and in any event, unanimity is no more important for less-than-12-member juries than for 12-member juries). Choice **C** is incorrect because the local district does not have power under FRCP 48 to dispense with the requirement of unanimity — only a stipulation by the parties may do that.

22. **A** A JML motion may only be made after the verdict if the movant moved for a JML sometime before the case was submitted to the jury, and the motion was denied. (See FRCP 50(a), saying that the JML motion may be made "at any time before the case is submitted to the jury," and 50(b), saying that after the entry of judgment the movant may make a "renewed motion" for JML.) Since on our facts, D never moved for a JML before the case went to the jury, he has waived his right to seek a JML after the verdict was reached. This means that the most D can get, either from the trial judge or on appeal, is a new trial, not an entry of judgment in his favor. Therefore, Choice **A** is correct.

Choice **B** is incorrect because if the JML procedure were properly used (i.e., as a renewal of an earlier motion at the close of the evidence), there would be no Seventh Amendment problem with entering judgment notwithstanding the verdict. Choice **C** is incorrect because even if the trial judge agreed that a reasonable jury could not have found for P, the explanation given above means that the judge is not authorized to enter judgment for D due to D's failure to move for JML at the close of the evidence. Choice **D** is incorrect because even if the judge believed that the verdict for P was substantially against the weight of the evidence, this would only be cause for ordering a new trial, not cause for entering JML for D.

23. **C** Federal Rule 38(a) gives the right of jury trial "as declared by the Seventh Amendment to the Constitution." That Amendment applies only to suits "at common law." Therefore, there is only a right to a jury trial (unless Congress specifically otherwise provides) where the suit is one which is "legal" rather than "equitable." An injunction suit is always regarded as "equitable," so there is no right to a jury trial on an injunction claim. A claim for damages, by contrast, is virtually always "legal," so it does carry with it a right to a jury trial. Therefore I is false, and II is true.

If the court tries the injunction claim (without a jury) first, this will probably bind the jury when the jury hears the damages claim later, because of the doctrine of "law of the case." Yet if the jury is not given comparatively free rein in deciding the damages claim, D's Seventh Amendment right to a jury trial will be violated. Therefore, even though it may be somewhat inefficient, the federal judge should try the damages claim first, then the injunction claim, if there are significant issues in common between the two. (There are almost certainly such common issues here, e.g., the issue of whether P's trademark is valid and whether D has in fact infringed it.) See *Beacon Theatres v. Westover*, 359 U.S. 500 (1959). Therefore, III is true.

Choice **C** is correct, because it correctly states that II and III are true. The other choices are false for the same reason.

24. **A** First, note that the D's claim and P's claim arise out of two different "transactions or occurrences" (the accident and the contract). Therefore, under FRCP 13(b), D's counterclaim was ***permissive***, not compulsory. Thus I is correct.

Next, since the counterclaim is permissive, it does ***not*** fall within the court's ***supplemental jurisdiction***. (Under 28 U.S.C. § 1367(a), supplemental jurisdiction does not apply to a claim that is so different from the main claim that it is not part of the "same case or controversy" as the main claim; that's the case here.) Consequently, most courts say that the permissive counterclaim must independently meet the $75,000 amount-in-controversy requirement, which it doesn't here. Therefore, II is incorrect.

Finally, since the counterclaim is permissive rather than compulsory, D need not assert it here — he can wait and assert it in a separate later action in either state or federal court. Therefore, III is incorrect.

25. **D** The circumstances under which a plaintiff may join two or more defendants are governed by Federal Rule 20(a)(1)'s "permissive joinder" provision: "Persons ... may be joined in one action as defendants if: (A) any right to relief is asserted against them jointly, severally, or in the alternative with respect to or arising out of the same transaction, occurrence, or series of transactions or occurrences; *and* (B) any question of law or fact common to all defendants will arise in the action."

Here, the first requirement in 20(a)(2) — that all claims involve the "same transaction, occurrence, or series of transactions or occurrences..." — is not satisfied. It is true that the transactions are roughly similar, but they are not the *same* — they involve alleged infringement of different sorts, against different copyrighted properties, by different defendants not acting in concert. Just as a plaintiff cannot join in one federal action all defendants who owe him money where each defendant is liable under a separate contract, so it is the case that a plaintiff cannot join independent copyright violators. Therefore, Choice **D** is correct.

Choice **A** is not correct because the case is based on a federal-question claim (copyright infringement), and there is no amount-in-controversy requirement for federal-question claims. Choice **B** is not correct because, again, the case raises a federal question and diversity is therefore not required. Finally, Choice **C** is not correct because the multiple-defendant joinder is not proper under FRCP 20(a)(2) as described above.

26. **C** One of the requirements for a federal class action, according to Rule 23(a)(1), is that the class be "so ***numerous*** that joinder of all members is impracticable...." Twelve is such a small number that it is hard to see why the individual co-op members cannot simply join together as co-plaintiffs under Rule 20(a). (Groups smaller than 21 are rarely granted class action status.) Also, the degree to which the prospective class members are geographically dispersed is a factor, with the greater the dispersion, the more impracticable joinder would be; this factor cuts heavily against class-action status here, since the plaintiffs all live in the same building and could thus easily join as ordinary co-plaintiffs. Therefore, Choice **C** is correct.

Choice **A** is not correct because of the problem of numerosity already discussed. (But this choice otherwise correctly states the requirements for a 23(b)(3) action, which is the type of class action this would have to be if it went forward at all.) Choice **B** is not correct because the entire group has elected the named representatives, and there is no reason to distrust the named reps' ability or willingness to fairly protect the interests of the absent class members. Choice **D** is incorrect because the fact that the defendant "acted on grounds that apply generally to the class" is one of the requirements for a 23(b)(2) injunctive-relief class action (which this could not possibly be — it seeks damages, not equitable relief), not for a 23(b)(3) action.

27. **A** Here, Paul is not only a stranger to the first action but also an ***"offensive"*** user of collateral estoppel, so his case for getting the benefit of the doctrine is weaker than if he had been either a participant in the first action or a defendant in the second action. Nonetheless, the court will probably find that Paul is entitled to use collateral estoppel. First of all, Paul might not have been allowed to intervene in the first suit even if he had wanted to, since individuals are not always permitted to intervene in suits brought by government bodies (so Paul can't be accused of unfairly sitting out the first suit and then taking advantage of its results). Second, there is every reason to believe that Natural Foods had an incentive to vigorously defend the first suit. Finally, there is no evidence that Natural Foods would have procedural opportunities in the second suit that were not present in the first suit. All together, there seems to be very little risk of unfairness to Natural Foods in collaterally estopping it from relitigating the issue of whether Oat Bits reduces colon cancer risk. This fact pattern is somewhat similar to that of *Parklane Hosiery Co. v. Shore*, 439 U.S. 322 (1979), where the Supreme Court held that offensive collateral estoppel should be allowed on those facts. Therefore, Choice **A** is correct.

Choice **B** is wrong because courts are increasingly willing to allow a stranger to the first action to make offensive use of collateral estoppel, and the reasons listed above are in fact good ones for allowing such use here. Choice **C** is incorrect because the iron-clad requirement of mutuality of estoppel has long been abandoned everywhere. Choice **D** is incorrect because the requirement of Full Faith & Credit applies only where a party to the first action is seeking to enforce a judgment, not where someone is seeking merely to prevent a factual issue from being relitigated.

ESSAY EXAM QUESTIONS & ANSWERS

The following questions were adapted from various Harvard Law School First-Year Civil Procedure examinations of the past. The questions are reproduced almost exactly as they actually appeared, with only slight changes to the facts. The sample answers are not "official" and represent merely one approach to handling the questions.

QUESTION 1

Muenster Airways, Inc., is a small airline flying regularly scheduled flights between points in New Jersey, New York, and New England. It is incorporated in New Jersey and has its principal place of business there. Amos Stilton, a passenger on the ill-fated flight described below, is a citizen of Ames, a small midwestern state located between Indiana and Illinois.

In December 2017, Muenster conducted an advertising campaign in Ames and other midwestern states offering a special flying tour of New England in the spring of 2018, featuring stopovers in Tiverton, R.I., Worcester, Mass., and White River Junction, Vermont. Stilton, attracted by the advertisement, bought a round-trip ticket from an independent travel agent in Ames and was put into a group of Ames travelers who would be leaving on the tour on April 1 from Ames City. The agent, after selling the ticket, immediately listed Stilton (care of his Ames address), on Muenster's reservation system as a passenger for the upcoming trip. Transportation to Newark, N.J., the starting point of the tour, was provided to Stilton and other tour participants by another airline.

Stilton and his fellow travelers arrived in Newark on the appointed day and boarded a Muenster plane for Tiverton, but the plane was forced to make an emergency landing in Bridgeport, Conn., and although no passengers were killed, many (including Stilton) were seriously injured.

One of the passengers, Charlene Cheddar, brought a diversity action for $125,000 damages against Muenster in a New Jersey federal court. The case went to trial and the jury found Muenster liable but awarded only $500 to Cheddar, apparently rejecting her claim of serious injury. No appeal was filed.

Stilton has now brought a diversity action of his own against Muenster in an Ames federal court, seeking $100,000 damages. The only portion of the Ames long-arm statute that might plausibly give *in personam* jurisdiction over Muenster in a state-court action is §103(a)(1). Section 103(a)(1) confers on the Ames state courts personal jurisdiction over "any person who acts directly, or by an agent, with respect to a cause of action arising from the person's transacting of any business in this state." Stilton made service of process on Muenster by registered mail (without any acknowledgement-of-service or request-for-waiver-of-service form enclosed) at Muenster's home office in New Jersey; this form of service on out-of-state defendants is authorized by the Ames long-arm.

Stilton, in addition to relying on §103(a)(1) of the Ames long-arm, has sought to establish jurisdiction in the Ames federal court by attachment of an airplane owned by Muenster and currently under two-year lease to Gorgonzola Airways, a company doing business solely in Ames, at an annual rental of $20,000. The Ames long-arm says nothing about the validity of jurisdiction based on such attachments.

A. What are the arguments for and against Muenster's motion to dismiss the action in its entirety for lack of jurisdiction? How should the motion be decided?

B. Assume that all motions addressed to jurisdiction are denied and that Stilton, relying on the New Jersey decision, moves for summary judgment on the issue of liability. If the issue is one of first impression, what decision should be made on the motion and why?

ANSWER TO QUESTION 1

Part A: The most difficult jurisdictional questions in this case relate to jurisdiction over the parties. However, there are two preliminary subject-matter jurisdictional issues which will be dealt with first: (1) Is there diversity? and (2) Is the amount in controversy requirement met?

(1) *Diversity:* Under 28 USC §1332(c), Muenster is a citizen of New Jersey, since that state is both the state of incorporation and the principal place of business. Stilton is a citizen of Ames, so diversity is established.

(2) *Amount in controversy:* The satisfaction of the $75,000 amount in controversy requirement is clear. Stilton has claimed damages of $100,000; under the *St. Paul Mercury* case this amount will control unless it appears to a legal certainty that Stilton cannot recover more than $75,000. Since Stilton's claim appears to be in good faith, and he is seriously injured, the amount in controversy requirement is satisfied.

(3) *In Personam Jurisdiction:* Turning to the question of *in personam* jurisdiction, the first point to keep in mind is that since this is a diversity action, the federal court for Ames will exercise personal jurisdiction over the out-of-state Muenster only if the Ames *state courts* would exercise such jurisdiction. So even if the Ames courts could constitutionally exercise jurisdiction over Muenster (i.e., even if Muenster had minimum contacts with Ames), if the Ames long-arm wouldn't reach Muenster, the federal court sitting in diversity can't exercise jurisdiction either.

§103(a)(1) of the Ames long-arm may grant personal jurisdiction over Muenster. Muenster will undoubtedly argue that the travel agent who sold Stilton his ticket was not its agent, and that §103(a)(1) therefore does not apply. Muenster might on this ground escape those decisions holding that where a foreign corporation uses an in-state agent to perform in-state functions (e.g., to advertise in the forum state on behalf of the foreign corporation), the foreign corporation has the minimum contacts necessary for jurisdiction.

In determining whether the travel agent was Muenster's agent within the meaning of §103(a)(1), the volume of Muenster tickets the agent sold and the existence of communication between Muenster and the agent should be considered. If the agent sold so many tickets that had he not been in business Muenster would have set up its own Ames office, the travel agent would likely be found to have been Muenster's "agent." Conversely, if the agent only very rarely sold a Muenster ticket and few Ames residents took the Muenster tours, the agency relationship would likely be found lacking. Note that §103(a)(1) only applies to those in-state contacts which are related to the *particular cause of action* in question. It is also possible that Muenster's other contacts with Ames, unrelated to the Conn. crash, may be sufficient to confer jurisdiction over Muenster.

Even if the Ames long-arm reaches Muenster on account of the agent's activities, Muenster could still plausibly argue that the Ames federal court's exercise of personal jurisdiction over Muenster, an out-of-Ames corporation, would violate Muenster's right to *due process under the 14th Amendment of* the U.S. Constitution. As noted, a federal court sitting in diversity won't hear a case that wouldn't fall within the personal jurisdiction of the state where the federal court sits. In this case, it seems likely that the Ames federal court will need to exercise only ***"specific"*** jurisdiction over Muenster, not "general" jurisdiction. (Specific jurisdiction is jurisdiction for a claim arising at least in part out of the defendant's *in-state activities.*) Ames' claim arises from a flight taken on a ticket that Stilton bought while an Ames resident (and that Muenster *knew* from the beginning was bought by an Ames resident); also, Stilton bought the ticket in response to an in-Ames ad campaign conducted by Muenster. Thus Stilton's claim would likely be found to arise in significant part from Muenster's in-Ames activities, so that specific jurisdiction would suffice. For suits based on specific jurisdiction, an out-of-state corporate defendant's due process rights are not violated so long as the defendant had "minimum contacts" with the forum state. So here, there will be no violation of Muenster's due process rights as long as Muenster had minimum contacts with Ames. Here, the combination of Muenster's use of an in-Ames agent to sell tickets in Ames, combined with Muenster's decision to advertise its tour in the state, would almost certainly be sufficient to establish minimum contacts between Muenster and Ames. Thus the federal court should be found to have specific personal jurisdiction to hear the case (assuming that the Ames long-arm was found to apply).

Notice that if the claim *didn't* arise out of any voluntary contacts between Muenster and the state of Ames — as would be the case if Muenster operated and advertised only in New England, and Stilton bought the ticket in New England — then the Ames federal court would need *"general,"* not "specific," jurisdiction over Muenster. General jurisdiction over a defendant corporation may constitutionally be exercised *only* in the corporation's state of incorporation or its state of principal place of business. *Daimler AG v. Bauman.* And Muenster is not incorporated in Ames, nor does it have its principal place of business there. So if general jurisdiction were required (i.e., if the suit didn't arise out of any in-Ames activities by Muenster), the required general jurisdiction *would not* exist.

An additional issue arises with respect to *notice*. Was registered mail service a sufficient form of notice to Muenster? Federal Rule 4(e)(1) allows service by any method (e.g., registered mail) allowable under the law of the state in which the federal court sits. Since we're told that registered mail service on an out-of-state defendant is acceptable for Ames state-court suits, registered mail service here is sufficient.

Part B: Summary judgment ought to be denied Stilton. He is seeking an offensive use of collateral estoppel. That is, he is, as a plaintiff, trying to apply the finding of liability in the Cheddar case against Muenster in this case. Such offensive use of collateral estoppel was allowed by the Supreme Court in *Parklane Hosiery*. But in *Parklane*, only two lawsuits were involved; here, there is the likelihood of not only the Cheddar and Stilton actions, but of actions by each of the other injured passengers as well. It seems unfair to require Muenster to play this "heads you win; tails I lose" game in each of the many possible suits. This is the "multiple plaintiff anomaly" situation.

The issue becomes even more stark when one considers the possibility that the jury's finding in *Cheddar* was not really one of liability-but-no-serious-injury, but rather a finding of serious-injury-but-doubtful-liability. In other words, the jury may have mixed elements of liability and damages, and decided to give Cheddar something for her trouble (and save her from paying court costs) even though it didn't really think Muenster was liable. If this is what in fact happened, then there is all the more reason not to hold that the *Cheddar* litigation was conclusive on the negligence issue.

It is true, of course, that to deny the use of collateral estoppel in this instance may promote additional litigation — the negligence issue will be retried, perhaps many times over. But this prospect is somewhat offset by the likelihood that Muenster will not wage as long and desperate a defense. If estoppel were applied, then in the first of a string of suits, the defendant would drag out the litigation as long as possible, and defend as ardently as it could, even if only a few dollars were involved. If estoppel is not applied, then the defendant in Muenster's position can afford to defend a small claim half-heartedly — the amount of increased litigation may thus not be as great as might at first glance be feared.

A further injustice is implicit in allowing the use of collateral estoppel in this situation — Cheddar is effectively penalized for having gone first. Assuming that the jury did in fact render a compromise verdict because of its uncertainty on liability, Cheddar would have been better off waiting until someone else won against Muenster, and then using collateral estoppel. Thus each plaintiff has a powerful incentive to wait for someone else to go first, and to refuse to consolidate with other plaintiffs. When this judicial inefficiency is coupled with the likelihood that the plaintiffs will all agree to let the most appealing plaintiff sue first, it can be seen that Stilton's case for estoppel is about as poor as it could possibly be.

QUESTION 2

Staley's Tire Store, Inc., a retail outfit located just across the Rancid River in Langdell City, Langdell, until recently was a franchise dealer for the Plastic Tire Company, Inc., a manufacturer whose principal place of business is here in Ames. Staley's just recently decided to carry a line of tires manufactured by our client, Vinyl Tire Company, Inc., whose plant is also located in this state.

Staley's has just brought suit under the federal antitrust laws against Plastic in the Langdell federal court, alleging that its franchise agreement with Plastic violated those laws and seeking rescission and damages. Plastic has filed an answer denying any violation of the antitrust laws, and has counterclaimed for damages for breach of the franchise agreement. Plastic has sought to add our client, Vinyl, as a party to the counterclaim, alleging that Vinyl induced the breach. Service of process was made by a federal marshal at Vinyl's home office here in Ames City.

Can Vinyl be forced to litigate this case in Langdell, or is there some way we can have the action against it dismissed?

ANSWER TO QUESTION 2

The question is a very close one, and involves many complexities. Vinyl may or may not be amenable to suit in Langdell federal court; if it is, service may or may not have been valid. If the requirements of personal jurisdiction are met, federal subject-matter jurisdiction is probably present, even though Plastic and Vinyl are citizens of the same state.

Personal jurisdiction: Two issues arise with respect to personal jurisdiction over Vinyl: (1) Is Vinyl *amenable* to suit in Langdell?; and (2) If it is, was service on Vinyl made within the geographical boundaries for service specified by the Federal Rules?

(1) *Vinyl's amenability to suit:* In federal question cases, the federal courts have generally held that a corporation is amenable to suit (i.e., suable) as long as it has minimum contacts with the state in which the district court sits sufficient to meet the *International Shoe* test (p. 23); in other words, the fact that the state courts might not exercise jurisdiction over this particular out-of-state defendant on a state-law claim would be ignored in determining the defendant's amenability to a federal suit. In cases not raising a federal question, however, the prevailing rule is that the federal courts exercise *only* the jurisdiction that would be exercised by the courts of the state in which the federal court sits, even if the state courts do not extend their jurisdiction as far as is constitutionally permissible.

Although the underlying suit here is based on a federal question, the supplemental claim by Plastic against Vinyl is a state-law breach-of-contract claim, so Vinyl's amenability to that claim should probably be analyzed as if the case did not involve a federal question. Under that analysis, if (and only if) the Langdell state courts would have exercised personal jurisdiction over Vinyl had the Plastic claim against it been brought there, the *federal* court in Langdell should also exercise jurisdiction. Plastic's claim against Vinyl seems to involve "specific" jurisdiction. (That is, Plastic's claim that Vinyl induced a breach is probably correctly viewed as growing out of conduct allegedly committed by Vinyl *in Langdell,* namely inducing a Langdell-based company, Staley, to breach a contract connected with Langdell.) A state court's exercise of specific jurisdiction over an out-of-state company requires merely that the company have minimum contacts with the forum state. So the Langdell state courts would have constitutionally-sufficient specific jurisdiction over Plastic so long as Vinyl has minimum contacts with Langdell. *Burger King* (pp. 46-49) establishes that an out-of-stater's signing of a franchise contract that's closely related to the forum state is normally enough to constitute minimum contacts between the out-of-stater and the forum state. By extension from *Burger King*, probably an out-of-stater's inducement of a *breach* of a contract that's closely tied to the forum state *also* constitutes minimum contacts with the forum state. By this analysis, the Langdell state courts could constitutionally exercise specific jurisdiction over Plastic for the inducement claim. Consequently, the Langdell *federal* court should and will also exercise such specific jurisdiction, as long as the federal court also believes that the Langdell state courts would elect to *exercise* that specific jurisdiction over Vinyl.

If, on the other hand, the federal court believes that the Langdell state courts would *not* choose to exercise jurisdiction over Vinyl, the issue becomes more difficult. As noted earlier, since the claim against Vinyl is based solely on state law, the federal court should probably treat the problem of amenability as if the claim were based purely on diversity. And in diversity cases, the federal courts will generally not exercise jurisdiction if the courts of the state where the federal court sits would not exercise jurisdiction. So if the

Langdell state courts would not exercise jurisdiction over Plastic (even though those courts *could*, consistently with due process, do so), then the federal court for Langdell would not do so either.

(2) *Geographical boundaries for service:* If we conclude through the above reasoning that Vinyl is amenable to service, there is an additional requirement that service be carried out within the geographical limits specified in the Federal Rules. According to Rule 4(k)(1)(A), service on Vinyl may be made anywhere that the laws of Langdell permit. If the Langdell long-arm would permit service on Vinyl's Ames offices, then the federal service which occurred is valid. If Langdell law would not permit such service, the service may nonetheless be valid under the "100-mile-bulge" provision of 4(k)(1)(B). That provision allows service on persons who are brought in as additional parties to a counterclaim pursuant to Rule 19 at a place not more than 100 miles from the court where the action is pending. Thus, if Rule 19 allows Vinyl to be brought in as an additional party to Plastic's counterclaim, and if Vinyl's Ames offices are within 100 miles of the Langdell federal courthouse, service was valid.

It is unclear whether Vinyl may be brought in pursuant to Rule 19. That Rule allows joinder of certain persons who are subject to service of process and whose joinder will not destroy subject matter jurisdiction. Assuming for the moment that Vinyl meets these two tests (the subject-matter question is discussed below), it is joinable under Rule 19 if it "claims an interest relating to the subject of the action and is so situated that disposing of the action in [its] absence may . . . as a practical matter impair or impede [its] ability to protect the interest[.]" Since Vinyl has an interest in having Staley stay in business so that it will continue to distribute Vinyl products, it is arguable that Vinyl satisfies the provision of Rule 19 just cited. If so, service within the 100-mile bulge is permitted.

Subject-matter jurisdiction (supplemental jurisdiction): Plastic and Vinyl are both citizens of Ames. Plastic's claim against Vinyl therefore fails to satisfy independently the requirements of diversity. Unless the claim can be "tacked on" through supplemental jurisdiction, the claim must be dismissed.

The doctrine of supplemental jurisdiction, codified in 28 U.S.C. §1367, allows a federal court which has jurisdiction over an initial claim to also hear a related claim, even though that related claim would not independently satisfy the requirements of federal subject-matter jurisdiction (diversity and amount in controversy). One of the ways supplemental jurisdiction can apply is to allow a court to hear a state-created claim closely related to a federal question claim that is the "core" claim supplying original jurisdiction. (In other words, supplemental jurisdiction can be used to supply what was known before the 1990 enactment of §1367 as "pendent" jurisdiction.)

For a court to exercise its supplemental jurisdiction, the two claims must form part of the "same case or controversy under Article III" of the Constitution. This test is usually deemed satisfied if the state-created claim and the federal claim derive from a "common nucleus of operative fact"; see *UMW v. Gibbs*. Since both the federal claim (that the franchise agreement violated the antitrust laws) and the counterclaim against Staley and Vinyl (alleging that Vinyl induced Plastic to breach the franchise agreement) relate to the franchise agreement, probably the "common nucleus of operative fact" test would be satisfied. Therefore, supplemental jurisdiction would govern the counterclaim against both Staley and Vinyl.

§1367(a) allows "claims that involve the joinder or intervention of additional parties." So Vinyl does not get any comfort from the subject-matter jurisdiction aspect of the case — supplemental jurisdiction as implemented by §1367(a) allows Vinyl to be brought into the counterclaim, even though a claim by Plastic against Vinyl would not independently meet federal subject-matter-jurisdictional requirements.

All of this assumes, of course, that there is something in the Federal Rules which allows the joinder of Vinyl to Plastic's counterclaim against Staley, apart from questions of jurisdiction. The operative Rule is 13(h), which allows additional parties to a counterclaim to be brought in in accordance with the provisions of Rules 19 and 20. While there is some doubt as to whether Rule 19 would allow such joinder, Rule 20(b)(2) almost certainly does. That rule allows joinder of persons as defendants "if: (A) any right to relief is asserted against them jointly, severally or in the alternative with respect to or arising out of the same transaction, occurrence, or series of transactions or occurrences; and (B) any question of law or fact common to all defendants will arise in the action." (A defendant to a counterclaim is presumably a defendant for the purposes of Rule 20.) If the Staley claim and the claim against Vinyl are closely enough related so that the supplemental jurisdiction doctrine applies, then they are certainly close enough so that Rule 20 applies. In that case, Rule 13(h) joinder is allowable. Since such joinder is at the discretion of the counterclaimant, there is nothing Vinyl can do.

QUESTION 3

Our client, William Byer, entered an agreement with Stanley Cellar to purchase a parcel of Ames land from Cellar for $500,000. A down payment of $100,000 has been made by Byer and the transfer was to occur on May 1. Byer claims that he was induced to enter the contract by Cellar's fraud, and when Cellar refused to call the deal off, Byer brought suit in Ames federal court, on April 1, for cancellation of the contract and refund of the down payment. (Byer and Cellar are of diverse citizenship).

Last week, after getting an extension of time to file his answer, Cellar interposed an answer denying the alleged fraud and counterclaiming for the remainder owing on the contract. He has demanded a jury on all issues triable as of right by a jury. So far as I can tell, the only contested issue in the case is the alleged fraud of Cellar. Does Cellar have a jury trial right on that issue?

ANSWER TO QUESTION 3

Cellar is raising a legal counterclaim (damages for breach of contract) to an equitable suit (rescission). The question of fraud is a factor affecting both claims, since it would be a defense to the counterclaim and is the basis for the original suit. In *Beacon Theatres*, the U.S. Supreme Court held that a trial judge did not have discretion to order the trial of legal and equitable issues in such a way that the right to jury trial of the former would be lost. Since the issue of fraud will only be tried once (the rules of *res judicata* and "law of the case" require this), it must therefore be tried to a jury, in order to protect Cellar's right to jury trial of his legal counterclaim.

QUESTION 4

The State of Ames has enacted the following statute: "No person engaged in the business of a contractor shall be permitted to present any judicial demand before any court of this state for the collection of compensation for performance of any act for which a license is required by the law of this state without alleging and proving that he was a duly licensed contractor at all times during the performance of such act." Dauntless Construction Co. is a Thayer corporation engaged in the business of installation and construction of telephone facilities. Dauntless contracted with Pacific Telephone Co., an Ames corporation, to construct certain facilities and install them in Ames. This was a contract for performance of which a license was required by Ames law. Dauntless was a duly licensed contractor in Thayer but neglected to obtain a license in Ames, apparently through ignorance of the Ames requirement. A dispute arose between the parties during the performance of the contract, and Pacific brought an action against Dauntless in the Ames Superior Court for breach of contract. Proper service of process was made. Dauntless removed the action to the U.S. District Court for Ames and filed an answer denying plaintiff's allegations, setting up certain affirmative defenses, and also asserted a counterclaim claiming damages for misrepresentation in the negotiation of the contract and breach of various conditions therein. Pacific has moved to dismiss the counterclaim because of noncompliance with the Ames licensing statute. There is an Ames decision, *McCord v. Dean Waterworks Co.*, 321 Ames 400 (1972), holding that an unlicensed contractor cannot maintain a counterclaim arising out of a contract performed in Ames. You are the law clerk to the federal judge who is about to hear the motion. He has asked you for a memorandum to aid him in dealing with the problem. Prepare the memorandum.

ANSWER TO QUESTION 4

This is a classic *Erie* problem, in which the federal interest in consolidation of litigation conflicts with a state interest in enforcing licensing requirements. An additional wrinkle is presented by the fact that it is a counterclaim, rather than an original claim, which is in question.

The *Erie* doctrine applies to those situations in which there is no Federal Rule on point, and the underlying claim is a state-created one. That's the case here. If the court decides to follow Ames law, the Dauntless counterclaim will be barred.

The "twin evils" to which the *Erie* decision was addressed are: (1) discrimination against the citizen of the forum state; and (2) forum-shopping. Both of these evils would result to a certain extent if the court here refuses to follow Ames common law (the *McCord* decision), and allows Dauntless to pursue its counterclaim. Dauntless, as non-citizen of Ames, has had the opportunity to select a federal forum by means of the right of removal. (Your honor is aware, of course, that a defendant may remove only if he is not a citizen of the state in which the action is originally brought). Dauntless has thus been able to "shop" for a forum which it hopes is the more likely to be hospitable to its claim — it knew that it would fail in Ames state court, so it chose to remove to federal court. If your honor permits Dauntless to prosecute its counterclaim in the face of Ames law, this "forum-shopping" will have paid off.

Prior to the Supreme Court's decision in *Byrd v. Blue Ridge*, the problem could have been easily disposed of by resort to the "outcome-determinative" test first espoused in

Guaranty Trust v. York. *Guaranty* held that state law must be followed if it would "significantly affect the result of a litigation for a federal court to disregard a law of a State that would be controlling" had the action been brought in state court. The effect of ignoring Ames law here is nearly the same as the effect would have been in *Guaranty* of ignoring the state statute of limitations. *Guaranty* held that it was "outcome-determinative" to ignore a statute of limitations, since this would allow prosecution in federal court of a claim which would be completely barred in state court. Here, similarly, the effect of ignoring the *McCord* decision would be to allow a claim in federal court which would be barred in Ames state court.

As *Byrd* indicates, however, (1) there are varying degrees of outcome-determinativeness, and (2) the fact that the decision of which law to apply will be somewhat outcome-determinative does not settle the matter — there may be stronger countervailing considerations. Thus, the decision whether to try an issue to a judge or to a jury is less likely to determine the outcome of a lawsuit than is the decision whether to bar an action as untimely. *Byrd* held that the former issue is so little outcome-determinative that strong countervailing federal policies may compel a refusal to follow state decisions on the allocation of judge/jury roles.

It might seem, at first glance, that there is not any strong federal interest in favor of allowing the Dauntless claim. However, there is a strong federal interest in *consolidating* all the related litigation between two parties into one single action. This interest in consolidation is not evident at first — one might argue that if the Dauntless claim is barred, then it can't be brought in either Ames state ***or*** federal court, and will not reappear to be litigated in a separate, judicially wasteful, action. However, this argument that no consolidation interest is present overlooks a crucial consideration: *the Dauntless claim may be triable as an original action in the state or federal court of some other jurisdiction, perhaps Thayer*. If it is in fact the case that the Dauntless claim can and will be tried elsewhere, then there is a strong federal interest in disposing of all claims between Pacific and Dauntless in one action. Thus, the situation is quite different from that in *Guaranty*, where the federal courts had no strong reason to try a claim time-barred in state court (assuming that no other state court would have allowed the *Guaranty* claim).

It is difficult to tell from the record as it has so far been developed whether the Thayer state courts would entertain the Dauntless claim. Personal jurisdiction over Pacific can be constitutionally exercised by Thayer courts — the making of a contract with a citizen of the forum state is generally a sufficient contact to permit jurisdiction in a suit arising out of that contract. (See *Burger King*.) Thus, if the state of Thayer has a long-arm which would reach Pacific, the Dauntless action might be maintainable in Thayer. It is possible, of course, that the Thayer court will defer to the Ames statute (and the *McCord* interpretation of it), and bar the Dauntless claim. This is a question of conflict of laws. If Dauntless would be allowed to sue in Thayer state court, then a federal court sitting in Thayer would have to allow the suit, under the rule of *Klaxon v. Stentor*, which compels a federal court sitting in diversity to apply the conflicts rule of the state in which it sits.

It is therefore quite possible that if this court bars the Dauntless claim, it will later be brought in either the state or the federal court of Thayer. In that event, this court will have promoted a kind of "lateral forum-shopping"; defendants in the position of Dauntless will select a forum like Thayer instead of bringing their claims as counterclaims in Ames. Such an inducement to hold back from asserting a counterclaim promotes judicial inefficiency, as well as forum-shopping. This possibility indicates that Ames law should be disregarded, and the Dauntless claim allowed.

However, one additional possibility may negate the above reasoning — if the Dauntless counterclaim is *compulsory*, then it may be waived if it is not brought in this action. Since the counterclaim arises out of the same contract that is the subject of Pacific's claim for breach, it probably meets the "transaction or occurrence" test of Rule 13(a), and is thus compulsory. However, it is not clear whether Dauntless is barred from bringing the claim as an independent action in Thayer if it has done everything it could to assert the counterclaim in this case, and has failed. It would probably *not* be held to be barred from suing on the claim as plaintiff in Thayer state or federal court. Therefore, the fact that the counterclaim arises out of the same transaction or occurrence as the Pacific claim is irrelevant. The above argument for ignoring Ames law and letting Dauntless assert the counterclaim would thus still hold.

One difficulty with this argument, however, is that it compels a district court faced with the kind of problem presented in this case to examine the jurisdictional and conflicts policies of every other potential jurisdiction, in order to determine whether the action will be brought somewhere else if the present court dismisses it. Such an examination may be time-consuming and ineffective. Nonetheless, I think it would not be burdensome for this court to set forth a principle that where the federal court *knows* that there is some other jurisdiction, either state or federal, that will hear the claim, it should not give excessive weight to the door-closing rule of the state in which it sits.

Thus if your honor later determines that Thayer, or some other jurisdiction, would in fact permit the Dauntless claim as an original action, this court should allow the claim.

QUESTION 5

Your client, Peripheral Products, Inc., brought a treble damage action against Devious Corp., in the U.S. District Court for Ames under the Clayton Act for alleged antitrust violations. The defendant's answer included a defense based on the four-year statute of limitations provided by Congress for actions arising under the antitrust laws. After a hearing on a motion for summary judgment based on that defense, the court entered this order: "It is ordered, adjudged and decreed that the defendant's motion for summary judgment be, and the same hereby is, granted with costs to be taxed." Peripheral has now brought another action in the Ames Superior Court, alleging virtually the same facts and claiming damages for unfair competition. The Ames statute of limitations allowing six years for such actions has not yet expired. Devious has pleaded *res judicata*. Prepare a memorandum on the problem.

ANSWER TO QUESTION 5

The basic prerequisites for the application of *bar* are the following: (1) The present and former suits must represent very similar "causes of action;" (2) The parties to both suits must have been the same; and (3) The former adjudication must have been "on the merits."

(1) Similarity of causes of action: I think our best hope of defeating the claim of *res judicata* lies in showing that the two claims are not sufficiently identical for bar to apply.

While it was formerly the case that absolute identity of the two claims had to be shown, the courts have now adopted a looser test which serves to bar a greater number of claims. Devious will be able to cite the principle that a judgment is conclusive, not only as to matters which were decided, but also as to all matters which ***might have been decided***. Of course, this principle does not mean that any claim which could have been asserted in the first action is barred — if that were the case, there would be no hope for us at all, since we could have asserted the unfair competition claim by the doctrine of supplemental jurisdiction (see discussion below). The test for determining whether the second cause of action is so closely related to the previously litigated claim as to be barred by it is a pragmatic one: if two actions allege very similar facts, and claim violation of the same legal right, bar will apply, even though two different legal theories for recovery are involved. We should argue that the elements of unfair competition are different from those of antitrust violation, and that the protected legal right is not the same in both cases. However, I am not optimistic.

It should be noted that if the kind of relief we now seek was not available from the court in which we tried the previous action, we will not now be barred. If we can, for instance, show that the unfair competition claim could not have met the requirements of federal subject-matter jurisdiction, and could not therefore have been joined with the antitrust claim, we will be in the clear. Unfortunately, the doctrine of supplemental jurisdiction would almost certainly have permitted the unfair competition claim to be joined to the antitrust claim, since the two claims involve a common nucleus of operative fact.

(2) Identity of parties: The parties to both actions are identical.

(3) Adjudication on the merits: Our only remaining hope for avoiding bar is to demonstrate that the original adjudication for untimeliness was not "on the merits." However, this approach is not promising. While a 12(b)(6) dismissal for failure to state a valid claim might arguably be considered not on the merits, a summary judgment is as final and dispositive of the issues as a jury trial. Therefore, I don't think we will get anywhere with this line of attack.

In my opinion, unless we can persuade the court that the two claims are not sufficiently identical for bar to be applied, we will be prevented from litigating the unfair competition claim.

TABLE OF CASES

This table includes references to cases cited everywhere in this book, including in the various Exam Q&A sections.

SUBJECT-MATTER INDEX

This index includes references to the Capsule Summary and to the Exam Tips, but not to Q&A or Flow Charts.

www.ingramcontent.com/pod-product-compliance
Lightning Source LLC
LaVergne TN
LVHW080025210926
848481LV00011B/3106

* 9 7 9 8 8 9 4 1 0 9 7 5 6 *